THE CHURCHES OF INDIA

THE CHURCHES OF INDIA

Joanne Taylor

NIYOGI BOOKS

Published by
NIYOGI BOOKS
Block D, Building No. 77,
Okhla Industrial Area, Phase-I,
New Delhi-110 020, INDIA
Tel: 91-11-26816301, 26818960
Email: niyogibooks@gmail.com
Website: www.niyogibooksindia.com

Editor: Mohua Mitra
Design: Shashi Bhushan Prasad

ISBN: 978-93-86906-99-1
Publication: 2019
Reprint: 2026

Printed at: Niyogi Offset Pvt. Ltd., New Delhi, India

To my grandsons Lachlan and Oliver Taylor
who will inherit this world and make it a much better place

CONTENTS

FOREWORD

India's architectural heritage is as enormous as it is varied. The history of the country is written in the buildings that stand out from their backgrounds. Some are magnificent edifices self-consciously designed to create a sense of awe. Others are small works hidden in the back streets of cities and villages; it is easy for them to be passed unnoticed. As a set of individual structures, the religious buildings give India its identity as a nation of diverse people with their own cultures and aspirations expressed within a broad definition of 'being Indian'. These aspirations can be seen in the religious architecture of the nation. Hindu temples, Muslim mosques, Buddhist stupas and Parsee fire temples enrich the morphology of settlements and countryside in the sub-continent. They are immediately recognisable and full of meanings for people to read into them. Some are pure types; others are hybrid because religious groups have borrowed impressive elements from the buildings of others. So too with Christian churches.

Churches in India date back to the very beginnings of the common era identified with the birth of Christ. Their presence surprised the Portuguese when they first set foot on Indian soil. Churches have been built in greater numbers from the middle of the last millennium when settlers such as the Armenians and colonisers, Portuguese, French and British, brought their own branches of Christianity and religious architecture with them. The church rituals and their architecture either became, self-consciously or unselfconsciously, indigenised or they remained as symbols of aloofness of the colonisers by retaining their architecture in its pure form to the extent that the climate would allow. The sculptures and decorations show the aspirations of their congregations.

Joanne Taylor's latest work *The Churches of India* with its fine illustrations gives the reader a deep feeling for the range of churches, from the grand to the humble, and their architecture that has been built in the country. It is also a fine history of the search by those who design or adapt buildings for a self-identity through the symbolism.

Jon Lang
Emeritus Professor of Architecture
University of New South Wales, Australia

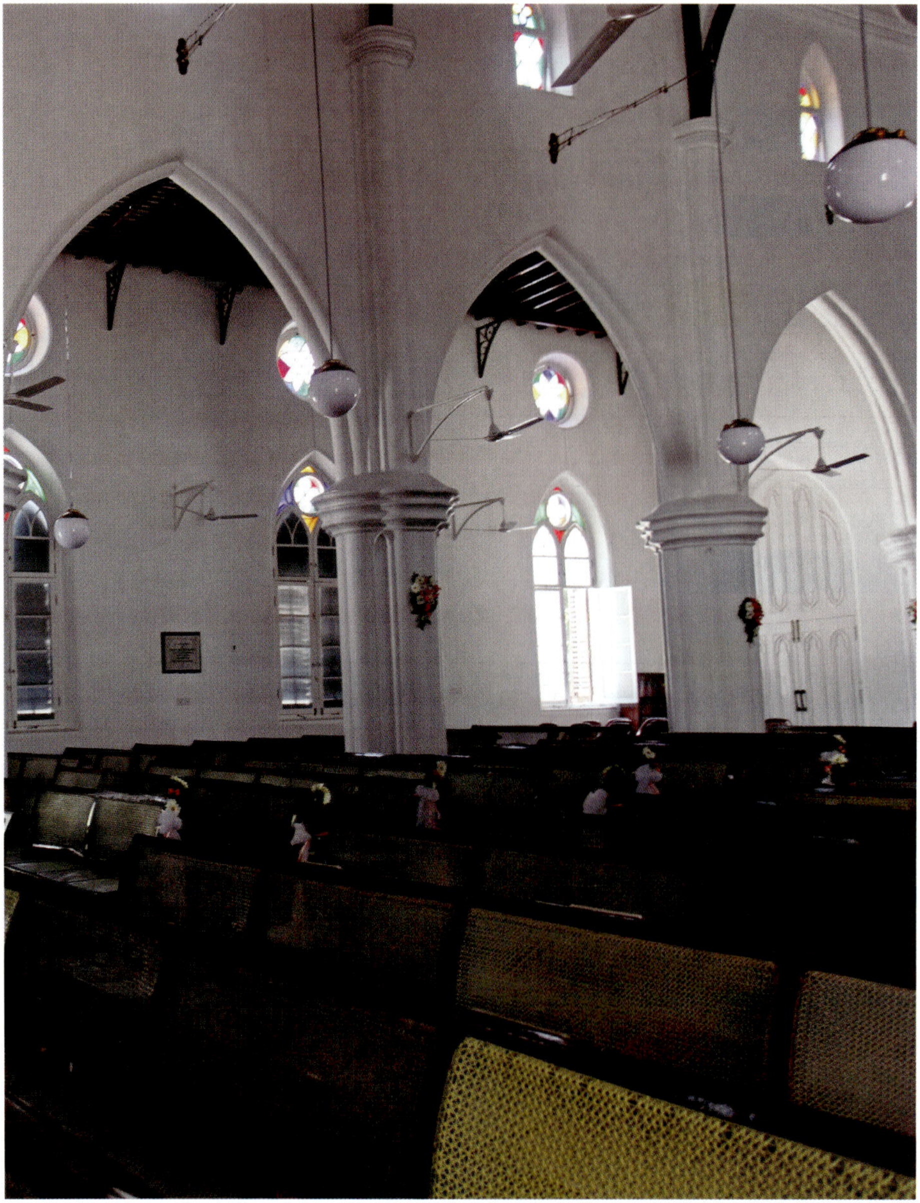

Interior view of St. Mark's Cathedral, showing arched doorways and massive pillars. This is the oldest Anglican church in Bengaluru

INTRODUCTION

'Architecture has recorded the great ideas of the human race. Not only every religious symbol, but every human thought has its page in that great book'

—Victor Hugo

Though India is known as a land of Hindu temples and Islamic mosques it is also home to an extraordinary number of Christian churches. Contrary to what many believe Christianity did not arrive in India with colonisation but is one of India's most ancient religions and it is widely believed, began with the arrival of St. Thomas the apostle who brought the religion to the west coast of India in 52 AD. It was after the arrival of the Portuguese in 1498 that church architecture in India did become inexorably linked with the history of colonisation. These churches represent the faith of the religious orders which built them and the colonisers' need to establish their identity in India. They also exhibit the artistic abilities of India's master craftsmen who decorated them. More recently, Indian architects are reinterpreting church architecture and creating a Christian identity for Indians in the built form.

Over the centuries the architecture and design of India's churches has evolved and flourished, though more in some regions than others. In Kerala churches can be seen everywhere one looks while in Gujarat or Rajasthan it would be difficult to find one. How they came to be part of India's landscape is a fascinating story which began in the first century AD and continues today.

This book has been written for readers interested in Indian history and church architecture. From simple chapels to grand cathedrals, it showcases a diverse number of church buildings from all over India.

The work has drawn on the most commonly believed or most probable facts. I have endeavoured to be as accurate as possible. The very early churches have had numerous incarnations and much has changed over time. Many churches have been demolished and rebuilt, sometimes in quite different styles. In addition, the dates of Indian churches are not always reliable and many churches have changed in response to cultural patterns. What has happened over time can be convoluted.

Though much church photography concentrates on the massive exteriors and soaring interiors of churches the photographs in this work also focus on the small details; a piece of exquisite carving or the simple garland of marigolds at the feet of a saint's statue. Details such as this show the human element of a church.

It would be impossible to record all of India's churches. The goal here has been to present a diverse collection from across India. Each chapter begins with an introduction to the region followed by the church and its accompanying photographs. The similarities and differences are what make these churches intriguing. Some have fascinating histories and inspiring architecture, while others are eclectic. Many are simply charming.

People of all religions have expressed their faith for centuries by constructing buildings for their gods. Though faith may be the same the world over the architecture it inspires is diverse and fascinating. I invite you to discover the Churches of India.

Unless stated all the photographs throughout the book are mine. Though much church photography concentrates on the massive exteriors and soaring interiors of churches I have also focused on the small details.

—Joanne Taylor

ANCIENT BEGINNINGS
Early Christians in Kerala

Churches of the Eastern World

Christians came to India in early times by sailing across the Arabian Sea and along the flourishing spice trade routes, not to trade but to escape persecution. It is widely believed that the first was the apostle St. Thomas who arrived on the west coast of India in 52 CE, long before Christianity reached the rest of India. There is no documented evidence particularly over the first few hundred years so oral traditions have been relied on, handed down and treasured over centuries. At that time India was well connected to the Middle East by trade and St. Thomas was known as the most travelled of the apostles. It is certainly possible. However, what we do know is that from the third or fourth centuries onward there is clear evidence of a Christian presence in Kerala. Nonetheless St. Thomas is regarded by many as the founding father of Christianity in India by Christians and Hindus alike and the tradition of St. Thomas is cherished and embedded in India's as well as Kerala's own history.

It is said St. Thomas established churches in seven locations in Kerala after arriving at Muziris, an ancient port which has now vanished but believed to be near today's Kodungallur. These churches would have been simple, possibly house-churches or palm thatched cottages. Several groups of Christians arrived in the 4th to 6th century CE including several hundred escaping persecution from Edessa, in what was then Persia, led by Thomas of Cana. There are a number of versions as to who this later Thomas was; a merchant warrior, a bishop…and so on. However once safely in Kerala these early Christians settled and flourished by combining their faith with Hindu culture. These early Christians became known as St. Thomas Christians or Nazrani, the followers of Jesus of Nazareth. Today's St. Thomas Christians are said to represent one of the oldest Christian traditions in the world. They would have brought with them traditional church designs from the east. However over the next centuries the non-

Catholic Syrian Christians, having Hindu backgrounds and being isolated built their churches to resemble what they saw around, the three-tiered gabled temples of Kerala.

Over time many other Christian communities developed. From the 6th century on they became known simply as Syrian Christians or Eastern Christians referring to the Syriac-Aramaic language they had in common, a dialect of the language probably spoken by Jesus. Divisions and sub-groups formed later, the result of which is complex and too numerous for a work such as this. However simply put, todays Christians of Kerala can be divided into two groups; non-Catholics and Catholics (introduced by the Portuguese in the late 15th century). The first group are the Jacobite Syrian, Marthoma Church and the Church of South India. The second group are the Syrian Latin, Roman Catholics, Syro-Malabar Catholics and Malankara Orthodox.

These early churches had begun by the 9th century and by necessity would use local, perishable building materials. Consequently none of these early churches exists today. It is

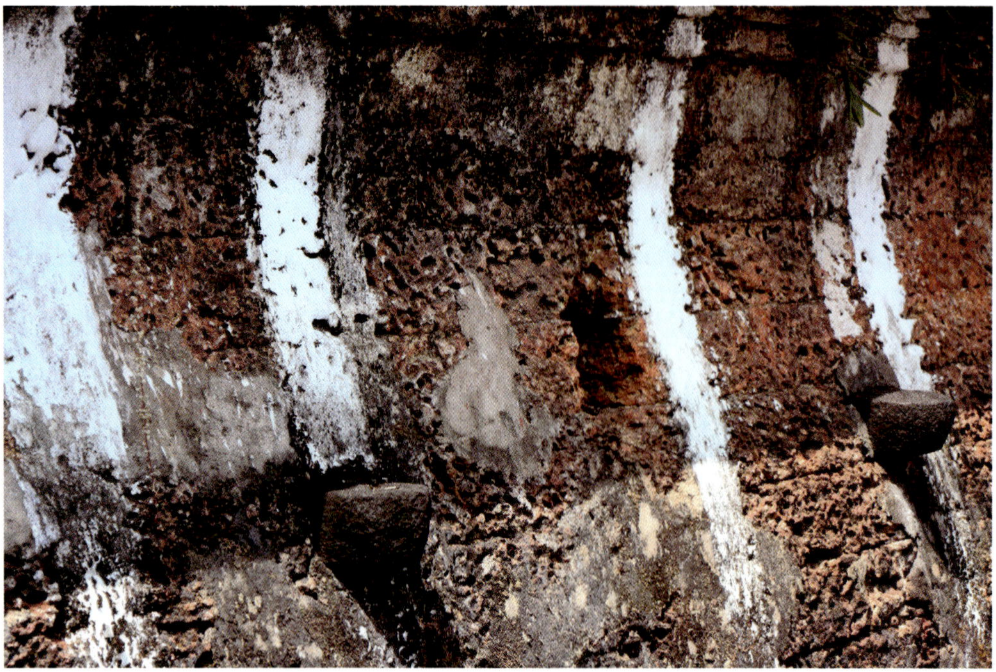

Rock oil lamps can still be found in the crevices of church walls in Kerala

difficult to fully understand what they looked like. However accounts from travellers and prominent writers agree that the churches were modelled on the three tiered gabled architecture of Hindu temples. The only difference between a Hindu temple and a Christian church was the cross at the front or at the top.

In 1599 Antonio de Gouvea who accompanied the Archbishop of Goa to Kerala used the term 'pagoda of the Hindus'. In his famous book *Jornada* he described a pre-Portuguese indigenous Kerala church:

> The buildings were small…so narrow and long that it was scarcely possible to raise the Most Holy Sacrament at the altar… very dark, inside there were no windows….' and further, Kerala Christians had 'made around the church a very high wall which could only be crossed with ladders because of the height…some churches were built of bamboo.

Later the churches became more substantial, built from readily available laterite stone cut into blocks, timber, usually teak, coconut and jackwood, a tree common in south-west India. These churches incorporated many Hindu temple elements, the most visible being the *dhwajastambha* or flagpole still seen in newly built churches today. Made of teakwood enclosed in copper or brass these flagpoles symbolise the connection between heaven and earth. The flagpoles of Hindu temples are topped with three horizontal branches symbolising the three main Hindu gods, Brahma, Vishnu and Shiva whereas Christian flagpoles are topped with a cross.

The lamps are made of a brass stand with a wick soaked in ghee or oil at the

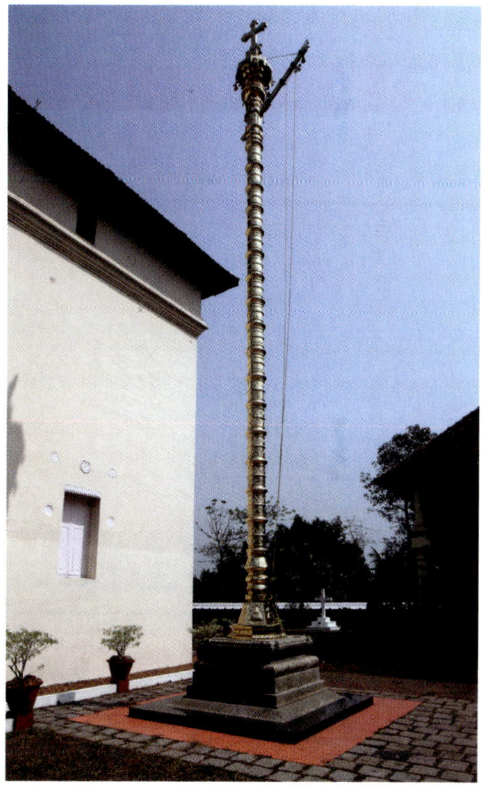

The wick oil lamp, nilavilakku, *inside or outside the entrance is another component of Hindu temples in churches, topped with a cross*

top or graduating multiple trays holding a number of wicks. Ornate circular lamps can also be found hanging by chains from the ceiling inside the temple. These consist of graduated round trays, each holding tiny bowls containing oil and wicks. When lit they create steps of light. The lighting of the *nilavilakku* is an important part of all rituals and ceremonies and is considered to be auspicious. Syrian Christian families also keep these lamps in their homes as do Hindu families. They are important to both religions and are lit at prayer times. The high stone wall mentioned earlier is another element borrowed from Hindu temples. It is usually painted white with an arched entrance, some of which are quite elaborate. The entrance to the church is often on the side of the building and approached through a carved teakwood portico or *shala.* Large churches may have particularly long *shala*s connected to an alternate entrance, built to shelter people during religious services and festivals. Without a *shala,* heavily carved teak doors open directly to the nave of the church.

Similarly the practice of taking garlands of flowers to a church and laying them on the cross or beneath images of saints is a connection to the Hindu ritual of placing multiple garlands of flowers, usually marigolds, on the images of Hindu gods. These many traditional practices and rituals are certainly of India but a unique culture has developed within the framework of Syrian Christian traditions. What is particularly interesting is that many aspects of Syrian Christian worship have not changed and in some non-Catholic orthodox churches such as the Jacobite, the ancient Aramaic language is used in their liturgies.

Antonio Gouvea, Portuguese envoy to Malabar, mentions in his 16th-century work *Jornada* that almost all the churches of the Syrian Christians followed the models

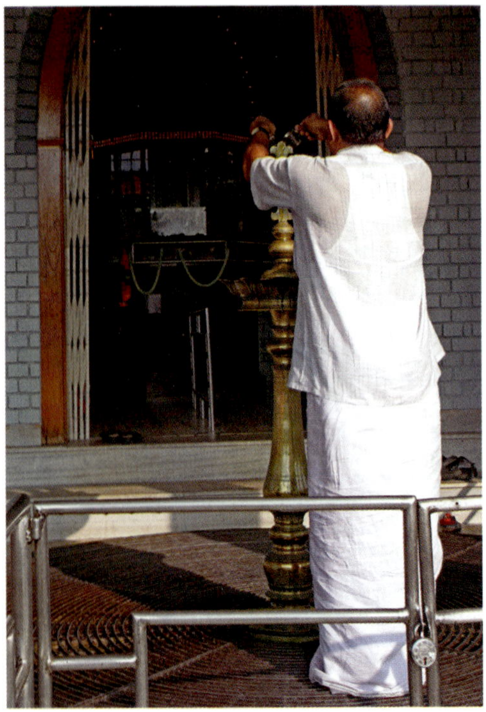

Nilavilakku—*A priest lighting a wick oil lamp*

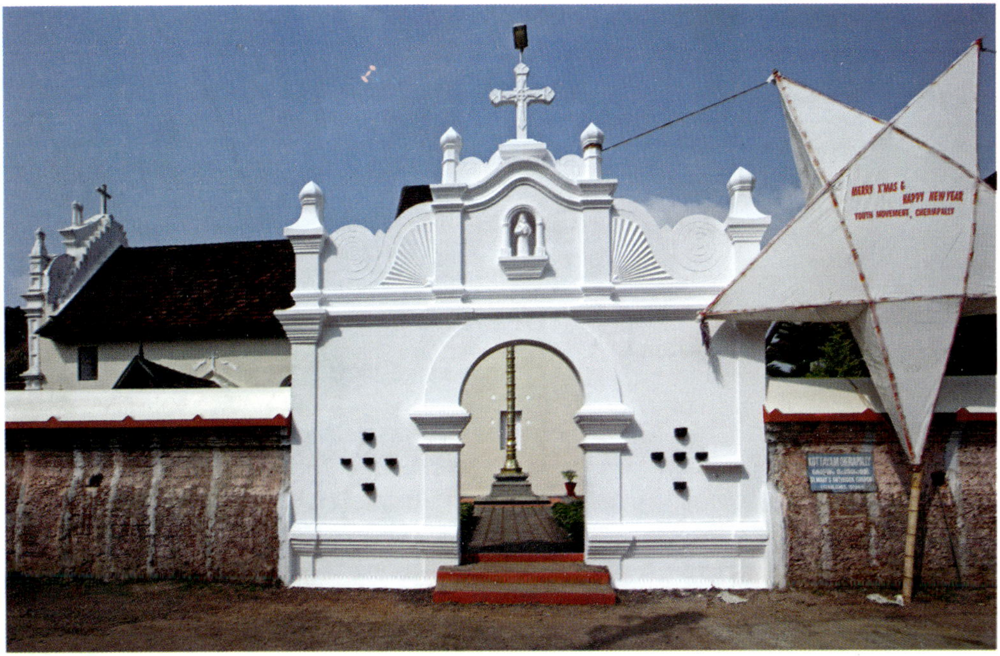

Walls, an element from Hindu temples, are common, though lower, with elaborate entrances. St. Mary's church, Kottayam

of Hindu temples of that period but were distinguished by the huge granite cross in the front yard of the church. These stone crosses, *vilakukumadam,* are just as important today. The practice of parishioners pouring oil over the granite cross is similar to the Hindu practice of pouring milk, oil, or coconut water over various deities (a 'ritual bath'). This ritual of anointing is to wish for an auspicious future, to help someone or simply for peace and prosperity.

Traditionally the interiors of Kerala's Syrian Christian churches are positioned east to west and are bare of furniture; the congregation sits on mats on the floor as they do in Hindu temples. There are three low elevations; the sanctuary, *madbaha*, the choir, *qestroma* and the nave, *haykla*. The sanctuary is on the upper level at the eastern side of the building and represents heaven. The main altar is on the eastern wall while to the north of the sanctuary is the sacristy, *diaqonikon.* To the south is the baptistery. The sanctuary is surrounded by brass rails to protect it and covered by a red curtain, opened rarely but always during the *Qurbana,* the Eucharist.

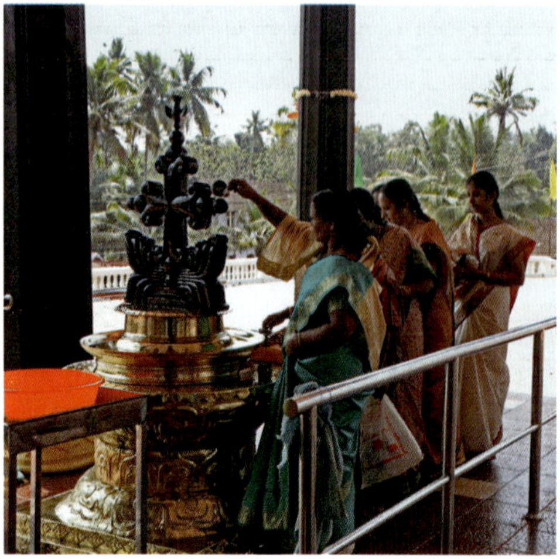

Enna Nercha—anointing the ancient granite cross with oil as an offering to God

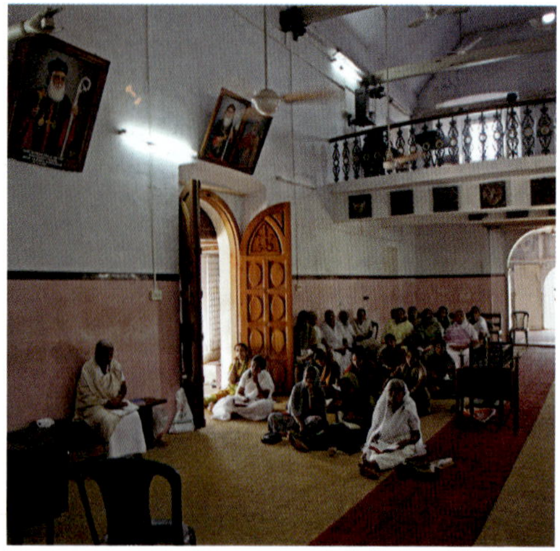

Seating arrangement inside St. Mary's Valliapally Church, Kottayam

Within the sanctuary the presence of God is represented by a constantly lit oil lamp. Unless a church is Syrian Catholic crucifixes or images of saints are not found. Father Placid J. Podipara, a scholar in the Syriac language has said Kerala's churches are 'Christian in religion, Hindu in culture and Syro-Oriental in worship.'

Before the Portuguese arrived traditional indigenous churches appeared regional and native in style. There were no imposing facades, simply a plain front wall with a simple tile and wood roof jutting over it. This changed after the arrival of the Portuguese who changed the existing churches to what was familiar to them. Today there are no original 15th century churches that have been preserved without having some extension or alteration.

EUROPEAN BEGINNINGS
The Portuguese

During the mid to late 15th century Spain and Portugal were the two greatest maritime nations on earth and competed fiercely to be the first to discover the important sea route to India. It was the 'Age of Discovery' and faraway India was irresistible as it was known as a land of spices and Europeans were desperate for them. Pepper was much sought after and worth its weight in gold. Used as a food preservative pepper made meat last longer and taste better. With no refrigeration and after a poor harvest heavily salted meat with added pepper kept many from starving. Other spices were used

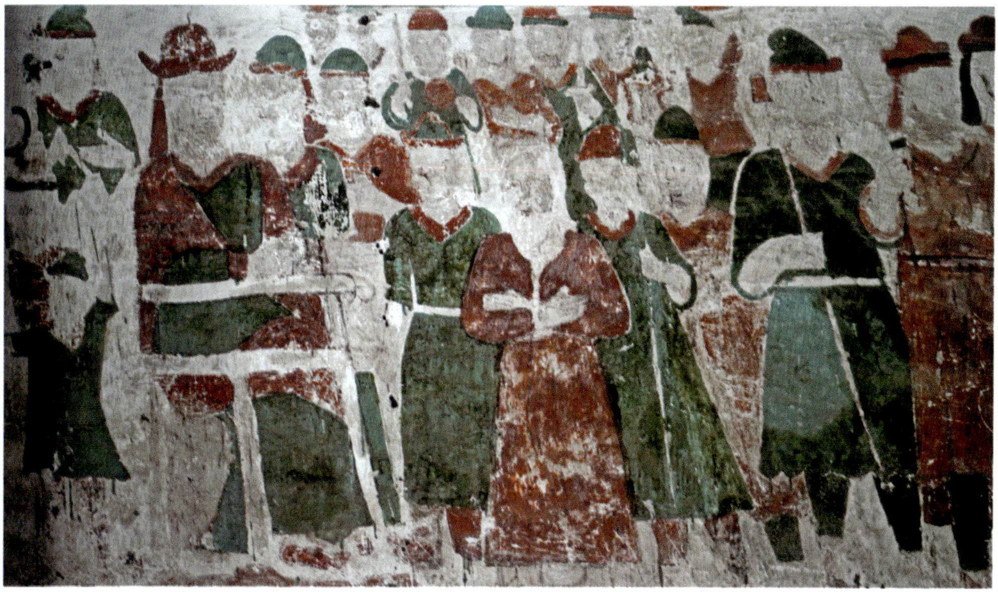

Ancient murals of Portuguese soldiers, St. Mary's Church, Kottayam

to add flavour to ale or mulled wine and as an ingredient in medicines, to embalm the dead and were even thought to cure the plague. Spices however were rare, far away and difficult to procure and therefore very costly.

The spice trade began in the Middle East over 4,000 years ago and several ancient trade routes such as the famous Silk Road were used by Arab traders to transport spices and other goods from India to the western world, some by land, and others by sea or by a combination of both. The Arabs monopolised the spice trade and became fabulously wealthy travelling by camel caravans to take exotic spices to the Mediterranean countries, North Africa and Europe via trading cities such as Venice. At that time spices were not only valued for their flavour, they were also such an important commodity, literally worth their weight in gold. The Arab traders told fabulous tales of the origins of spices to deter competitors. These tall tales included exotic creatures, the phoenix, dragons and huge winged beasts. Pepper could only be found in deep canyons guarded by snakes, or on a mountain top in Arabia guarded by vicious birds of prey that made their nests from spices.

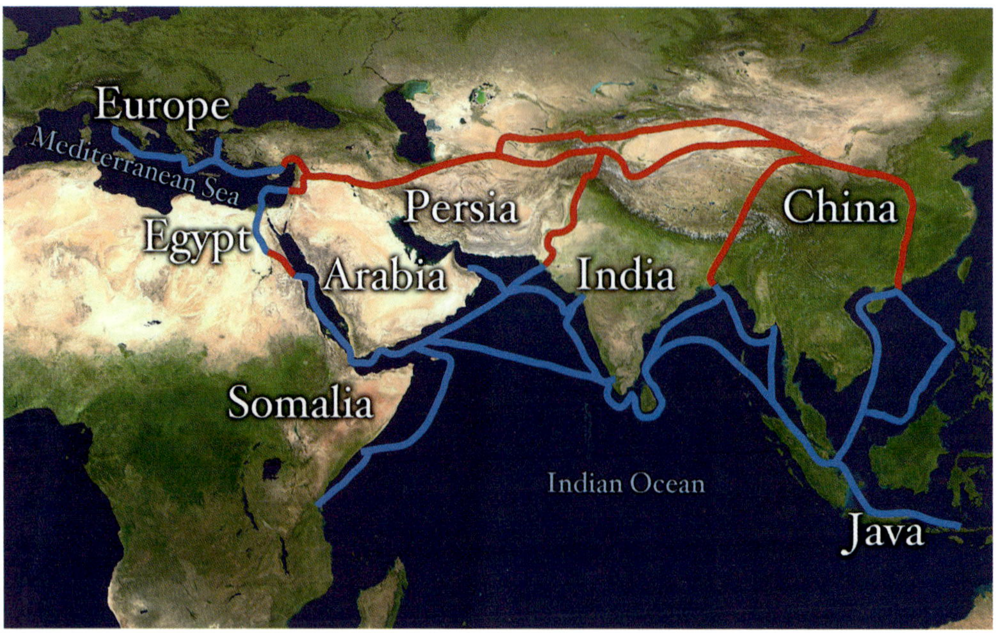

The early overland and maritime spice routes

To obtain spices in the 15th century Europeans had to take the dangerous journey via the Red Sea and Egypt or across Persia, Iraq, Syria and Anatolia. The Islamic empires were competing for control of the trade and merchant caravans were often robbed. For the Europeans the goal was worth the risks involved. However when the Ottoman Turks captured Constantinople and began closing overland trade, the equations changed. Constantinople was a major centre of trade between the Mediterranean and the Black Sea and bypassed not only the Arabs but the Venetians who charged huge tariffs. When Europe's spice trade became subject to Turkish dictates a great urgency rose to discover a sea route from Europe to India which would completely bypass Venice, Constantinople and the Arab traders.

It was Portugal's great navigator Vasco da Gama who was victorious, sailing around Africa and across the Indian Ocean to Kerala on India's west coast in 1498. At the time Kerala was called 'the spice garden of India' but the regions also traded in exotic merchandise such as precious stones, pearls, teak, gold, ivory and peacocks. This route became known as 'The India Route,' *Carreira da India* and its discovery was a monumental triumph in the history of navigation. It marked the beginning of establishing the Portuguese Empire in the east. However for India it was the beginning of a succession of colonial rulers that would last for centuries.

Portugal's King Dom Manuel 1 had appointed Vasco da Gama to not only find spices but the lost and persecuted Christian tribes ruled by a legendary Christian King, Prestor John—a fictitious figure Europeans believed in at that time. King Manuel needed Christian soldiers to form an army to achieve his goal of becoming 'Emperor of the East' and taking control of the spice trade from the Arabs. Having reached Calicut Vasco da Gama believed he had found the legendary Christians of the East:

> '1498. Calicut. [Arrival.] That night (May 20) we anchored two leagues from the city of Calicut …
>
> 'The city of Calicut is inhabited by Christians … Some of them have big beards and long hair, whilst others clip their hair short or shave the head, merely allowing a tuft to remain on the crown as a sign that they are Christians … They pierce the ears and wear much gold in them. They go naked down to the waist, covering their lower extremities with very fine cotton stuffs. Further on; … When we arrived (at Calicut) they took us to a large church, and this is what we saw: The body of the church is as large as a monastery, all built of hewn stone and covered with tiles. At the main

> entrance rises a pillar of bronze as high as a mast … In addition to this, there was another pillar as high as a man, and very stout. In the centre of the body of the church rose a chapel, all built of hewn stone, with a bronze door sufficiently wide for a man to pass, and stone steps leading up to it. Within this sanctuary stood a small image which they said represented Our Lady…
>
> 'We did not go within the chapel, for it is the custom that only certain servants of the church, called '*quafee*'s, should enter. These '*quafee*'s wore some threads passing over the left shoulder and under the right arm, in the same manner as our deacons wear the stole. They threw holy water over us, and gave us some white earth, which the Christians of this country are in the habit of putting on their foreheads, breasts, around the neck, and on the forearms… Many other saints were painted on the walls of the church, wearing crowns. They were painted variously, with teeth protruding an inch from the mouth, and four or five arms. Below this church there was a large masonry tank, similar to many others which we had seen along the road.'

Vasco da Gama had clearly mistaken Hindus for Christians and a Hindu temple for 'the church'. 'Our Lady' was in fact the goddess Devaki, the mother of Lord Krishna.

When the Portuguese did find India's Christians they were surprised to find their churches resembling Hindu temples, the 'Houses of the Idols.' In the eyes of a 15th century European, the Syrian Christians were seen as heretics who were loyal not to the Pope in Rome but the Syrian Orthodox Church based in Antioch (now Turkey).

When Da Gama returned to Portugal in 1499 he was greeted as a hero. Other expeditions followed which led to the establishment of the first European colony in India. Trade with India made Lisbon one of the greatest cities in Europe for spices and luxury merchandise but just as imperative as trade in the early days was church building. With more religious zeal than ideas of political control the Portuguese had their own notions of what a 'proper' church building should look like and made a concerted effort to change the architectural style of Kerala's Syrian Christian churches to something familiar to them. The simplest way of achieving this was to add a large flat fronted Portuguese façade between the nave and the portico of the indigenous churches. As these Baroque facades became common, interiors also became richer and more decorative and stained glass began to appear. One of the best examples is St. Paul's church on the island of Diu. Portuguese churches were meant to impress. Later Portuguese

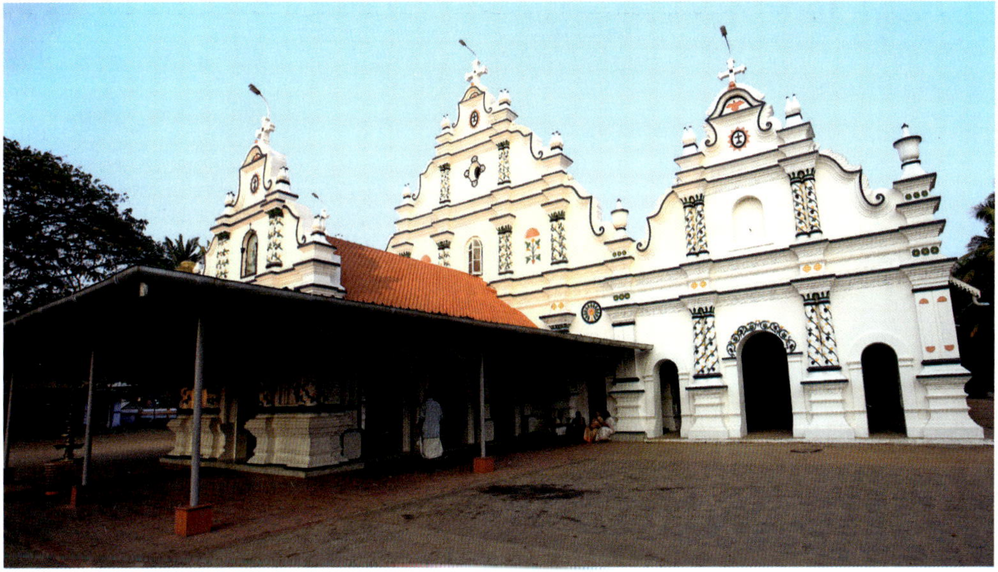

Three facades of St. George Syro-Jacobite Church on the way to Kottayam, is a mix of cultures

churches built on Indian soil would rival the great cathedrals of Lisbon.

Fort Kochi and Diu

Trade relations with India

After Vasco da Gama's voyage King Manuel sent Pedro Alvares Cabral in AD 1500 to establish trade relations in India and return to Portugal with spices. Cabral's mission failed but a successful Portuguese trading post came up in the Kingdom of Cochin, a group of islands and narrow peninsulas and built a fort around 1503 which became known as Fort Cochin, now Fort Kochi. Arabs and Jews had settled there in the 1st century CE and prospered due to support from local rulers. Kochi was the first of Portugal's Asian holdings and remained in Portuguese hands until the Dutch gained supremacy in 1663. Over a century later the British took control. Kochi is one of India's busiest sea ports and has been an important spice trading centre from the 14th century. It has a narrow channel between Willingdon Island and Vallarpadam which serves as an entrance to the Arabian Sea and beyond. Its position made it possible for trade to such diverse countries as China, Egypt and Portugal. The fort no longer exists but the name has remained. The area was under foreign rule for over four hundred years and

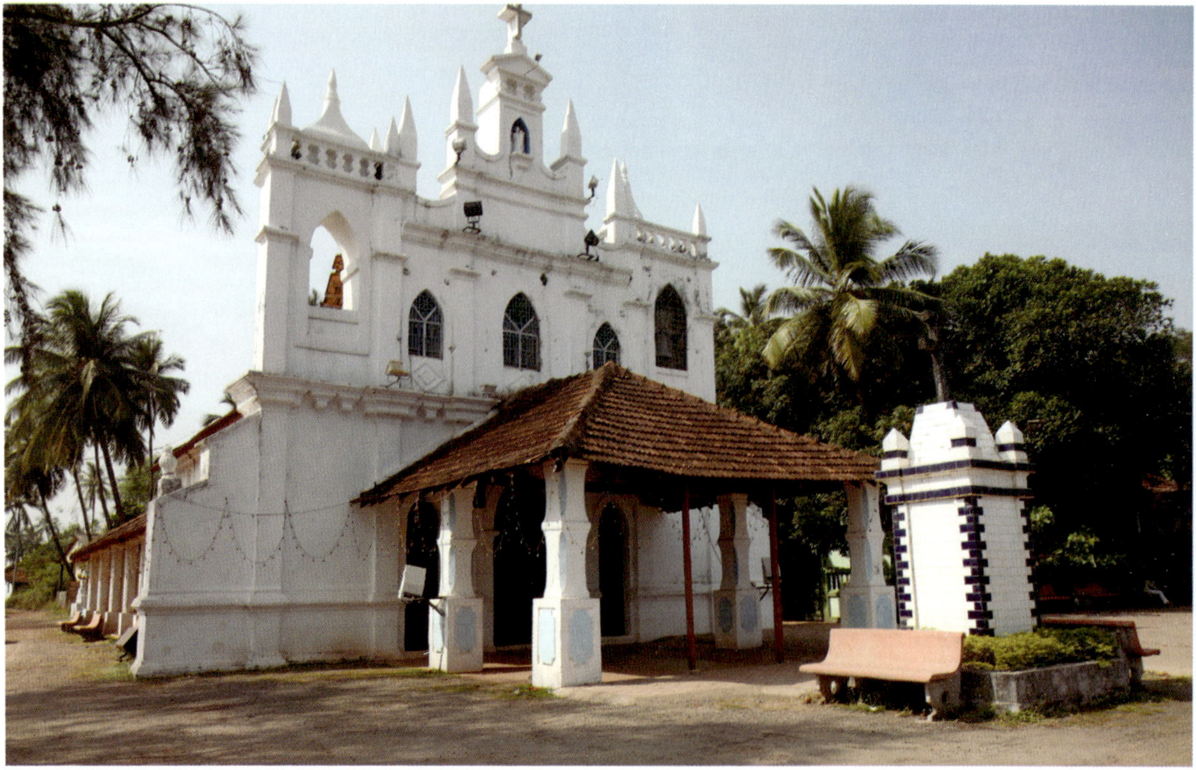

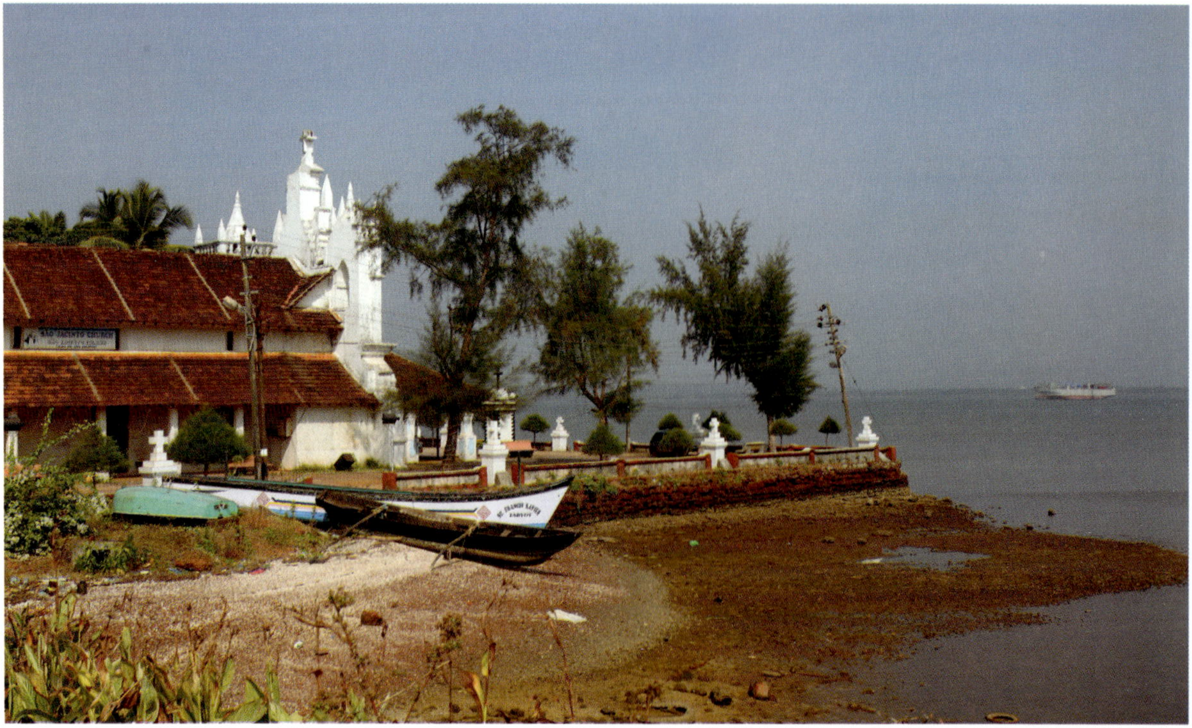

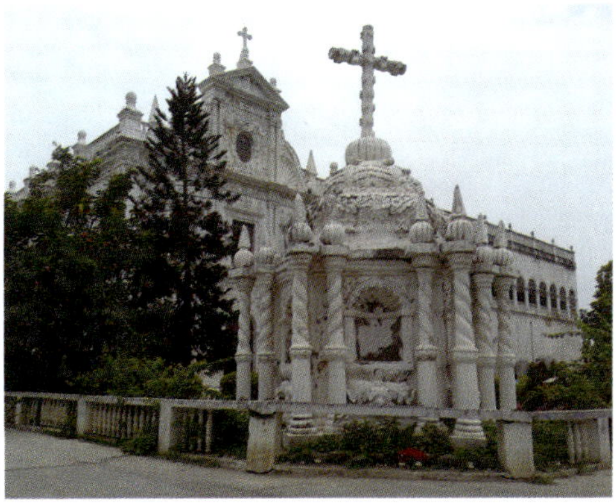

St. Paul's Church, Diu Fort, Diu (collection of Joanne Taylor)
FACING PAGE BOTH: *Two views of Sao Jacinto Church, Island of Sao Jacinto, Goa show an 'inserted' Portuguese façade*

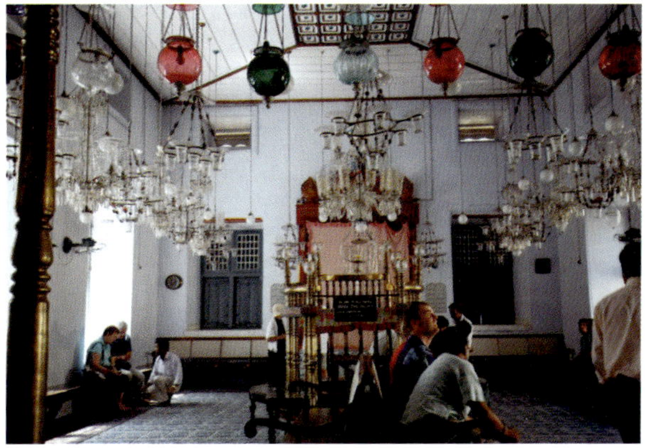

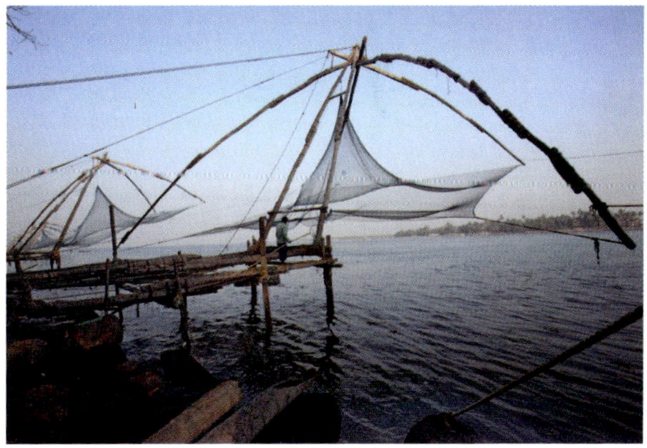

TOP: *The Paradesi Synagogue maintained by a Jewish family*
BELOW: *One of Fort Kochi's unique fishing nets*

saw many different cultures, traditions and diversity of rulers and trades, all concentrated in Fort Kochi. Foreign control ended when India gained independence in 1947.

Today's Fort Kochi is a relaxed place with tiny lanes housing spice wholesalers. Shelves heave with the weight of huge glass jars selling every imaginable spice while outside mountains of spice are ready to sell to wholesalers. This area is incongruously called Jew Town, the oldest surviving Jewish settlement and neighbourhood in India. All of Kochi's Jewish population have left except one family who can trace their roots back to some 2,000 years. The family members take care of the small Paradesi synagogue which can be found at the end of a narrow lane. Along the shore large wooden structures support funnel shaped fishing nets that are suspended into the sea by a pulley system of rocks tied to rope. Today Indian fishermen work these unique nets which are thought to be from China, brought to India by Chinese merchants in the thirteenth century.

An area of beautiful Dutch villas attests to the influence of the Dutch who came to

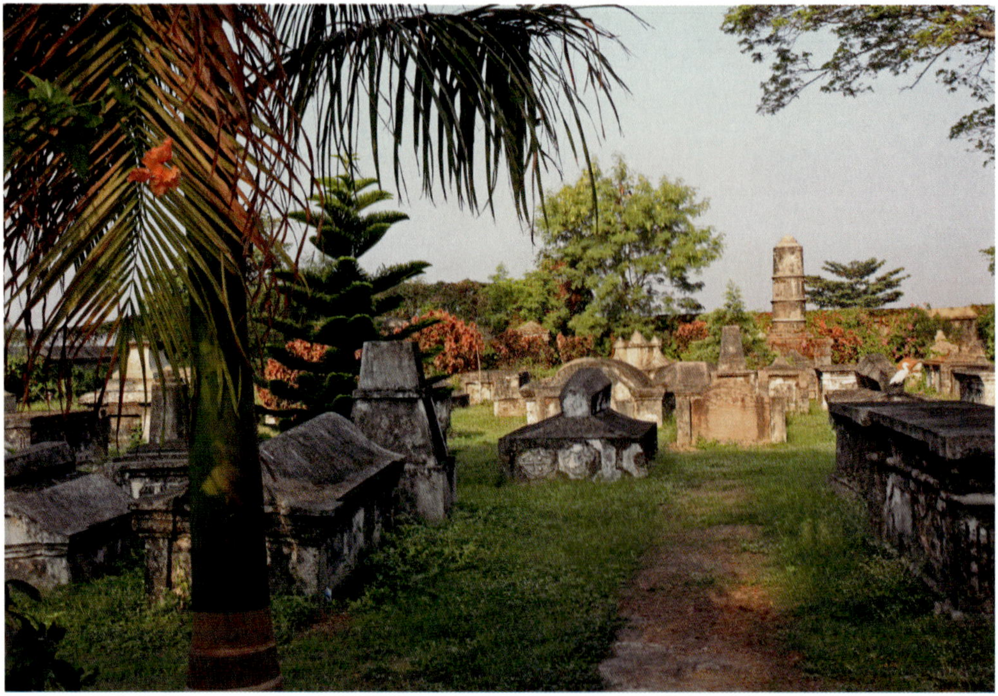

The Dutch cemetery

India's west coast in 1604. Now they are home to the wealthy of Fort Kochi; this is also where the Church of St. Francis, India's oldest European church can be found. The famous Church of St. Francis is the first church built by the Portuguese and the first church of its type in India.

The Church of St. Francis, 1516

C.S.I. The Church of South India

This unassuming Portuguese church with its flat fronted facade is the oldest European church in India with a history that reveals Europe's struggle for power. It is the most important building in Fort Kochi and at one time housed the tomb of Vasco da Gama.

When the Portuguese adventurer Francisco de Albuquerque, 'Francisco the Great' sailed to Cochin in 1503 he was accompanied by Portuguese Franciscan friars who built a small church within the simple Portuguese fort by the river. It was built from the trunks of coconut trees and held together with iron bands. In 1516 the Franciscans

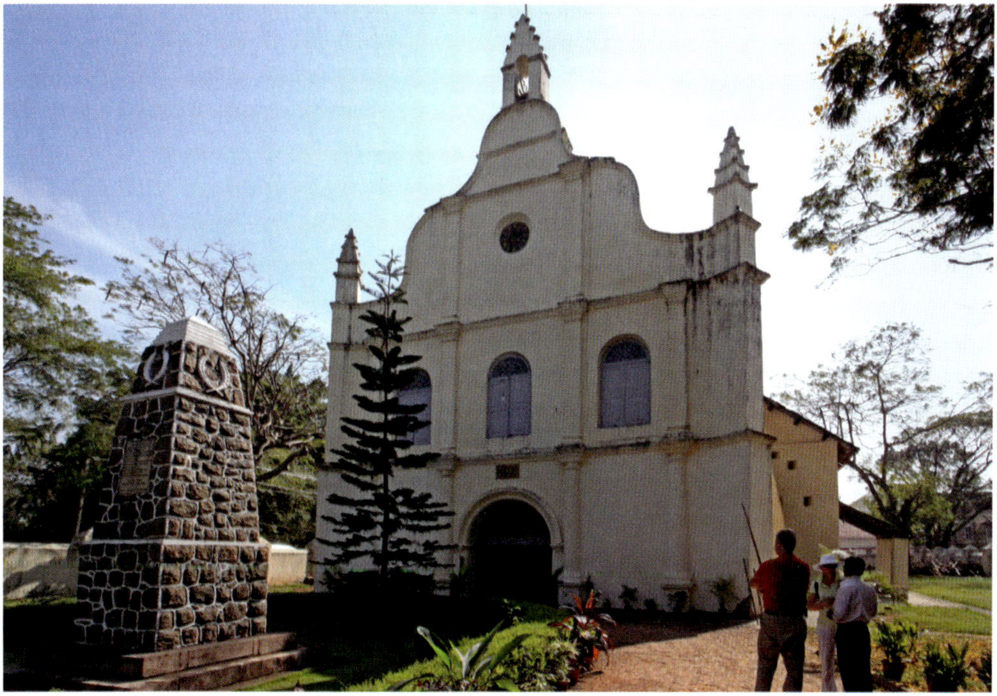

The Church of St. Francis, India's oldest European church in Fort Kochi

replaced it with a permanent structure, the building we see today, and services were performed with all the pomp and ceremony of Roman Catholic worship.

The Protestant Dutch attacked Kochi again in 1662 and the Portuguese surrendered the following year. The religious policies of the Dutch were on the whole more tolerant. Subsequently it was the beginning of a peaceful era until the British army attacked Kochi in 1795. The Dutch surrendered the church to the Anglicans in 1804 by which time it was in a sorry state, its roof had partly caved in and its walls were bare. Restoration began in 1886 and once fully restored, the British renamed it the Church of St. Francis.

The exterior comprises of a tall gabled facade with a large arched doorway. Three arched windows above are set at equal intervals and a clock sits in the centre of the façade. Above is the bell tower. On either side are small towers which give balance to the exterior. Shutters successfully keep the church cool in the Indian climate. It

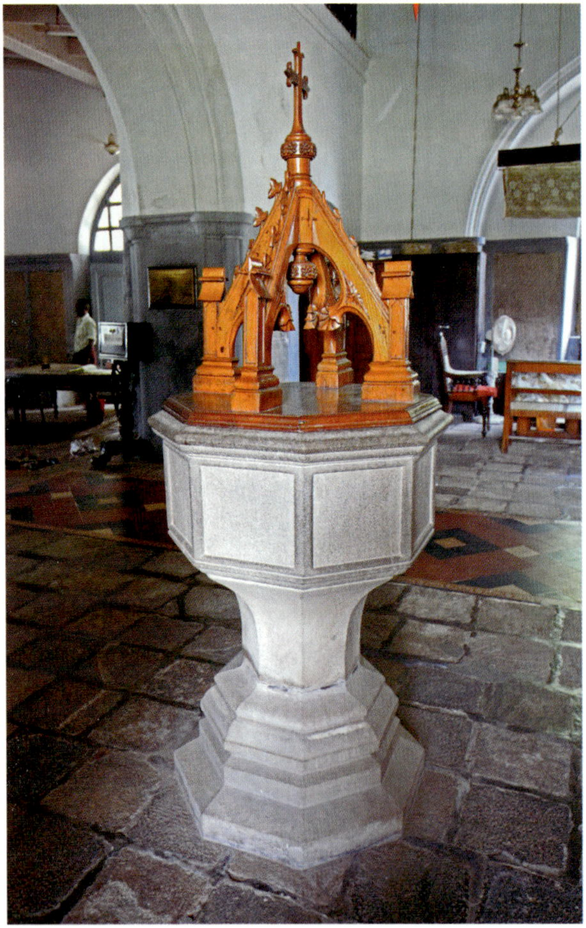

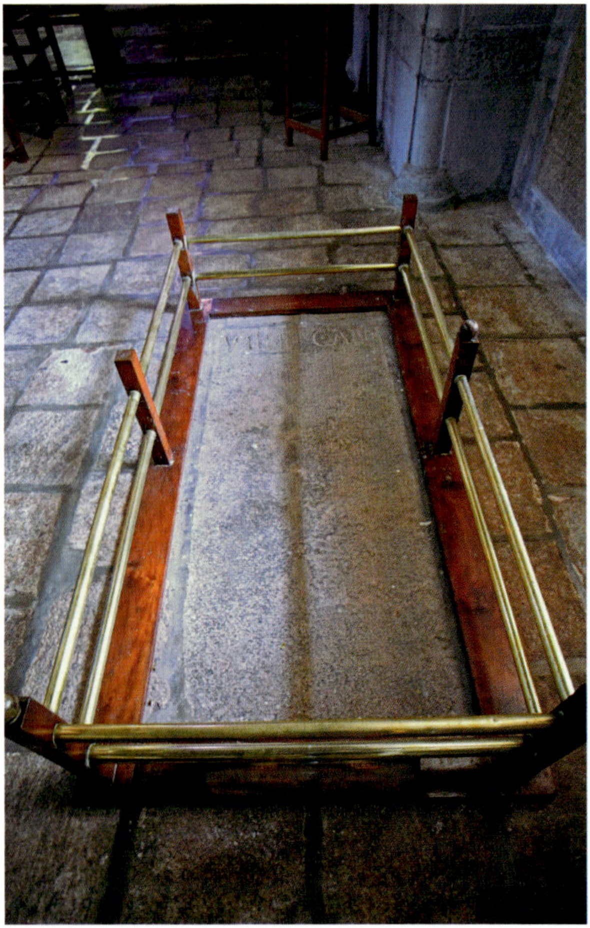

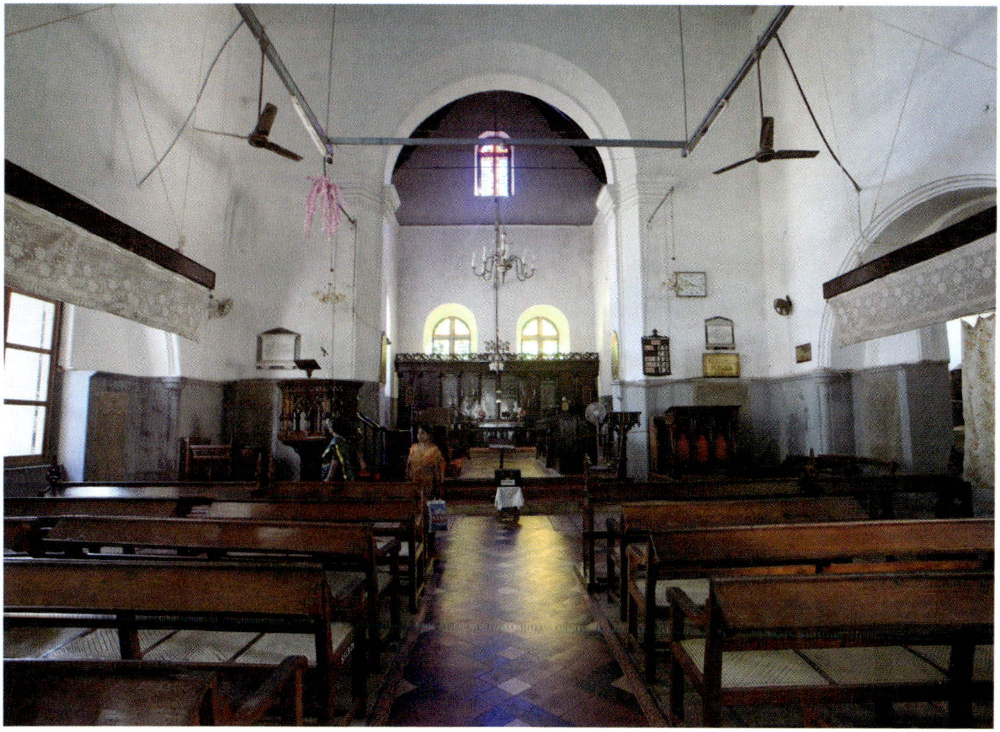

ABOVE: *Looking towards the altar inside St. Francis*
FACING PAGE TOP & BELOW LEFT: *Detail of the lace punkhas; The font, the flagstone and mosaic floor*
FACING PAGE BELOW RIGHT: *The original site of Vasco da Gama's tomb*

is a modest church and as such it has an appealing honesty.

Once inside the eye is drawn to the beautiful collection of *punkhas*, large lengths of cloth attached to wooden rods that hang from the ceiling—an ancient Indian method of cooling interiors. Lengths of string are attached which lead through the walls to the outside of the building where the *punkhawalla* would sit, moving the fans backwards and forwards keeping the British congregation cool. During the hottest months, from April to June, *punkha*s would be dipped in water and the evaporating effect would add to the cooling. *Punkha*s were usually made from gunning sacking so they wouldn't flap and frills would sometimes be added for a more decorative effect. The *punkha*s in St. Francis Church are particularly beautiful. Made of the finest muslin they are decorated with fine hand-worked embroidery. Above the

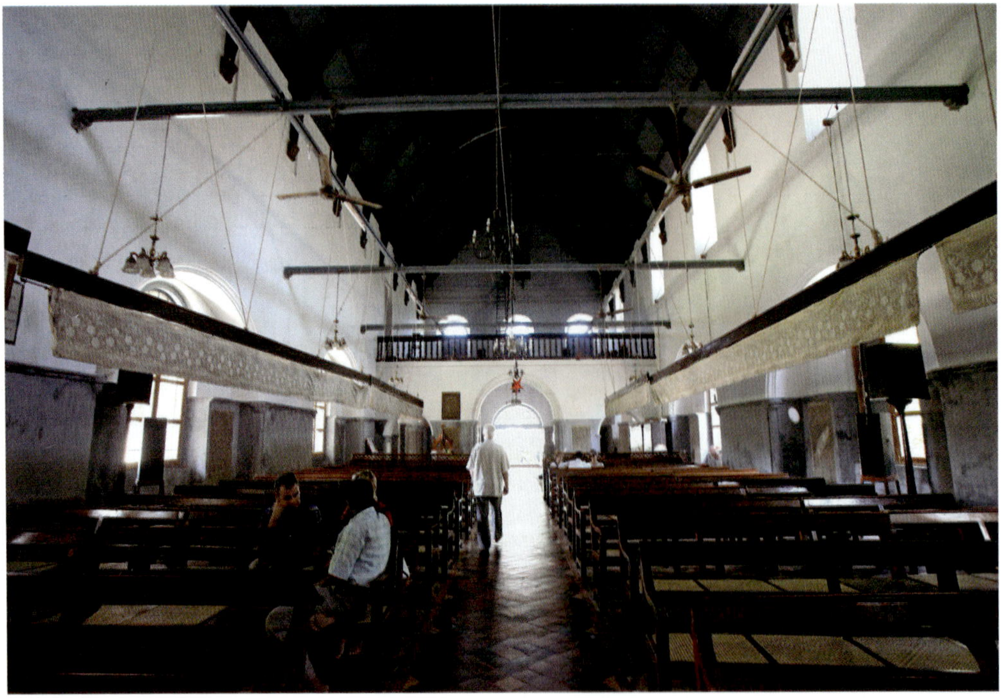

Looking away from the altar, the punkhas and the choir loft at St. Francis, Fort Kochi

punkhas the dark timber arches of the roof contrast with the simply adorned white walls. Overall the main body of the church is pleasantly cool and airy.

A broad spanned arch separates the chancel from the nave which interestingly is from the Latin *navis* which means 'ship,' a very apt description of the ribbed timber ship like ceiling in the Church of St. Francis. Behind the communion table is a richly carved screen or *reredos*. The choir loft is above the entrance. The original gravestone of Vasco da Gama can be found in the chancel of the church on the southern side of the building. His body was taken back to Portugal and is now re-interred in an impressive tomb in St. Jeronimos Monastery, Vidiguera.

After the church's long history it is now part of the Church of South India, CSI, which is a union of the Protestant and Anglican churches in South India. It replaced the Church of England in India after 1947 when India became independent. A cenotaph in the church garden was established in 1920 and dedicated to the people of Kochi who died in World War 1. The Church of St. Francis and the Church of Santa Cruz were the first churches built by the Portuguese after their arrival in Kerala.

The Cathedral Basilica of Santa Cruz, 1557

Roman Catholic

The first Church of Santa Cruz was built by Francesco de Almeida, the first Portuguese viceroy, who used the sale of goods acquired during Portuguese sea battles to finance the building. The foundation stone was laid in 1505.

The facade of the Cathedral Basilica of Santa Cruz can be described as Indo-Gothic in style. There are three timber entry doors on the ground floor and three corresponding timber windows on the second, each flanked by bi-foliate windows. These doors and windows are round, not Gothic in style but the earlier Romanesque. A decorative floral frieze, Gothic tracery and fanlights can be

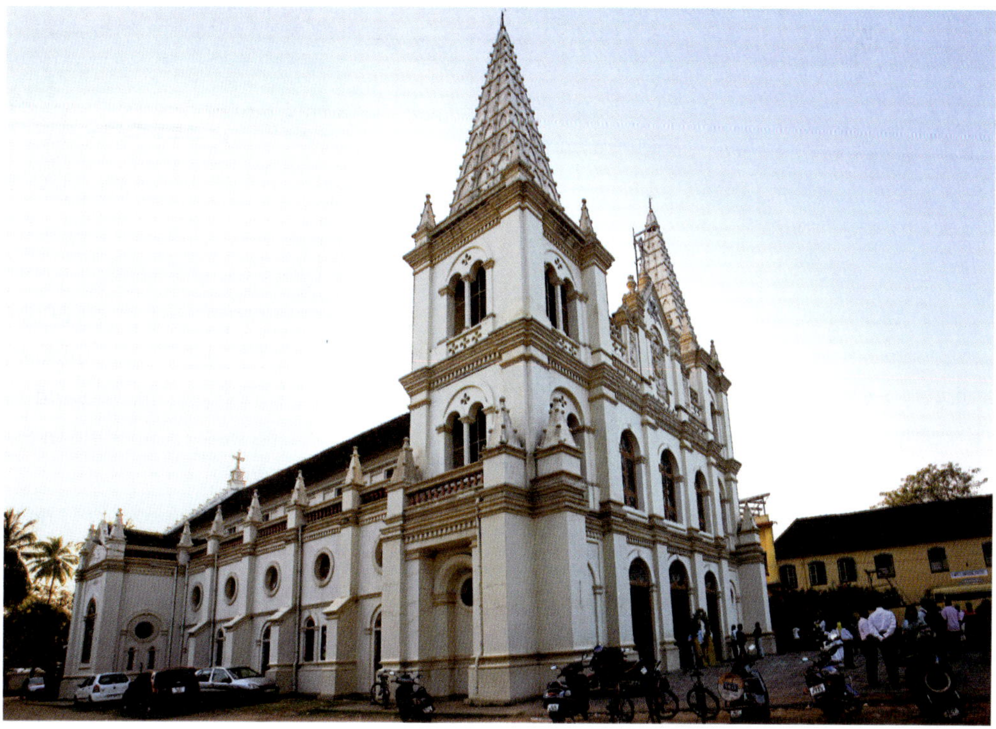

The Cathedral Basilica of Santa Cruz, rebuilt and opened for worship in 1903

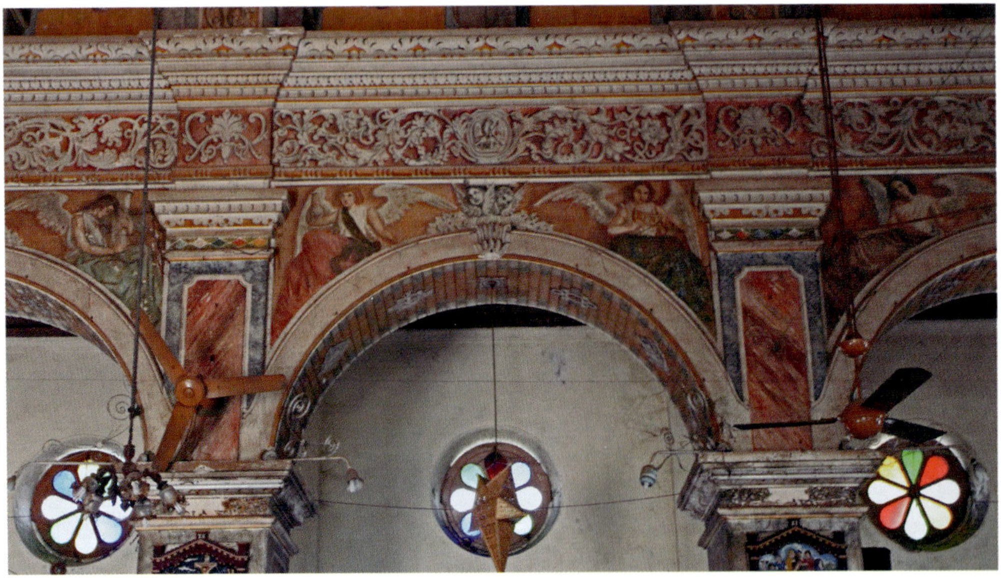

Faux marble and murals at the Cathedral Basilica of Santa Cruz, Kochi

seen and on either side are two more bi-foliate windows above which are tall, Gothic style towers adorned with crockets, a hook-shaped ornamentation. On the third level the gable is richly carved with religious figures and a coat of arms.

The interior of the cathedral is decorative with Indian elements. Bright blue pillars decorated with a white foliate design separate the nave, drawing an invisible line between areas of simple rough wooden pews at the entry to more elegant pews beyond and closest to the altar. Large square columns support arches enhanced with faux marble or 'trick of the eye' paint affects, the work of the famous Italian Jesuit Antonio Moscheni who also decorated the main altar. Seven large oil paintings attached to the ceiling show scenes from the Fourteen Stations of the Cross and a replica of The Last Supper after Leonardo da Vinci's famous work, hangs high above the altar. It took two years to complete the interior paintings.

After a six month siege in 1663 the Dutch seized Cochin from the Portuguese and the clergy were sent away. Their monasteries, churches, hospitals and chapels were completely destroyed except for the Church of St. Francis and the Santa Cruz Cathedral, which they used as a storehouse. When Fort

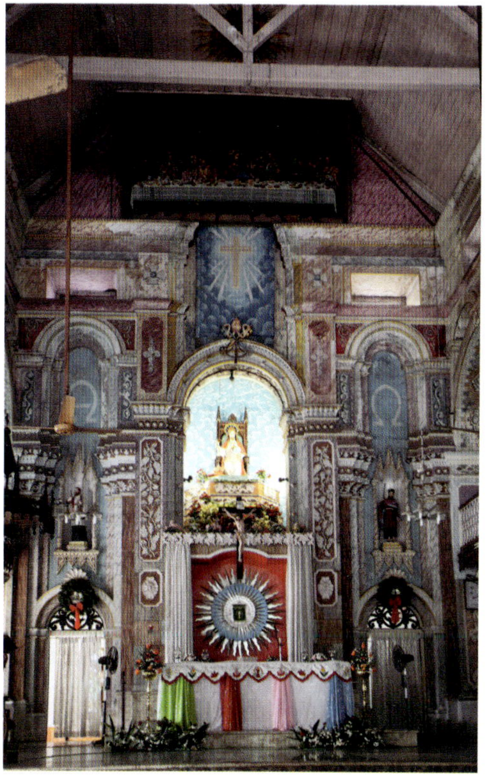

The colourful altar

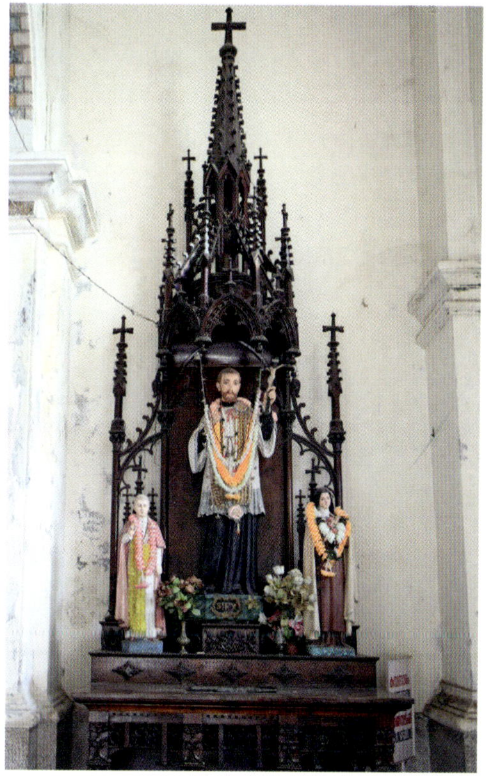

A Gothic shrine to Saint Francis Xavier

Kochi fell into the hands of the British they used St. Francis as their house of worship and all was relatively peaceful until 1806 when the British blew up the Cathedral of Santa Cruz for fear of an upsurge of Dutch power. The church was destroyed save for one granite pillar which can be seen in the south-eastern corner of the church.

The cathedral was eventually re-erected by Bishop Ferreira of Cochin in 1896 but collapsed just before completion. The Bishop died later the same year. It was Bishop Oliveira Xavier who rebuilt the cathedral until it was finally opened for worship in 1903 and was consecrated in 1905. The Cathedral of Santa Cruz, like the earlier Church of St. Francis, has had many lives over the centuries; built by the Portuguese, transformed by the Dutch, demolished by the British and then rebuilt to its former glory. Fort Kochi finally shook off European power with Indian Independence in 1947. In 1984 Pope John Paul II granted the Santa Cruz Cathedral the title of Basilica.

Kottayam

St. Mary's 'Valiyapally' Church, 1550

Orthodox Syrian

Kottayam is a beautiful district in Kerala bordering Lake Vembanad. This early church was built by Syrian Christians who are believed to be descendants of the Christians from the east who arrived in India with Thomas of Cana. It was built in 1550 CE and known in Malayalam as Valiyapally or 'big church'. In those early days the area was part of a small princely state ruled by the Thekkumkur Raja who invited the Christians to build a church near his fort. Though altered over the years it is remarkable that this ancient church has retained its original structure.

BELOW LEFT: *St. Mary's 'Valiyapally' Church*

BELOW RIGHT: *The ornate gilded altar in the church*

FACING PAGE TOP: *The interior of St. Mary's Valiyapally with a typical red curtain protecting the altar*

FACING PAGE BELOW: *Close-up of the ornate gilded altar*

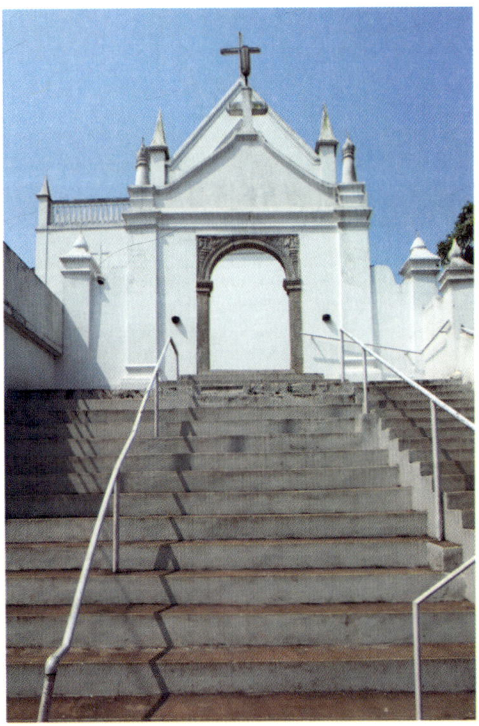

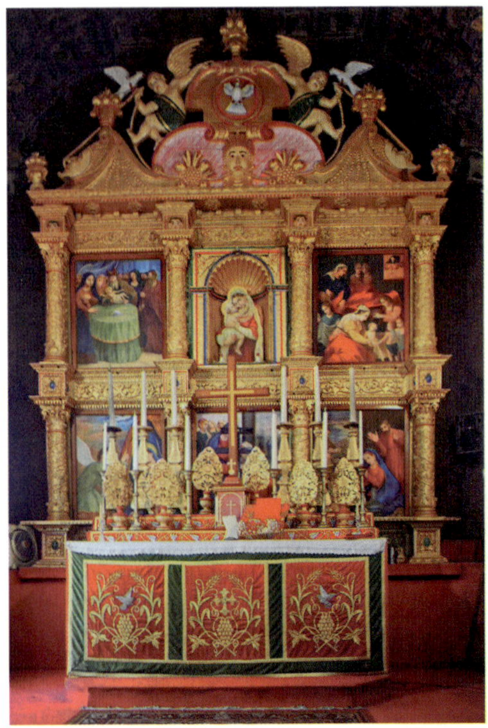

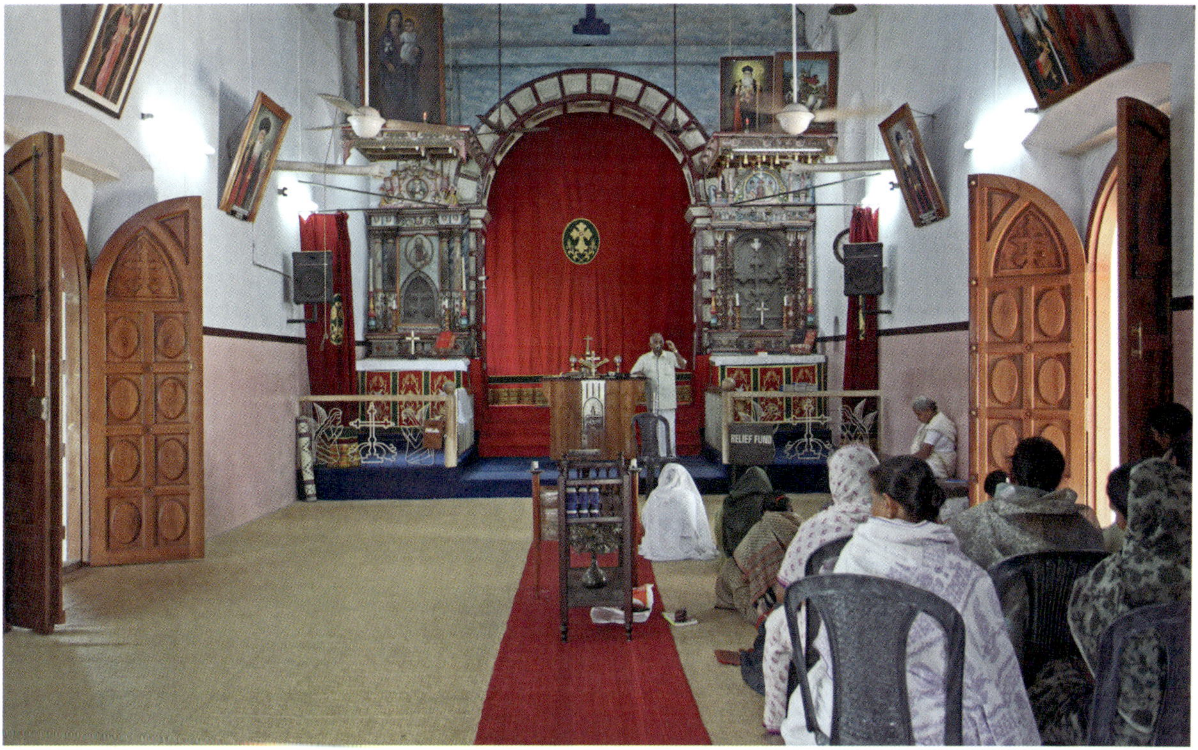
RELIEF FUND

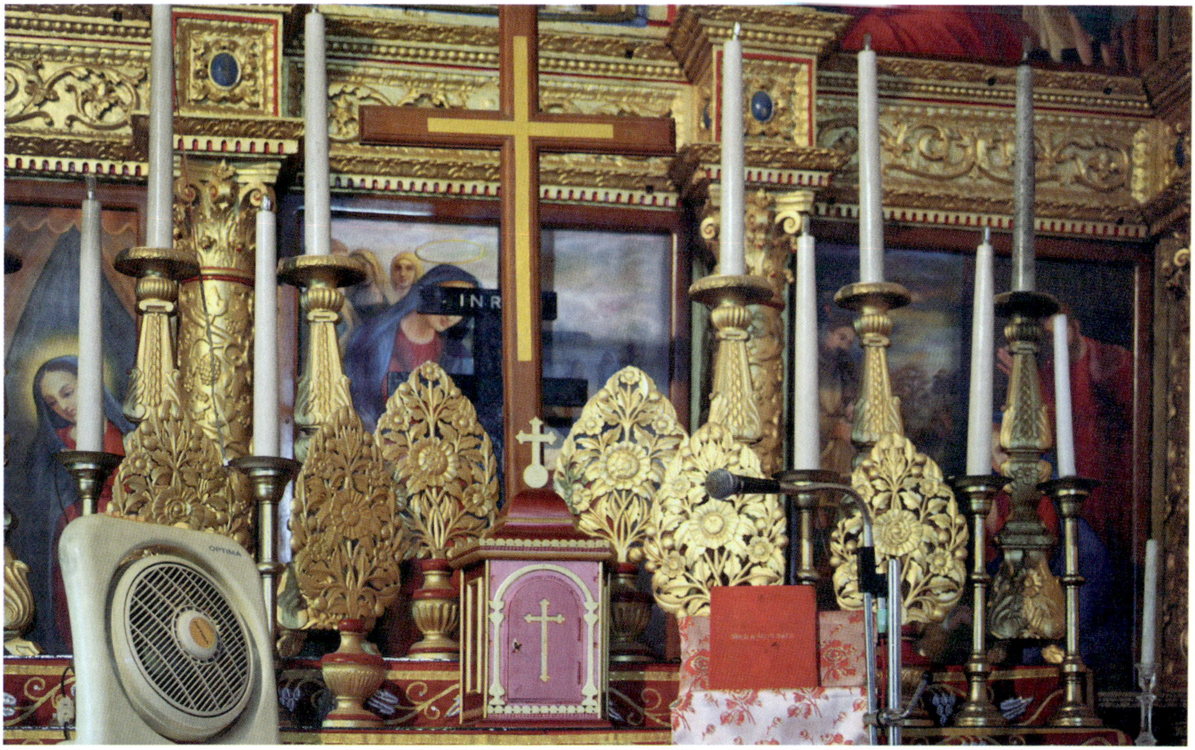
INRI
OPTIMA

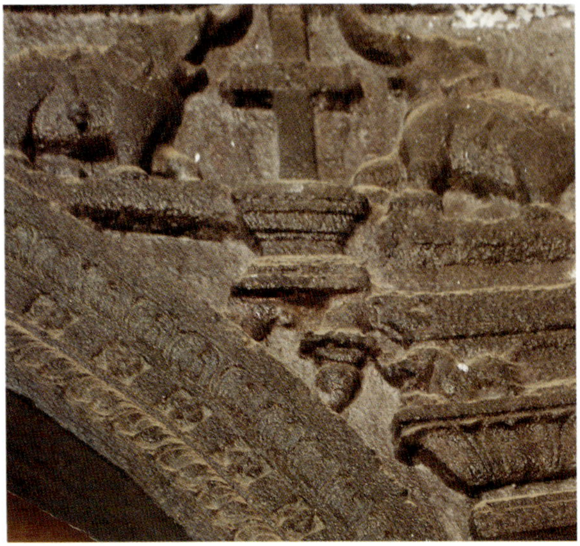

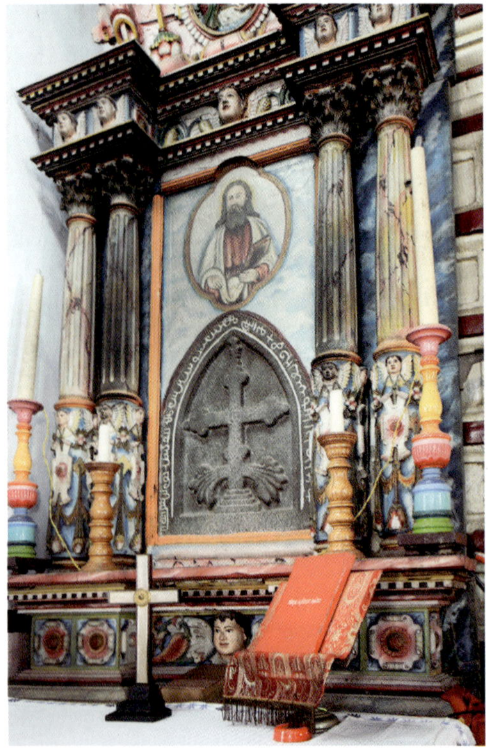

ABOVE: *A stone carving at the entrance shows elephants paying homage to a cross at St. Mary's 'Valiyapally'*
RIGHT: *One of the important ancient stone plaques*

Some vernacular forms can be seen in the church; the series of steep steps ascending to a hilltop, small turrets in Hindu temple style decorating the façade, a false entrance arch in granite and a true entrance on the side of the church opening into the centre of the nave. On the walls outside are plaques revealing the names of famous visitors to the church which include among others, the Emperor of Ethiopia, Haile Selassie and Lord Irwin, Governor General and Viceroy of India from 1926 to 1931. The church's interior has a few chairs for the elderly but otherwise the congregation sits on the floor which is traditional in all Syrian Christian churches. The interior holds two very famous 8th century granite plaques carved with ancient Persian crosses. They are originally from a much older church in Cranganore built by the Kottyam Christians' ancestors. Both have inscriptions in the ancient Persian language Pahalavi. The paintings on the main altar illustrate scenes from the bible.

When St. Mary's congregation became divided St. Mary's Orthodox Church was built nearby and completed in 1579. It is known in Malayalam as Cheriapally or 'Small Church'.

St. Mary's 'Cheriapally' Church, Kottayam, 1579

Orthodox Syrian

St. Marys is one of the oldest churches in Kerala and a typical Syrian Christian church apart from one major variation; the addition of a large flat fronted Portuguese style façade. The long gabled porch, *nadakasala,* was added in the 19th century. It is a beautiful structure with supporting pillars and ornate timber rafters, a characteristic of Kerala's temples. These European facades are an example of the most obvious of all architectural elements introduced to Kerala's churches by the Portuguese. It was a way of achieving what they thought of as a more Christian appearance to the Eastern churches. It was also relatively easy to achieve. These facades are numerous in Kerala and wholly European in style. However they are often mistakenly described by locals as 'pure Kerala style.'

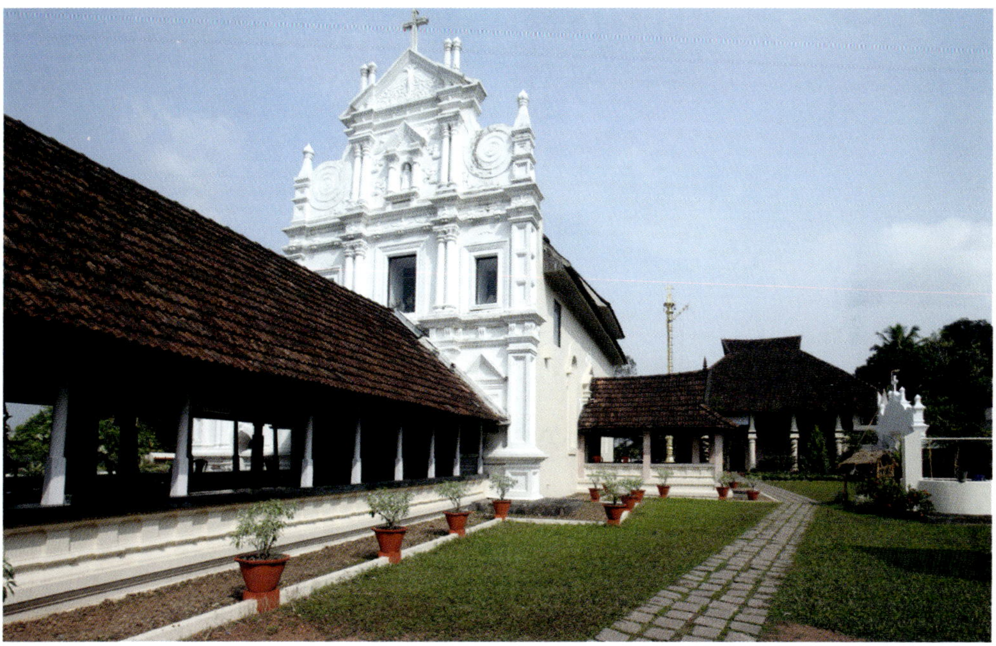

The European facade, the Syrian Christian porch and portico of St. Mary's 'Cheriapally Church'

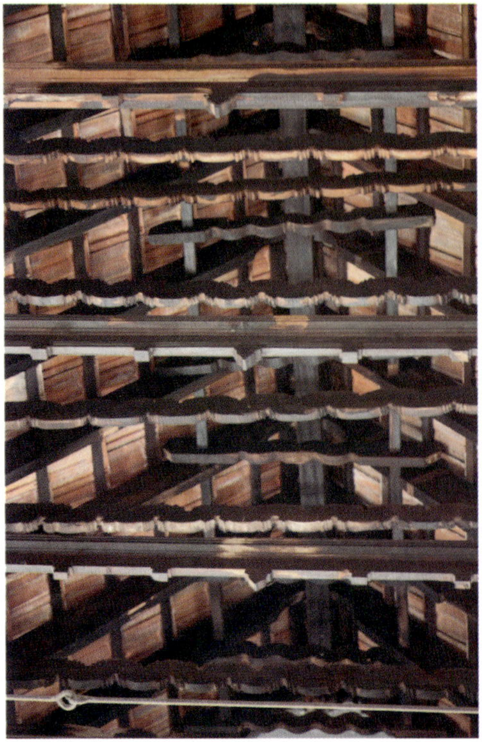

ABOVE: *Carved timber rafters of the St. Mary's porch*

FACING PAGE ABOVE: *The altar and extraordinary murals*

FACING PAGE BELOW LEFT: *Detail of Mary and the Baby Jesus (collection of Joanne Taylor)*

FACING PAGE BELOW RIGHT: *Detail of the façade with religious symbols*

Despite the facade being European the decorative bas-relief symbols are Indian in origin. They include large circular patterns either side of the pediment signifying the Hindu wheel of eternity; the double headed bird representing the dual nature of Jesus, both human and divine; the four small minarets at the top and the two below give recognition to the Muslim religion and the line of angels represent the Parsi religion. The cashew nuts and the deer symbolise aspects of Kerala life and culture. In the centre is a small niche which holds a statue of the Virgin and Child surrounded by angels.

St. Mary's is known for its murals. Behind the altar is a beautiful image of an Indian Madonna and Child surrounded by angels with the Holy Trinity above. Below are scenes from the life of Jesus. Painted Hindu motifs cover the barrel vault ceiling, carved from laterite stone, plastered then painted. Though less clear, the walls are covered with images of Portuguese soldiers, Christ on the Cross and motifs of Kerala life, borders of flowers, trees and animals. The murals in St. Mary's Church are extraordinary and show the influence of both European and Indian art.

The church was restored in 1993 and has been well maintained ever since. Kerala has many churches with ancient murals decorating their walls and ceilings and the tradition of mural painting in churches can be dated as far back as the 7th and 8th centuries CE. Religious and non-religious stories, some of them great epics, were painted on walls to convey ideas that would easily be understood. The images in St. Mary's have retained much of their vibrant colours. To create these murals artists used wooden bowls to mix

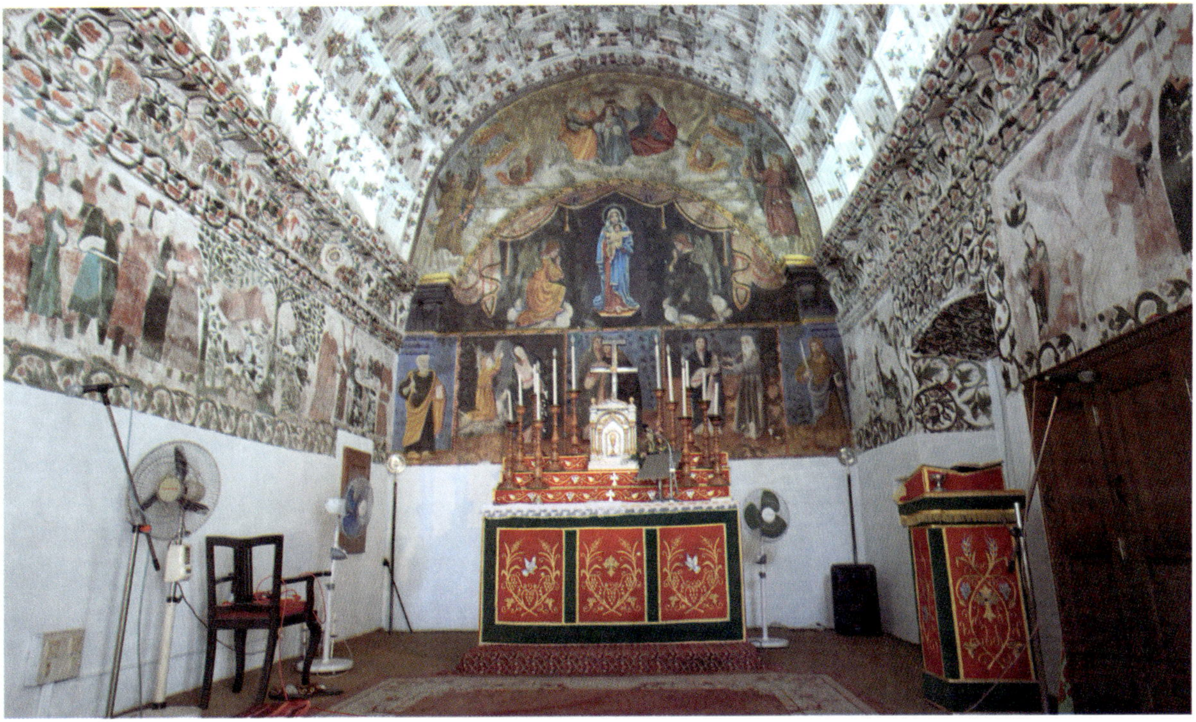

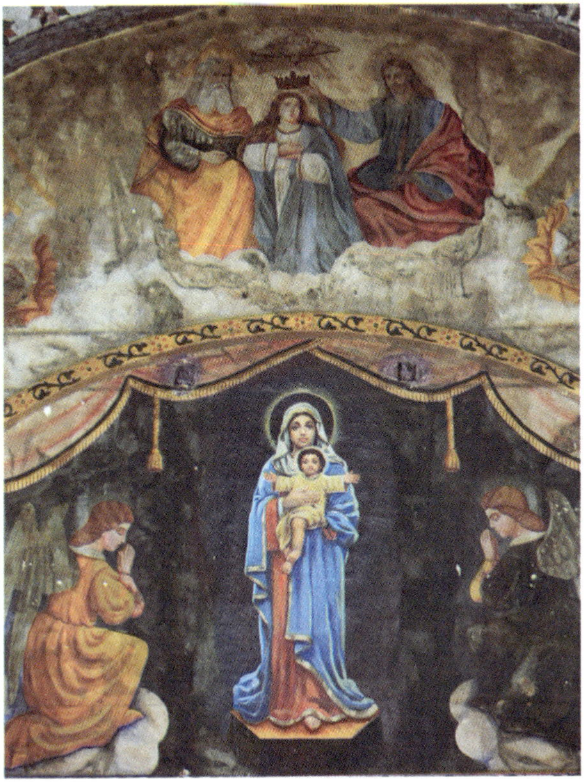

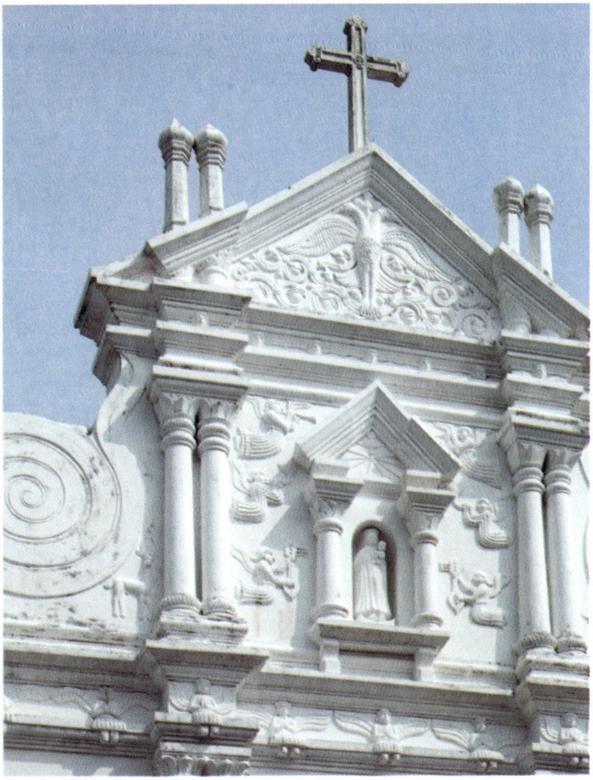

dyes made from vegetables, earth, roots and stones. Their brushes were made from a particular grass and lengths of bamboo were sharpened to create the fine outlines which can be seen in many of the paintings. Another church decorated with wonderful murals, some on display and others hidden, is St. Thomas Cathedral in Pala.

The Cathedral of St. Thomas, 18th Century, Pala

Syro-Malabar Catholic

This 18th-century cathedral is situated close to the River Meenachil. It is beautifully maintained with a dazzling white facade in the Portuguese style and a gabled nave in the Kerala style. The façade features statues

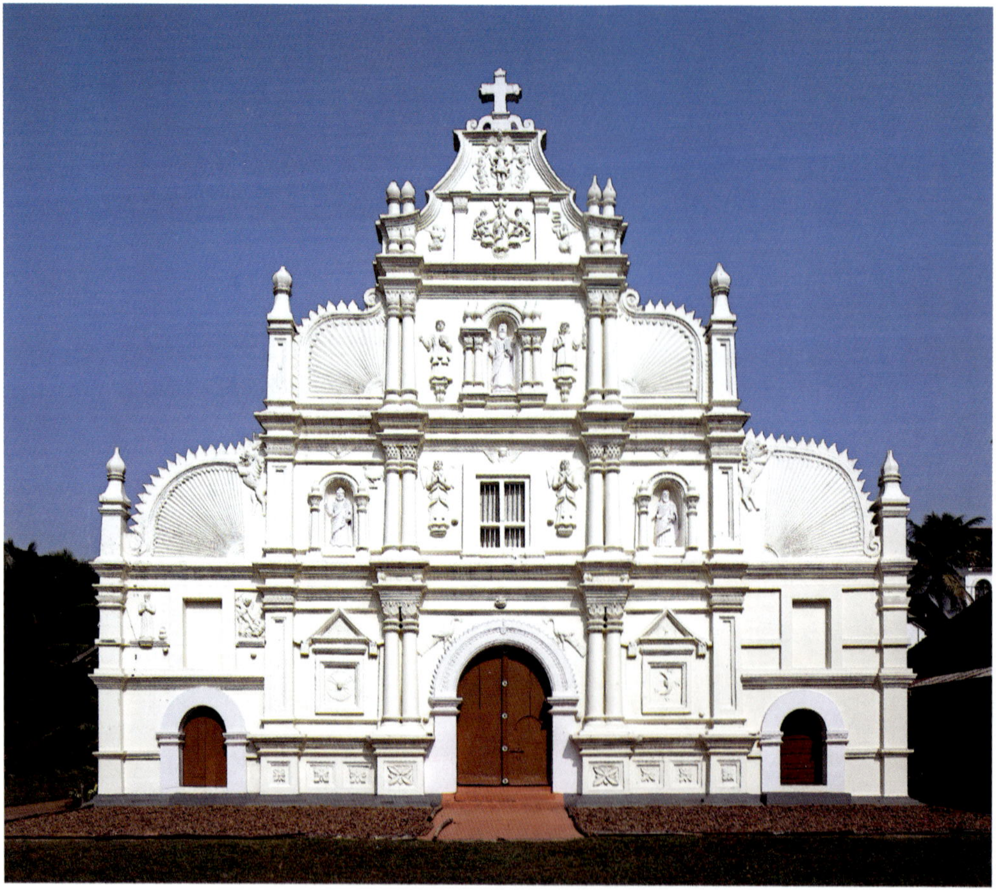

Cathedral of St. Thomas, Pala

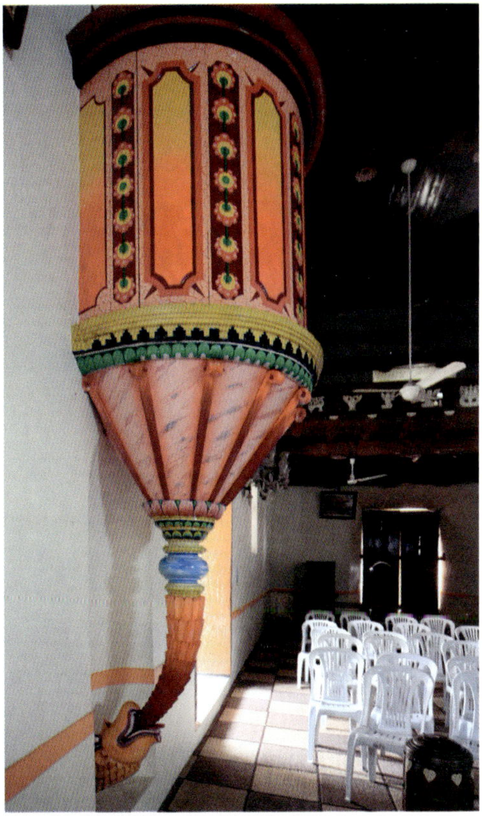

The flamboyant pulpit in the Cathedral of St. Thomas

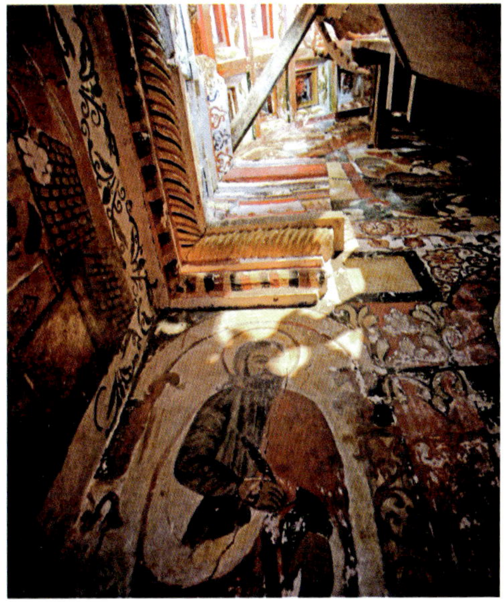

The ancient murals

of saints and a small number of Indian symbols. The original church of St. Thomas was completed in 1010 CE in Pala, a town inhabited by St. Thomas Christians from around 1000 CE and one of Kerala's main Christian cultural centres today. The church was built by four local Syrian Christian families and though we can speculate there is no evidence to show what that church looked like. The church was built in stone and mortar in the Portuguese architectural style In the 16th or 17th century and then renovated in the 18th century to what we see today. It was raised to the status of a cathedral in 1950 but when a bigger church was needed St. Thomas became known as 'the old cathedral'.

Inside the cathedral is an array of wonderful colours and ornate carvings. Pink, green, blue and gold, similar to the colours used in South Indian temples, are used on and behind the altar, pulpit and the moulded panels. Painted wood in the form of candlesticks and stylised flowers and trees make beautiful altar pieces. The *reredos* or screen behind the

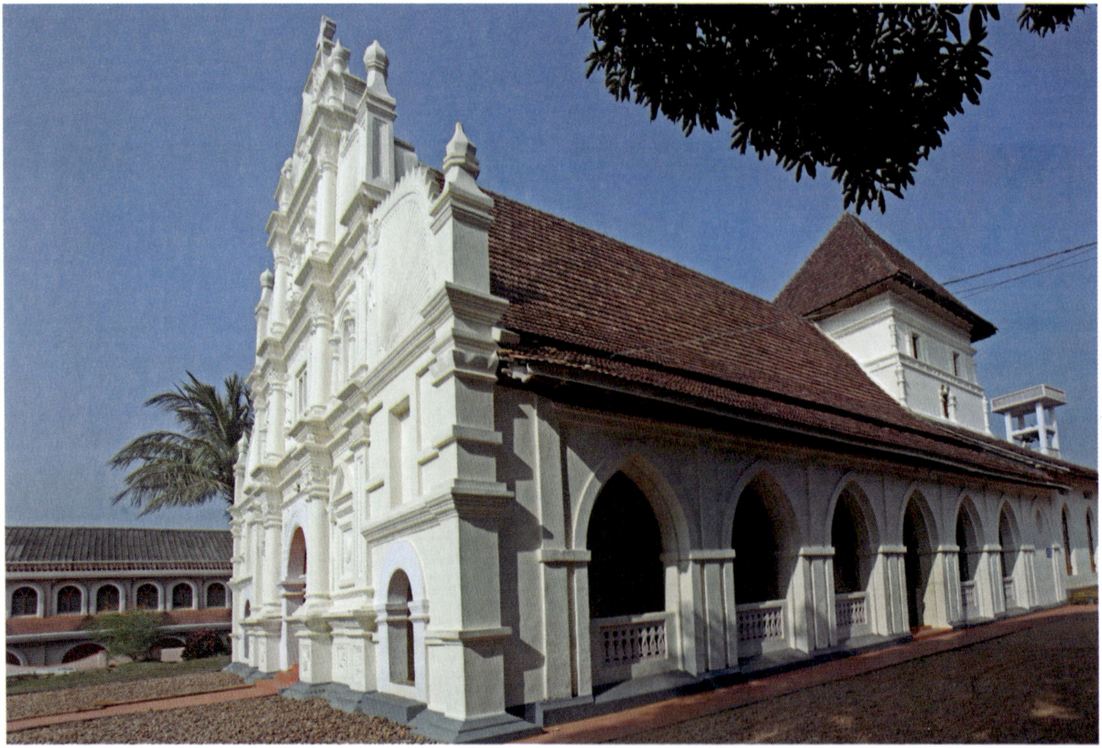

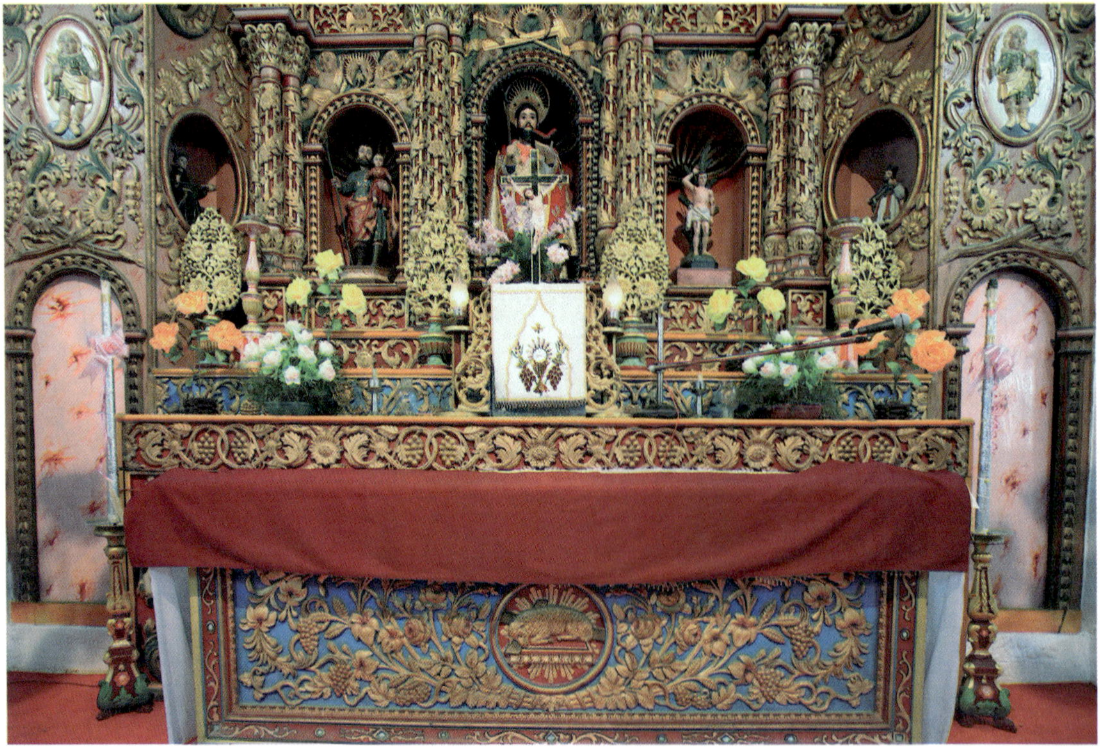

altar is highly decorative with pillars, painted medallions and arched niches holding figures of saints. In the centre is St. Thomas, on the right St. Sebastian and on the left St. Joseph. Suspended high on the church wall a flamboyant pulpit rises from the mouth of a serpent or *naga*. It is reached by exterior stairs allowing for a dramatic entrance. The design of the pulpit is distinctively South Indian.

The secret inside the cathedral's walls are the wonderful hidden murals. On either side of the altar behind what seem to be small arched panels, in fact doors, is a tiny space just wide enough to squeeze into. Inside it is dark but there is just enough light for my camera to detect ancient murals that cover the whole of the wall. The space is between the wall of the church and the more recently added *reredos* which is supported by wooden beams. The artist has used colours of ochre and terracotta to depict images of religious figures surrounded by the tropical plants and flowers of Kerala, similar to St. Mary's Church in Kottayam. At some time a new *reredos* was built hiding these ancient murals while at the same time preserving them.

St. John's Metropolitan Cathedral, Tiruvalla, 2004

Syro-Malankara Catholic

It is impossible to describe the wonderful St. John Cathedral in Tiruvalla without commenting on its famous architect Laurence Wilfred Baker, better known as Laurie Baker, a Quaker born in England in 1917. While in Mumbai waiting for a ship back to England he was introduced to Mahatma Gandhi who asked Baker to visit the concrete tenements, slums if truth be told that housed Mumbai's workers. Later he asked Baker "What is the alternative? We need people like you here," going on to explain that western architectural ideas would not succeed in India, to look at the rural areas instead of the cities and that it should be possible to build a home with building materials found within a five mile radius. As Baker's work was based on craft principles he was already Gandhian in spirit but this encounter changed Baker's life forever.

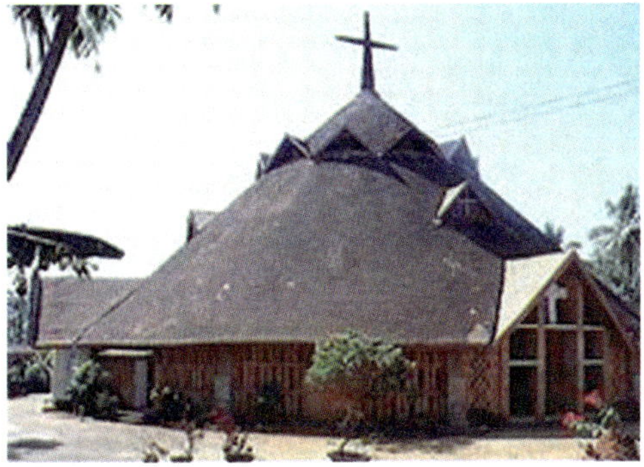

ABOVE: *The original St. John's by Laurie Baker (collection of Joanne Taylor)*

FACING PAGE TOP: *A side elevation of St. Thomas' Cathedral*

FACING PAGE BELOW: *The tiny doors in the* reredos *which lead to the hidden murals*

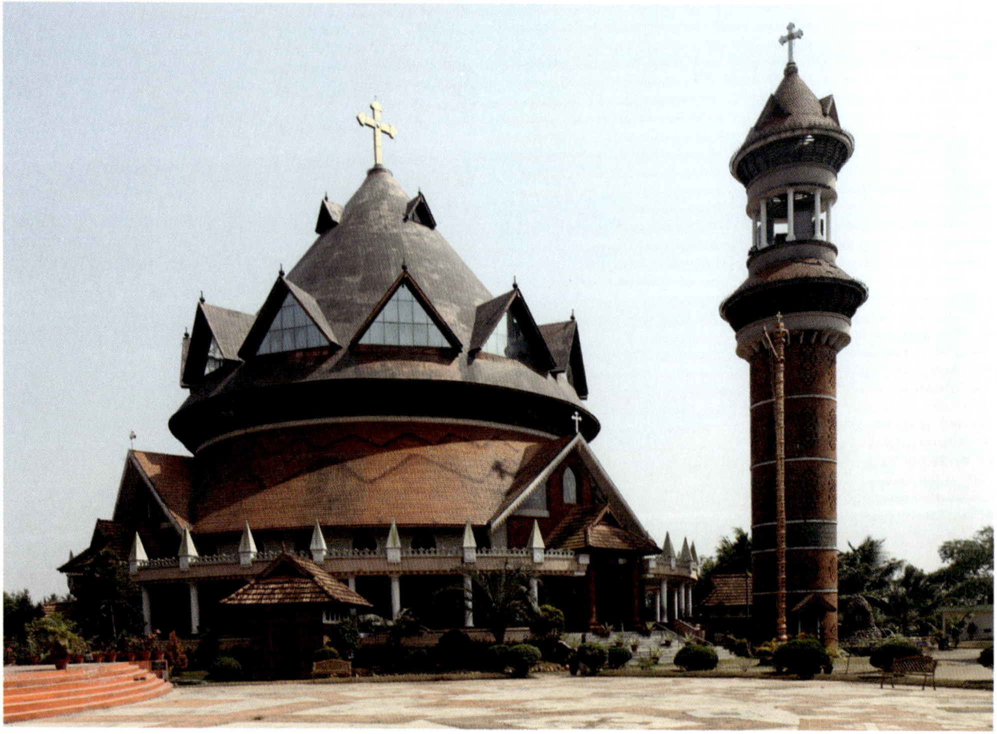

St. John's Metropolitan Cathedral

He returned to India in 1945 as chief architect of the Mission to Lepers, designing centres for leprosy patients. It was at one of these hospitals that he met his wife Elizabeth, a doctor and after working together in the Himalayas moved to Kottayam in Kerala in 1962. Kerala's tropical landscape suited the earthy, natural buildings that Baker was planning to design. By observing and studying the vernacular architecture he came to realise that indigenous methods were by far the most suitable. Baker spent the rest of his life in India designing, among other projects, low cost mud brick durable housing appropriate for the climate, the landscape and true to the Indian craft tradition. He became known as 'The Brick Master of Kerala'.

When Bishop Mar Athanasios from Tiruvalla attended the Second Vatican Council in Rome (1962-1965) which encouraged Eastern churches to reclaim their cultural heritage the bishop became

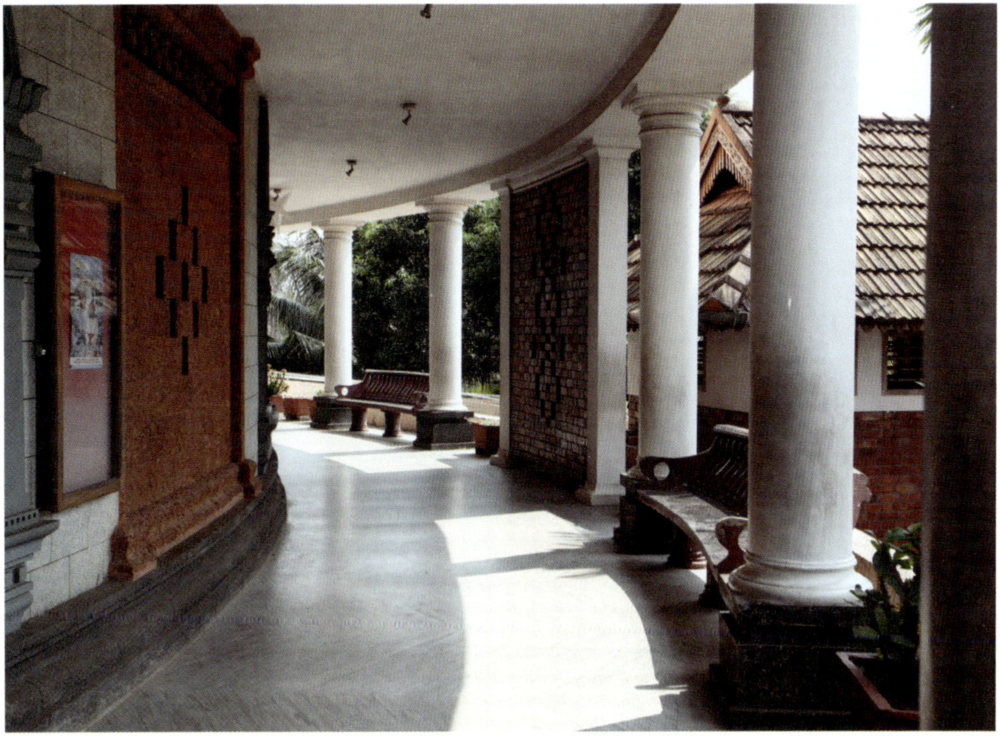

Exterior walls showing the panels of brick jalis

passionate about building a cathedral in the style and tradition of Kerala. He invited Laurie Baker to design the building using local materials.

Baker's design was influenced by the local bamboo structures and the Southern Indian tradition of patterned wooden grill-work or *jalis* which allowed air and daylight in while diffusing the glare of direct sunlight. Instead of wood Baker used brick, reducing the cost of windows, and an over-sloping roof, typical of Kerala architecture which helped protect walls from rain and direct sunlight. The roof of the circular building was supported by twelve pillars, symbolising the twelve apostles. It looked like a Hindu temple which appealed to the local people, something that was important to Baker.

The foundation stone was laid in 1970 and completed and consecrated in 1972. It became a landmark in the town. However by the 1990s the pillars began to weaken due

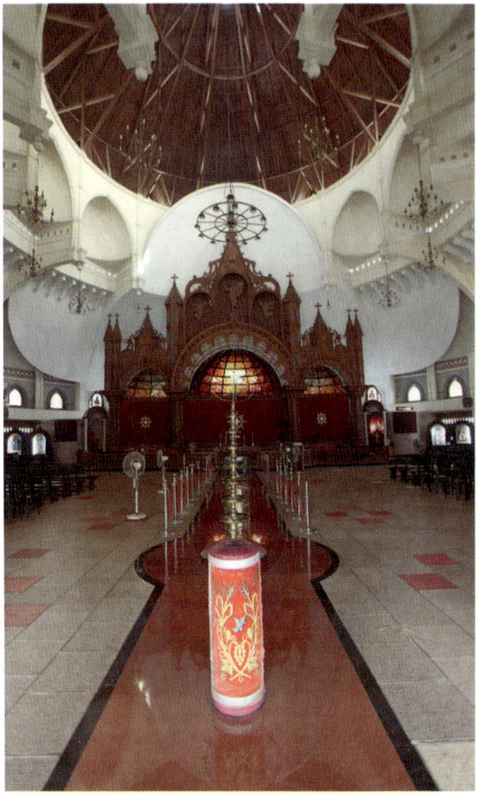

ABOVE: *View of the interior from the entrance of St. John's*
FACING PAGE TOP: *View of the ceiling with shell-like niches*
FACING PAGE BELOW: *Entrance to the churchyard and the roadside shrine*

to the weight of the wooden roof and the climatic conditions. A decision was made to demolish the building and build a new cathedral close by. The Rev. Dr. Mulamoottil, whose father had worked with Laurie Baker, was assigned the task of designing the new cathedral which was completed in 2004.

The exterior of the new church follows the same lines as the original. It is Hindu temple-like in appearance and circular in plan but is an immense structure. The ten foot high outer walls are of laterite piers interspersed with panels of tiles and brick *jali*s, used as in-fill panels creating a cool interior to combat Kerala's tropical climate. The gabled roof of the first cathedral, a feature of Kerala's architectural style, was low in height but the gabled conical roof of the new cathedral is massive and extends to form a porch supported by pillars which circles the whole structure. The upper section of the roof is copper topped with a cross at the twenty-one-metre-high apex.

The interior is truly vast and can accommodate 2,000 people. Like the original church there are no pillars to block the view of the altar. The altar itself is intricately carved and Gothic in style. Light from the *jali* behind the altar changes throughout the day and diffused light also enters from surrounding skylights, all creating the numinous, mystical quality of Christian space. The vaulted ceiling is supported by laminated wooden trusses. Large shell-like niches circumscribe the church below. Stained glass windows are central to the atmosphere. They portray biblical scenes, particularly of the relationship between God and man.

The cathedral and associated buildings are in a large walled compound entered from the

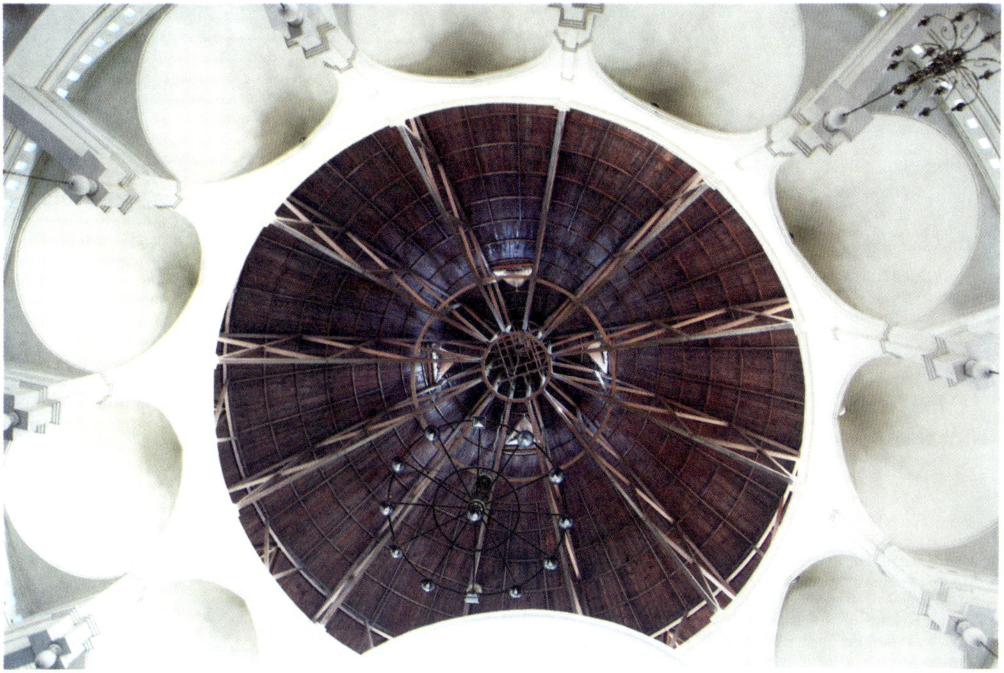

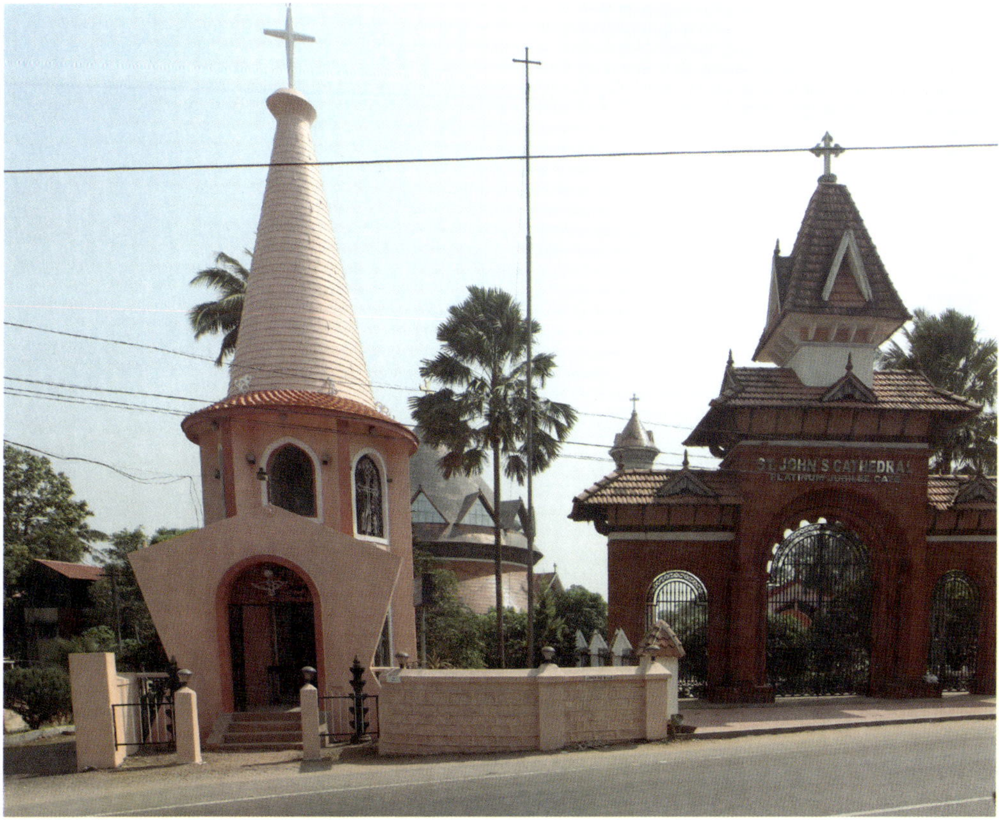
ST. JOHN'S CATHEDRAL

street through an elaborate gateway, styled like a miniature Hindu temple. On the left is a whimsical cylindrical shaped roadside shrine with a tall conical roof. An unusual tower takes the place of the flagpole or *dhvaja stambha* seen outside all Hindu temples and many Kerala churches. Like everything at St. John's it is enormous.

Laurie Baker died in 2007 in Trivandrum, aged ninety. His design for St. John's Metropolitan Cathedral expresses Christian concepts within an Indian context. By incorporating aspects of Keralan architecture, Hindu temple architecture and Eastern Christian traditions he created an inspiring landmark in Tiruvalla. Throughout his life he was guided by Gandhi's principles making India his home, working there for over fifty years and winning many awards. He obtained Indian citizenship in 1988 and was much loved for his work, particularly in Kerala.

Kerala's Backwater and Roadside Shrines

Kumarakom is one of many starting points for touring the backwaters of Kerala, famous

BELOW: *Bethlehem Church*
FACING PAGE TOP: *The beauty of the backwaters*
FACING PAGE BELOW: *Backwater shrines*

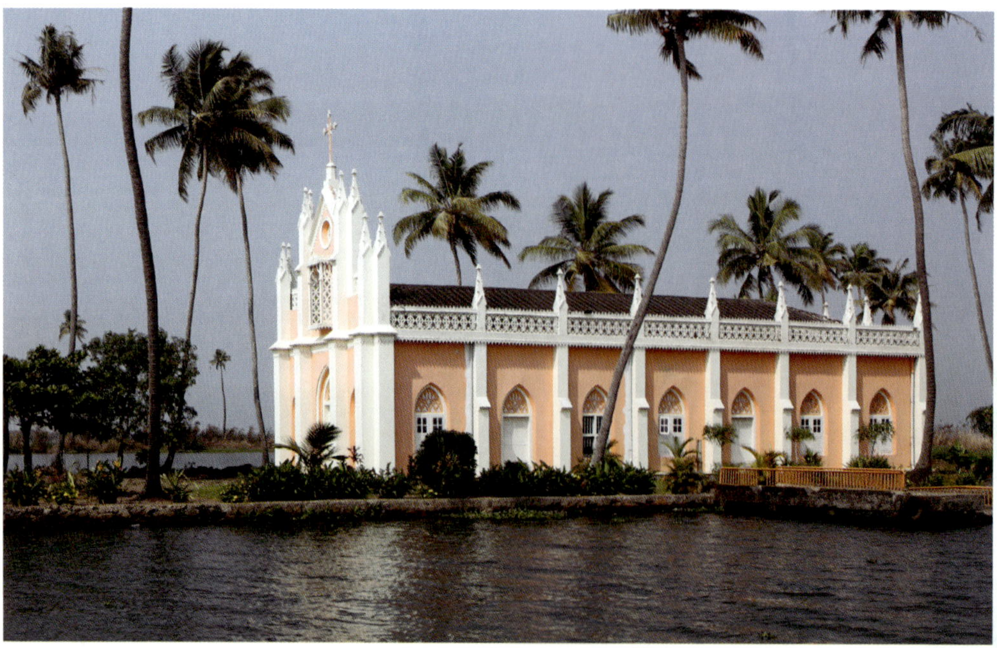

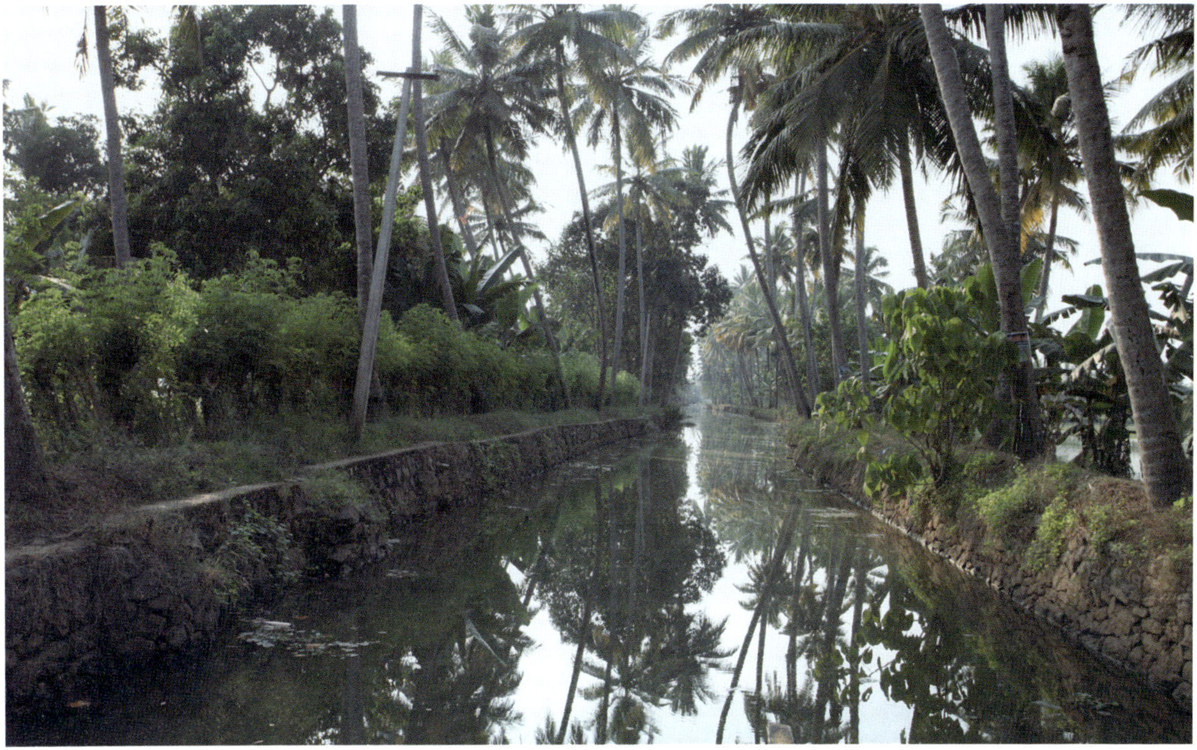

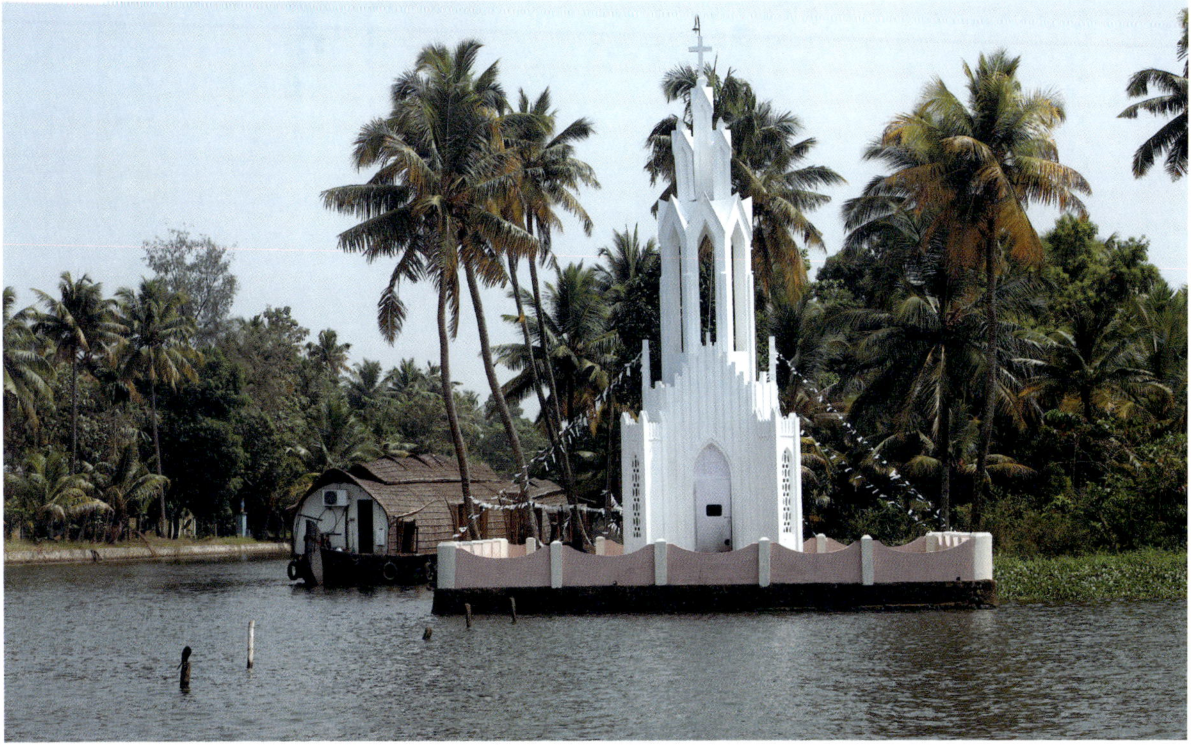

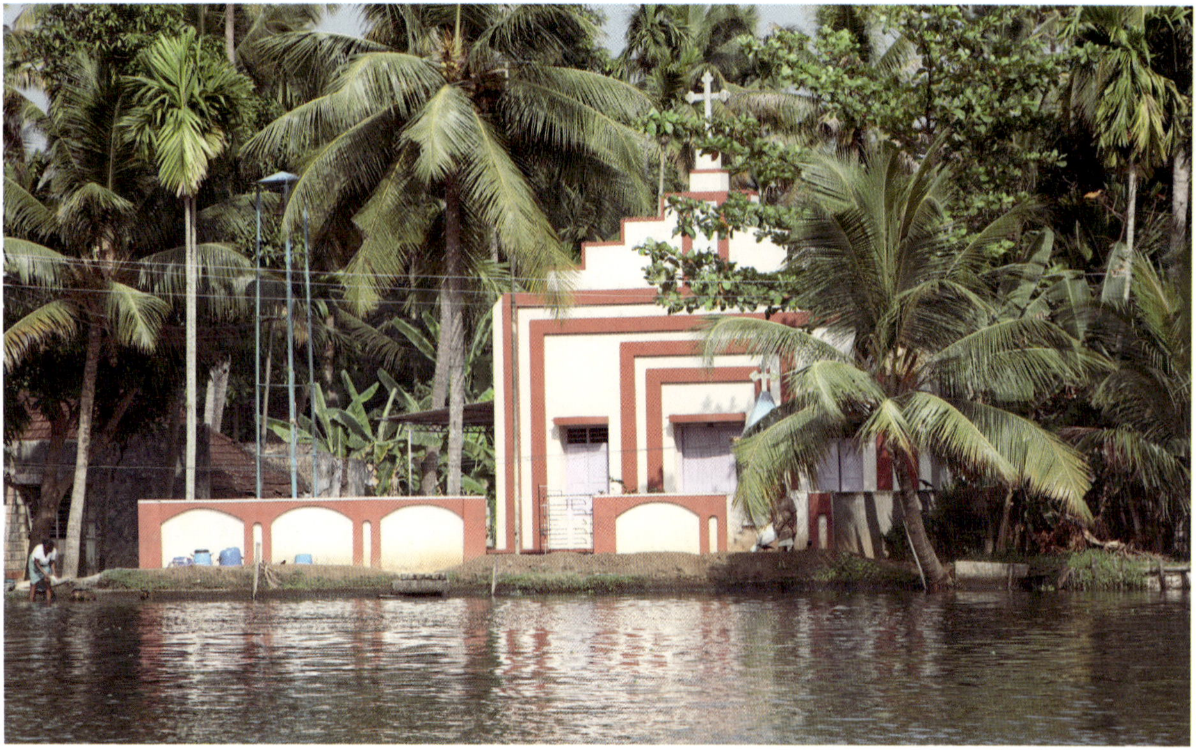

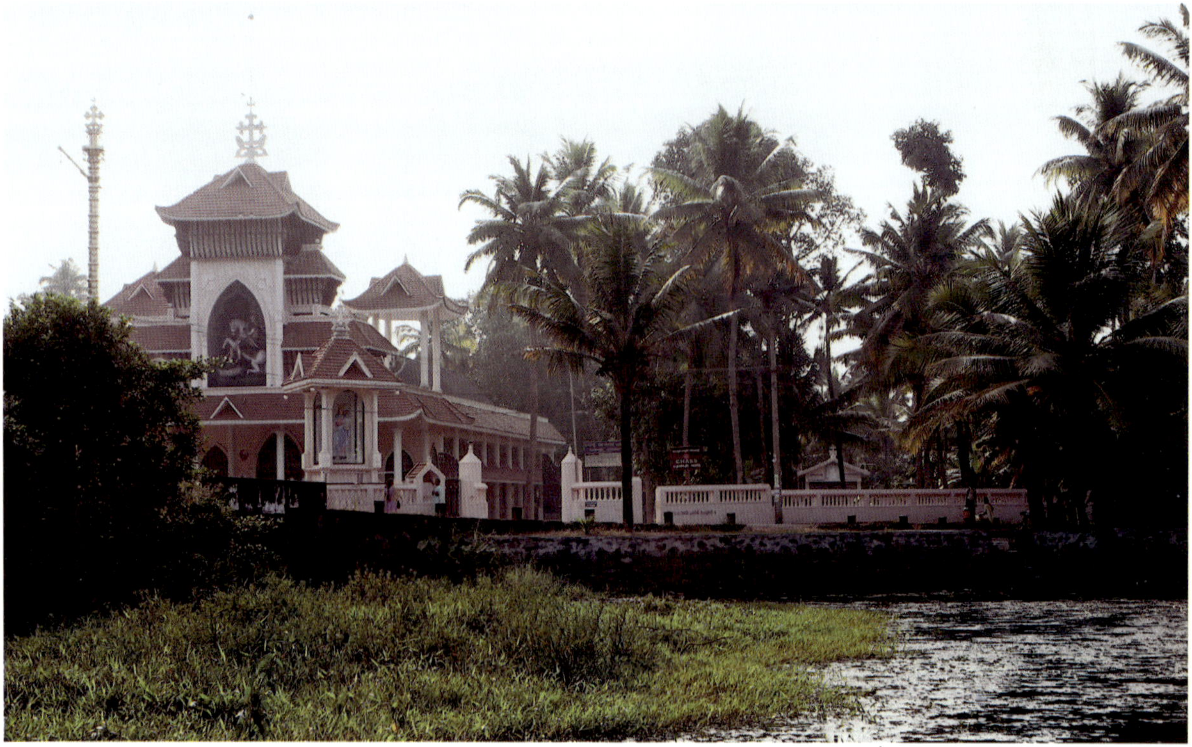

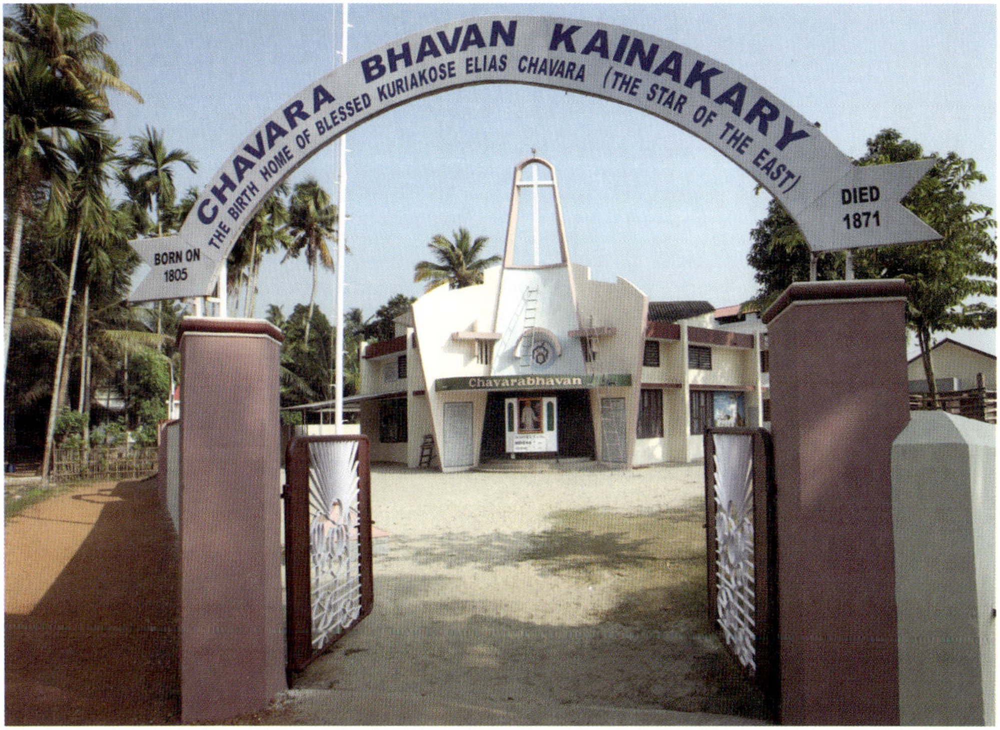

ABOVE: *The entrance to the chapel dedicated to Kuriakose Elias Chavara*
FACING PAGE TOP: *A small chapel among the palms*
FACING PAGE BELOW: *A Syrian Christian church*

for their beauty and serenity. Approximately forty monsoon-fed rivers originating in the high Western Ghats flow across the land into lakes which are connected to canals, some natural and others man-made. Lake Vembanad is the largest, its waters opening into the Arabian Sea at Port Kochi. Nine hundred kilometres of backwaters form an indispensable means of transport for the villages and towns of the area. They are a lifeline for the local community.

Rice fields below sea level are surrounded by swaying coconut palms and banana plantations. The fields reclaimed from the lake are separated from it by long fingers of land protected by clay walls which prevent further flooding. Single lines of small, brightly coloured houses run along the higher land, each with steps leading to the water and often with boats tied there. The backwaters are a dreamy place to glide through by boat and now and then a picturesque riverside shrine

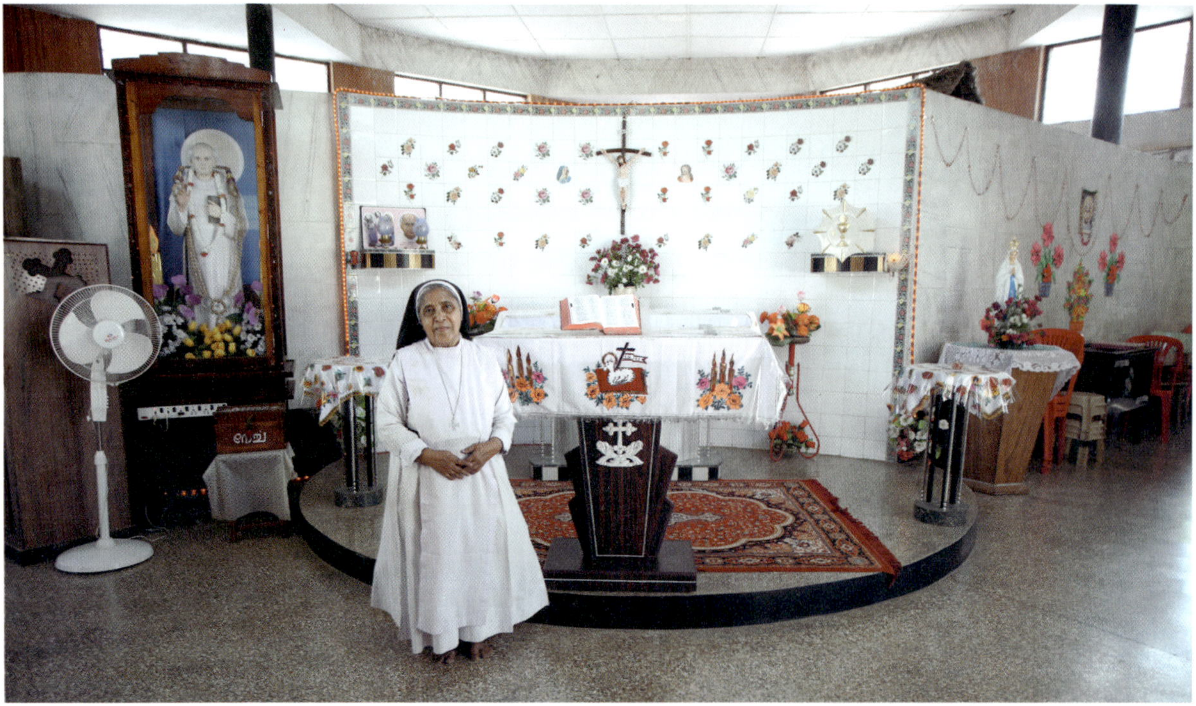

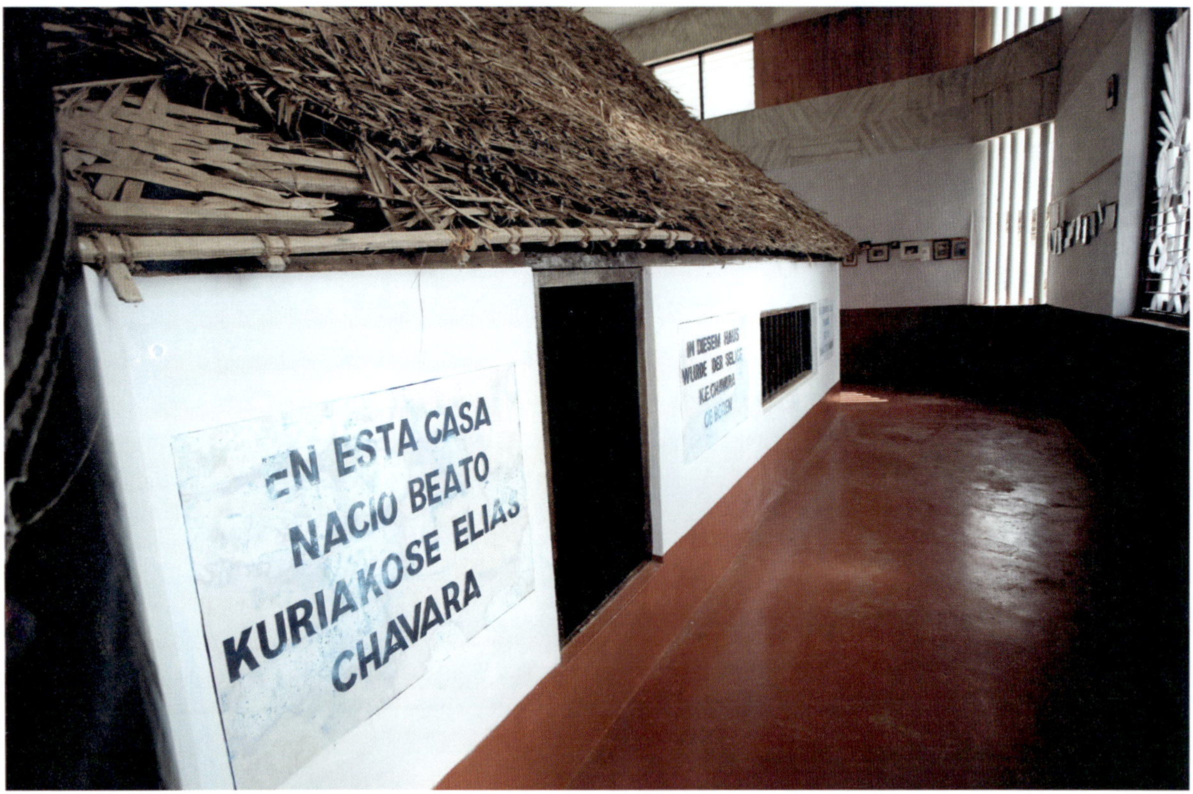
EN ESTA CASA
NACIO BEATO
KURIAKOSE ELIAS
CHAVARA
IN DIESEM HAUS

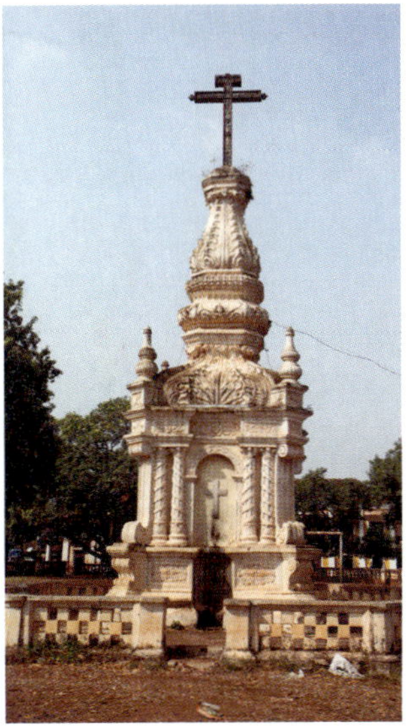
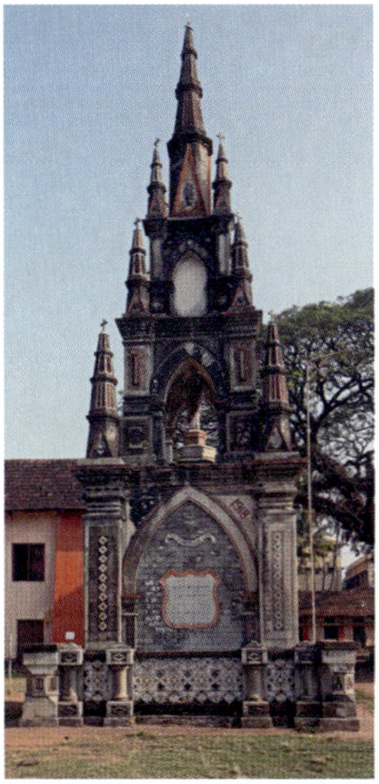
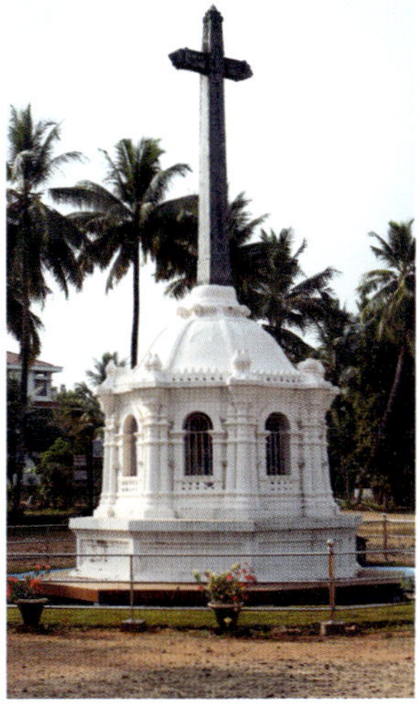
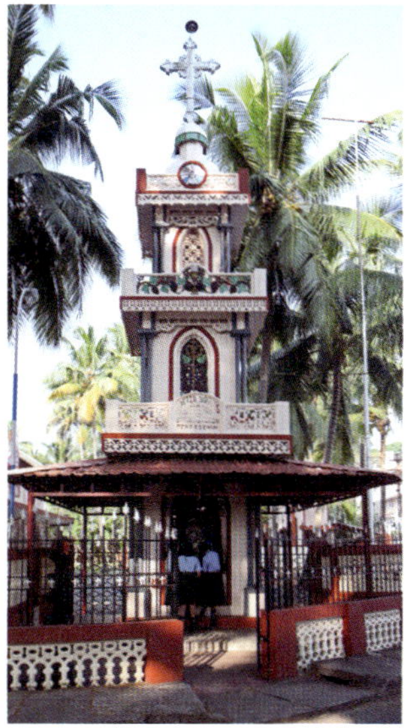

ABOVE (L to R): *Roadside shrines and piazza crosses*
FACING PAGE TOP: *Interior of the shrine*
FACING PAGE BELOW: *The exterior of the little thatched house*

or small church comes into view. The writer Arundhati Roy would have passed such shrines as she lived on the edge of the Meenachi River in Aymanam, close to Kumarakom. The house and the river feature in her much loved book. *The God of Small Things.*

One of the backwaters' most charming shrines is dedicated to Kerala's beloved saint, Kuriakose Elias Chavara. It is accessible only by boat and a pleasant walk along a palm fringed strip of land after pulling in at the landing stage in the village of Kainakary. The little round shrine is built on sand and inside is the remarkable 250-year-old one-room thatched cottage; the birthplace of Kerala's 'Blessed Chavara'.

Chavara was influential in the education of Kerala's women and believed in 'a school along with every church' which helped make education free. He had great foresight and worked for reform within the clergy of both Latin and Syrian churches, creating a peaceful co-existence of Christian life in Kerala.

Religious Festivals of Kerala's Churches

Common practices have crept into many religious faiths in India, particularly in Kerala where religious festivals are shared by all communities and all religions. The church is the heart of Kerala's villages. On the feast day of a church's patron saint a festival can last for days. Drummers or a local band often lead the image of the saint decorated with marigolds. Villagers dress in their best and follow the procession. These festivals are sometimes reverential but most are joyous and chaotic with excited crowds jostling to catch a glimpse of the saint.

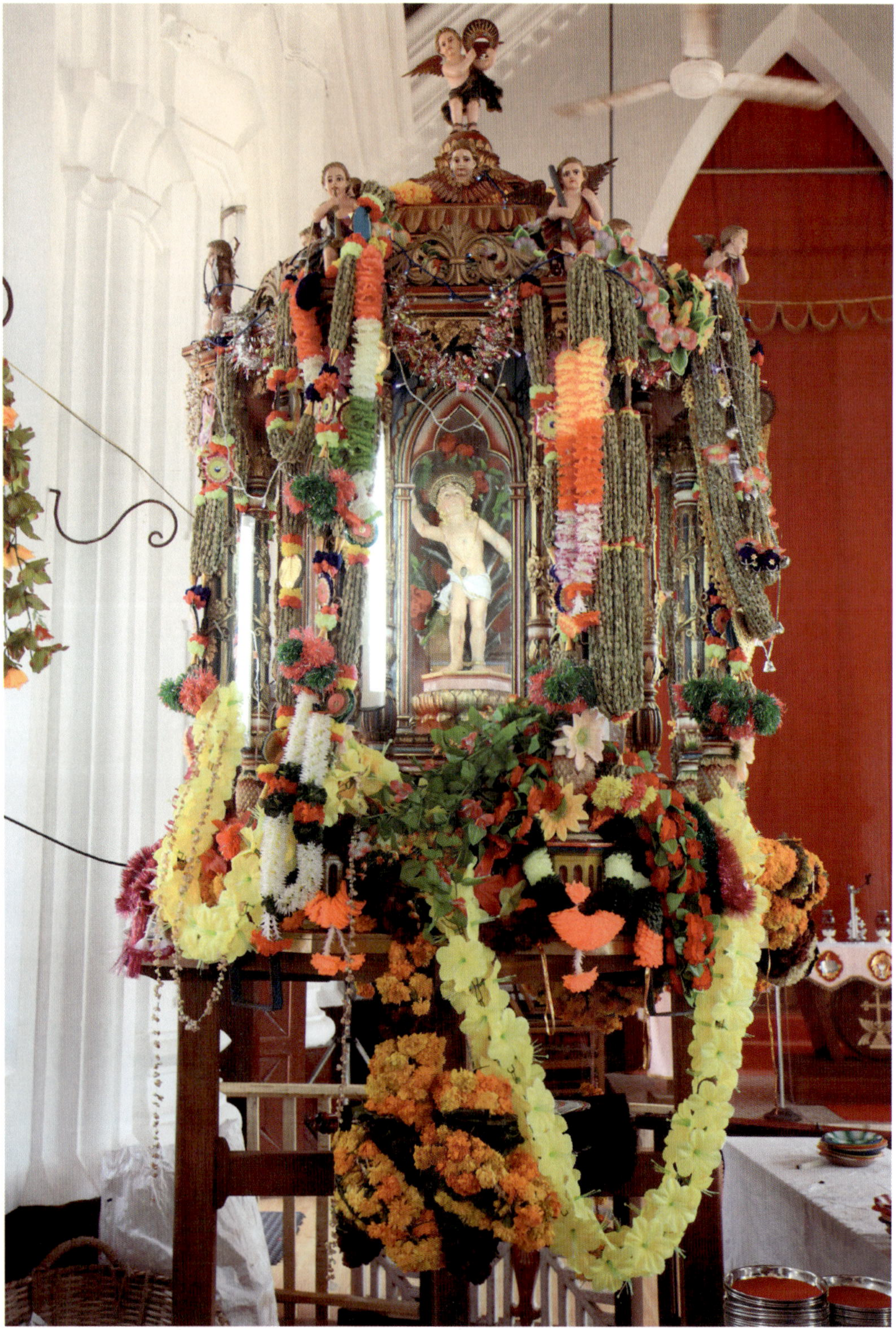

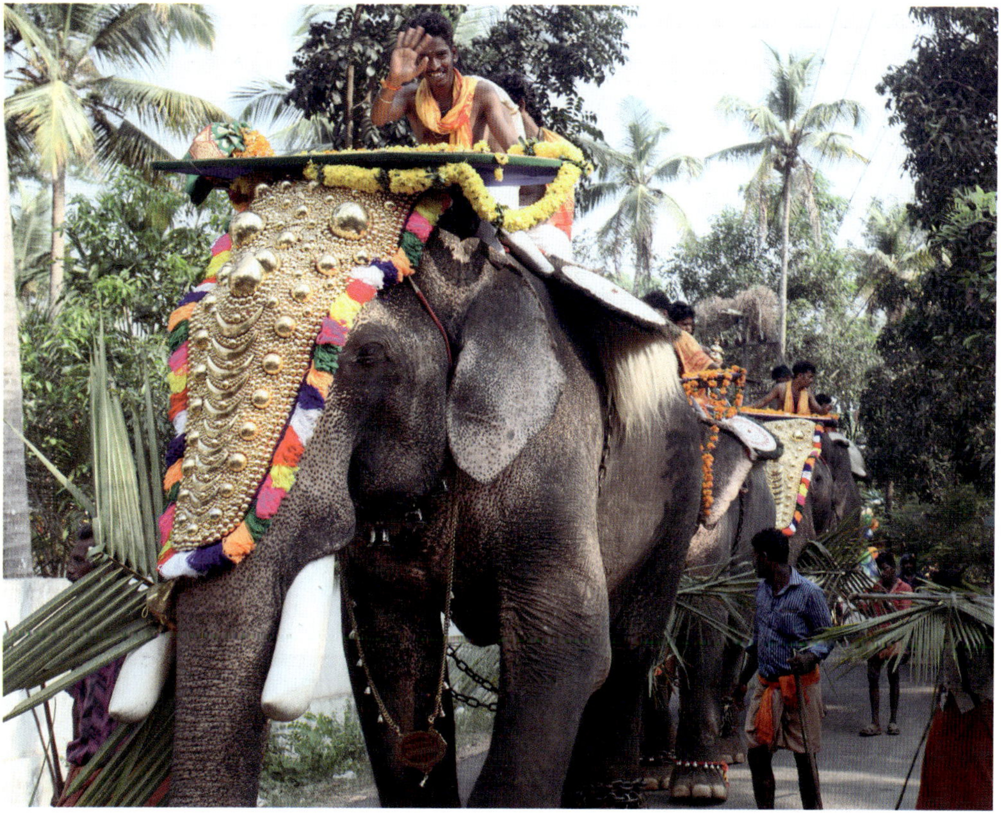

Caparisoned elephants on their way to a religious festival
FACING PAGE: *Shrine decorated during a religious festival*

Decorated elephants are common to Hindu festivals but in Kerala they are also part of many Christian processions and celebrations. In Thrissur, a lush tropical region close to the sea, the famous and most exciting of all Kerala's festivals is celebrated. The Thrissur Pooram is staged at the ancient Vadakkunnathan temple and each year thousands of people come to watch the highlights, the amazing sight of thirty bejewelled elephants with three priests on each rhythmically exchanging colourful umbrellas to the sound of hundreds of drums and trumpets. The festival continues unabated for thirty-six hours and begins with fifty or more elephants passing through the centre of the city towards the temple, all beautifully decorated with gold headpieces, *nettipattam* and other ornaments.

Our Lady of Dolours Basilica, Thrissur, 1940

Syro-Malabar Catholic

Even though Thrissur is known as a religious city it is still surprising to discover the enormous Christian Basilica of Our Lady of Dolours which looms over the relatively smaller buildings surrounding it. It is not far from the famous Hindu Vadakkunnathan temple known for its elephant festival. The Basilica's feast day in November is the second biggest festival of Thrissur. The building itself is an enormous Gothic structure covering an area of 2,300 square metres; the largest church in India, and the tallest in Asia. The original, built in 1814, was Thrissur's first Catholic Church.

When Bishop Vazhapilly travelled to Europe in 1929, he was inspired by the architecture of the cathedrals he saw, particularly those in Rome. On his return he began planning a new cathedral but lack of funds delayed construction. Engineers Jnanaprakasam and Ambrose Gounder supervised the building which took eleven years to complete. Finally, with the support of the Maharajah of Cochin Sri Rama Varma Bishop Vazhapilly consecrated the finished building in 1929.

The church is overwhelming in size. Three enormous towers; two in the front are over 44 metres high and the third – centred and towards the back of the church – is over 79 metres high. The building is painted entirely in dazzling white with an impressive entrance, the massive 'elephant door.' Above are three rose windows. A flagpole sits to the

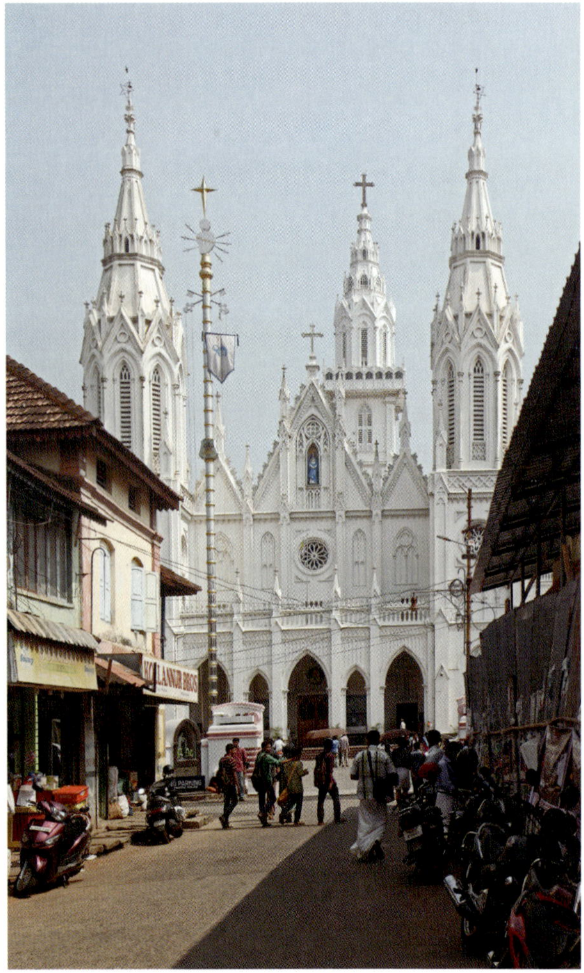

Basilica of Our Lady of Dolours

right of the church's entrance, the 'elephant door' which is enormous. Inside on either side of the main altar are ten altars holding statues of various saints including St. Thomas and St. Francis Xavier. The main altar holds a statue of Our Lady of Dolours and the statues of angels; Michael and Raphael. Above is an enormous dome decorated with murals that tell of the saints' lives. Beneath the altar lie the tombs of the bishops. Pope John Paul II visited the church in April 1992 and elevated the church to the status of a 'Minor Basilica'. It was then consecrated in May of the same year by Cardinal Antony Padiyara and was named the Basilica of Our Lady of Dolores. The pulpit and throne used by Pope John Paul II are preserved within the basilica and after his death the body of Bishop Mar Francis Vazhapilly was interred there.

In 2002 construction began on the inspiring Bible Tower, a vision of the Thrissur Catholics from the 1940s. Finally in 2006 the tower was opened and dedicated to World Peace. It holds a Christian art gallery showing the life of Jesus in a collection of murals and paintings. Wood carvings and stained glass also tell the stories of the miracles performed by Jesus and his suffering. The life of St. Thomas is also part of the collection. A platform at the top of the tower offers a wonderful view of the surrounding city and beyond.

St. Andrew's Basilica, Arthunkal, 1584

Roman Catholic

St. Andrew's Basilica in Arthunkal is an important church. It is the largest shrine dedicated to St. Sebastian in the world. Originally built by the Portuguese in the 16th century it celebrates 'Arthunkal Perunnal' the feast day of St. Sebastian who is known for healing serious illnesses and protecting followers from accidents. This amazing festival has made Arthunkal one of the biggest and most famous pilgrimage centres in Kerala. On the 10th of January each year thousands of Christian and non-Christian worshippers come from all parts of southern India to take part in the eleven day celebration which begins with music and fireworks.

The famous statue of St. Sebastian was sculpted in Milan in 1647. It is a startling image of the saint's body pierced with arrows. Seen just once a year, the statue is particularly moving and powerful to the faithful. The rest of the time it is kept hidden. St. Sebastian was shot with arrows on the orders of the Roman Emperor when it was discovered he was a Christian. During the festival the standing statue of the saint in an elaborate gold case is placed on a palanquin, a large mobile altar and carried at the head of the procession which makes its way from the church to the beach and back. It moves at a slow pace surrounded by worshippers and each year an eagle is seen

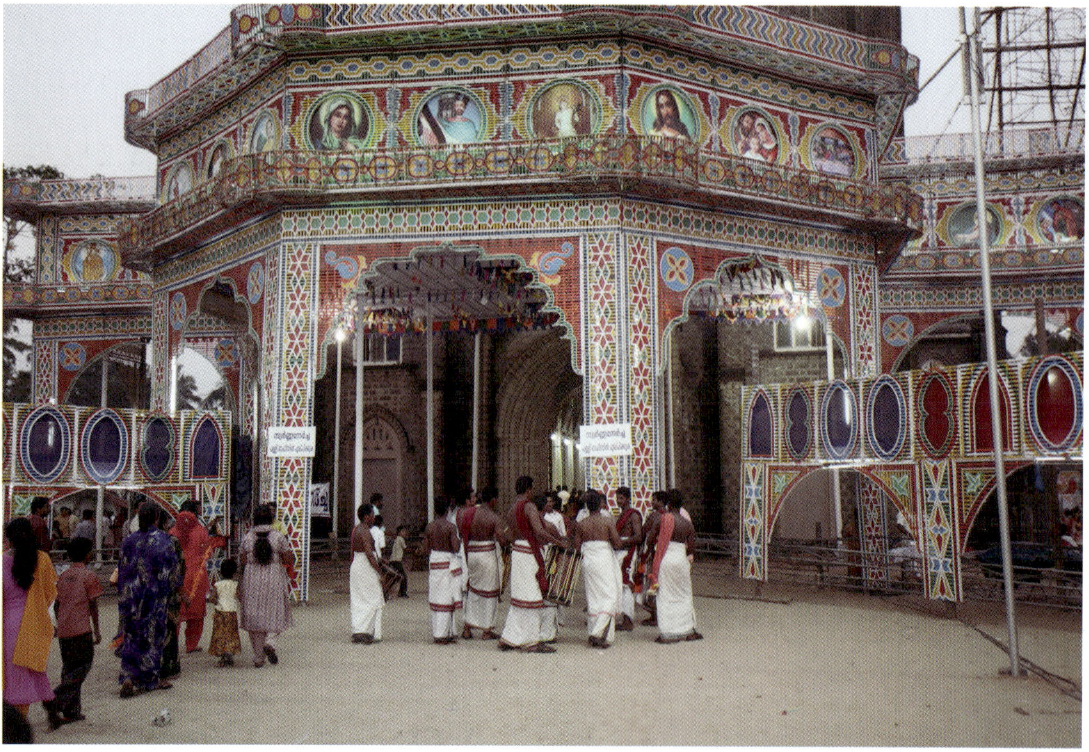

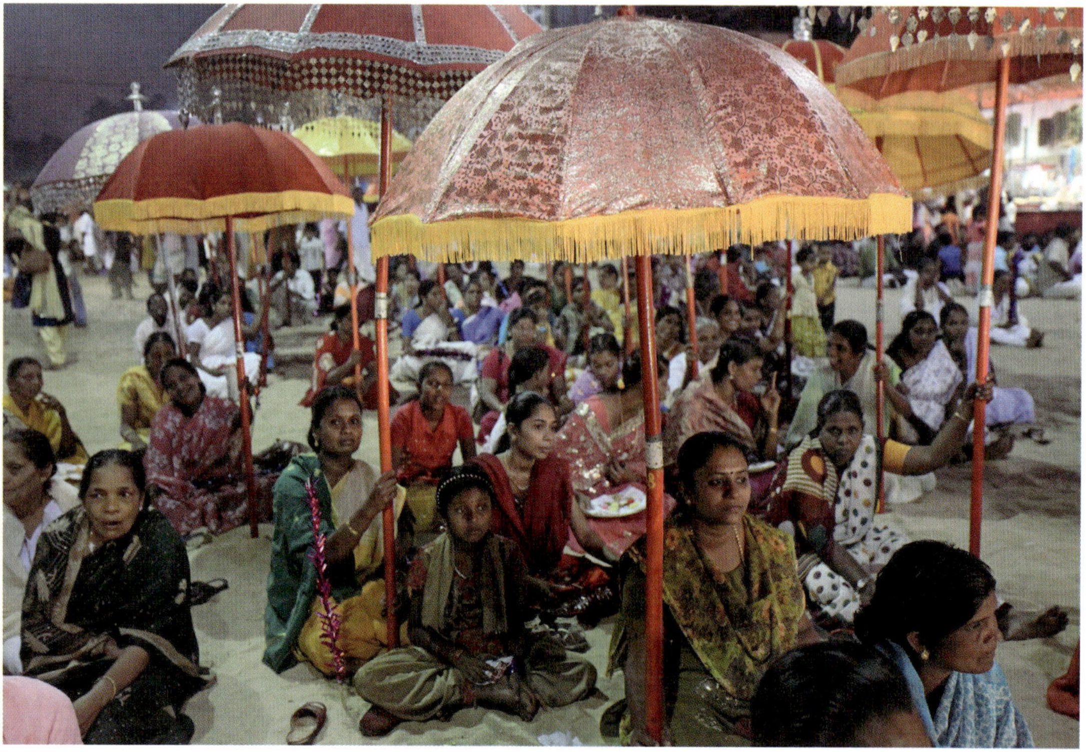

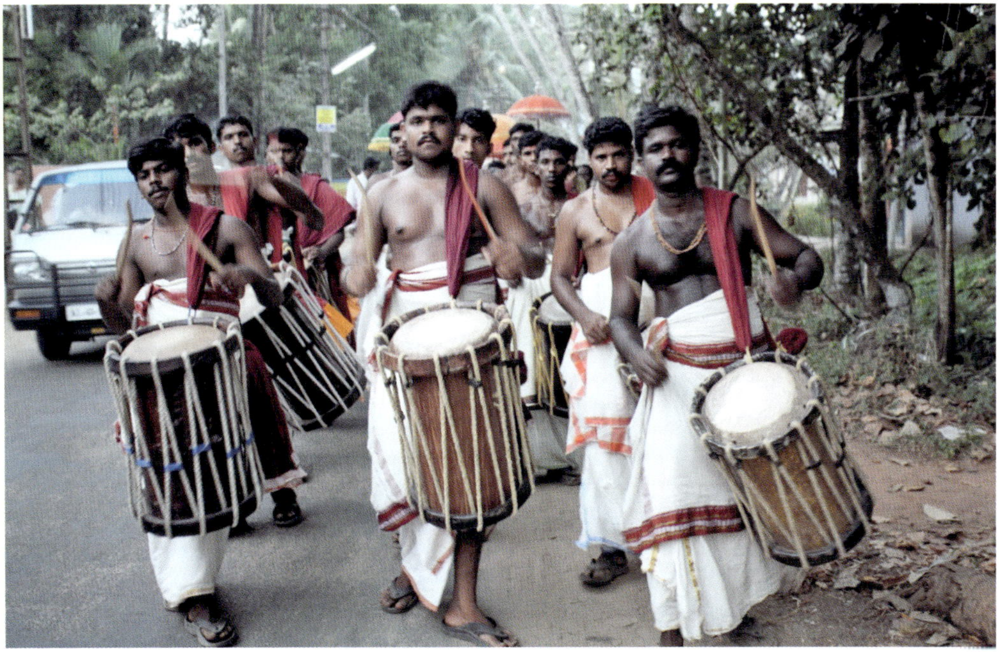

Above: *The procession with the statue of St. Sebastian progressing to the beach from the church*

Facing page top: *A decorative entrance to the church specially built for the feast day*

Facing page below: *Crowds at St. Andrew's on feast day*

flying high in the sky, seeming to follow the procession. Many devotees perform particular penances during the procession such as crawling or rolling the one kilometre between the church and the beach. This astonishing ritual known as *uralal nercha* is to show their respect and gratitude. Some hold gold or silver tokens, *ambum villum*, made in the shape of bows and arrows and even human limbs while others give a range of diverse offerings.

Each day the large area surrounding the church comes alive. Dozens of stalls sell a variety of food, sweets, drinks and even household goods such as plastic buckets and brooms. Long lines of women and children holding gaily coloured silk umbrellas sit patiently on the sand waiting their turn to see the statue of St. Sebastian while groups of drummers and jugglers entertain the crowds well into the evening. By nightfall the lights decorating the facade of the church begin to glow and revolve in concentric circles. The combination of the lights, heat and dust, incense and the smell of the ocean create a hypnotic atmosphere. This is when one

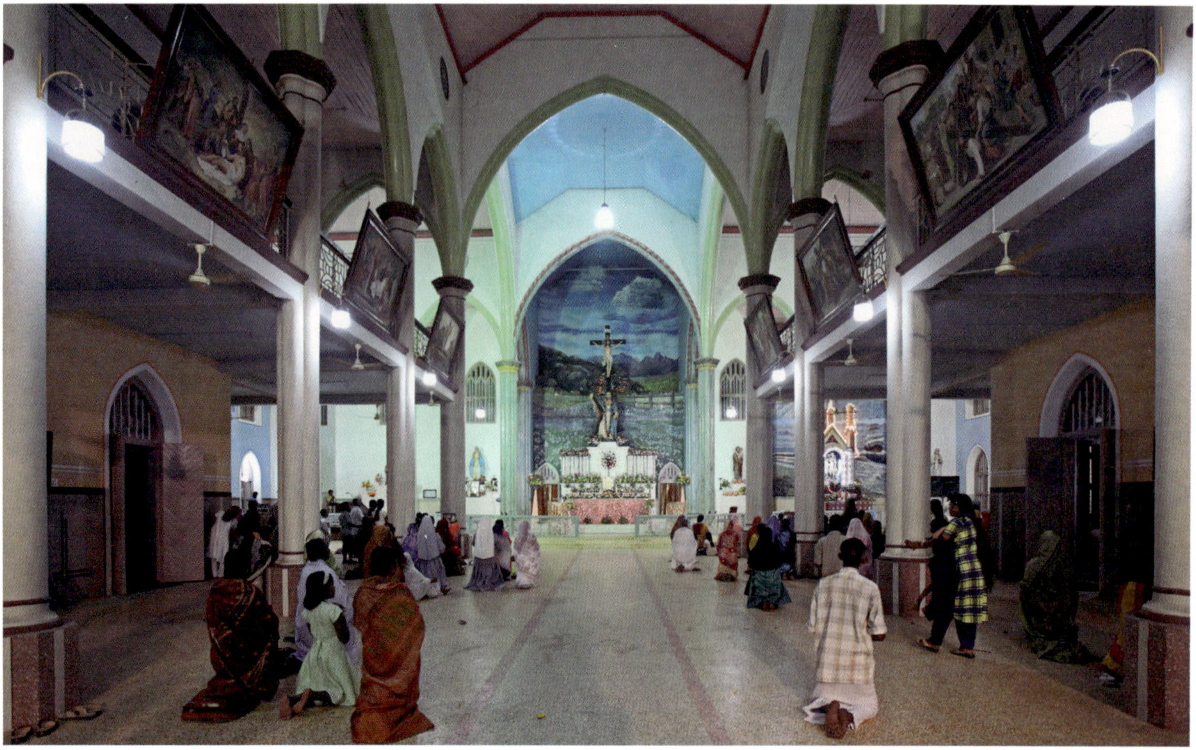

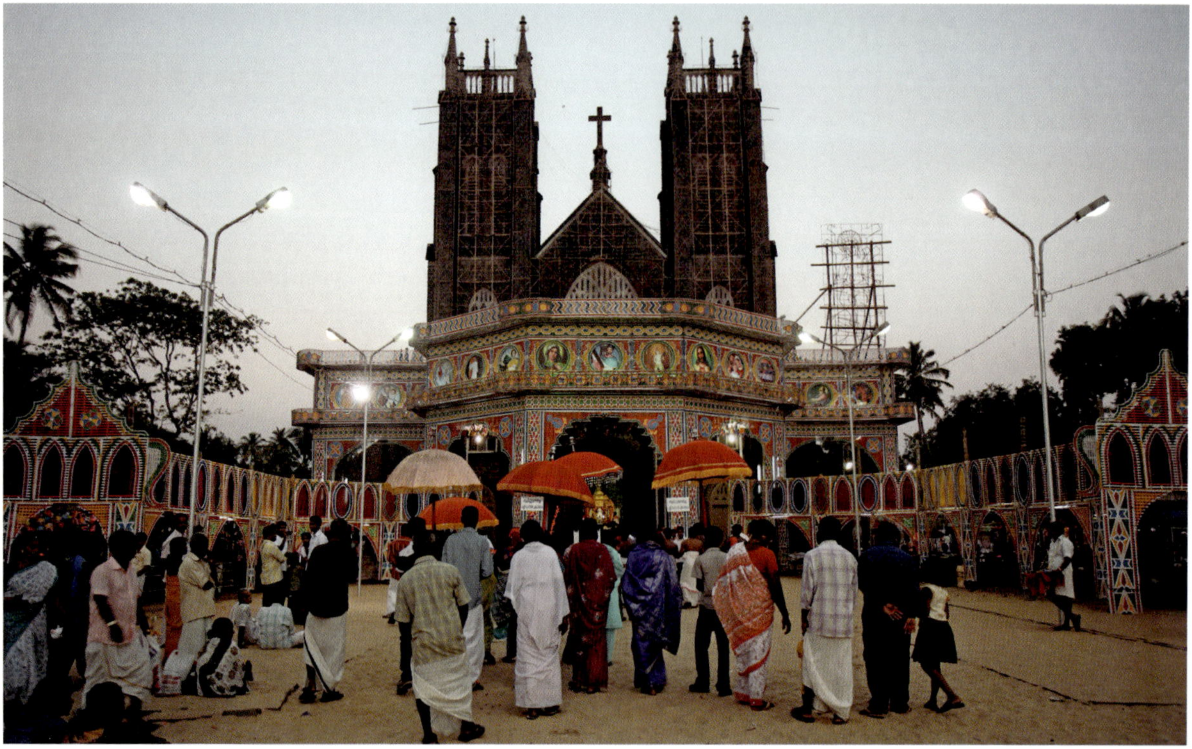

experiences India's intense religious passion and fervour.

The church welcomes Hindu pilgrims who worship Lord Ayyappa at the famous Sabarimala temple, 160 kilometres away. The Sabarimala festival is one of the largest Hindu pilgrimage sites in the world. Over fifty million people of all denominations visit each year. After returning to Arthunkal the pilgrims pay their respects to St. Sebastian, who they believe is the brother of Lord Ayyappa. They then bathe in the pond attached to the church or swim in the ocean. St. Andrew's Basilica is an example of religious harmony, a characteristic common to many churches and temples in Kerala.

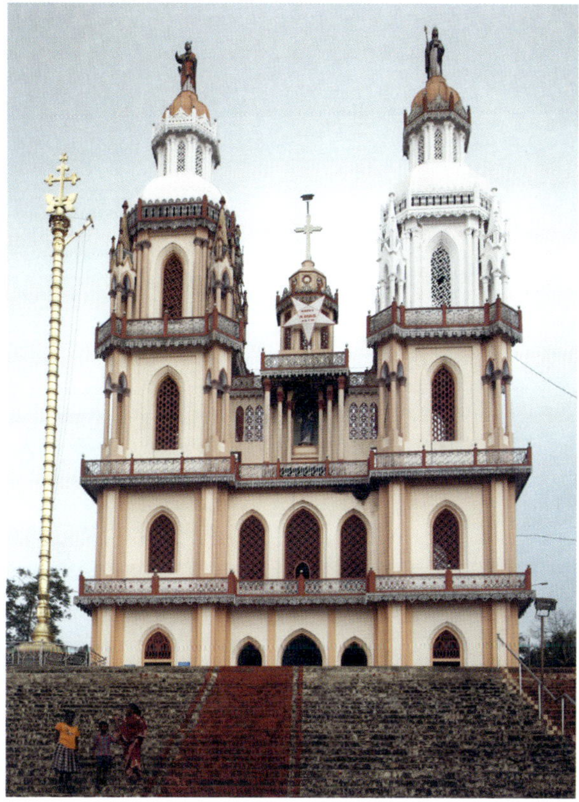

ABOVE: *St. Mary's Forane Church, Kuravilangad*
FACING PAGE TOP: *The pastel interior with wall murals*
FACING PAGE BELOW: *Worshippers continue arriving well into the evening*

St. Mary's Forane Church, Kuravilangad, 1960

Syro-Malabar Catholic

Known locally as Martha Mariam this interesting church is believed to have been first established in 355 CE. Like so many ancient churches in Kerala it has changed over the centuries up to the present church which was constructed in 1960.

St. Mary's feast day is an unusual event held over three days in January in honour of St. Sebastian, one of Kerala's most popular saints. The Moonnu Nombu festival tells the biblical story of Jonah, centred on a procession where local people carry a twelve metre long brightly painted timber ship around the church, down the steep steps and into the streets. The ship is complete with carved wooden sailors and on one side is the figure of Jonah. The festival has its origins in the sea going traditions of the early Christians, the Nazranis.

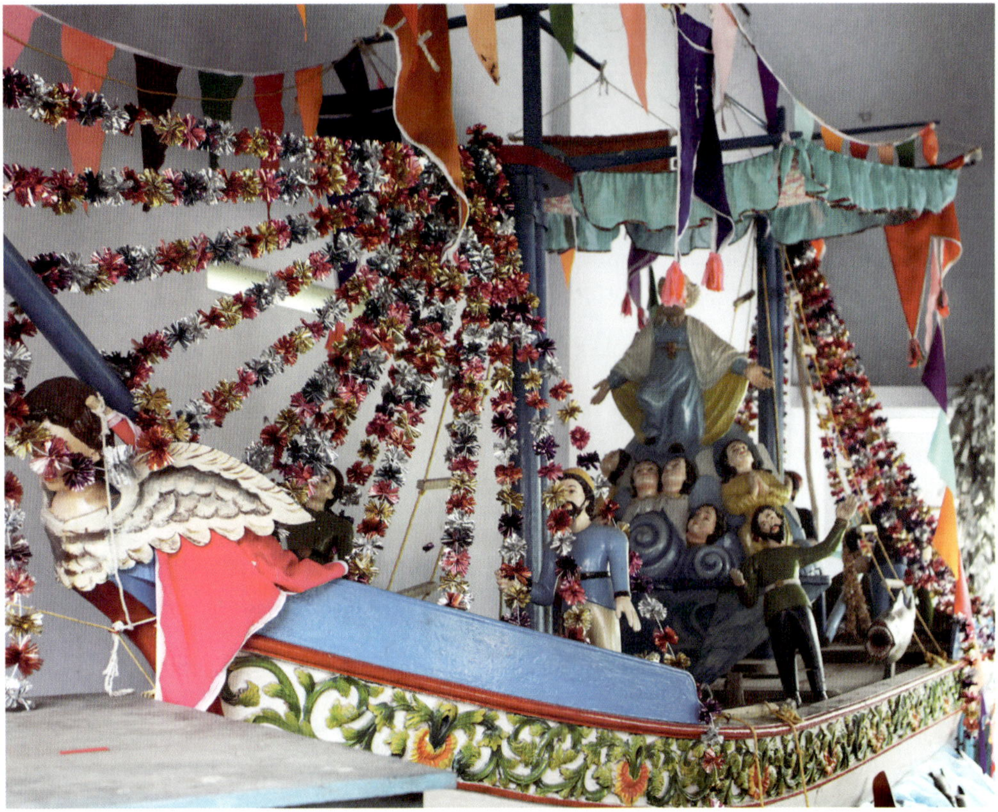

ABOVE: *The painted wooden ship carrying Jonah and his men*

FACING PAGE TOP: *The small church of 1829*

FACING PAGE BELOW: *Quiet contemplation at the St. Mary's Forane Church, Kuravilangad*

The ship's carriers run backwards and forwards, rocking the ship to imitate a rollicking vessel in an angry sea. At the same time thousands of people surge towards the ship to be part of the action. It is a chaotic scene. Add to this some decorated elephants, colourful embroidered umbrellas, music, a feast and worshipping of the cross and you have the kind of religious festival that can only be found in Kerala. It has to be seen to be believed.

The church cross is carved from a single piece of granite. Erected in 1597 it is enormous at 15 metres tall. At the base are 124 small wick lamps into which devotees pour coconut oil. There is also a small Hindu temple-like church devoted to St. Sebastian

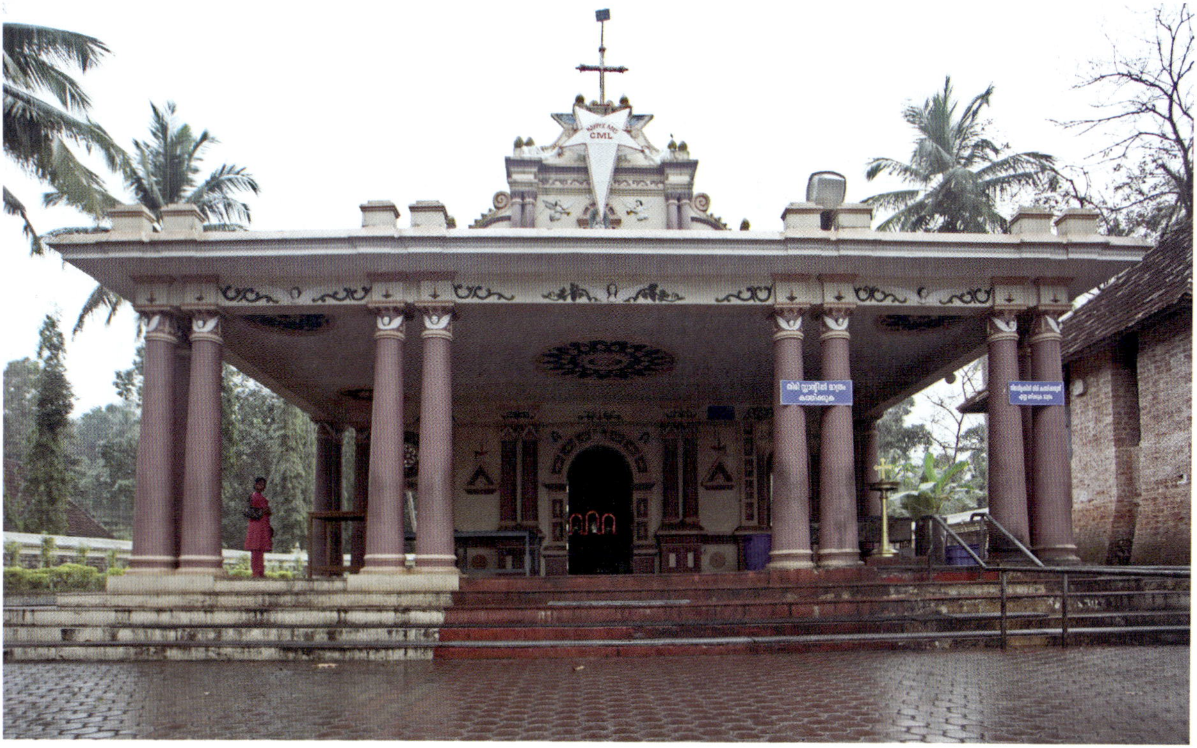
CML

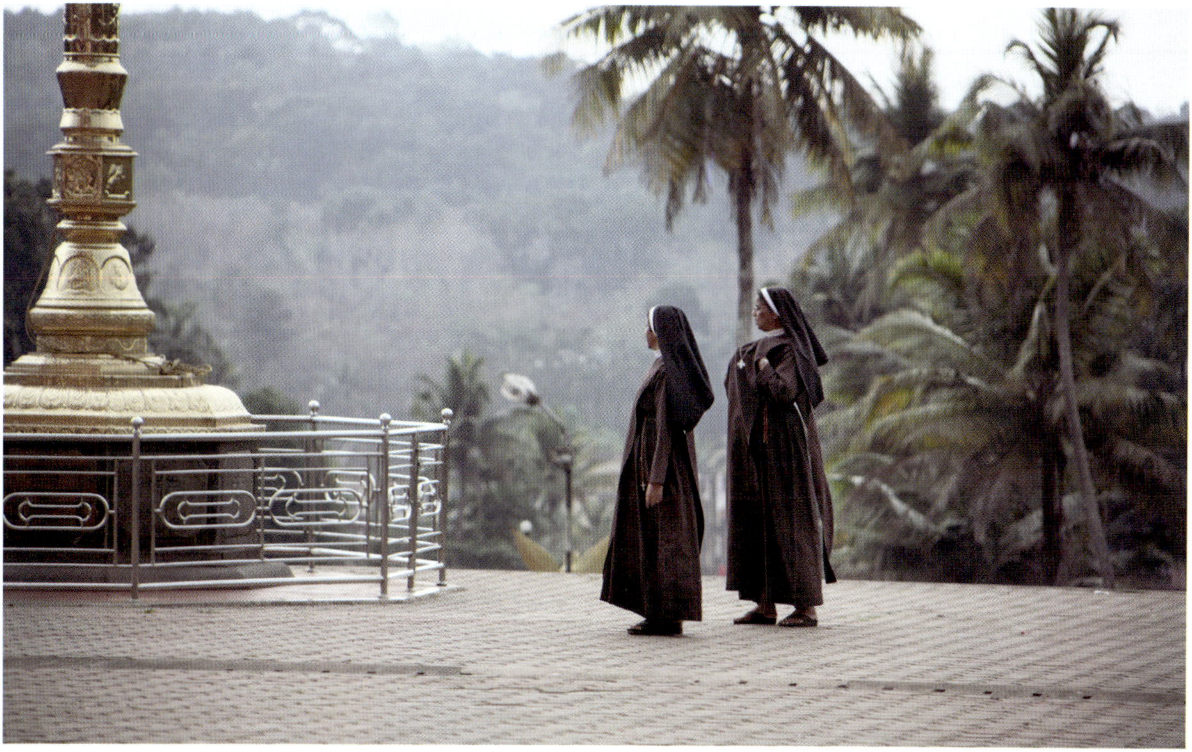

dating from 1868. It has three ancient bells, one weighing 1829 kg. One of these bells, thought to be from the late 16th century has an inscription in Syriac which reads; *'Ameh dalah'*, or 'Mother of God'.

St. Mary's Forane Church, Athirampuzha, 1962

Roman Catholic

Two churches make up the wonderful church complex of St. Mary's in Athirampuzha. The 'big' church was renovated in 1962. The façade has Art Deco similarities as well as the *navaratna* or Hindu temple style. It is an unusual design for a Keralan Hindu temple or Christian church. The 'small' church is temple-like though it has three Gothic-style arched openings on the facade.

Linking the two churches is a 200 metre long road lined with small shrines representing the Fourteen Stations of the Cross. Each Friday evening parishioners gather to walk the stations and follow the tradition of pouring oil on the cross as an offering to God. In St. Mary's the cross is of Persian design and made from a single piece of granite. A larger cross, also made of granite and some two hundred years old, is thirty feet high and sits on a platform with stone steps and oil lamps all around. Devotees light the lamps in the same way that candles are lit in western churches.

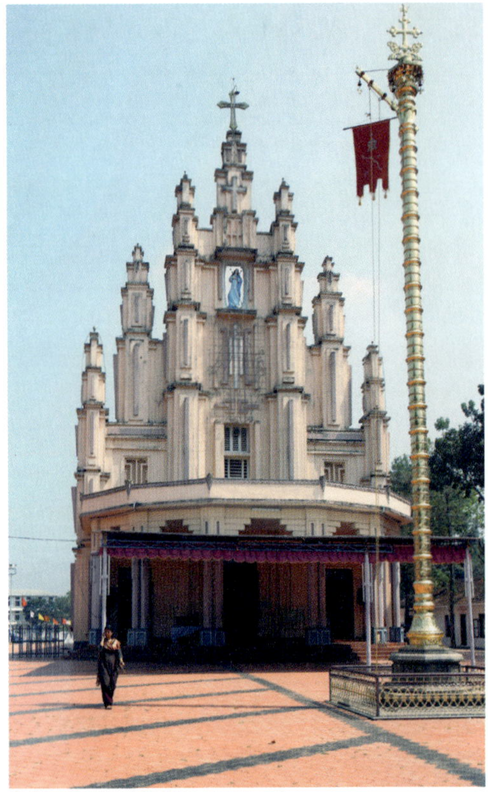

ABOVE: *The exterior of the 'Big Church' of St. Mary's with the brass flagpole*

FACING PAGE TOP LEFT: *Image of St. Sebastian the decorated Saint on feast day*

FACING PAGE TOP RIGHT: *Eager participants share in carrying the cross*

FACING PAGE BELOW: *The 'small' church with Gothic entrance and wiring to illuminate the church at night*

Over 10,000 people come here to pray and more so during the two famous feast days each year. The Feast of St. Mary in September is a special occasion when church elders in beautiful robes walk in a solemn

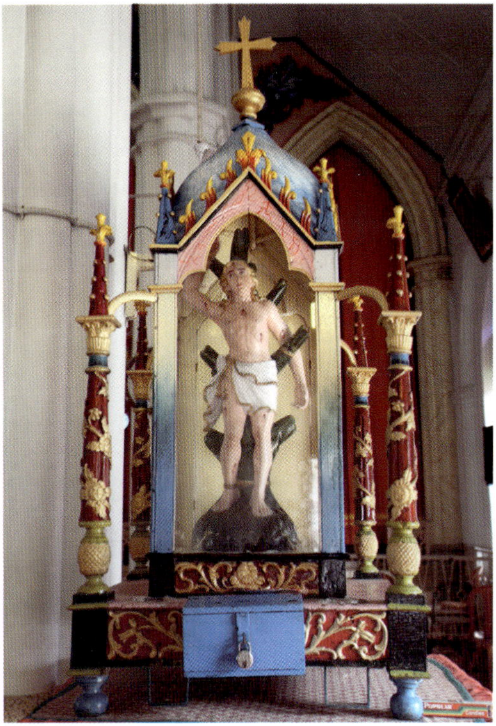

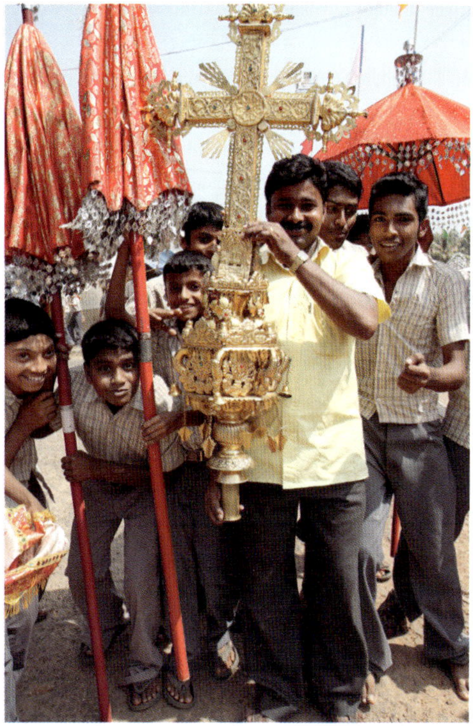

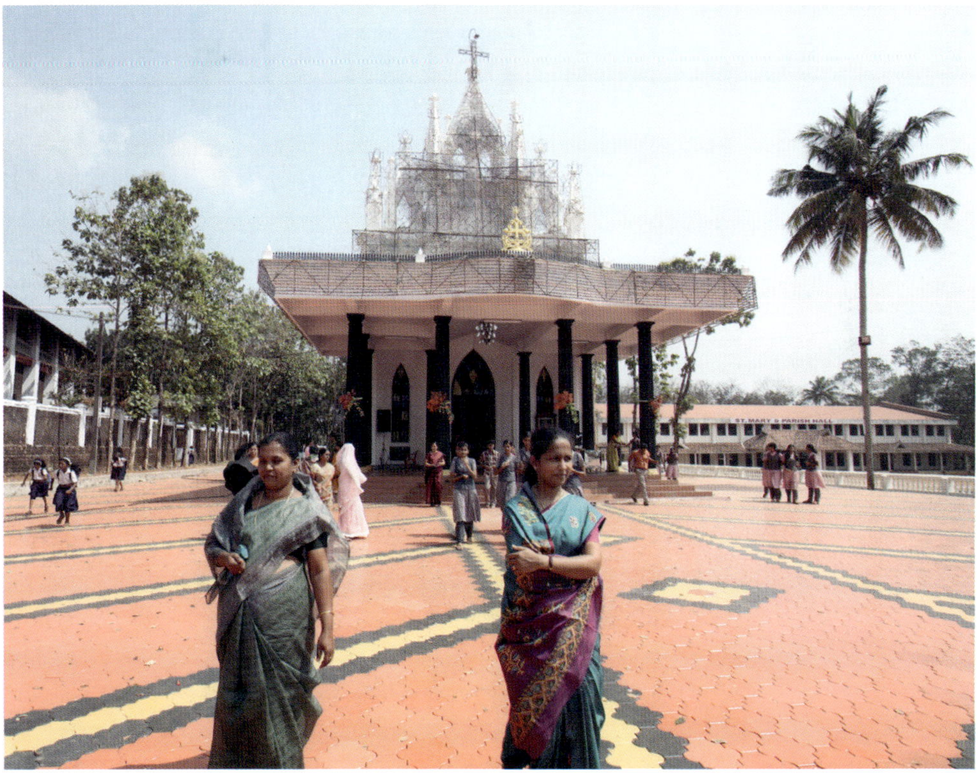

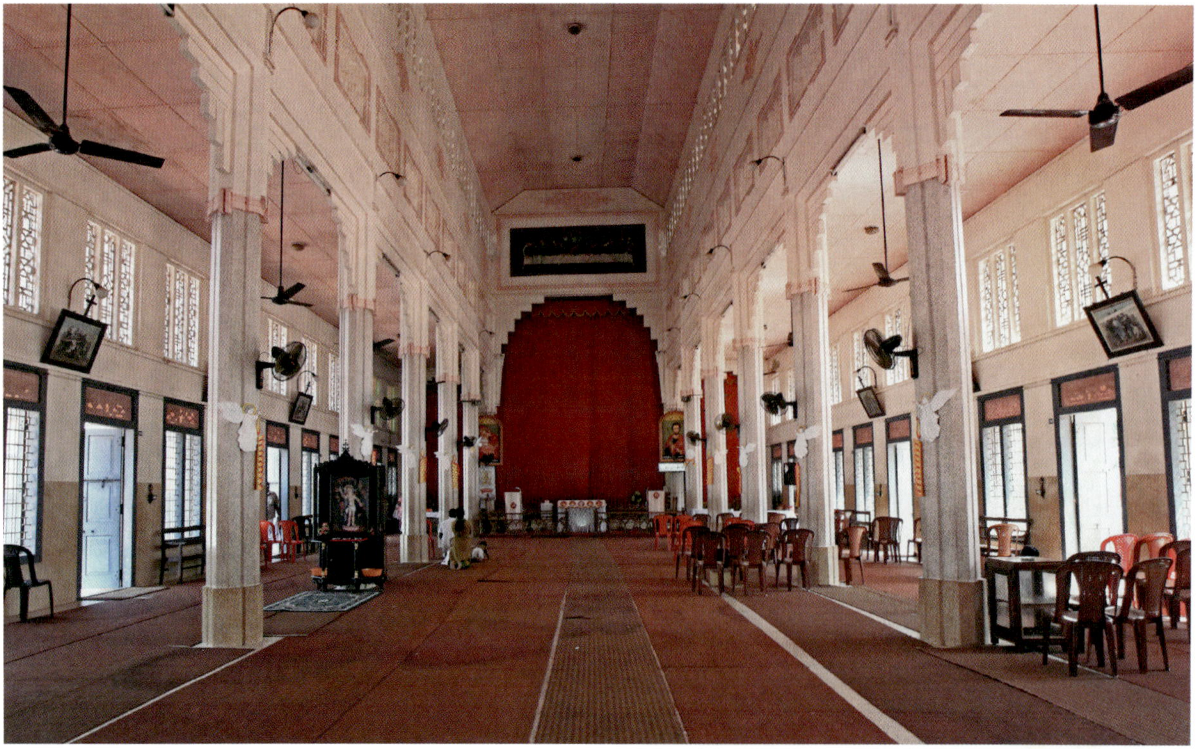

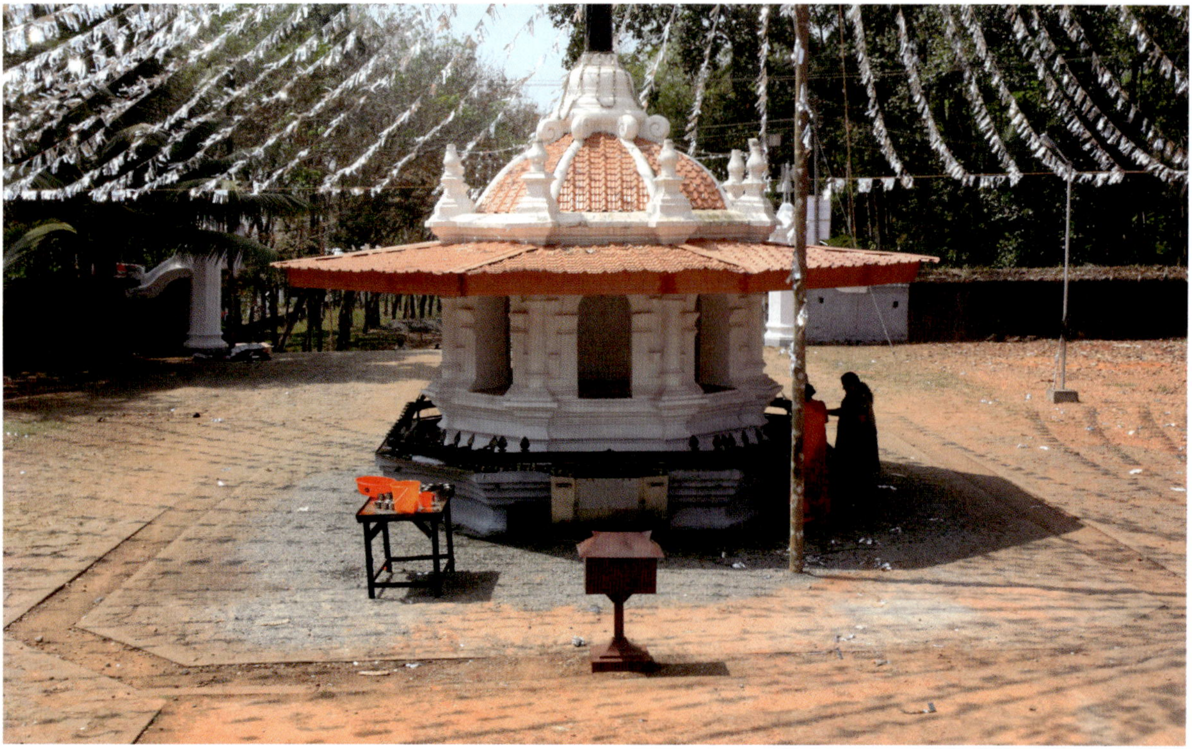

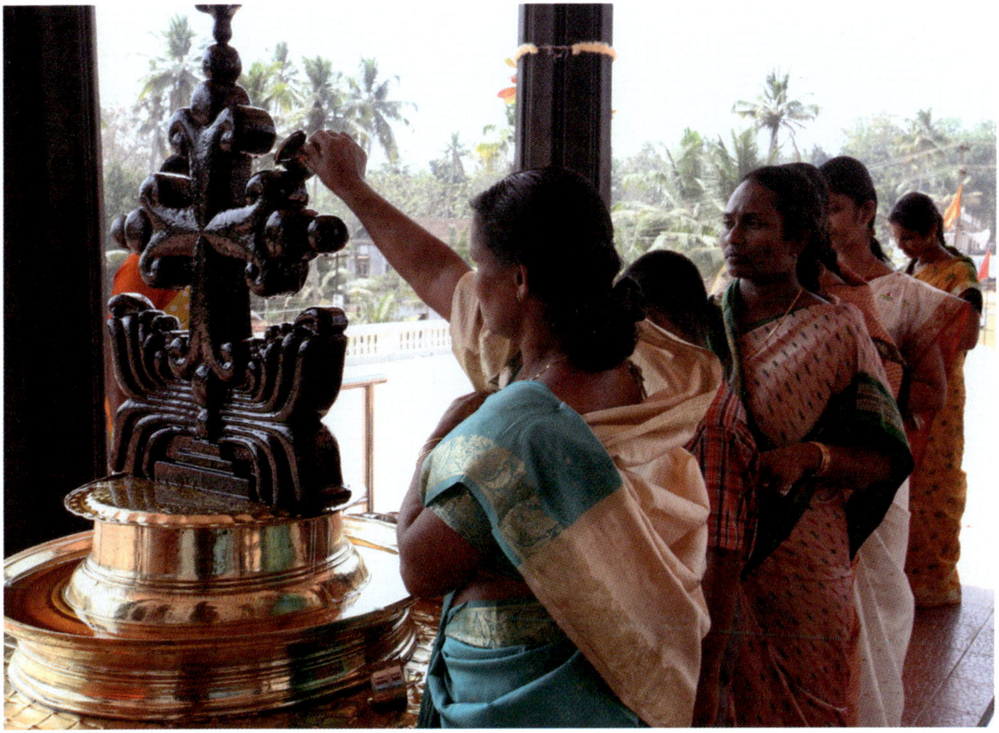

ABOVE: *Pouring oil over an ancient granite cross*
FACING PAGE TOP: *The typical Syrian Christian interior*
FACING PAGE BELOW: *Oil lamps at the base of the cross*

procession with a statue of St. Mary in a small shrine enveloped in flowers and strings of jasmine. The Feast of St. Sebastian began in 1647 and today pilgrims come from far and wide to be part of the event. The statue of the saint is ensconced in an elaborate shrine and carried on a palanquin for all to see. Crowds clamour to catch a glimpse of the beloved saint's statue which is believed to have been brought to India by the Portuguese navigator Leonard Gonsalves D'cuz in 1687. The crowd swells and the incessant beating of drums, ringing of church bells and loud music create a chaotic and hypnotic atmosphere. An Indian Christian church festival is nothing like the sombre Christian festivals of the west; instead it is a happy, noisy outpouring of faith. The feast day celebrates St. Sebastian as well as St. Mary's.

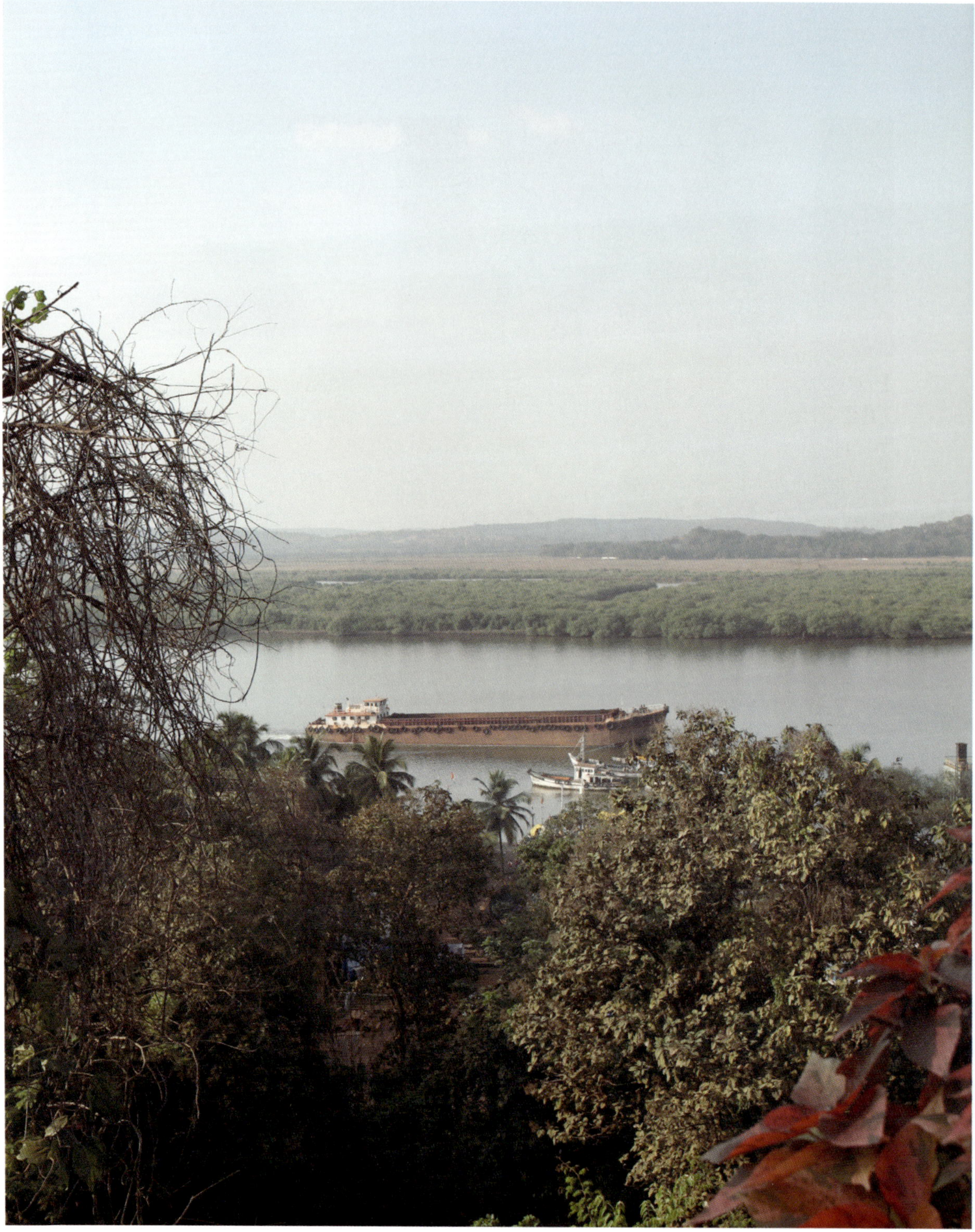

SPLENDID REMAINS
Goa

Portuguese History: Old Goa

To the north of Kerala lies the small but fascinating state of Goa. Like Kerala it has a rich assortment of Portuguese churches, a significant reminder of Portugal's strong influence on the west coast of India and the importance the Portuguese placed on church building in the early stages of their rule.

Goa's first major encounter with the Portuguese was between March and May of 1510 when Portuguese General and 'military genius' Alfonso de Albuquerque captured the city. By August Albuquerque had abandoned the city due to lack of support by his men and the local inhabitants. Three months later he returned making a surprise entrance into Goa's harbour with an impressive armada. The city surrendered and he was hailed as a conqueror, entering the city in triumph on an ornamented horse to the sound of drums and trumpets and surrounded by mounted Portuguese noblemen, *fidalgos*, all bearing their standards and gilt crosses.

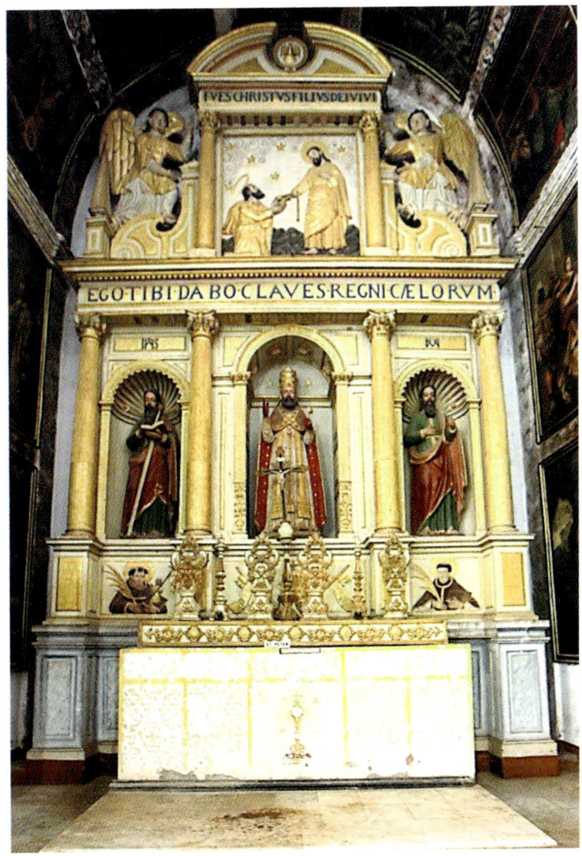

ABOVE: *Side altar, the Sé Catedral de Santa Catarina*

FACING PAGE: *The Mandovi river from Our Lady of the Rosary church*

By capturing Goa from the Muslim ruler Ismail Adil Khan Albuquerque established Portuguese rule, not only a triumph for Portugal but a clear sign to both Hindu and Muslim rulers that the Portuguese were there to stay. In a relatively short time Albuquerque had prepared Goa to become the future *Estado da Portuguesa,* the capital of the Portuguese Empire in India. Albuquerque secured the spice trade for Portugal. Like Kerala, Goa's position facing the Arabian Sea on the west and the Western Ghats mountain range on the east allowed the Portuguese to rise and rule with little interference for over four hundred years.

The first of the various religious orders began to arrive in 1517. The first were the Franciscans. The Jesuits came after spreading their message through the work of Spanish Jesuit St. Francis Xavier who arrived in 1542. Other orders followed and Christian communities began to grow. Most of the early churches in Goa were built by European Roman Catholic monastic orders that had the wealth to build massive churches that echoed the size of churches in Europe. Almost all of Goa's churches are Roman Catholic. As enthusiastic church builders the Portuguese allotted funds from the Royal treasury as well as through donations and taxes for their church building spree.

In 1543 Goa's rise was brought to a standstill when cholera broke out and each church bell announced another funeral, striking fear in the population. Though there was great suffering, the epidemic was short lived, Goa rose again and new buildings emerged. Once again it was a city worthy of Portugal's Empire in the East.

The architectural style of the churches evolved over time and reflected the varying wealth of the Empire, the changing taste and styles of Europe and the amalgamation of work by Indian artisans. The earliest churches, between 1510 and 1550, were built in a combination of Gothic and Manueline architecture. The Manueline style was peculiar to Portugal and made fashionable during the rule of King Dom Manuel I (1495–1521). It celebrated the exploits of the great navigators and their discovery of new sea routes and trade. Motifs included ropes, ships in full sail, anchors, shells and waves. It was a highly decorative style but unsuitable for Goa's climate so very few have survived. A good example is the entrance to the Church of St. Francis of Assisi.

The majority of Goa's churches were built in the Baroque style though less ornate than those in Portugal. Fighting wars and supporting massive armadas was expensive. A typical Baroque church built in Portuguese Goa featured a sombre exterior which belied the splendours of the interiors which were sumptuously decorated, true to the Baroque style. This is evident in the *reredos* (the backdrop behind the altar) of many churches, rich with decorative details and sculptural figures of saints carved in wood with much gilding. The veneration of saints reached its greatest heights in Portugal and Spain.

Fundamentally, the style of Baroque art and architecture belongs to the Roman Catholic faith. The Portuguese used the splendours of these churches and the power of their Roman Catholic religion to impress and subjugate the people they had colonised. Within the span of a generation however Indian craftsmen were creating their own designs in the churches they were decorating. Saints and angels began to look Indian and tropical foliage, flowers and cashew nuts began to appear, images of Christ showed gruesome, realistic wounds. The Basilica of Bom Jesu, the Se Cathedral and the Church of St. Cajetan built from the mid-16th century to the mid-17th century are excellent examples of the contribution of Indian craftsmen. These Christian churches show how the influence of Indian aesthetics created an interesting indigenised style.

Though Goa had been a thriving city before the Portuguese it certainly became a wealthier city of glamour and riches after their arrival. At its height the population was made up of merchants and the wealthy, not only from Portugal but also from Arabia, Armenia, Persia (Iran), Siam (Thailand), and Malacca, Bengal as well as Europeans from Venice, Italy, Germany, Spain and England and a small number from France. The streets were lined with mansions and gardens. Beautiful buildings housed musicians, tailors, money lenders and slaves. Certain streets specialised in one of a kind goods, Chinese porcelain or velvet fabric, ladies ornaments and of course many streets sold precious stones, pearls and coral jewellery. A 1698 description by artist Francesco Ramponi tells of merchants from Gujarat carrying sacks full of precious stones, bags of diamonds, rubies, emeralds and topaz to sell at the port before the ships left for Europe. Every eight or ten days fleets of twenty or thirty boats would be loaded or unloaded brimming with pepper, linen or spun cotton and chests were piled high with turbans and coloured cloth. From China came porcelain of every colour and size to decorate the drawing rooms of Europe. Everything was available for a luxurious way of life. Soon Goa's fame spread and people arrived from Europe to see the magnificent Portuguese capital of India, the 'Pearl of the Orient'. The importance Portugal placed on the building of churches continued and

Goa became the centre of Christianity in the East. An architectural style subsequently emerged between 1660 and 1760 in Goa's churches known as Indian Baroque, or Indo-Portuguese Baroque.

As Goa reached its peak of wealth and luxury, things began to change. Provisions and food became so expensive and scarce that the city suffered a famine, after which another epidemic broke out. The area was surrounded by marshy swamps and stagnant ponds and the river's muddy banks were covered in waste, breeding disease in Goa's hot climate. Little attention had been paid to the care of the population's health from the very beginning. The city continued to decline and the Portuguese realised too late that the site they had chosen for their capital in India had been a mistake.

To make things worse the Dutch and the English had become great naval powers and by 1625 they were determined to weaken the dominance of the Portuguese. With these two nations on the high seas and Goa's decline in trade, Portugal could hardly maintain its naval armament. The civil order Albuquerque had earlier put in place became undone and decadence and corruption rose. In 1650 French traveller J.B. Tavernier was struck by the abject poverty of Portuguese families in Goa. In 1666 M. de Thevenot spoke of a decaying city and by 1683 the population was suffering terribly. Through lack of money houses could not be maintained and decay set in, forcing the inhabitants to abandon their homes. The Minutes from the Senate of Goa mention "...the great poverty and general misery of the inhabitants, most of whom have not even means of subsistence'. Despite all this churches were still being built, albeit smaller. Funding for the religious orders began to dry up resulting in Indian builders and craftsmen having a greater input in the architecture, design and decoration of Goa's churches.

In 1759, with Goa in decline the Viceroy moved to the former palace of Adil Shah in Panjim, a small port city and military outpost, now known as Panaji. After more deaths from disease it was decided to transfer the whole Government in 1775. Goa's buildings were demolished and their materials transported to Panaji or what became known as 'New Goa'. The transfer led to the eventual desertion of the city except for its remaining religious buildings. Between 1834 and 1835 Lisbon instructed that all religious orders were to be suppressed, which forced the only inhabitants left, the monks, friars and nuns, to abandon their convents and monasteries. It was after this, in 1843, that the capital's official move from Goa to Panaji was complete, almost a century after it

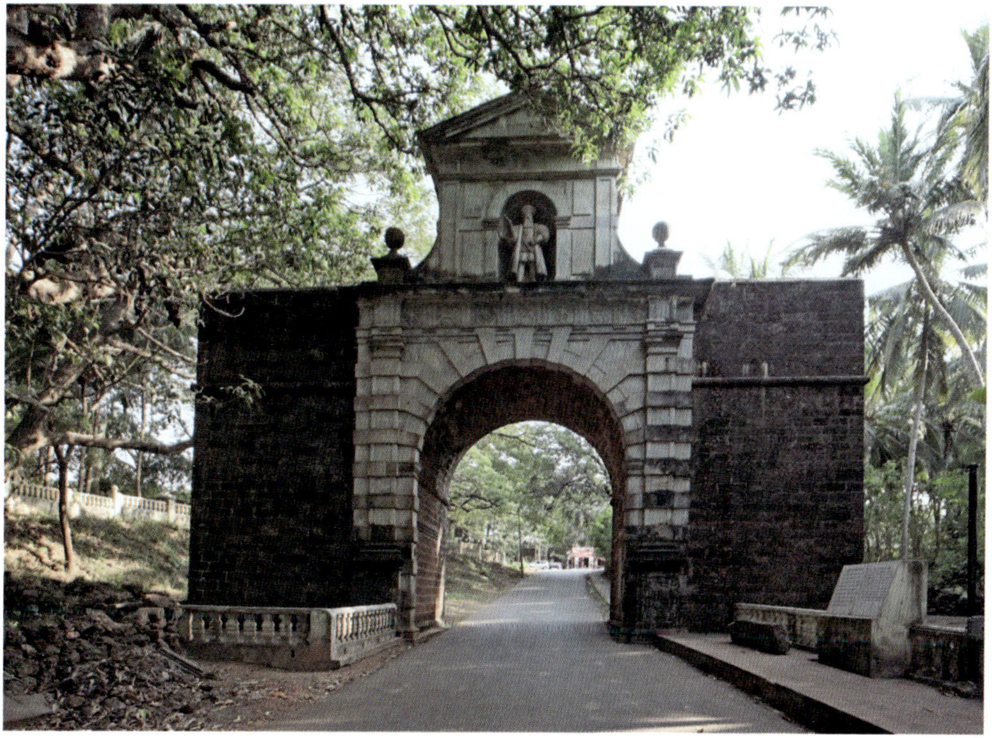

The maritime entrance to Goa; the Viceroy's Arch 1597 with a statue of Vasco da Gama above

began. At last Panaji had enough inhabitants to make it Portugal's largest settlement and to guarantee its position as Portugal's official capital in India. With no finances to preserve the splendid religious buildings their fate was sealed.

Today the vibrant, wealthy city of Goa is a silent puzzling place which causes visitors to wonder 'what happened here?' Unlike the rest of India time seems to stand still in what is now known as 'Old Goa'. There are no traffic jams or blasting car horns common to most other Indian cities. Instead the wide Rua Direta or 'True Path' is strangely empty of vehicles and people. Nothing is left of the city's old streets or the grand Portuguese mansions except a collection of the greatest monuments to Christianity in India. Once known as the ' Rome of the Orient' and a city that rivalled Lisbon for its splendour, it is now an incongruous remnant of what was once one of the greatest cities in the world.

The Church of Our Lady of the Rosary, 1547

Roman Catholic

'From this hill Alfonso de Albuquerque on 25 November 1510 witnessed Portugal's reconquest of Goa'

—Inscription placed in the church in 1931

This important church stands on Monte Santo, the Hill of the Rosary, on the site believed to be the spot where Alfonso de Albuquerque directed the battle that defeated Sultan Yusif Adil Shah. It is possibly the oldest building remaining in Old Goa and even though the exact date is not known the church was probably built between 1544 and 1547. The church has an austere, fortress like facade of three stories with small windows that look down on to the River Mandovi to Divar Island and beyond.

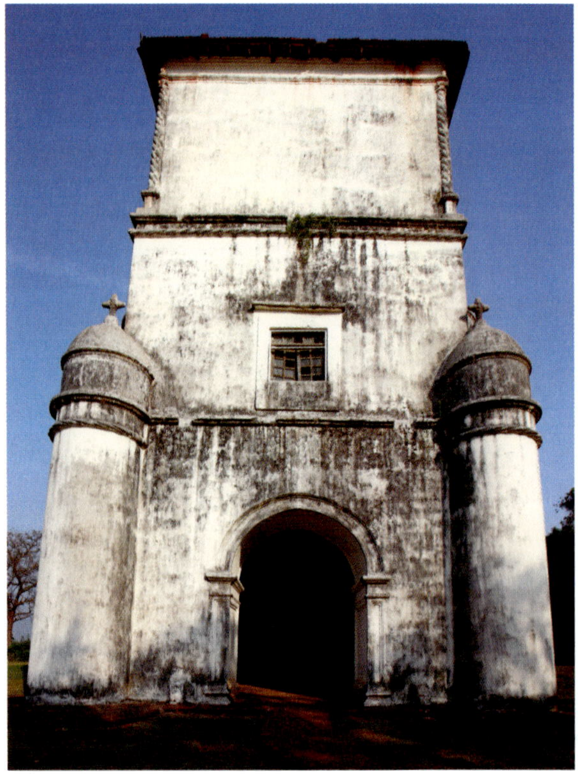

The Church of Our Lady of the Rosary

The most striking features of the church are the four rounded late-Gothic styled towers which, like buttresses, give support at each corner of the square portico which has three entrance archways. The towers at the front have cupolas and are topped with crosses. The towers at the back of the portico are taller and have no crosses. The south tower has a winding staircase which gives access to the choir loft. On the ground level of the north tower is the baptismal font. The top floor of the façade features narrow columns in a rope twisted design and at the back and sides are open arched windows hung with bells. The rope twist columns are a symbol of Portugal's dependence on sea trade and an indicator of the early 16th century Manueline style of architecture which became fashionable during the reign of Portuguese King Manuel. These columns and the towers are similar to churches in the Portuguese region of Alentejo

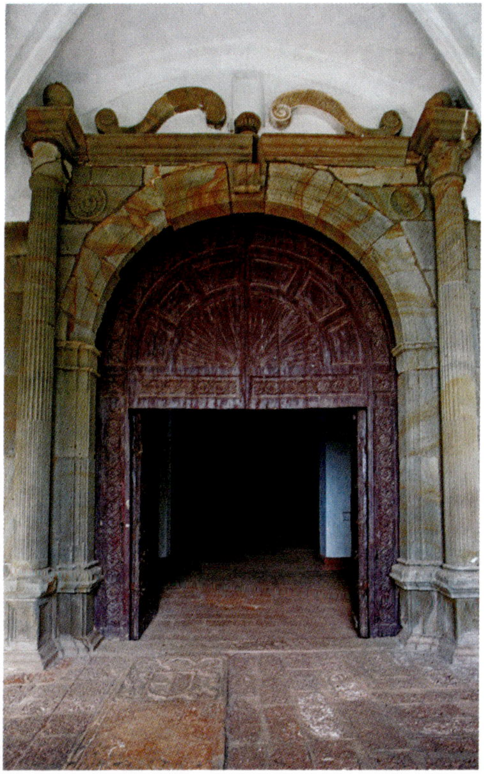

The entrance

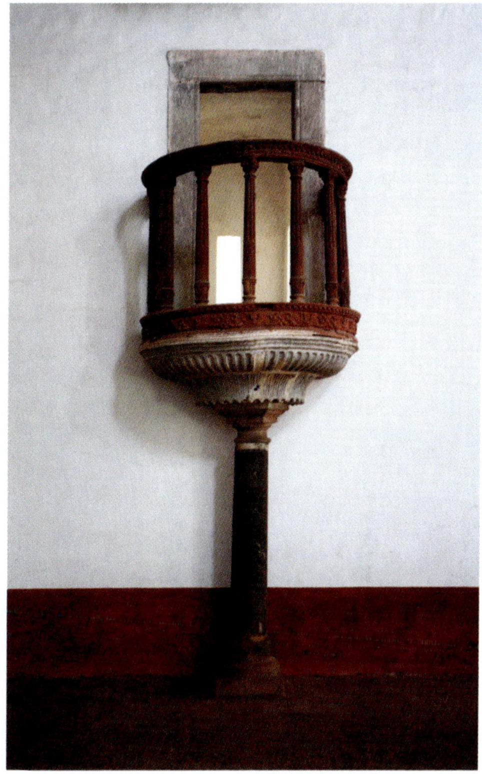

The elegant simplicity of the pulpit

and the exterior of the Church of Santa Maria Magdalena in Olivenza in particular.

The church is built of laterite, a local stone used extensively in Goa, and plastered with lime mortar. The porous qualities of laterite can be seen on the floor of the church. The ornate entrance opens onto an austere interior, very different to the elaborate churches that came later. Wooden beams support the roof and a chancel and two side chapels are next to the apse. In the chancel is an altarpiece dedicated to Nossa Senhora de Rozario, Our Lady of the Rosary and beside this is an alabaster monument in Indian style commemorating Dona Caterina, the wife of Garcia de Sa, the 14th Portuguese Governor of India. St. Francis Xavier is said to have officiated at their wedding and it is believed the saint gave his first sermon in the church after his arrival in Goa.

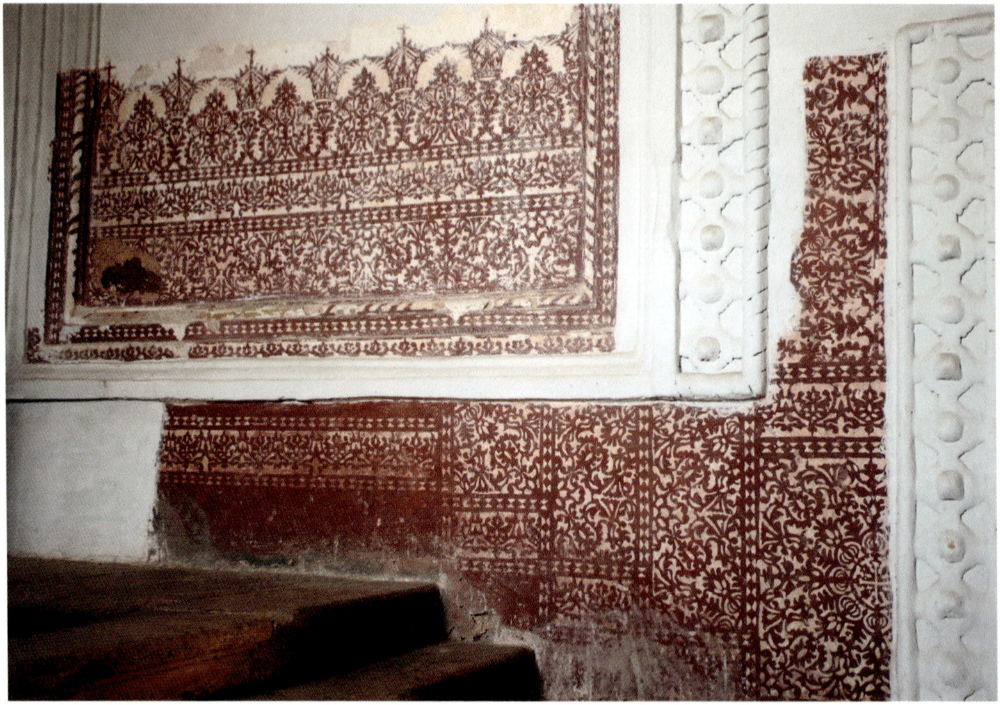

Graffiti and decorative designs on the walls

Near the altar are the remnants of Hindu ochre-coloured decorative stenciled designs on the walls. This folk art is created by applying a layer of red coloured plaster which is then painted over with a white layer. Before it hardens patterns emerge by carefully scraping away the white layer. It is often found in Goa's Hindu temples. There are two other altars and two side chapels entered through archways. Both chapels and the chancel have star-form rib vaulted ceilings. A simple but beautiful pulpit is reached by exterior stairs.

Today the Church of Our Lady of the Rosary is in the care of the Franciscans and is only opened at certain times of the year. Alfonso de Albuquerque had vowed to build a church on Holy Hill if the Portuguese were successful in conquering Goa. However the church of Our Lady of the Rosary was not completed until after his death.

Our Lady of the Rosary is the oldest existing church built in the earliest phase of Christianity in Goa. Other churches of the period have disappeared or become victim to being altered in some way. Our Lady of the Rosary is therefore one of Old Goa's most important churches, not only for its age but for its part in a significant period of Goa's history.

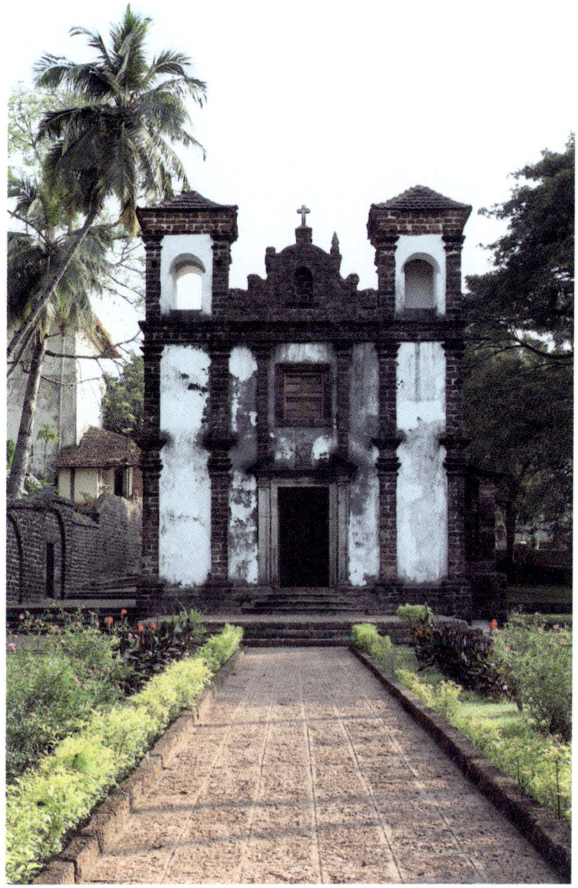

The Chapel of Saint Catherine

The Chapel of Saint Catherine, 1550

Roman Catholic

The site of this lovely chapel is believed to be the place where Alfonso De Albuquerque and his army entered the city and captured Goa from the Muslim rulers in 1510. It was St. Catherine's Day and to commemorate his victory and to give thanks he built a simple mud chapel with a thatched roof of palm leaves. Later it was replaced with a stone structure; later in 1550 the chapel was enlarged and a new altarpiece was added, placed by the Governor George Cabral who erected a stone slab on a side wall of the Chapel which reads;

"Here in this place existed the door through which entered the Governor Alfonso de Albuquerque and captured the City from the Muslims on the day of Santa Catarina in 1510, in whose honor and memory Governor George Cabral ordered this house to be built in the year 1550 at the cost of His Highness."

Until the last Portuguese Governor left India, St. Catherine's feast day was celebrated with a very solemn procession of dignitaries including the viceroy, senators and high church officials all dressed in the red gowns of the Confraria of Saint Catherine. During the Mass a twenty gun salute was fired.

The chapel sits inside a walled garden at the end of a narrow path. It is a very pretty

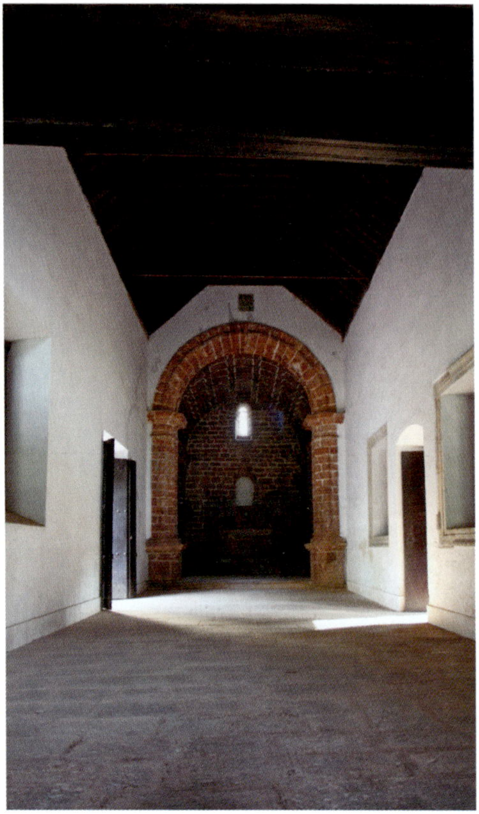

The interior of the chapel

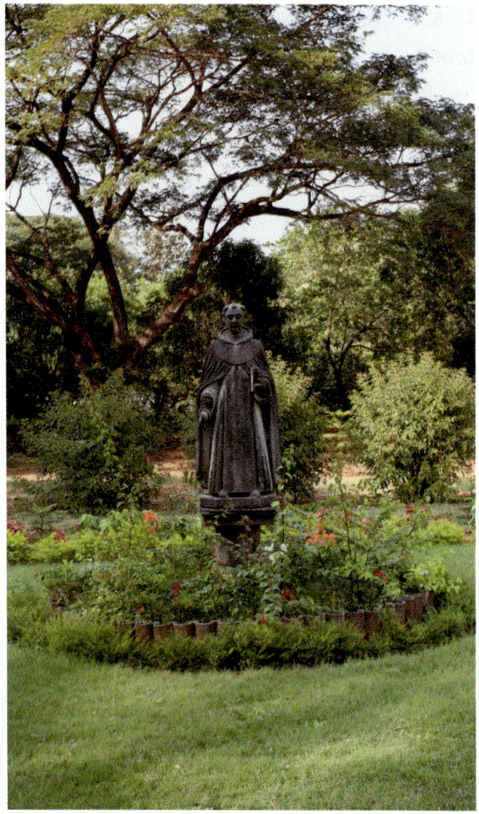

The statue of St. Francis

structure, built of Goa's red laterite stone with contrasting whitewashed plaster panels. The chapel's facade comprises three stories with a triangular pediment supported by four Tuscan pilasters. These extend to twin square towers with terracotta roof tiles on top. The arched openings between these towers hold a small niche which once held a statue of Saint Catherine. The cross above remains intact, and despite some decay of the laterite stone, the chapel is in good condition. The apse has a coffered, vaulted ceiling despite earlier removal of the plasterwork. The interior is simple and undecorated. In 1534 the chapel was raised to a Cathedral by Pope Paul III. It remained that way until the new Cathedral of St. Catherine (the Se Cathedral) was built nearby.

Reis Magos Church, 1555

Roman Catholic

On the Mandovi river is a village, a fort and a church, all bearing the name Reis Magos, which means Three Wise Men; the oriental kings of the bible who travelled to Bethlehem bearing gifts of gold, frankincense and myrrh for the Baby Jesus. The church is reached by a relaxed drive beside the river before the majestic building comes into view at the top of a hill. Built by Franciscans between 1551 and 1555 the church is dedicated to St. Jerome. In the mid-18th century pillars were added to the facade and sometime later the church was renovated. Today the three storied church is painted in bright white with a high scroll-like gabled facade outlined in blue. It sits dramatically at the top of an impressive flight of stairs. Though there are some Hindu temple elements, particularly in the shape of the gable (decorated with the insignia of the Portuguese crown and coat of arms) the church is Baroque in style. Five bays on the ground floor consist of a centred main door flanked by two smaller doors on each side. The second story follows this design with the placing of five windows directly above the doors. The third story has a window in the centre and one on each outer side. The other bays are plain.

The highest point of the facade above features two square towers, one of which is a belfry. The figures of two lions sit at the base of the steps, believed to be evidence that the church was built over the site of a Hindu temple, something that was common during Portuguese rule.

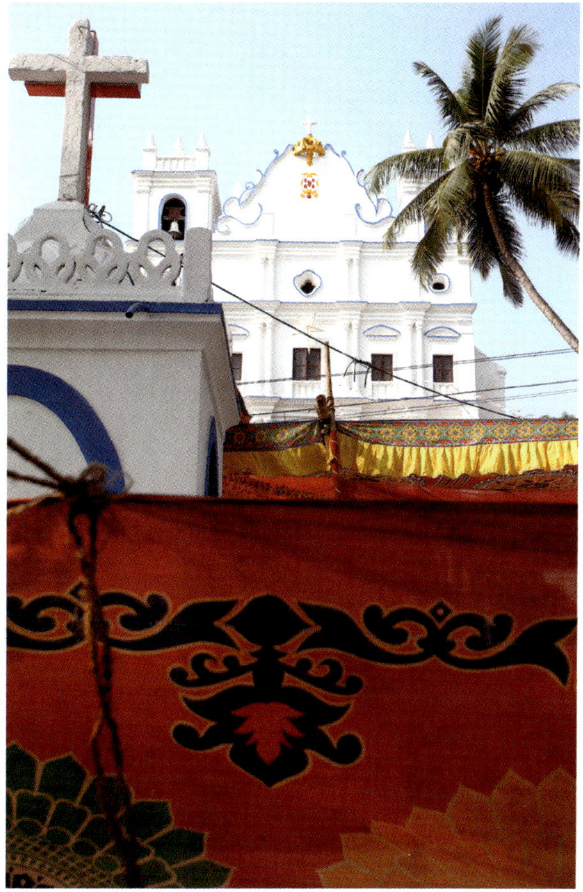

Reis Magos Church

The church interior is bright and richly decorated. The marble floor of the altar is

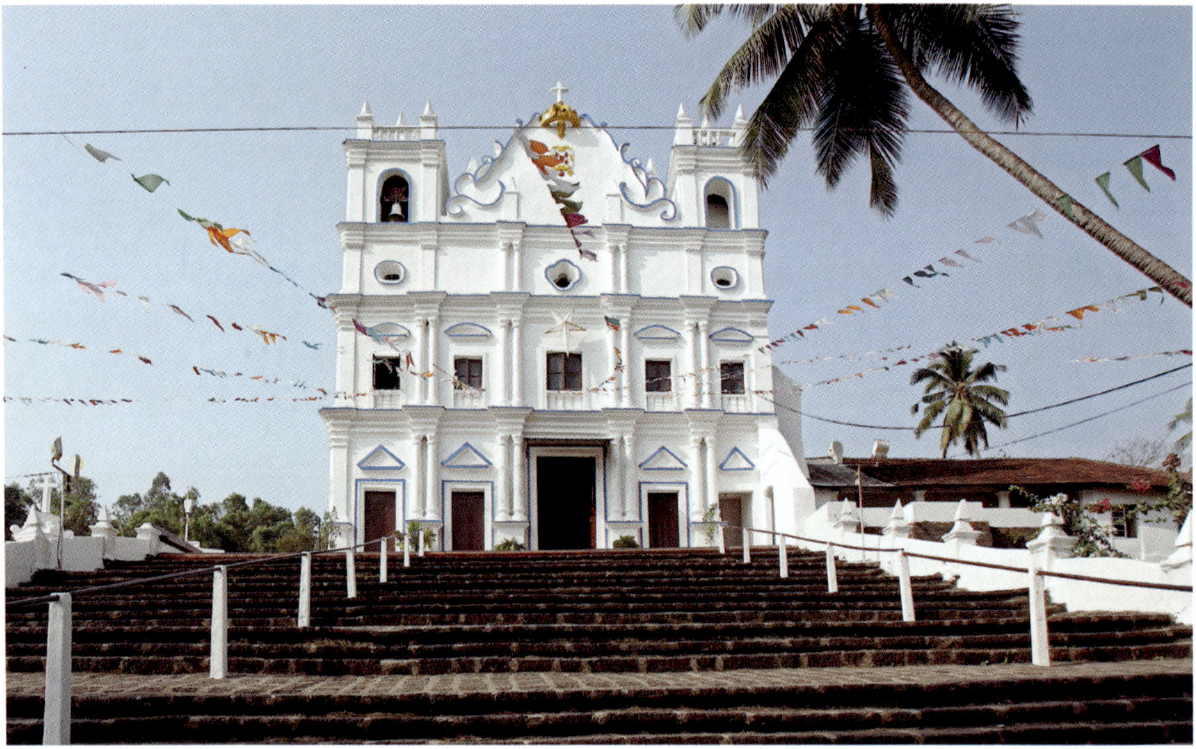

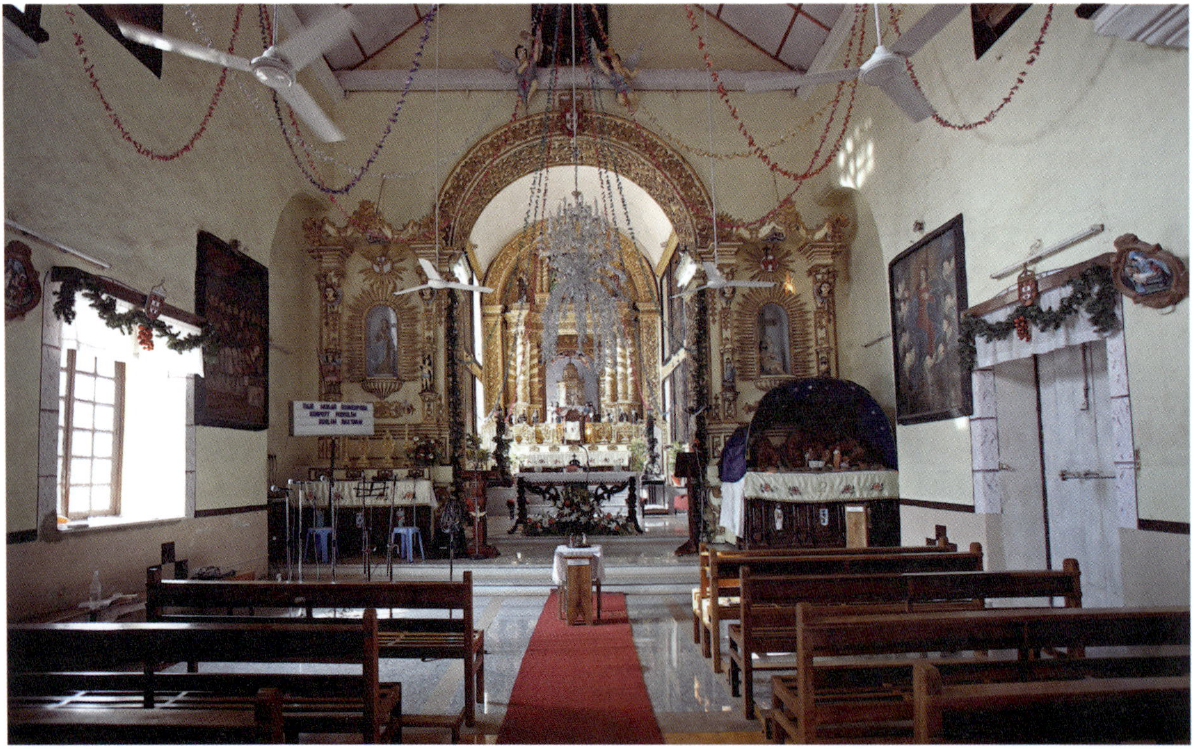

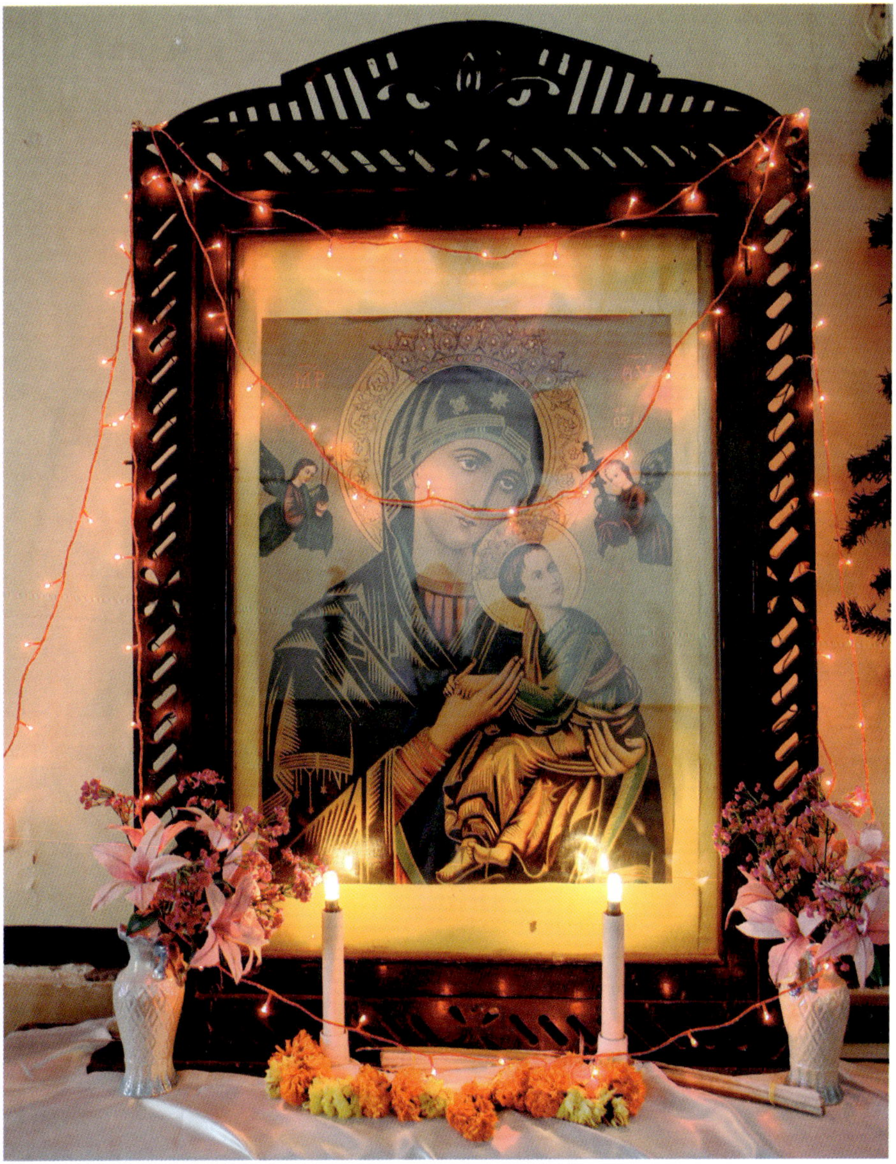

ABOVE: *Painting of the Madonna and Child*
FACING PAGE TOP: *The laterite steps leading up*
FACING PAGE BELOW: *Interiors of the church*

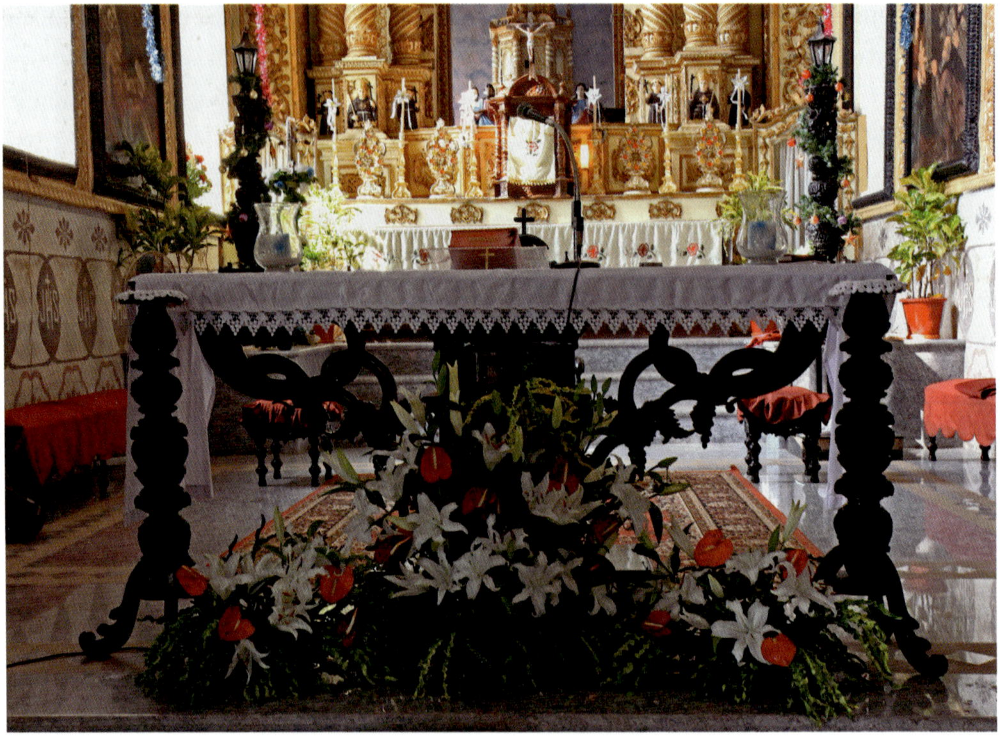

The church's interior

partly covered by a handmade rug and a delicate handmade cloth covers the altar under which is a large display of flowers. There are painted wooden figures of the three kings bearing their gifts to the baby Jesus. These figures are part of the decoratively carved and gilded *reredos* behind the main altar.

The Festa dos Reis Magos, Feast of the Three Kings, is celebrated on the sixth of January every year and tells the story of Gaspar, Melchior and Balthazar, the three kings from the Orient who asked; '*Where is the one who has been born king of the Jews? We saw his star in the east and have come to worship him*'. In Reis Magos the whole community is involved in the feast day beginning with a procession starting at the church and winding through the village. Young members of the community play the roles of the wise men and the baby Jesus. It is a festival where the whole community, not just Christians, celebrate love, faith and happiness.

The Convent and Church of St. Augustine, 1602

Roman Catholic

The most extraordinary sight on Monte Santo is the moving spectacle of a single damaged tower rising twelve metres above a pile of ruins. The tower is the last remaining fragment of the Monastery of St. Augustine and the Nossa Senhora da Graca, the Church of Our Lady of Grace built by the Augustinian Order in the 16th century. There were four towers originally, the remaining one was part of the facade and served as the belfry. St. Augustine's was completed in 1602. It was one of Goa's richest monasteries and the church was one of the largest in India.

This great church was completed around the same time as the Basilica of Bom Jesu

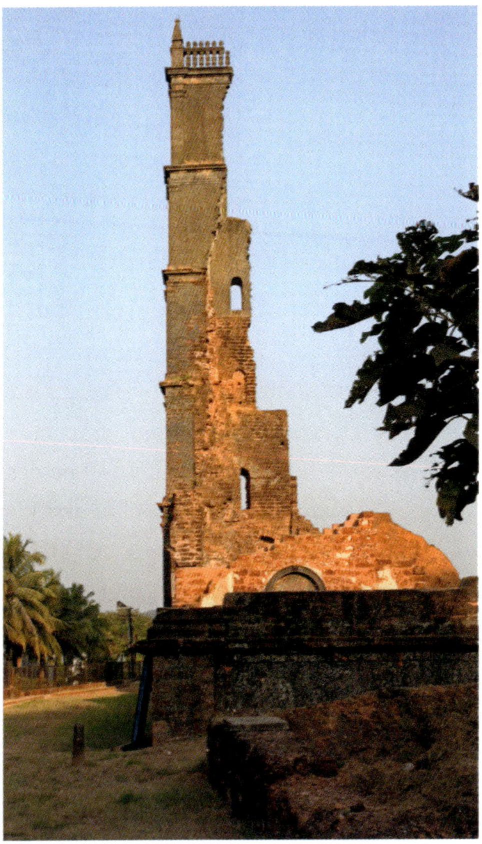

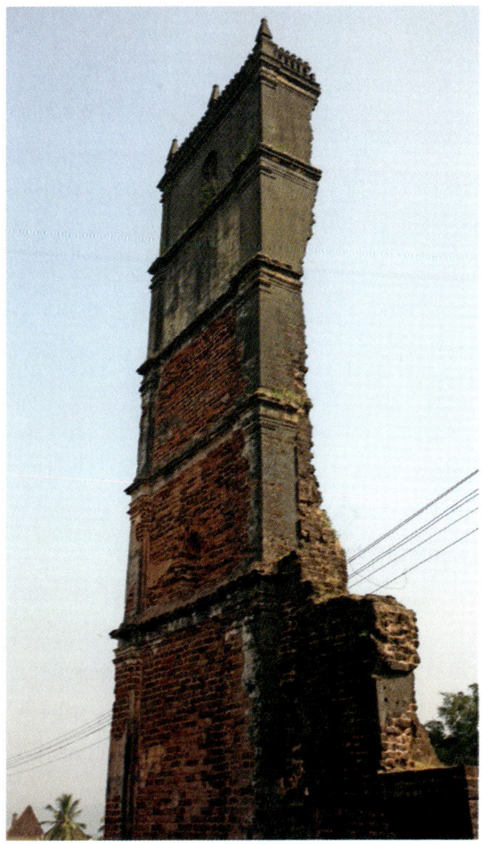

Two views of the Convent and Church of St. Augustine

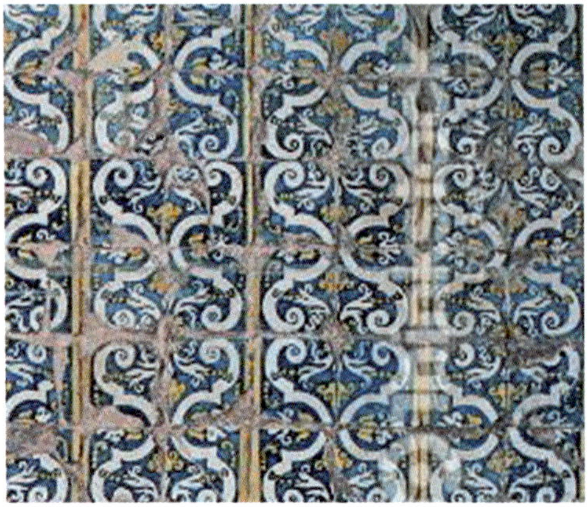

Portuguese azulejo *tiles in the ruins of St. Augustine's*

and the Se Cathedral. Julio Simao, Goan born Chief Engineer of the Indian colonies of Portugal was a possible architect though this is not certain. When the church was completed it was accepted as one of the three great Augustinian churches. The others were Spain's Monasterio y Sitio El Escorial near Madrid and Portugal's Mosteiro Da Sao Vicente de Fora in Lisbon.

The Augustinians were one of a number of religious orders who arrived in Goa during the 16th century. They built a small monastery then expanded it to include a church dedicated to Our Lady of Grace. Over time the complex grew to include twenty two monasteries each with a college attached.

Today it takes some imagination to picture the once splendid five-storied façade, the four enormous towers and the richly decorated interior. It was a collection of beautiful buildings with numerous altars, vast halls, galleries and cloisters, a magnificent library and a large collection of religious paintings. Some remains of the convent cells can still be seen amongst the ruins as well as fragments of broken walls covered in hand painted Portuguese *azulejo* tiles which were not only decorative but cooling. The nave of the church held a high altar with a large gilded tabernacle (a chest housing holy objects) set within an arch and seen through a partition of arched columns. These columns supported the enormous barrel vaulted nave, now open to the sky. In 1835 the Portuguese Government suppressed a number of Goa's religious orders, the Augustinians included. The monastery and church were abandoned and in just seven years the ceiling collapsed and later the monastery and college were demolished leaving just the empty church. In 1871 the tower's enormous bell was removed to the Church of the Immaculate Conception in Panaji where it remains to this day. Amazingly the facade survived until 1931 but once this collapsed only the tower remained, a lonely but defiant remnant of a once great religious past.

The ruins of St. Augustine are a reminder of long gone splendours but they also hide some intriguing secrets. Archaeological students discovered man-made and natural

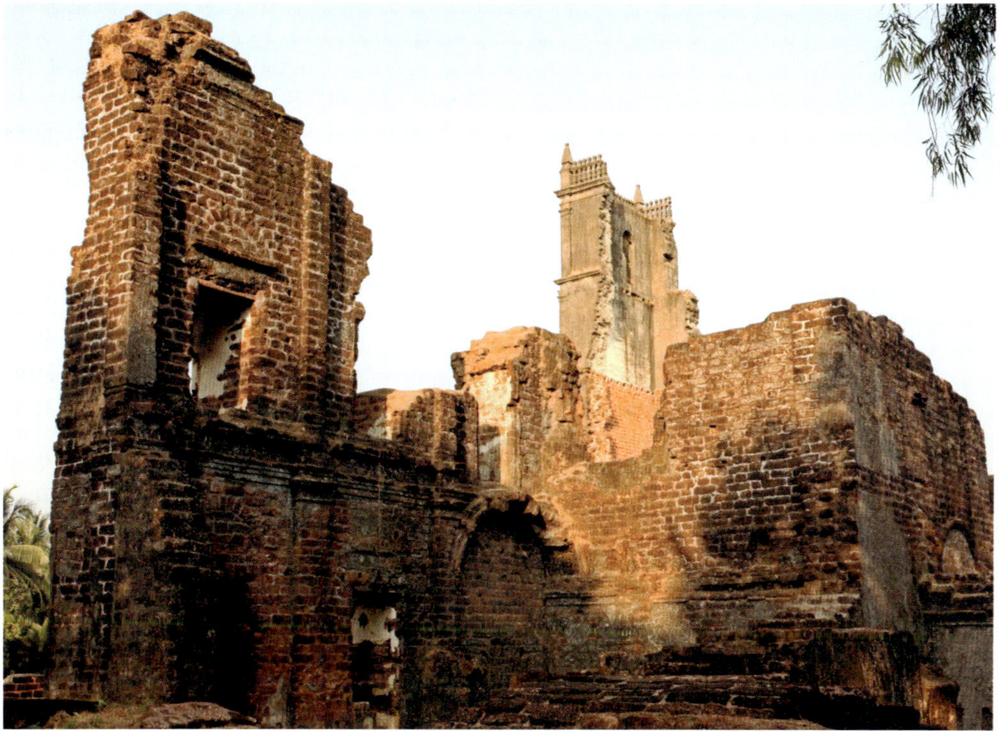

The ruins of St. Augustine

tunnels and passageways underneath St. Augustine's but more fascinating is the discovery of what archaeologists believe is the tomb of 17th century Georgian Queen Katevan, executed by Shah Abbas, the Persian ruler for refusing to join his harem nor convert from Christianity to Islam. Soon after her death she was canonised as a saint by the Georgian Orthodox Church.

Historical records reveal that between 1624 and 1627 two Augustinian friars who were devoted to the queen secretly unearthed her remains and transported them to St. Augustine's church in faraway Goa. Delegations from Georgia have been sent to work with the Archaeological Survey of India in locating the Queen Katevan's grave and in 1991 a search began after a request from the Russian embassy. More recently DNA testing has revealed the remains found are most likely to be those of Saint Queen Katevan of Georgia.

The Bom Jesu Basilica, 1605

Roman Catholic

The Basilica of Bom Jesu or Good Jesus is the most famous church in Old Goa. It was completed in 1605 and houses the famous Chapel and Tomb of St. Francis Xavier, the student and friend of St. Ignatius of Loyola who founded the Jesuits. St. Xavier came to Goa in 1542 and travelled to many areas of Asia. However his greatest success was in the Portuguese held areas of India. He was energetic and devoted which gave him a great following. Despite being in India for less than two years he is still revered by Christians and Indians alike. In Goa the Saint is known as '*Goencho Saib*', or 'Lord of Goa'.

St. Francis Xavier died on the Chinese island of Shangchuan in 1552. He was buried with a large amount of lime which is known to speed up the breaking down of

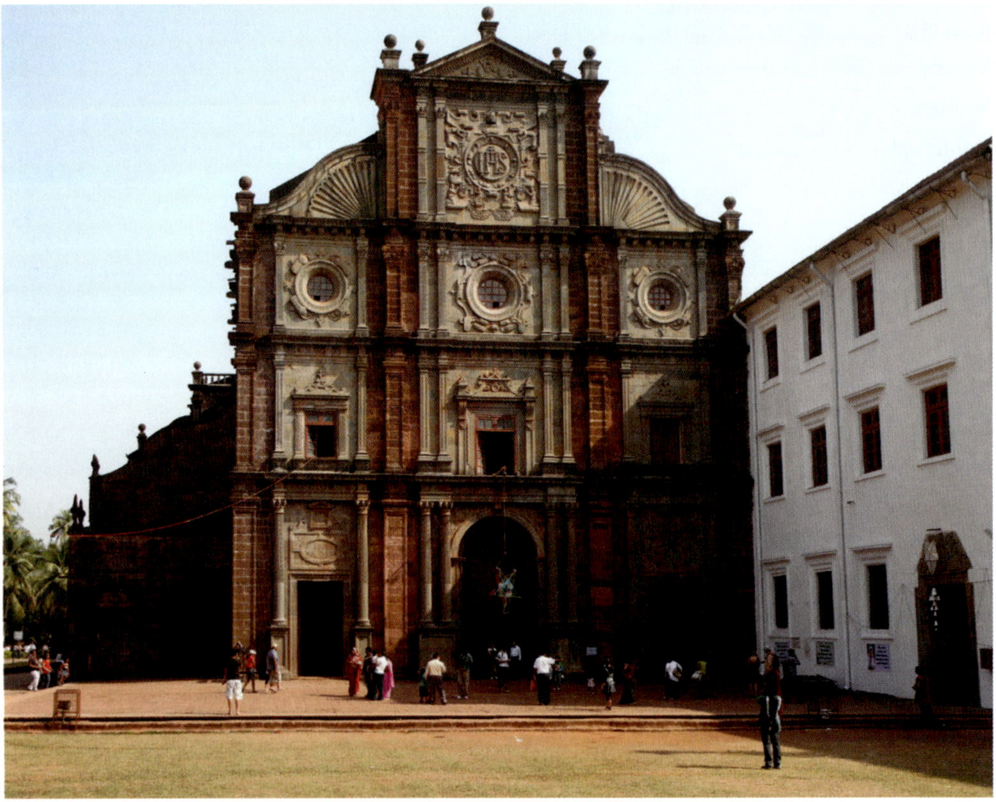

The Basilica and the Professed House on the right

the body to deter grave robbers and render it easier for his remains to be transported to India. Two years later when the casket was opened in Goa the body was miraculously intact. From that time the saint's remains became known as the 'Uncorrupted Body of St. Francis Xavier'.

The mausoleum of St. Francis is found in a side chapel near the altar. It is an astonishing mass of Baroque silverwork. The body of the saint can be seen resting in an elaborate silver casket above an equally elaborate catafalque (a framework which supports the coffin of a distinguished person). The three storied catafalque was a gift from the Grand Duke of Tuscany, the last Medici, in return for the saint's pillow. The casket was made by Indian silversmiths supervised by the Italian Jesuit Friar Marco Mastrilli. It was completed in 1637 on the Saint's Feast Day and is known as the Mastrillian Casket. There are thirty two silver plates on each side of the casket which depict the life of the saint. An angel near the saint's feet bears the words; '*Satis est, Domine, Satis ext*', which translates, 'It is enough, O Lord, it is enough', believed to be the saint's most common saying.

Today the remains of St. Francis Xavier are still preserved despite some misfortune. In 1952 the saint was displayed for three weeks. Over 8,17,000 people passed the casket to kiss the saint. One of them was so overwhelmed she is said to have bitten off one of the saint's toes and tried to smuggle it away! Whether this story is true or not it was decided that the touching of the body was accelerating the deterioration of the saint's remains. Consequently the body is

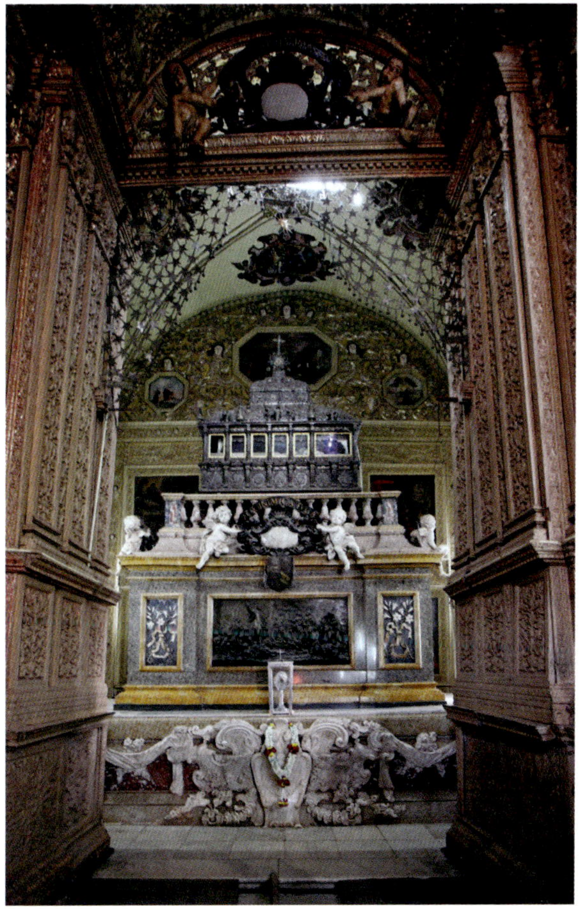

The mausoleum with the casket and remains of St. Francis Xavier at the top

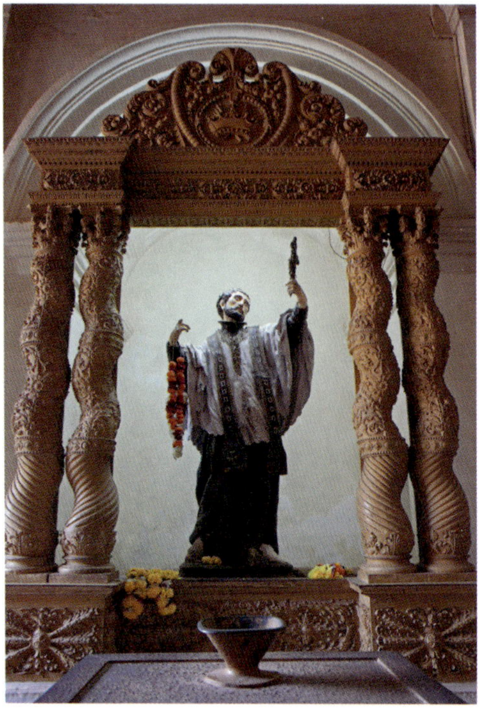

A finely carved and painted wooden statue of St. Francis Xavier

now shown in a glass casket. Interestingly however, one of St. Francis' toes is held in a glass case in the sacristy.

The Basilica is built of dark red laterite, a stone common in many of Goa's old religious buildings. It is a practical stone and easy to cut and carve. However it is very porous. Consequently with each monsoon the exterior carving becomes more eroded. Originally the Basilica was plastered with lime on the outside until 1950 when a Portuguese conservationist unfortunately decided to expose the original exterior. Light coloured basalt has also been used to decorate the three storied facade in a heavy scroll design with a mixture of three classical columns; Ionic, Doric and Corinthian. It is typical of the grand Jesuit style that became popular in Europe and Latin America during the 17th century although there are no towers which were usual in Portugal's Jesuit churches.

The ground level has three doors which open onto a single undivided nave, possibly the first church to introduce the three door entrance. Above are three corresponding long windows. The third level features three round windows and the uppermost level of the facade is a square shape carved with the IHS the first three letters of Jesus' name in Greek, the emblem of the Jesuits. Either side are fan shaped volutes. There is a belfry at the rear of the church and the entire structure includes two chapels, a main altar, a sacristy and a choir loft above the entrance. Construction of the church began in 1594 and was designed by Portuguese Jesuit Domingos Fernandes and Julio Simao Portugal's chief engineer in the Indies who may have built the Monastery of St. Augustine. It was consecrated in 1605 by the archbishop, *Dom Fr. Aleixo de Menezes*. The interior of the Bom Jesu is a large opulent space with numerous altars carved in wood

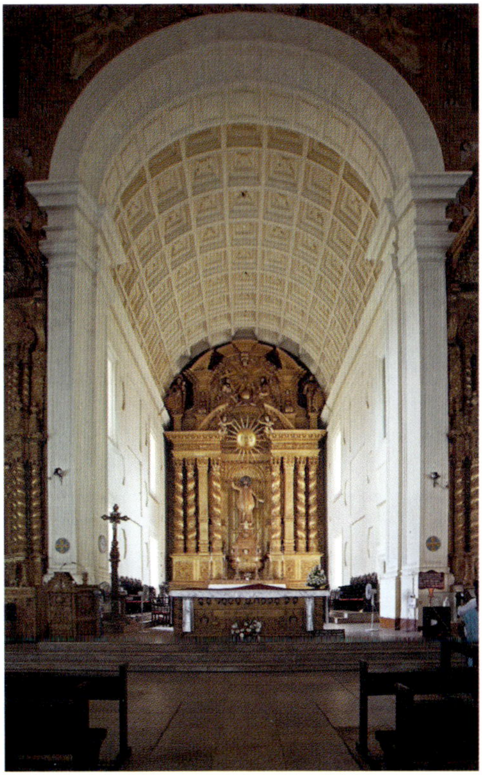

The altar and the gilded reredos

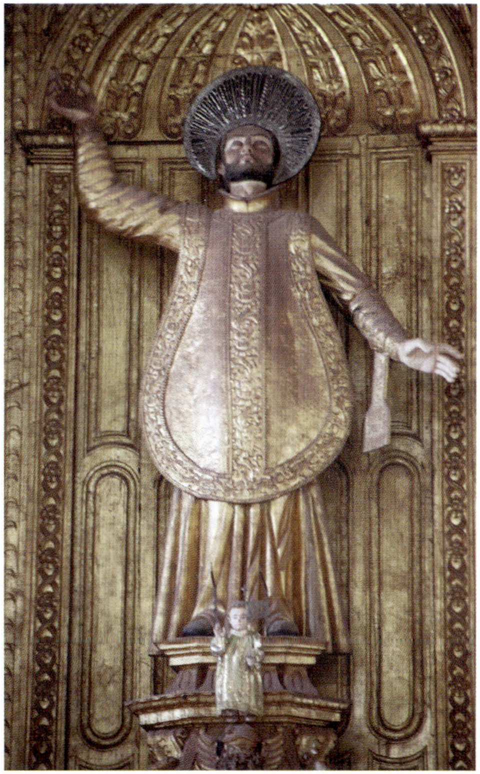

St.Ignatius of Loyola with a tiny Baby Jesus

and covered in gold leaf. The magnificent gold *reredos* soars up into the panelled vault of the arch which surrounds it, typical of the decorative Indian-Baroque style. The Basilica is a fine example of an artistic style common to Portugal and Spain which concentrated on two points; the façade and the *reredos*.

The interior seems to glow in burnished gold. The first thing to catch the eye is the striking three metre high statue of St. Ignatius of Loyola whose eyes look up to the medallion of the Jesuits above. Higher up is the Holy Trinity, the Father, Son and Holy Ghost. At the feet of the huge statue is a tiny statue of the infant Jesus. On either side of the main altar in the transept are two more altars, one dedicated to Our Lady of Hope and the other to St. Michael. Both are richly gilded. Several paintings on the walls portray the life of St. Francis Xavier.

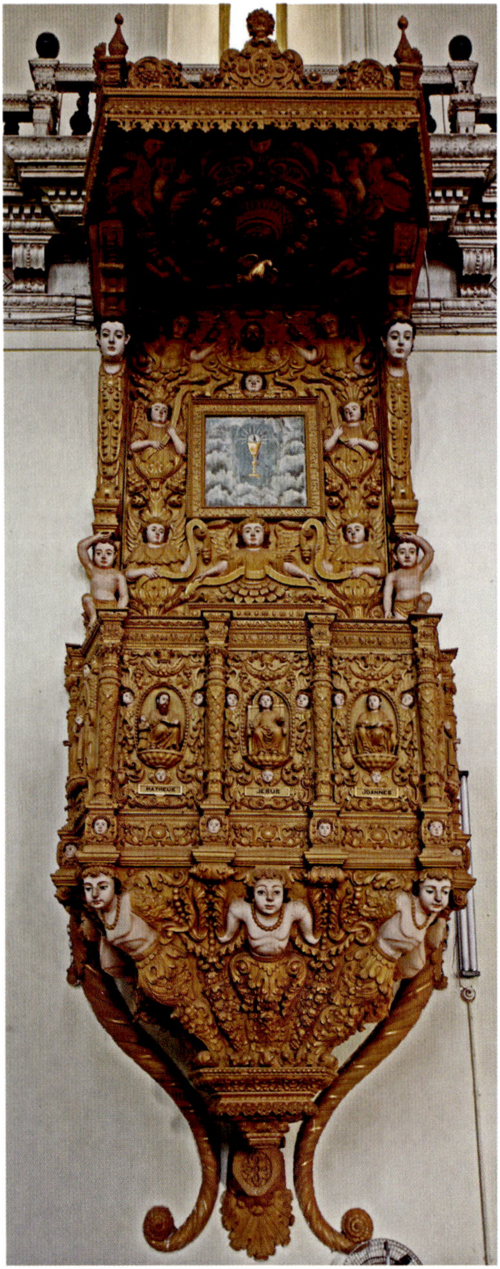
MATHEUS
JESUS
JOANNES

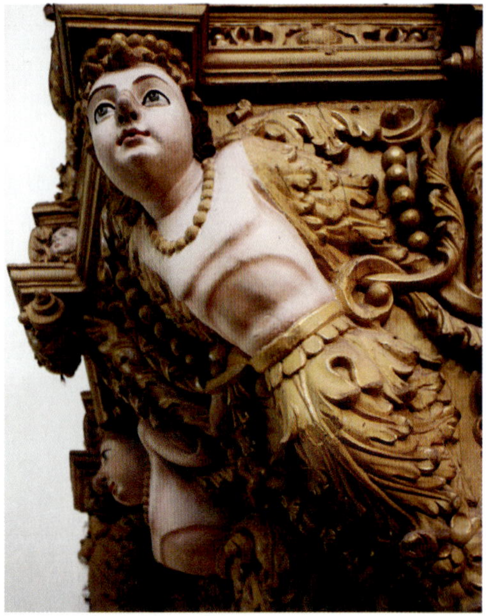

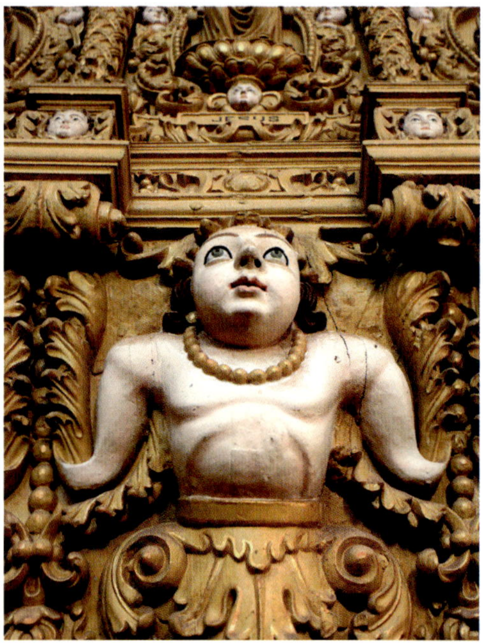

An astonishingly ornate canopied pulpit is incorporated in the southern wall and shows the skill of local Indian craftsmen. It is richly carved and depicts Jesus, four evangelists and four 'doctors', the special title given to certain saints. The whole structure is a mass of writhing serpents, lotus flowers, Hindu-like winged gods, Christian and Hindu symbols, columns and rope twists, all intricate and all clearly Indian in style. Seven nagas or imaginary creatures support the pulpit. They are related to spirits that dwell in the forests or in the water. Serpents are also associated with these creatures and they are worshipped by Hindus for fertility.

Next door to the Basilica is the older Casa Professa, the Professed House of the Jesuits where Jesuit missions to other eastern regions were planned and discussions took place with the Ministries on the ways in which the strict laws of the Jesuit ways of life could be upheld.

The Basilica of Bom Jesu is one of the richest churches in India and one of the most revered in India. Once every ten years there is an 'exposition' or public viewing of the body in the casket which attracts people from around the world. Many believe the saint has miraculous healing powers and that simply being there in the crowd has a healing effect. In 1946 the remarkable Bom Jesu became the first Indian church to be raised to a minor Basilica.

FACING PAGE LEFT: *The ornate pulpit at Basilica of Bom Jesu*
FACING PAGE RIGHT TOP & BELOW: *Details of the pulpit's imaginary creatures*

The Sé Catedral de Santa Catarina, 1619

Roman Catholic

'...a grandiose church worthy of the wealth, power and fame of the Portuguese who dominated the seas from the Atlantic to the Pacific'.

The Portuguese Viceroy Redondo (1561-64) issued the above words to describe the church he commissioned for the Dominican Order in 1562. The result is a beautiful cathedral, one of the oldest and most famous in Old Goa. It took more than sixty years to complete during which time six different Portuguese had reigned. It was used for services by 1619 but not consecrated until 1640.

The Sé Cathedral was built in commemoration of the day in 1510 that Alfonso de Albuquerque conquered Goa, and the feast day of St. Catherine of Alexandria. The church is dedicated to the Saint. The original church was a small chapel built of mud, straw and stones. Today's Cathedral is built of laterite blocks and lime plastered. It was begun by an unknown architect but passed on to engineers Julio Simao, the designer of the

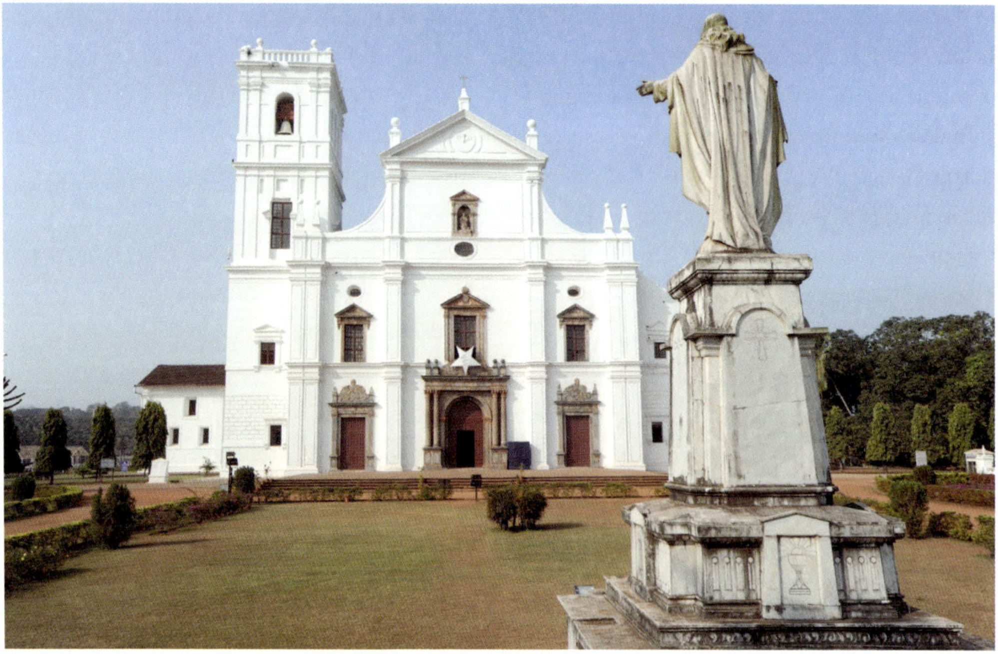

The Sé Catedral de Santa Catarina

Basilica of Bom Jesu, and Ambrosio Argueiro. The building replaced the smaller church of St. Catherine (shown previously in this chapter) which had functioned as a cathedral up to that time. The completed Cathedral was seen as the finest building ever built by a European architect in Asia.

The Cathedral is set on the west of a large grassy square, once the main square of the city, and faces a one hundred year old statue of Christ with arms outstretched. A distinguishing feature of the Se Cathedral is its missing tower on the southern side. Struck by lightning in 1776 it was never rebuilt. The remaining tower houses the famous 'Golden Bell', known for its beautiful tone. However during the Inquisition, from 1560 to 1812, the tolling of the bell announced the dreadful *auto da fe,* or 'act of faith,' the public ceremony held in the square during which suspected heretics were subjected to torture or even death. Try to imagine Old Goa in the past; the grassy square where the city's market was held, the Senate House to the left and the infamous Palace of the Inquisition to the right. The famous historian and writer Teofilo Braga wrote that when the Inquisition was instigated in Portugal, due to demands form Emperor Charles V of Spain, it signaled the downfall of the Portuguese. It is perplexing that the Inquisition was initiated in Goa by St. Francis Xavier who it is believed was present for the first *auto da fe* in Portugal in 1540. He did not live to see the horror of the Inquisition in Goa.

Today the cathedral square is a place of peace and most visitors know nothing of its past history. Instead the cathedral's thirty metre high Tuscan facade is the focus. The Manueline style doorway with two Corinthian columns on plinths either side is entered from a large patio. Inside the enormity of the great cathedral becomes clear. Over 76 meters long and 55 meters wide, it is the largest church in Asia. The interior space is spectacular. From the entrance the altar glows in the distance and the stark white walls contrast with the six intricately carved and gilded *reredos* which depict scenes from the life of St. Catherine. The altar with its imposing crucifix towers above. Nearby is the throne of the Archbishop of Goa. Overall the style of the interior is restrained and elegant. At the entrance is a painting of St. Christopher crossing the river carrying the Baby Jesus. On the saint's feast day the procession gives thanks to St. Christopher for saving the Cathedral's remaining tower.

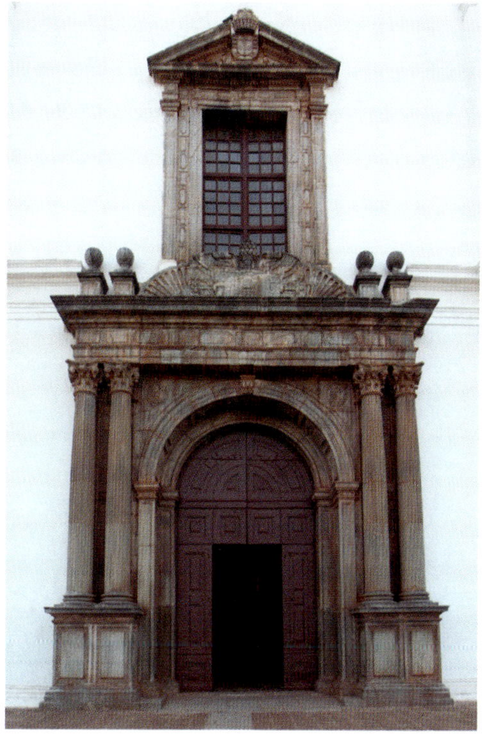

The Manueline entrance

Rows of enormous pillars support the barrel-vaulted nave and the choir. The aisles have four chapels each side and six at the transept. The Chapel of the Blessed Sacrament is exceptionally beautiful as every surface of the walls and ceiling is decorated and gilded. It is protected by a delicately carved wooden screen. The Chapel of the Cross of Miracles, Cruz dos Milagres, is also protected by a delicate screen as it houses a very important cross. Legend has it that this

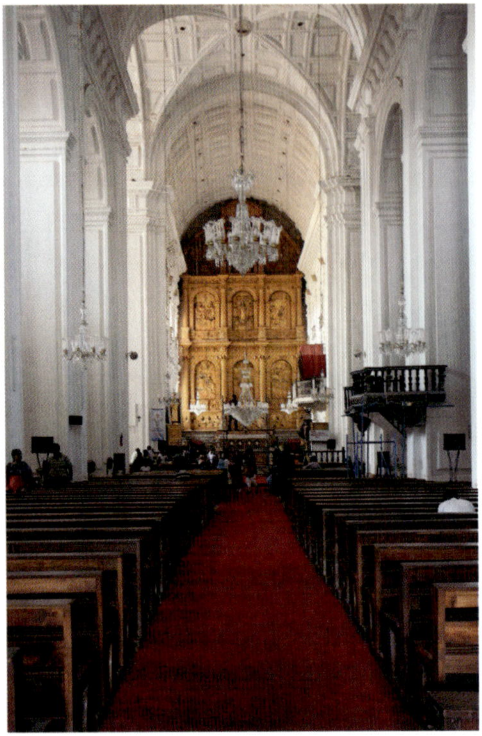

The interior

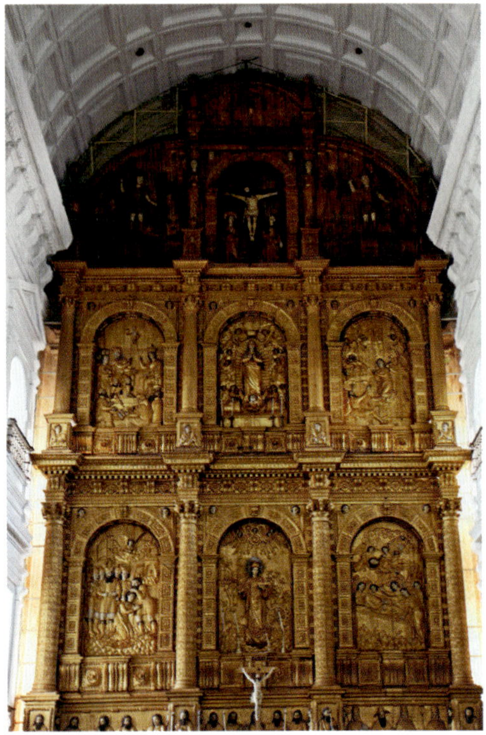

A closer view of the reredos

rustic wooden cross was first erected on a hill by shepherds in 1619. Soon locals began reporting that the cross was growing, and then several people saw a vision of Christ on the cross. As is often the case when a miracle occurs, a church was planned on the site where the vision had appeared. When the church was completed the cross seemed to have grown even more and the church doors had to be enlarged. In 1845 the now famous cross was moved to the Se Cathedral where it is believed to have miraculous healing powers and strangely, that it still continues to grow. A vision of Christ is said to have appeared in 1919. The sacred cross is contained in a large wooden case with a small opening, allowing the devout to touch the holy relic.

This beautiful Baroque cathedral is one of the most famous churches in Goa and an architectural high point reached by the Portuguese in India, a symbol of their devotion to the Catholic Church.

The Church of St. Francis of Assisi, 1661

Roman Catholic

Next to the Se Cathedral but separated by the Convent of St. Francis of Assisi is the beautiful Church of St. Francis of Assisi. The buildings were established by eight Portuguese Franciscan friars who arrived in Goa in 1517. They built a small chapel which was adapted to a church in 1521. In 1661 it was replaced by the present-day church. The lovely Manueline doorway is the only part of the earlier church left intact. Its design includes a Greek cross, the emblem of all Portuguese ships, two navigator's globes

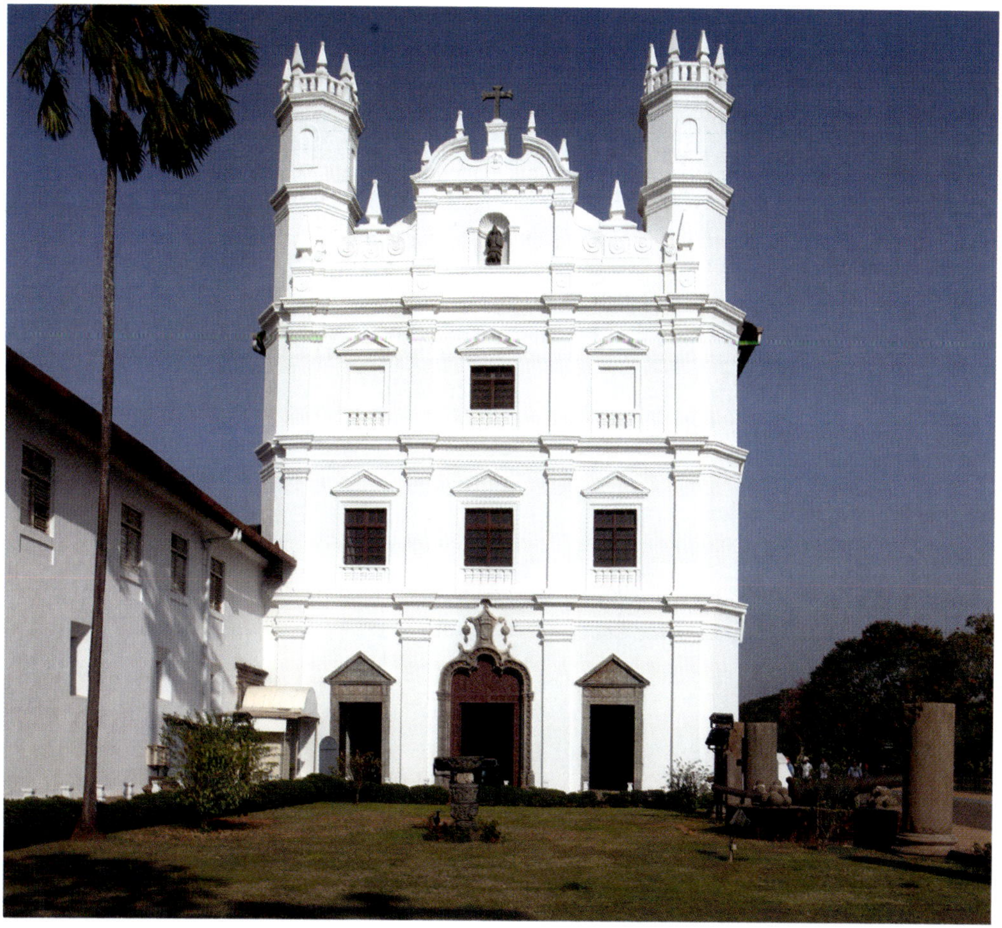

The Church of St. Francis of Assisi

and a coat of arms, all nautical themes symbolising the era of the Great Navigators. The entrance may have been carved by Leonardo Vaz who was involved in the building of the Manueline Tower of Belem in Portugal, the country where the true opulence of Manueline architecture reached its peak. The doorway and the Manueline turret-like octagonal towers contrast with the austere Tuscan facade, a style which became popular in the 17th century. Between the towers is a central niche with a statue of St. Michael and another which houses a statue of Mary. The three storied façade is built of laterite and covered with limed plaster.

The interior is surely one of the most beautiful of all churches in India. Rich gilding and frescoes with floral motifs in subtle shades of pink, green, yellow and gold line the walls and ceiling. There is an element of Islamic art, the influence likely from local artist's exposure to the Moorish art of Portugal and Spain. Portuguese tombstones dating back to the 16th century cover the floor of the vast nave and small chapels feature religious figures and paintings. There are no aisles, only a nave with a rib vaulted ceiling, all created to give the illusion that the upper level of the church is floating in soft light. There are floral frescoes on the internal buttressed walls and the main Baroque style altar and the *reredos* are beneath a high and deep chancel. On the walls inside hang large oil paintings on wood depicting the life of St. Francis of Assisi. The soaring *reredos* is in burnished gold leaf and fills the whole of the eastern wall of the church. Two pairs of slim columns rise from decorated bases between which are niches with statues of the apostles and a central space for the tabernacle, the

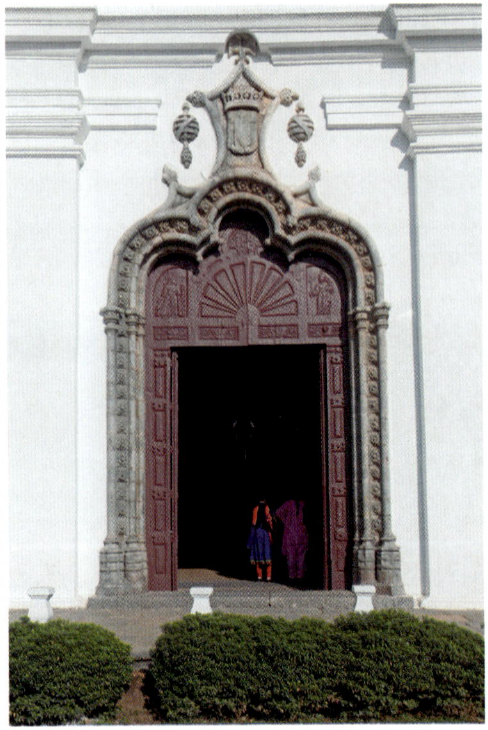

ABOVE: *The Manueline entrance*

FACING PAGE TOP LEFT: *The chancel*

FACING PAGE TOP RIGHT: *Ancient painting of the Virgin and Child and a wooden statue of St. Francis*

FACING PAGE BELOW: *Paintings of the life of St. Francis*

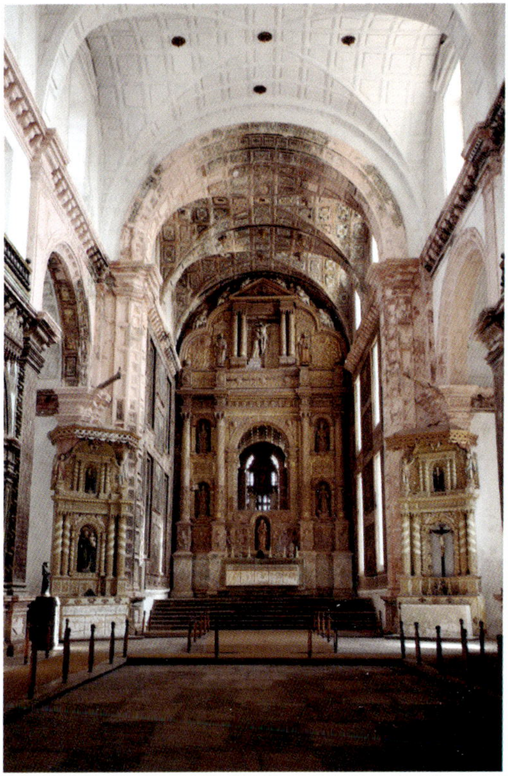
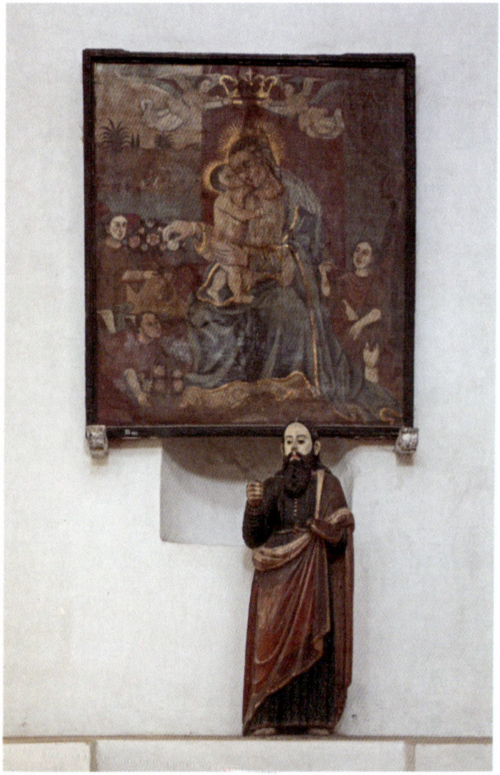
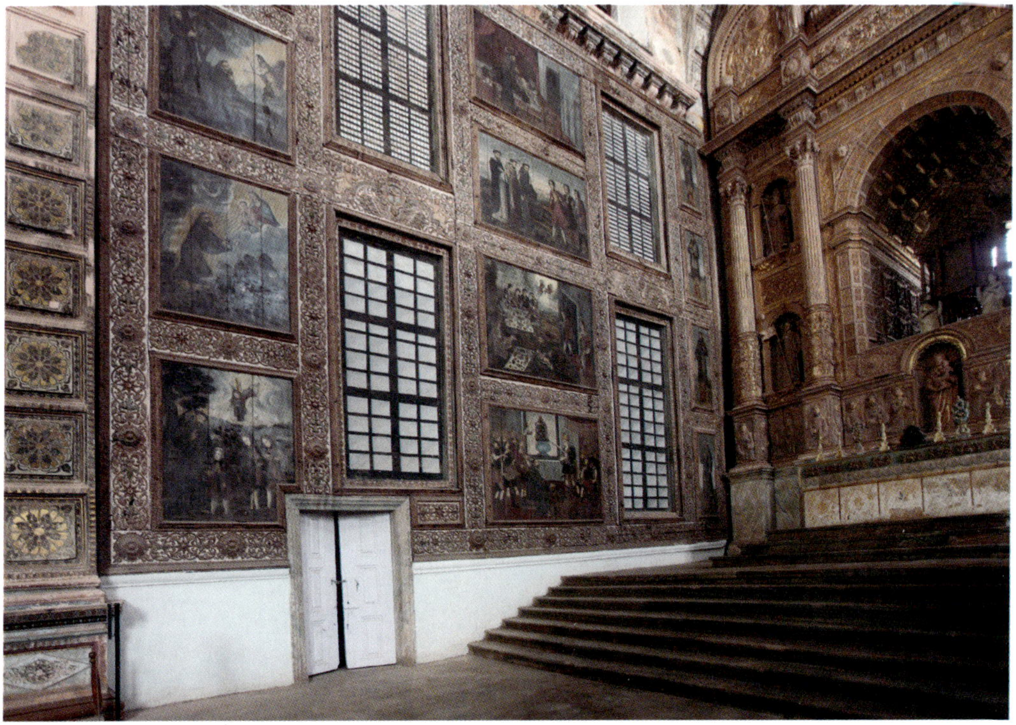

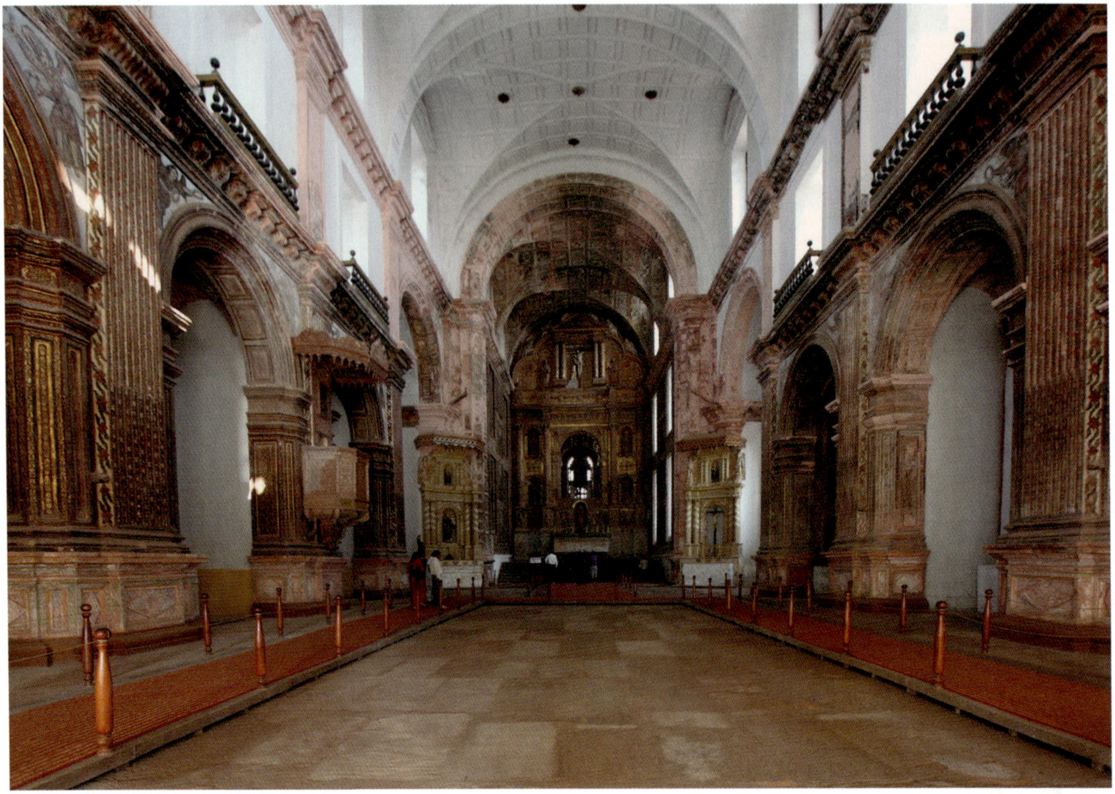

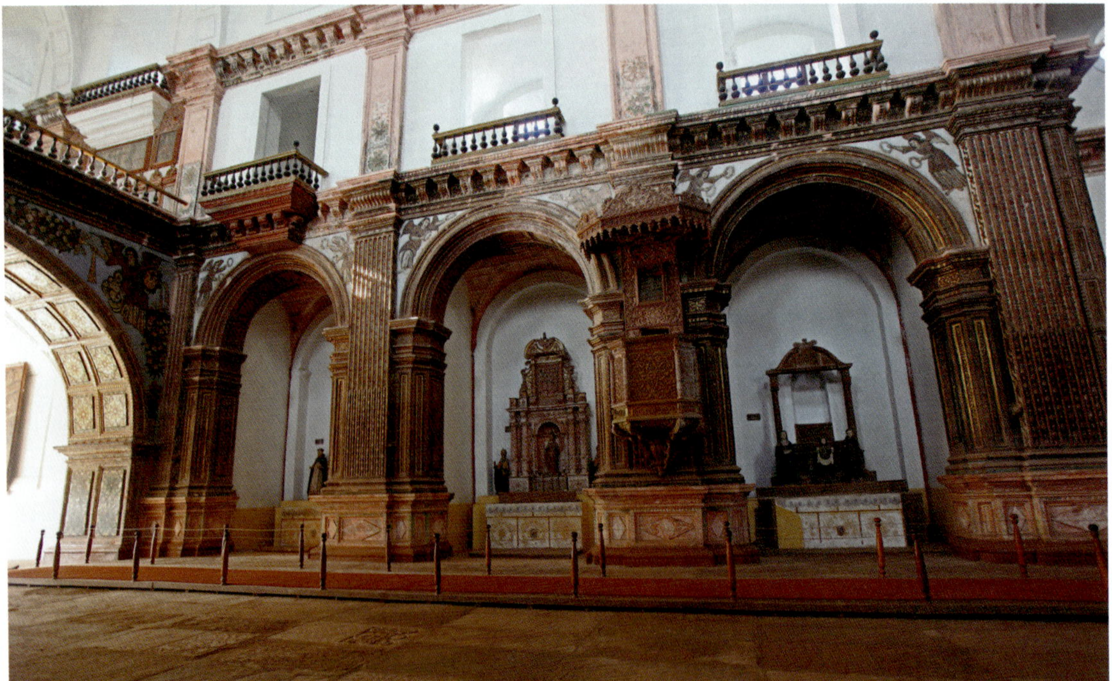

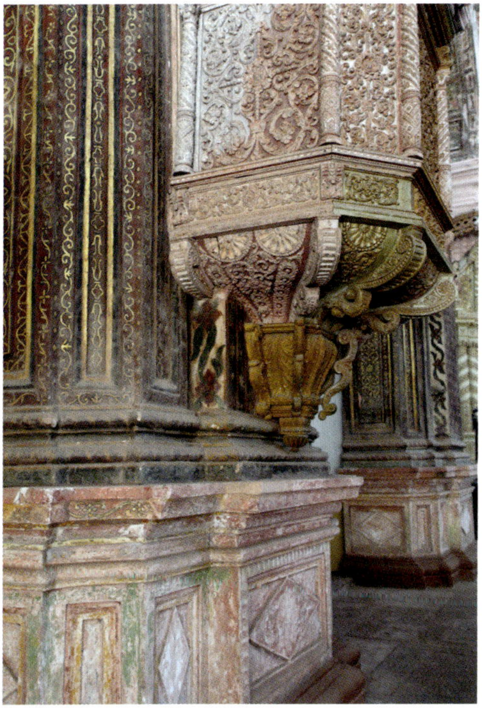

ABOVE: *Detail of the ornately carved timber pulpit*
FACING PAGE TOP: *Looking in towards the altar*
FACING PAGE BELOW: *Side altar*

box in which the Eucharist, the bread and wine, are kept in a Catholic church.

At the very top of the *reredos* is a statue of Christ on the Cross with one arm embracing St. Francis and below are the three vows of the Franciscans; Poverty, Humility and Obedience. To the right of the entrance, near the carved and canopied pulpit is an interesting basin holding holy water atop a pedestal which is part of a pillar from a Hindu temple. The church is full of decorative wonders.

Attached to the Church of St. Francis, the Convent of St. Francis of Assisi houses the Archaeological Museum and its collection of artefacts and religious paintings including portraits of the Portuguese viceroys and governors of Goa. Both the Se Cathedral and the Church of St. Francis are well maintained by the Archaeological Survey of India. With the Basilica of Bom Jesu opposite these three buildings are the last of the great churches of Goa.

The Church of St. Cajetan, 1661

Roman Catholic

Nossa Senhora da Divina Providencia, Our Lady of Providence or simply St. Cajetan's Church was built in the mid-17th century by Italian friars of the Order of Theatines, an exclusive austere order founded in 1524 by Gaetano dei Conti di Thiene (St. Cajetan) who was a contemporary of St. Francis Xavier and three others including Giovanni Pietra Carafa who was to become Pope Paul IV.

The designers were Italian father Carlo Ferrarini and Francisco Milazzo, a lay brother. Though smaller than many other important churches in Old Goa it is certainly one of the most beautiful. The church is totally European in architecture and

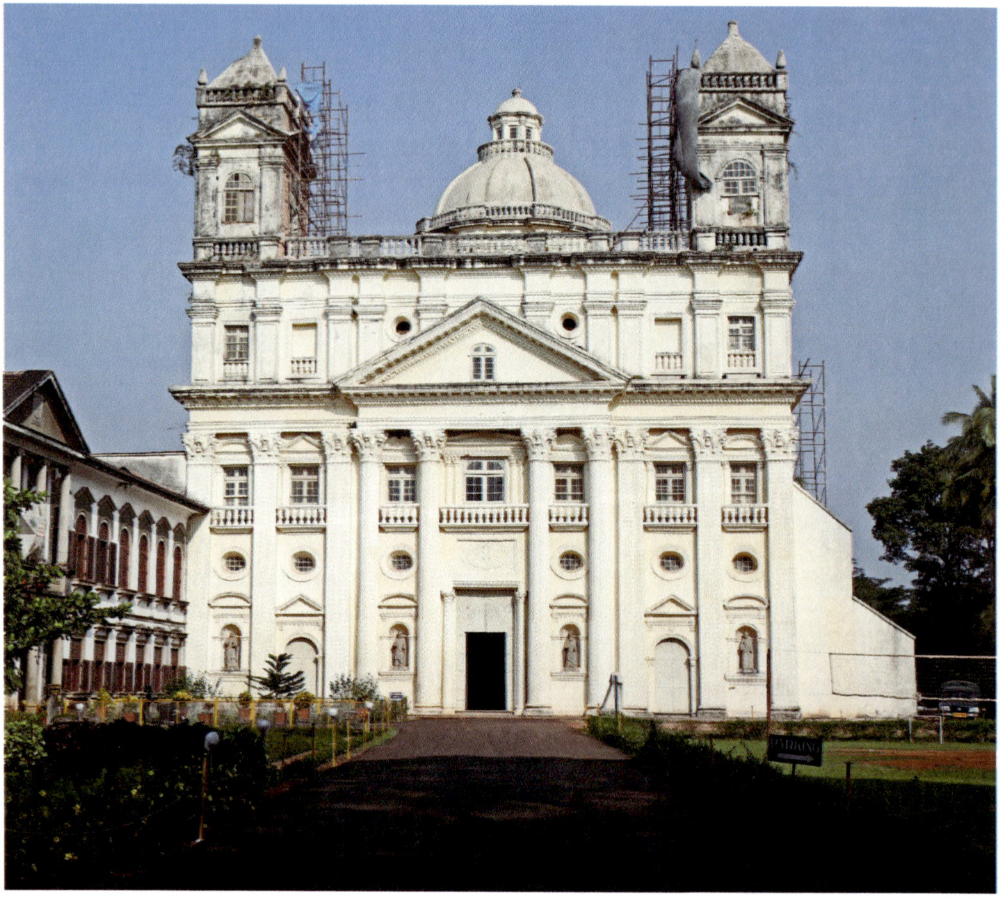

The Church of St. Cajetan

decoration with the dome and hemisphere cupola the most outstanding feature of the church's exterior. The dome and the façade were inspired by St. Peters of Rome and after it was completed Goa became known as the 'Rome of the Orient'. It is the only true domed church surviving in Goa.

Like so many in Goa the church is built of laterite blocks plastered over with lime giving the impression of stone. The facade features two belfry towers on either side with tall Corinthian columns and pilasters supporting a pediment in between. On the ground level statues of four apostles sit in their respective

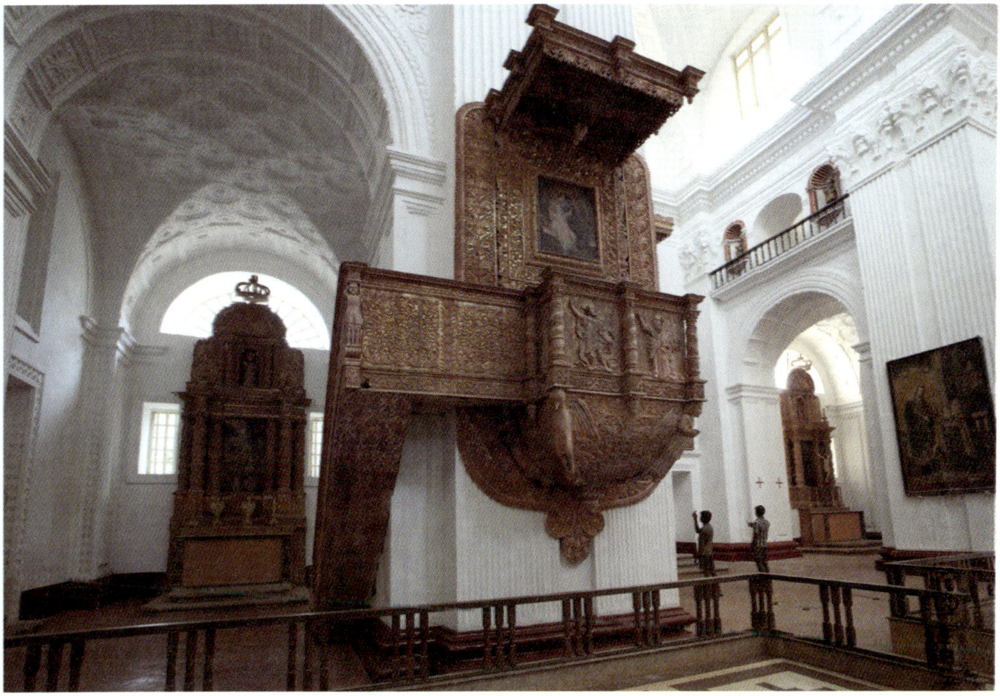

The beautiful pulpit

niches. Above and behind the façade can be seen the enormous yet elegant dome.

Inside four enormous piers faced by Corinthian pilasters support an octagonal drum on top of which sits the dome, an inscription around the base is from the gospel of St. Mathew; 'My house is a house of the words of Christ.' The dome is topped with a lantern, or cupola which serves to admit extra light and air and adds a decorative element to the dome's interior. Beneath the cupola is a fascinating ancient well, 22 meters deep and covered with a stone slab. It is thought to be the remains of the holy tank of an earlier Hindu temple. Another theory is that the architect built the well to drain rising water. Another covered well can be found in the verandah of the church.

The nave which varies in height has two aisles with three altars on each side. The largest is dedicated to St. Cajetan. Paintings depict scenes of the saint's life and wooden statues of saints are set in niches above and around the altar. Octagonal rooms either

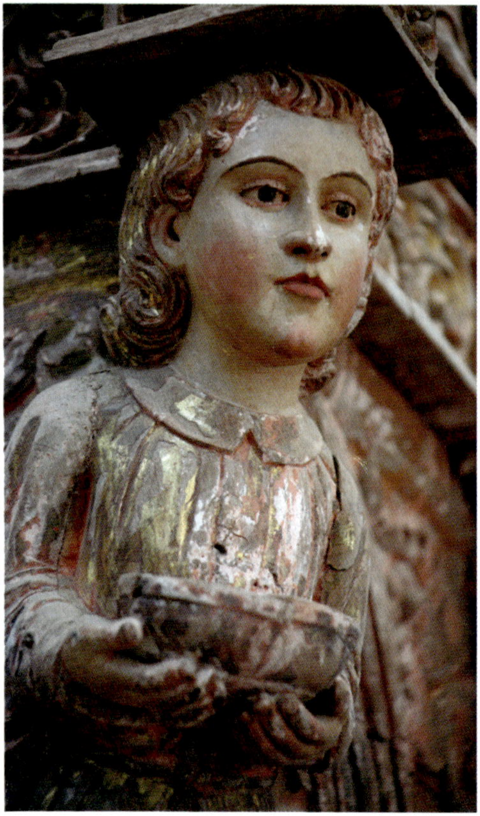

Detail, an angel at the base of the pulpit

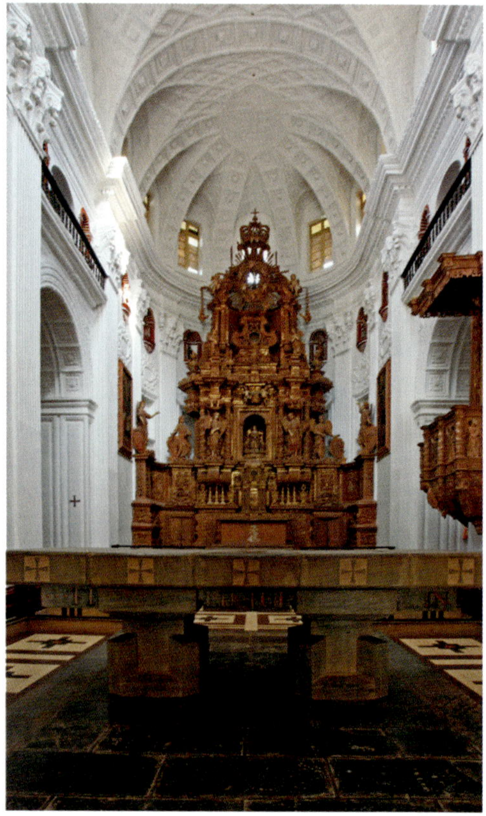

The altar, the Baroque reredos *and the pulpit*

side of the main altar serve as the sacristy. The beautiful Baroque *reredos* is unusual as it steps upwards. At the base are large carvings of angels while the uppermost carving is a symbolic sun topped with a golden crown.

The canopied pulpit sits out from one of the massive Corinthian piers and is covered in fine carving. It is supported by symbolic figures representing the four gospel writers, Mathew, Mark, Luke and John. Traditionally St. Mathew was a divine man, St. Mark a winged lion, St. Luke a winged ox and St. John a rising eagle. All the fine carvings in St. Cajetan's demonstrate the skill of Goan craftsmen.

There are catacombs beneath the church where Theatine priests were once buried. Later these catacombs became a temporary place to hold the bodies of Goa's Portuguese Governor Generals until they were taken home to Portugal. Also fascinating, the church grounds hold the only remains of the Islamic palace of Adil Shah, the ruler of Goa before the arrival of the Portuguese. Another domed church in Goa is the Church of St. Alex in the beach side area of Calangute. It is a dome of a different kind.

The Church of St. Alex, 1741

Roman Catholic

The Church of St. Alex is in Calangute near the beach made famous by hippy travellers in the 60s and 70s. The church was completed in 1741 and the twin towers added in 1765. The church has a large dome set between twin towers, similar to St. Cajetan's Church however the difference is that the dome of

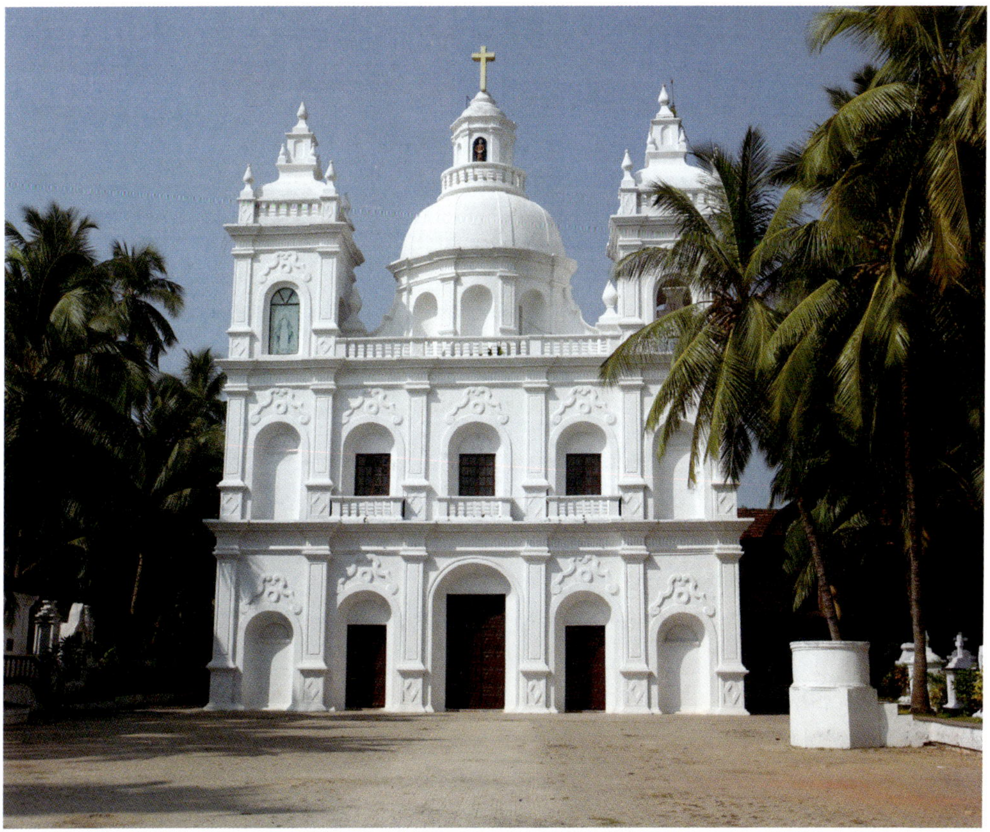

The Church of St. Alex

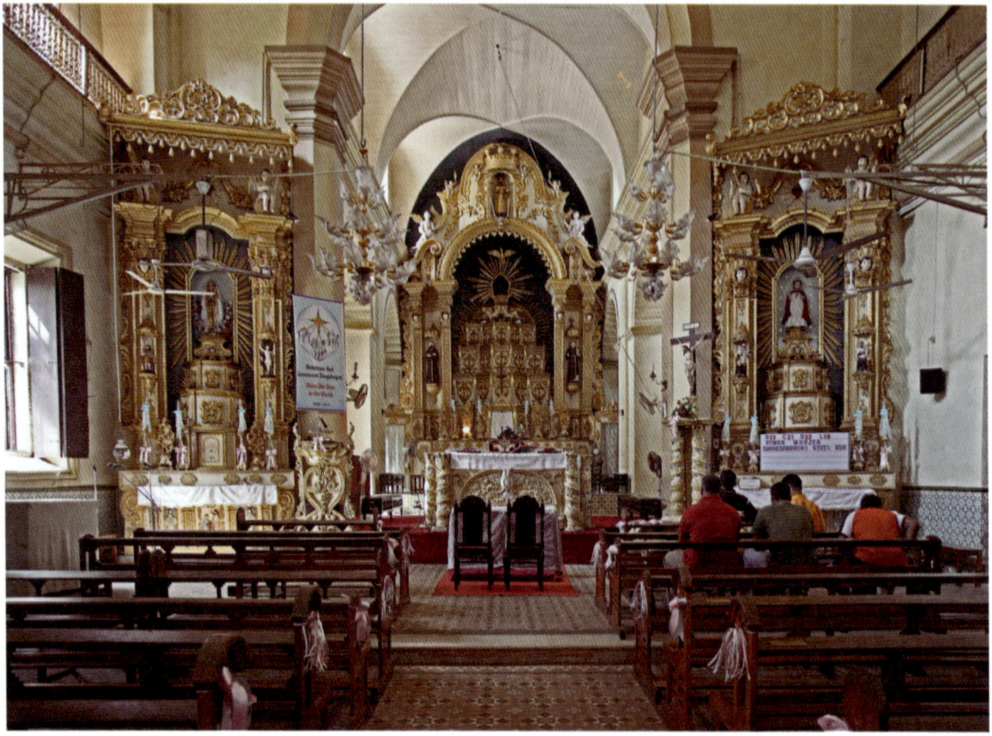

The gold and white canopied pulpit

St. Alex is a *cupola falsa*, a 'false dome' or a corbel dome. This 'optical illusion' is achieved by replacing the pediment of the façade with slightly curved elevated walls. In most cases the corbel dome is built entirely in one piece of masonry, giving a three dimensional illusion. In addition the masonry is etched replicating the shallow ribs of a dome. There are two other Goan churches with false domes; St. Stephens in Juem and the Church of the Immaculate Conception in Moira.

The first Church of St. Alex was built by Franciscan monks in 1576. It was a simple chapel thatched with palm leaves. In 1595 the Franciscans built a second church, traces of which have been found in the form of a cemetery and a cross. The third church is the one that stands today.

The church's exterior has an entrance door with two smaller doors either side and smaller mock entrances at either end. Six pilasters divide the five doors. The upper

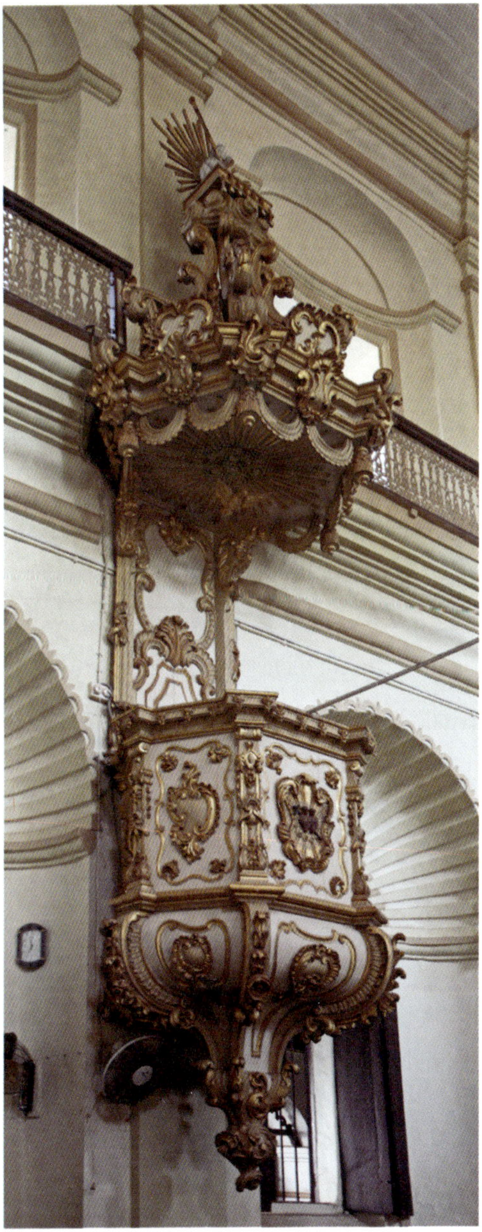

The ornate Rococo elements

level echoes the one below. At the top of the facade is the false dome and lantern with a niche for the image of St. Cajetan. Twin towers flank the dome, on the left is an image of Jesus, on the right is a belfry. St. Alexius, the patron of the Calangute church, was the only son of a rich senator of Rome, Euphemian and his wife Aglae. He was born and educated in the fifth century. He is said to have given away all his possessions to the poor and lived on alms.

The influence of St. Cajetan's is clear on the exterior of the church as well though it is smaller and less opulent. Inside the church is gold and white with decorative Rococo elements. The canopied pulpit is elegantly flamboyant in gold and white and decorated with sunbursts, volutes, tassels and pendants and topped with a figure of a lamb, a symbol for Jesus 'the lamb of God' portraying his innocence and his sacrifice.

The interior of St. Cajetan's has evolved from the Baroque of the 17th century, while the interior of St. Alex developed from the lighter mood of the Rococo of the 18th century. Their interiors and exteriors show interesting transitions over the centuries.

Mae de Deus Church, Saligao, 1873

Roman Catholic

The village of Saligao is a beautiful area full of coconut palms, fruit trees and rice

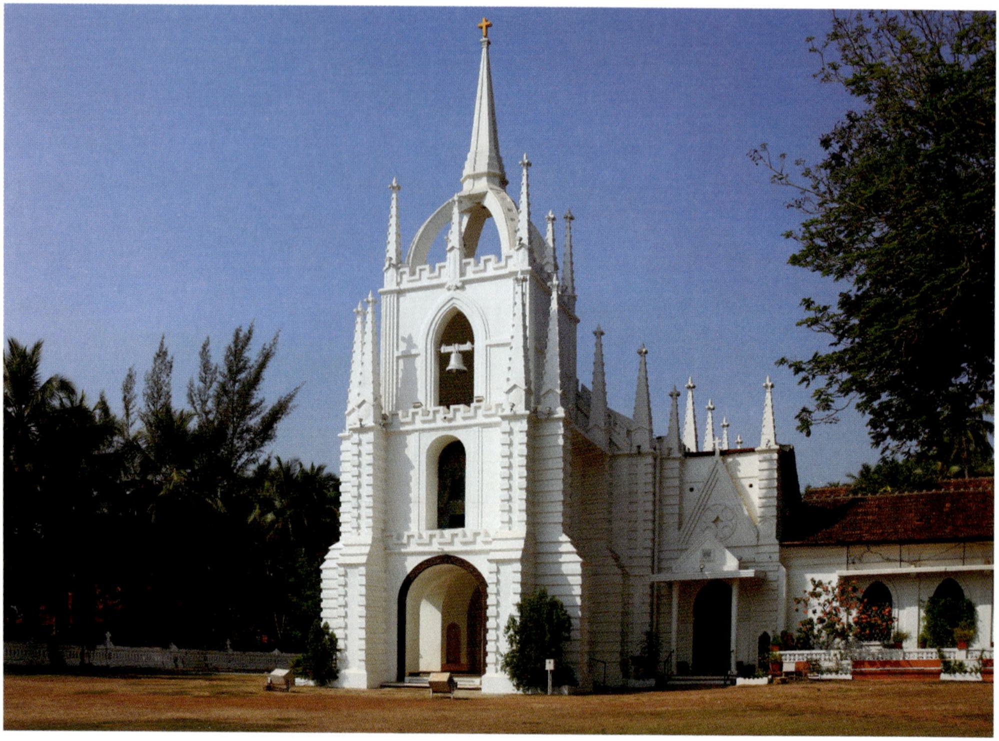

Mae de Deus Church, Saligao

fields. Saligao means 'wooded forest' and in the middle of this tropical setting is the rather incongruous Gothic styled Mae de Deus Church.

The original Mae de Deus Church was located in another place at another time like so many of India's churches. In this case it originated in the 16th century in Daujim where almost hidden by jungle a cross on a pedestal remains. The new bright white church in Saligao began in 1867 and was inaugurated in November, 1873. It is dedicated to Mae de Deus, the Mother of God.

A gilded wooden statue of Mary comes from the ruins in Daujim. It was transported ceremoniously across the Mandovi River in a decorated boat to Betim then taken further by a bullock cart decorated with flowers. On arrival at Saligao twenty one shots were fired, a band played and crowds of people cheered. The final and most sacred element of the church had arrived.

The church has a round archway at the entrance and the upper level of the facade. Above is the belfry which has a typical Gothic pointed arch. The tower-like facade is three storied while the body of the church is two. The overall staggered brick work adds to the church's 'spiky' Gothic appearance. Buttresses support its walls and in places black stones from the ruins in Daujim embellish the walls.

The interior of the church is an example of the decorative skills of Goan craftsmen in what can be called Indo-Gothic. Fret-worked timber arches span the ceiling and painted flowers in relief decorate a low arch. The usual verticality of most Gothic interiors has been reduced in keeping with the size of the church.

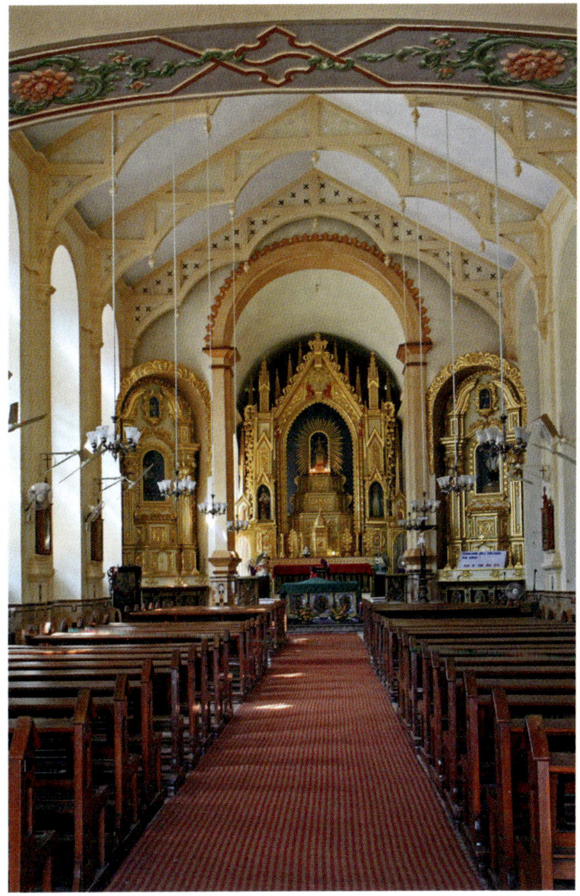

The interior

Each year, on the first Sunday of May the village wakes to the sound of church bells which herald the beginning of the Feast of Mae de Deus. The villagers make their way to the church in their best clothes and a brass band accompanies a display of fireworks which continues throughout the day. A procession to the altar is led by attendants carrying a cross and candles. A select number of villagers follow the procession and finally the clerics of the Saligao Feast follow, dignified in their vestments of gold and white. The celebration continues all day under Goa's hot sun. People shelter under ornate colourful umbrellas and are joined by friends from other villages and often relatives from other countries. It is the most important religious occasion for the village. Everyone touches or kisses the precious image of Mary until late in the night when the villagers of this tiny hamlet in Goa leave the procession and wend their way home.

Church of Our Lady of Bethlehem, 1949

Roman Catholic

In sleepy Chandor south Goa, at the end of the village square sits the simple Gothic styled Church of Our Lady of Bethlehem or Nossa Senhora de Belem. It was built in 1645 though the high three storied facade was replaced in 1949. Twin towers either side are smaller than the façade and each are topped with ramparts and four spear shaped finials. The towers hold Gothic pointed windows, two of which hold statues of saints while a third houses the church bell. A statue of the Madonna and Child is housed in a narrow niche at the apex of the facade. The exterior is painted white and decorated with bright yellow Gothic shaped mouldings. A beautiful piazza cross stands in the church square.

Chandor is one of three villages that celebrate the Feast of the Epiphany, the arrival of the Three Kings from the east who followed a star to greet the Baby Jesus. On a specific day after Christmas three boys from Chandor village travel a route strewn with palm leaves

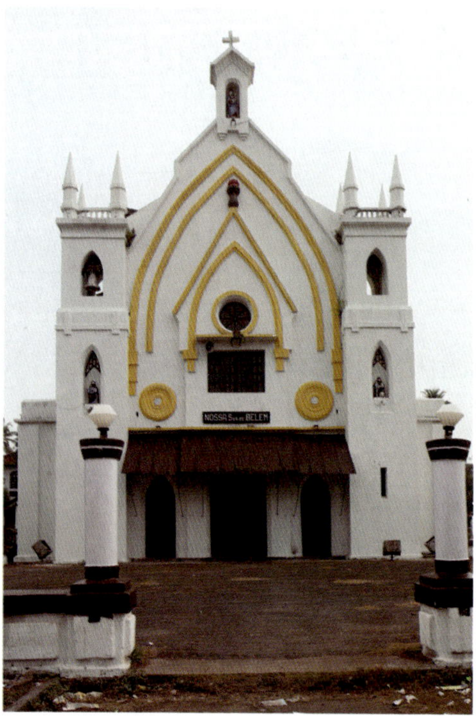

Church of Our Lady of Bethlehem

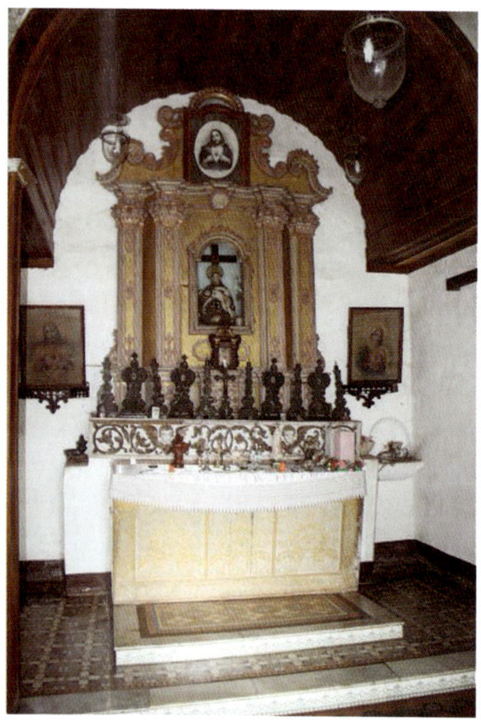

The 'Petite Chapel' in the Braganza home

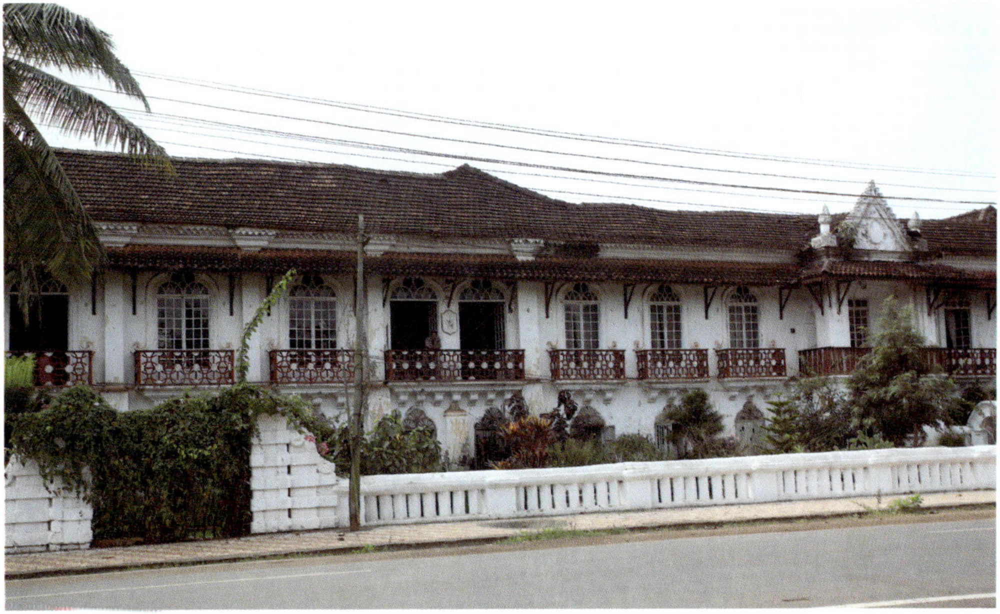

The Braganza House

to re-enact the journey of Gaspar, Balthazar and Melchior. The boys consider it a great privilege and sit astride horses at the head of the procession wearing colourful robes and crowns and carrying gifts. It is a long procession which winds around the streets of the town and culminates at the church. Small children cheer the boys from the roadside and the whole village is included in the festivities which feature the usual food stalls and dancing common to many Indian feast days.

The church is particularly interesting as opposite is the mansion of the wealthy Braganza family regarded as the grandest of Goa's colonial mansions. The family and their ways of life offer an insight into the pious nature of the colonial Portuguese. It is one of a number of large and elegant Portuguese homes built around the church square in the late 17th century. It occupies an entire side of the village square and incorporates an impressive twenty eight windows in its facade. The home is painted white with burgundy iron work on the balconies matching the colour of the terracotta roof tiles. The house is divided into two 'villas' with an entrance to each side by side. They are the homes of the Braganza's two sons.

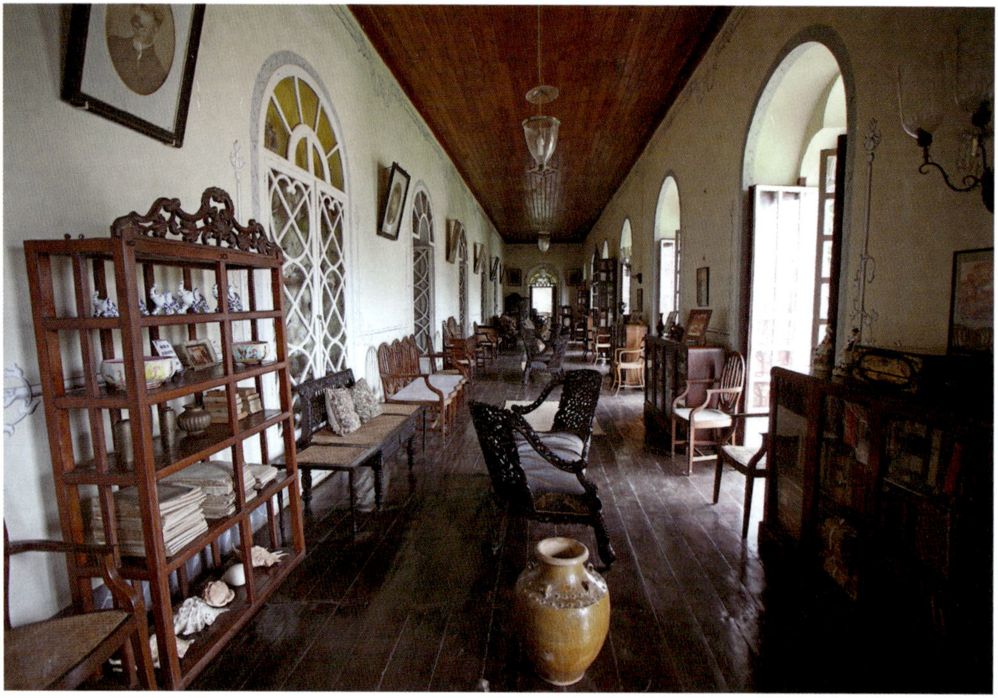

An interior room

In earlier times the two families would keep their doors open to come and go into each other's homes as they wished. After a family dispute however the doors were locked. The feud continues to this day.

The west wing is home to the remaining members of the Menezes Braganza family. It is filled with European furniture and decorative eclectic pieces. The home is cool and quiet and the old ways of life seem to live on in the rooms. The elderly matriarch explained that it takes six servants to keep the villa maintained. The east wing belonging to the Pereira Braganza side of the family is in need of restoration. However it is a splendid, atmospheric place with a grand ballroom. As in Portugal there is a small chapel. The pious nature of the colonial Portuguese can be seen in the Menezes Braganza House. Despite a church existing opposite the house their 'Petite Chapel' can be used by the family at any time. It is especially fascinating to learn that the chapel houses a relic of St. Francis Xavier; a gold and diamond encrusted fingernail!

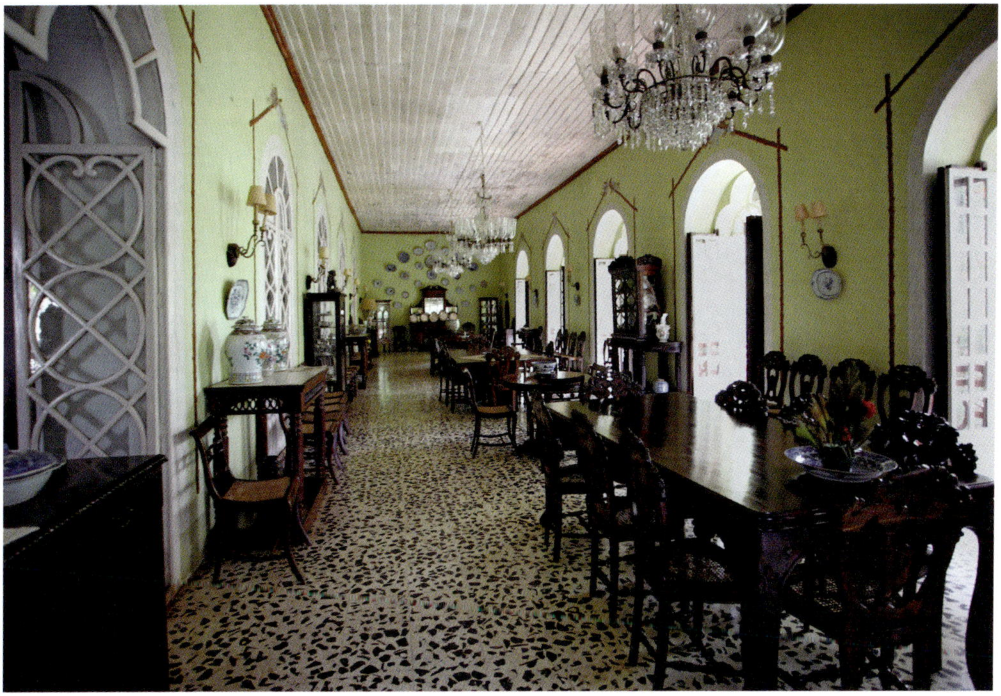

Chandeliers, Indian and Portuguese furniture and oriental ceramics

Braganza de Pereira, the great-grandfather of the present owner of Braganza House was the last knight of the king of Portugal. More recently Menezes Braganza was a famous journalist and freedom fighter, one of the few Goan aristocrats to oppose Portuguese rule and forced to flee Chandor in 1950. In 1962 the family returned to find their home untouched.

Panaji, 'New Goa'

Initially the small fishing village of Panaji was not a popular choice as like Old Goa it was an unhealthy place, full of stagnant ponds. With the exception of the palace of Adil Shah the village consisted of fishermen's huts and the dwellings of poor people spread amongst dense palm groves. It was still more promising than Goa as it was close to the sea and the cool sea breeze. Most importantly the harbour was suitable for ships and the embarking of troops. The palace of Adil Shah was seen as a suitable residence for the Portuguese Vice Regal. The magnificent buildings of the former

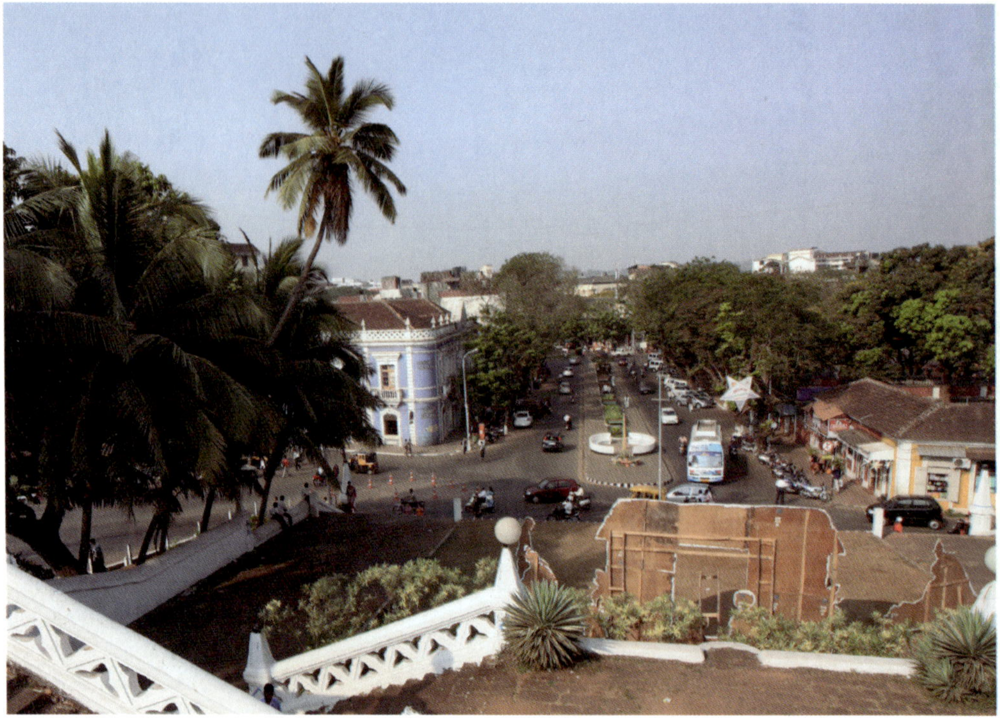

ABOVE: *Panaji from the steps of the Church of the Immaculate Conception*

FACING PAGE TOP: *The coat of arms at the entrance to the Archbishop's Palace*

FACING PAGE BELOW: *The Archbishop's Palace*

capital were dismantled and the stone used to build smaller houses and government buildings in Panaji.

With the arrival of Dom Manuel Francisco de Portugal e Castro (1828 1834) as colonial administrator, the city was raised from swampland to a peaceful, traditional Portuguese garden city. By 1846 the new capital, Nova Goa hardly resembled the old village of Panjim.

From the river, Panaji is very picturesque. The seven kilometre promenade is lined with attractive and colourful old buildings which evoke Panaji's Portuguese history. It is a slow paced, charming city with a distinct Mediterranean character. Above the town is the hilltop suburb of Altinho, once an exclusive area, retaining its elegant nature with some beautifully kept Portuguese mansions lining the winding roads. Panaji can be seen in the distance. Dense tropical

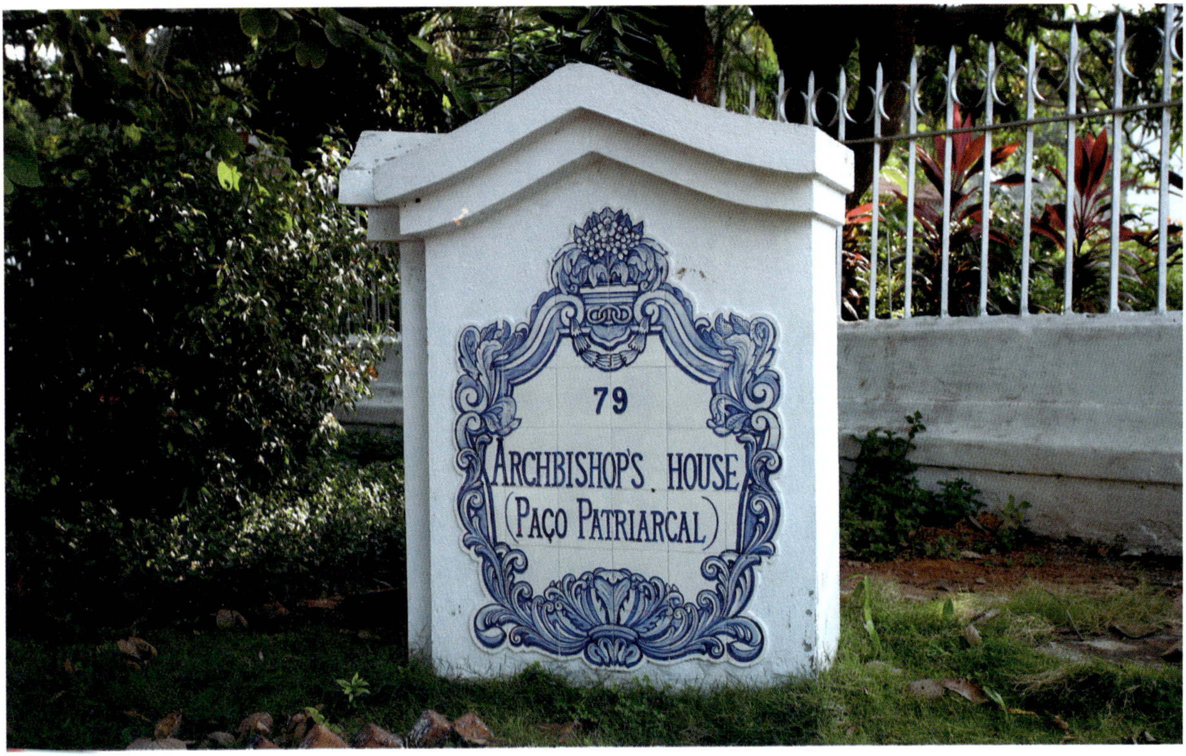
79
ARCHBISHOP'S HOUSE
(PAÇO PATRIARCAL)

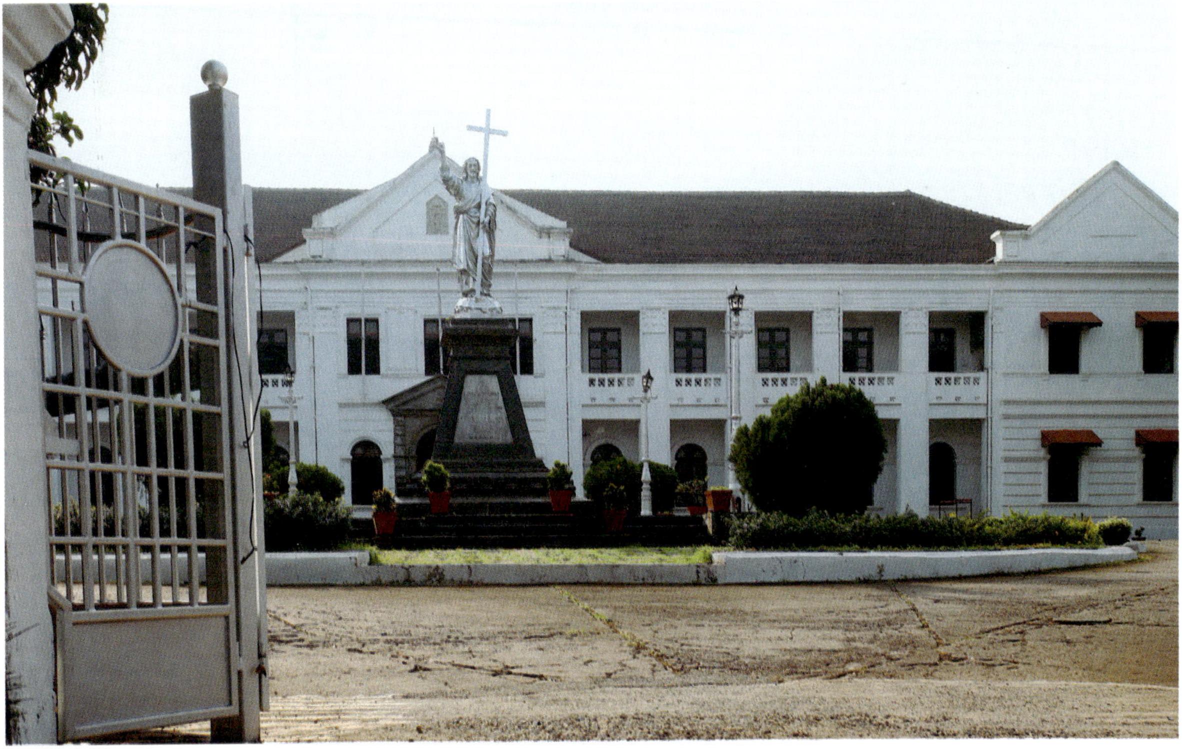

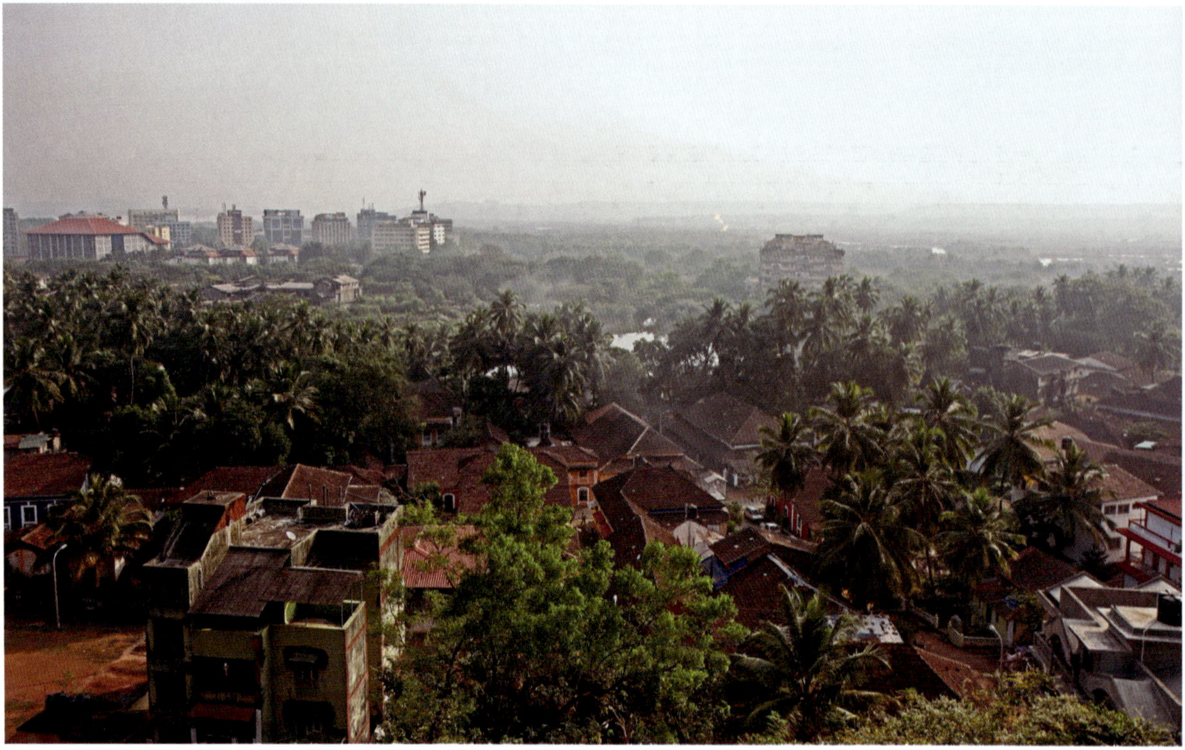

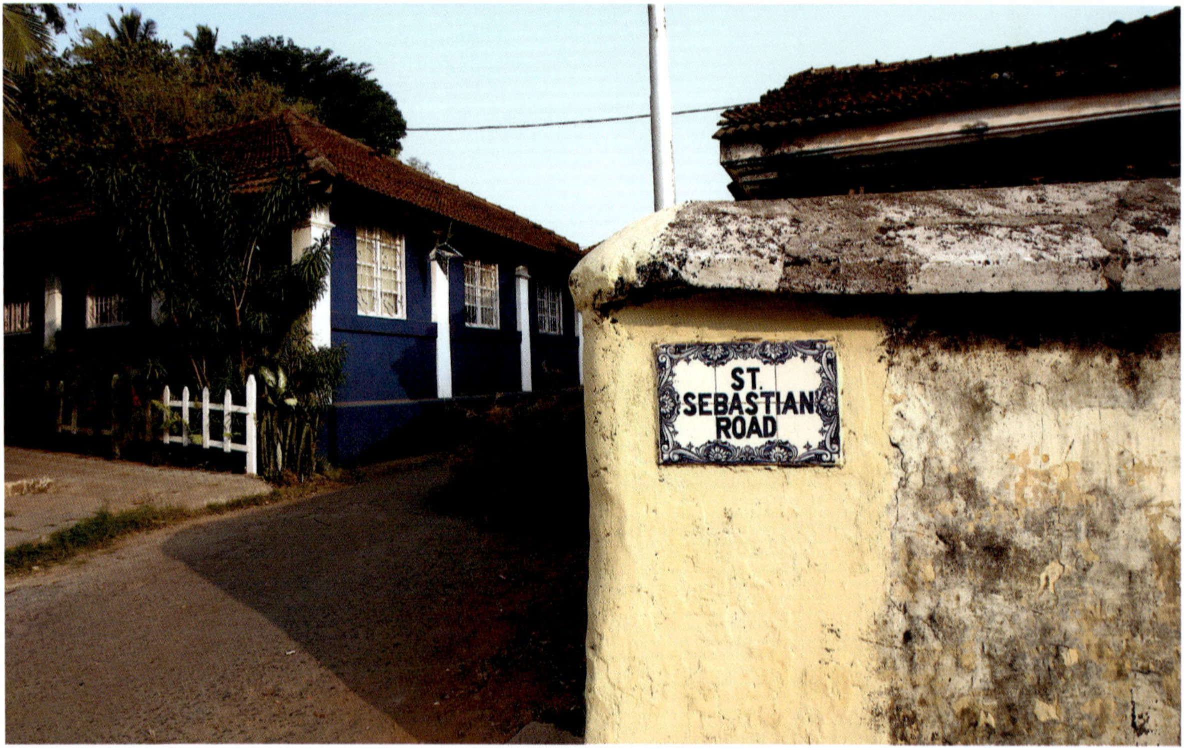
ST.
SEBASTIAN
ROAD

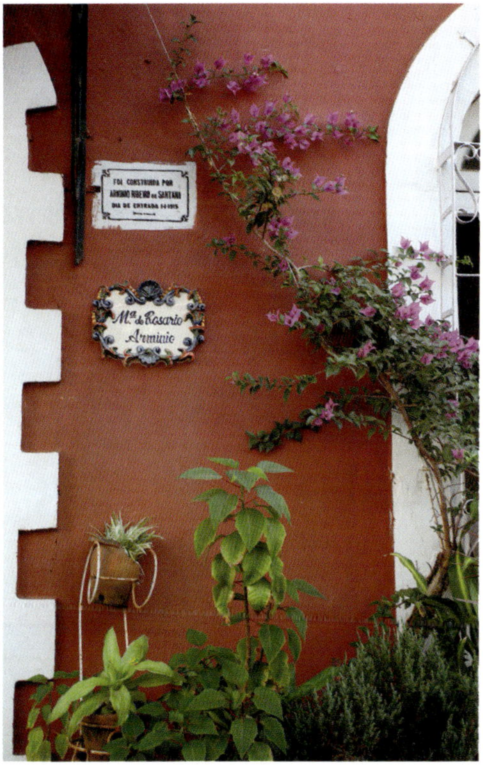

ABOVE AND FACING PAGE BELOW: *The Portuguese character of Fountainhas*

FACING PAGE TOP: *The view from the hillside of Altinho to Fountainhas and Panaji beyond*

plants tumble down the hillside to the village of Fountainhas with its pretty houses.

The most impressive building is certainly the 'Bishop's Palace'. It is an elegant two storied wooden building with a statue of Christ the Redeemer in the garden. The palace was completed in 1894 at a time when the Archbishop was elevated to a Patriarch. It was the last residence to date of a number of houses built for the archbishops. The hand painted Portuguese tiled coat of arms at the entrance is that of Goa's first patriarch, Dom Antonio Sebastio Valente.

The Church of Our Lady of the Immaculate Conception, 1619

Roman Catholic

From its elevated position this grand church presides over the heart of the city of Panaji. Its sheer size contrasts with the smaller buildings of the city and it can be seen from the port, making it a well-known landmark. It was built in 1619. However a chapel sat on the same site in 1541. Today's church is dedicated to Portugal's beloved Mary, the mother of Jesus, 'Nossa Senhora da Immaculada Conceicao'.

The exterior of the church is baroque in style with twin towers and a massive belfry at the top of the façade, above which is a cross. The bell was taken from the Augustinian Monastery in Old Goa after it collapsed. It is the second largest in Goa, the first being the 'Golden Bell' in the Se Cathedral. The symmetrical zigzag staircase is so striking it almost detracts from the church itself. It was added in 1871 replacing the original staircase consisting of seventy-eight steps. Today's staircase has a central landing with four side landings of equal size. It was influenced by the Bom Jesus de Braga church in Portugal.

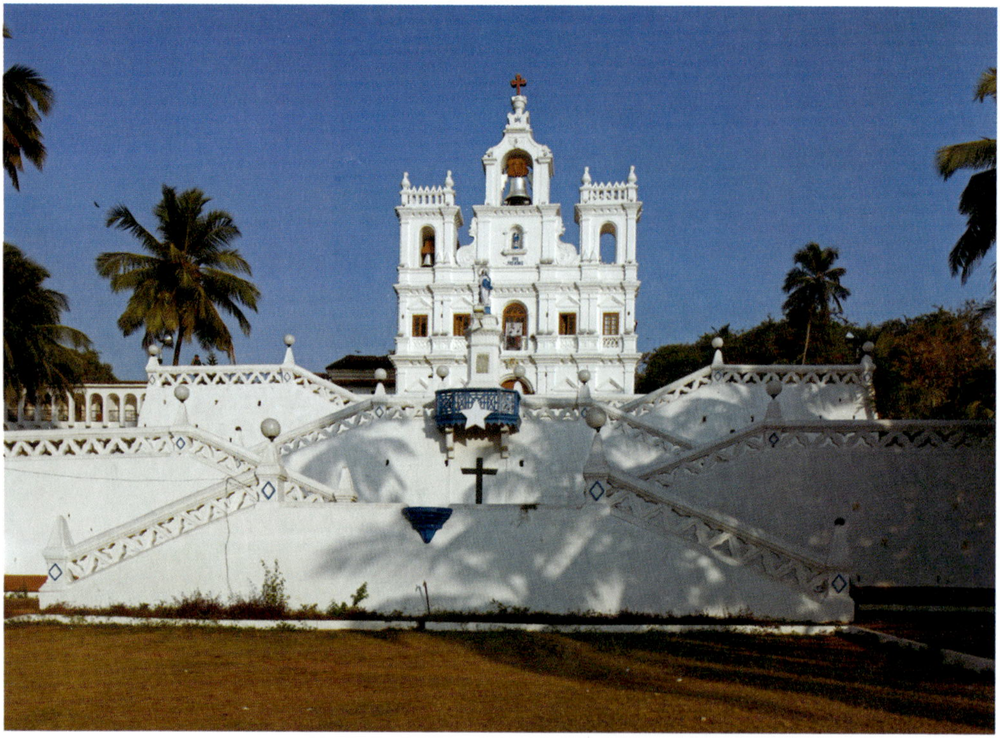

The Church of Our Lady of the Immaculate Conception

The stairs are bound by solid balustrades and on the first landing is a painted marble statue of Our Lady of the Immaculate Conception on a high pedestal. A small rounded balcony gives the impression of a pulpit and so the statue with arms outstretched seems to be blessing the city below and the port of Panaji beyond.

At night huge beacons would be lit on the hillside behind the church to guide Portuguese ships from Lisbon safely into Panaji's harbour. The sailors would then make their way to the church to give thanks.

Inside the church is simple but colourful. The main altar dedicated to Mary Immaculate is carved and gilded and tiles line part of the walls. Two other altars are dedicated to Jesus and Our Lady of the Rosary, both of which are richly decorated. Marble statues of St. Peter and St. Paul stand at the side of each altar. The most recent statue is that of Our Lady of Fatima which was placed there in 1945,

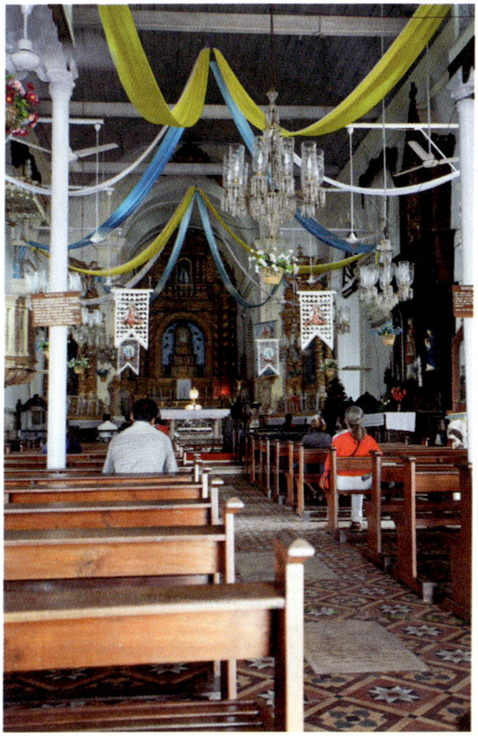

The interior

and blessed by Sydney's Cardinal Gilroy in 1950. This statue is formally carried through the city each year in a moving procession lit with candles.

The Chapel of St. Sebastian, 1880s

Roman Catholic

On the eastern side of Panaji is the quaint area of Fountainhas. It has the character of a tropical Portuguese village. The name Fountainhas means 'Fountain of Phoenix,' after a nearby spring from which a reservoir was built to provide fresh water for the community. Here the pretty chapel of St. Sebastian can be found.

Fountainhas has grown haphazardly with many dwellings built on various levels of the Altinho hillside. The higher of these are accessible by what locals call 'stepped streets' which join narrow winding lanes and pathways, sometimes meeting at small squares and fountains. Hand painted Portuguese tiles declare the names of streets and houses and though many houses have not been maintained they manage to look vibrant and colourful, perhaps an inherited idea from the Portuguese who insisted that every building in Goa should be painted after a monsoon.

Within this picturesque village at the end of a square sits the Chapel surrounded by lush greenery. The first Chapel was established in 1818 but to make way for a new road it had to be demolished and another built just at the opposite end of the small square! At one point both churches faced each other separated by a distance of just 100 metres. The foundation stone for today's church was laid in 1884 and consecrated in 1888 by the Patriach of the Indies, D. Antonio Sebastiao Valente.

The facade features pilasters on three levels. A simple classical pediment sits above the main door above which is a decorative wrought iron screen incorporating a cross in

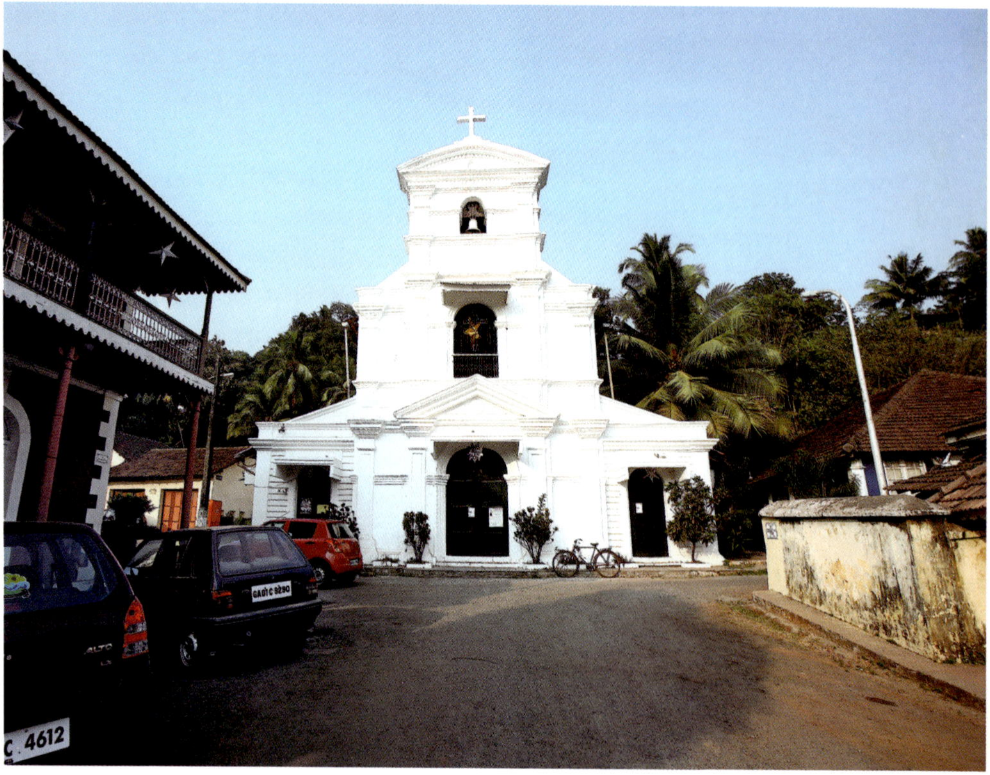

the design. The top level holds a niche in which hangs the chapel bell. Above is a pediment with a curved apex supporting a cross.

Once inside the gilded *reredos* dominates the church, its three glass-fronted niches for saints correspond to the three aisles, which also correspond to the three exterior entrances. The central niche is dedicated to St. Sebastian and side altars feature heavily carved twisted columns. There are an unusually large number of altars for such a small church.

ABOVE: *The Chapel of St. Sebastian*

FACING PAGE TOP LEFT: *Brightly painted house in Goa*

FACING PAGE TOP RIGHT: *The interior of the Chapel of St. Sebastian*

FACING PAGE BELOW: *Artefacts on display inside the chapel*

At the end of the right aisle is the chapel's most well-known artefact, the Crucifix of the Inquisition, one of the only relics of that terrible era which began in Goa in 1560 and lasted for over two centuries. The Inquisition took place first in Old Goa but was later installed in the chapel of the Viceroy in Panaji.

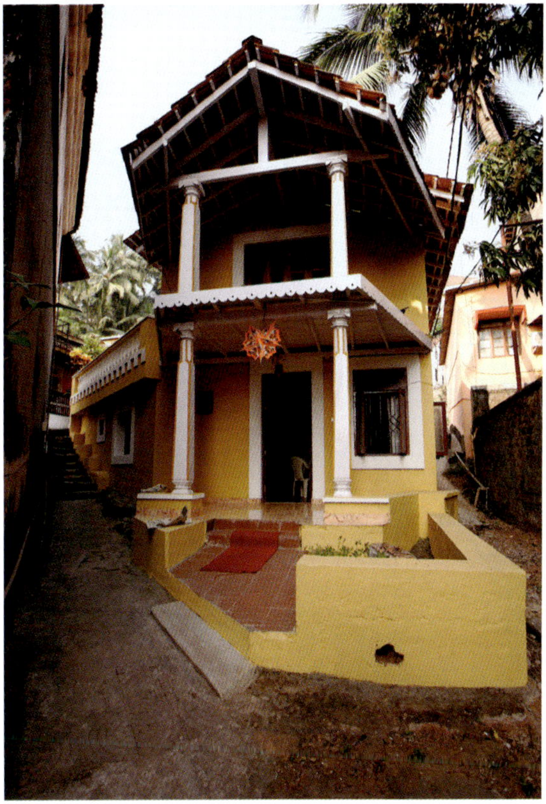

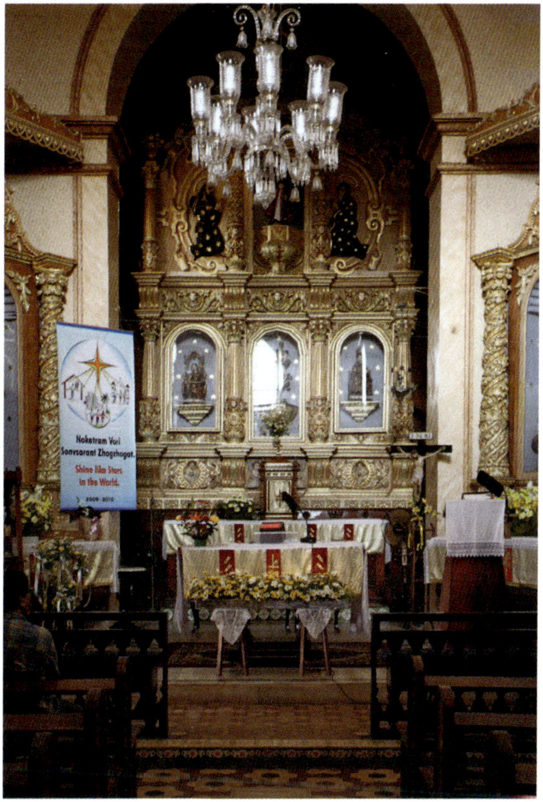
Noketram Vori
Sonvsarant Zhogzhogat.
Shine like Stars
in the World.
2009 - 2010

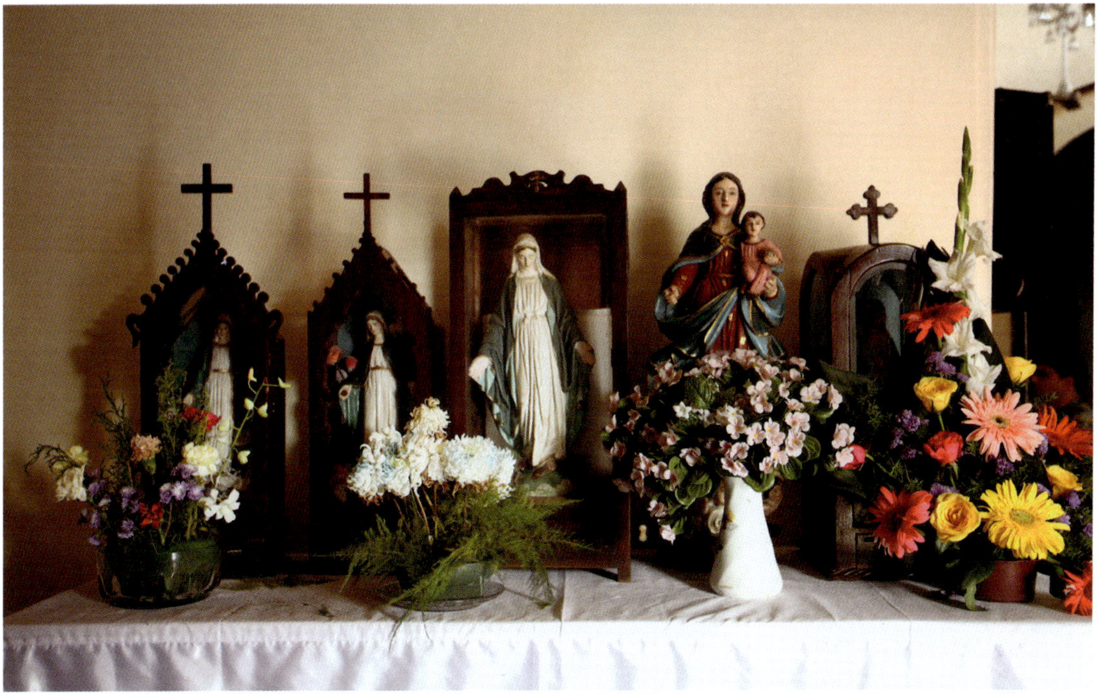

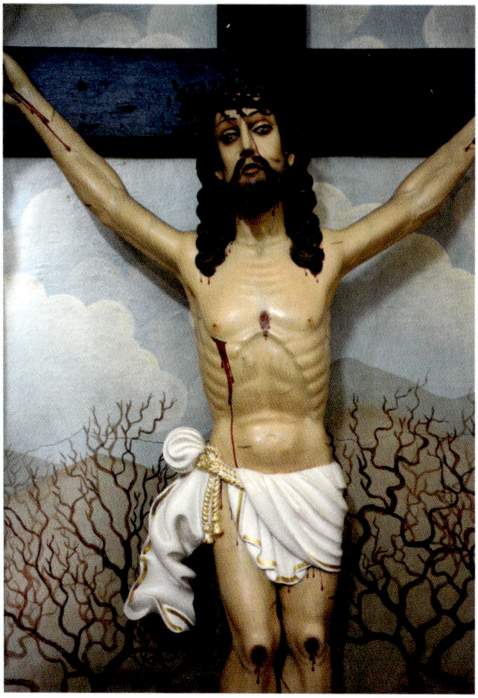

The famous crucifix

The chapel closed in 1918 and the crucifix was brought to the Chapel of St. Sebastian where it can be seen today. The large crucifix shows Jesus not with his head down and eyes closed but with his head raised and eyes wide open. This crucifix is very sacred and believed to be magical. Each November a street fair outside the chapel celebrates the Feast of Nossa Senhora da Livramento, Our Lady of Liberation, which seems fitting when contemplating the famous but frightening relic of the Inquisition which hangs inside.

TRADERS BECOME RULERS

The British

By the second half of the 16th century Portuguese power and their monopoly in India began to decline. Their suppression of Hinduism, the introduction of the dreaded Inquisition in 1560 and their failing in not recognizing the deep religious nature of Indians weakened their position. Muslim sultans of the Deccan attacked Portuguese bases in the south but the last hoorah for the Portuguese was in 1588 when a British naval force under the command of Francis Drake and Lord Charles Howard defeated Spain's 'Invincible Armada' off the coast of France. With this success Britain broke Portugal and Spain's domination of the spice trade and opened the way for British ships to travel to India via the Cape of Good Hope. These events heralded a race for domination of the spice trade between the Portuguese and the British that continued into the next century.

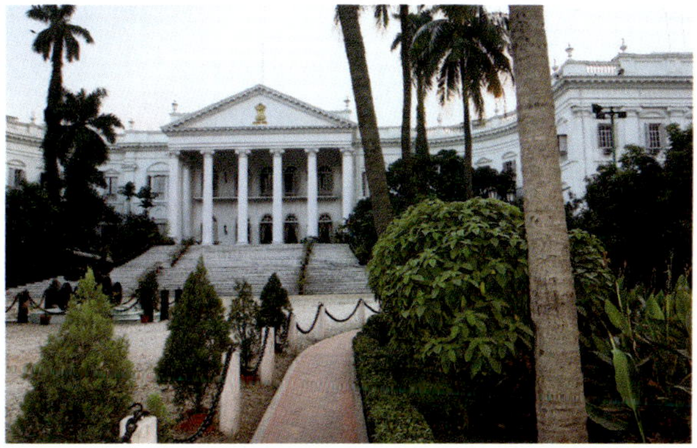

Seat of British rule, the Government House in Kolkata

Portuguese navigation maps arrived in Europe from Dutch merchant and historian Jan van Linschoten, secretary to the Portuguese Viceroy in Goa from 1583 to 1588. The "Sailing Guides to the Eastern Seas" were the secret routes to India fiercely guarded by the Portuguese. The maps were of great value to the British as they showed the passage to India thus ending Portugal's almost century old advantage.

On December 1600 Britain's Queen Elizabeth agreed that a charter be given to a large group of merchants to form a company to trade in the East. It was formally named 'The Governor and Company of Merchants of London, Trading into the East Indies,' better known as the East India Trading Company. It was a relatively simple beginning of a mercantile venture but one which would profoundly affect India's history.

In 1608 the East India Company's first naval endeavor to India landed in Surat, a port in the state of Gujarat. After obtaining permission from the Mughul ruler a simple warehouse was built which lead to other British trading posts developing along the east and west coasts of India. The most important of these became the port cities of Chennai (formerly Madras), Mumbai (formerly Bombay) and Kolkata (formerly Calcutta) which became known as the Presidency Towns. They allowed access to and from other regions in India and other countries.

Later forts were built to protect the European community. Within the walls were soldier's barracks, arsenals, residences for officers, the presidents and staff. Later administration buildings and banks were added. In essence a European fort in India housed and protected an entire community. Churches were also needed to meet the religious needs of the fort's inhabitants and often the churches were the sturdiest buildings in the forts.

The British forts began in Chennai. In 1639 the British purchased land on the Coromandel Coast, in India's south west. Three years later a fort was established and within its walls the sturdy little garrison church of St. Mary's was built. By 1687 Surat had been replaced by Mumbai as it was a deep water port and became important for British ships arriving from Europe. Mumbai's fort protected the growing city from pirates and Dutch invaders. Very soon the British needed a base on India's north-east coast. In 1690 they built a factory on the Hughli River, a branch of the Ganges with access to the Bay of Bengal. The area grew to become the city of Calcutta and eventually the capital of the British Empire in India. An outstanding number of British began to arrive across the country and trade reached astonishing levels.

Unlike the Portuguese who were as intent on saving souls as in trading the first British settlers had no interest in spreading their religion. They were only concerned with trade and the churches they built were for themselves. Many were designed by British military engineers who often replicated the style of buildings they were familiar with, such as the famous St. Martin-in-the-Fields in London or used architectural journals and reference books for designs.

Unlike the rectangular basilica plan of the Portuguese British churches were mainly in the plan of a cross (cruciform) that appeared in Gothic architecture. The east end was dominated by the altar and a decorative stained glass window behind would illuminate the interior. At the other end would be the baptismal font. To the north and south, the 'arms' of the cross, or the transepts, were for small side altars or sometimes the church organ.

The cruciform design allowed a bigger congregation and a clearer view of the important altar. The climatic conditions of India were taken into account with high naves, small sunshades projecting over windows, *punkha*s and sets of louvers set between overly tall exterior columns.

The East India Company expanded their trading posts across India while at the same time developing military and administrative divisions. The company which had begun as a traditional trading organisation was changing. One of the most significant episodes was the Indian Uprising or Sepoy Mutiny which occurred in 1857 at the Barrackpore military barracks near Kolkata. For Indians it was the First War of Independence and it shook the very foundations of the British Empire. Today the name of this important episode in India's history is being reviewed. 'The Revolt of 1857', is thought to be a less controversial choice.

The sepoys were Indian infantrymen employed by the Company. When rumours spread that the new rifle cartridges were greased with the fat from meat both Hindu and Muslim sepoys became incensed as they had to tear open the cartridges with their teeth. Their religions banned the eating of cattle and pork. With the leadership of Sepoy Mangal Pandey the Indian Army rose up against the British, who to their discredit had failed to change the cartridges or reassure the sepoys. The unrest spread rapidly to other army and civilian towns across central and north India until hundreds of thousands of people had been killed, some believe millions. India had changed forever and the British Government began disbanding the East India Company's power. By 1873 'the high and mighty, the noblest of exalted nobles, the chief of illustrious warriors, our faithful servants and sincere well-wishers, worthy of our royal favours,' (*The Annuls of Fort William, Calcutta*, 'Firmaun from the King Shah Allum, for the Dewanee of the Province of Bengal', August 12 1765.) the English Company that had ruled India for two and a half centuries no longer existed.

When the British Government took control the British Raj began and the world's most powerful empire was born. Though the British were supremely confident in their capacity to rule India during the 19th century they were still dependent on its large Indian Army and its monetary and military support from the princely states. As the Raj rose it was financed by plundering the subcontinent. It was always the economic interests of Britain that won out. In 1901 Lord Curzon stated, "As long as we rule India we are the greatest power in the world. If we lose it we shall drop straight away to a third rate power."

Originally the British built churches for their own communities, families, merchants and military personnel. Many were distinctly Anglican having been founded by members of the Church of England. The style of these churches was seen by many as a symbol of foreign occupation. Architecture, colonialism and religion went hand in hand. However today these churches are lovingly cared for and cherished long after the privileged rulers have gone. For that reason visitors can't help but feel a little sentimental whether they want to or not.

Chennai: Churches at the Sea Port

The Church in the Fort

The city of Chennai lies on the Bay of Bengal on the east coast of India. Its history can begin in 1522 when the Portuguese built a port, calling it Sao Tome after the apostle St. Thomas. It became a major stop on the maritime Silk Roads. European traders with different cultures, religions and ideas were attracted to the area which helped shape the future city of Chennai. Today the Sao Tome Cathedral is believed to hold the grave of St. Thomas. A number of other churches were built by the Portuguese in and around Chennai, all of which have a profound connection to the apostle St. Thomas.

In 1639 Francis Day, a British administrator with the East India Company gained the rights over the fishing village of Madraspatnam, a strip of land just ten kilometres long. A year later Fort St. George was established, becoming the East India Company's Coromandel headquarters. It was the first trading post in India to be fortified, a necessary precaution as profitable key ports along the maritime Silk Roads could control sections of the routes and also levy taxes. As such, Chennai's development as a centre of trade made it an attractive acquisition. The French tried attacking the British fort twice, capturing it for two years and then attacking again between 1758 and 1759. Hyder Ali, the Mughal ruler of Mysore also attacked the fort twice in the late 18th century.

Inside the fort the army lived close to the walls while the civilians lived near the warehouses, later followed in other British-held areas of India. The military zones became known as cantonments, a term still used today. By the turn of the century Fort St. George had grown to become a large, well planned city with tree lined streets. Today Fort St. George is a huge sprawling complex of buildings that houses the seat of government of Tamil Nadu and other official buildings including Fort House, Fort residencies, the Grand Arsenal, King's Barracks, Clive's House and the Exchange House. A garrison of troops is also housed in the fort.

St. Mary's Church is an integral part of the fort's history and a place of peace and calm within its bustling walls. Though small it is certainly the most important building in the fort. In his handbook on the church published in 1905 Reverend Charles Herbert Malden wrote;

> *"It is not only the oldest place of worship built by the English settlers in India and now in use, but it is believed to be the oldest British building of any kind in the whole of India."*

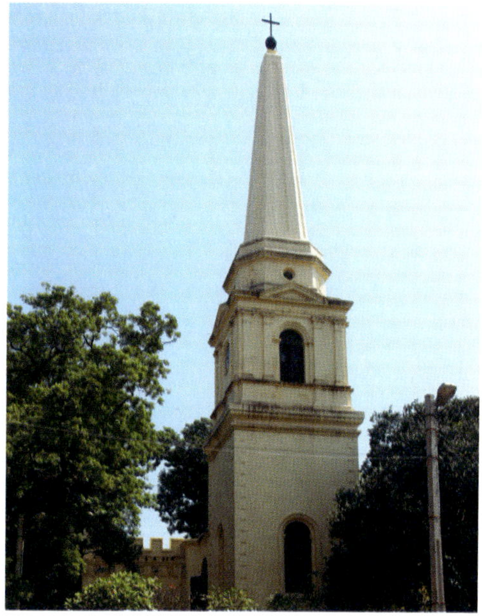

The spire of St. Mary's

The British made a great effort to replicate what they had left behind; the look and the feel of England. Among the most beautiful and well preserved structures in the British forts are the Christian churches. The best example is St. Mary's Anglican Church in Fort St. George.

In a quiet corner of Fort St. George and almost obscured by neem trees a gate with an old lamp can be seen. It is the entrance to St. Mary's, a treasure trove of history. It was Streynsham Master the Governor of Madras who was the driving force behind the building of St. Mary's. When appointed governor in 1678 he found that a common room was used as a chapel. Master decided that a proper church was needed for the settlement and within the same year building had begun. Funds for the church came from Master himself, his colleagues and the merchants who were dealing with or in the East India Company's service.

Though common to British garrison churches the small interior of St. Mary's holds a remarkable number of funerary monuments, statues, tombstones and marble wall plaques. Most are dedicated to British military heroes long gone. More uncommon is the fine memorial plaque dedicated to the Indian soldier. It reads in part:

> 'This tablet is erected in this church of St. Mary Fort St. George Madras as a memorial to the long and loyal service of the undermentioned regiments on the final disbandment of the 1st Battalion 3rd Regiment of the last remaining Battalion of the Madras Infantry...erected by the officers past and present.'

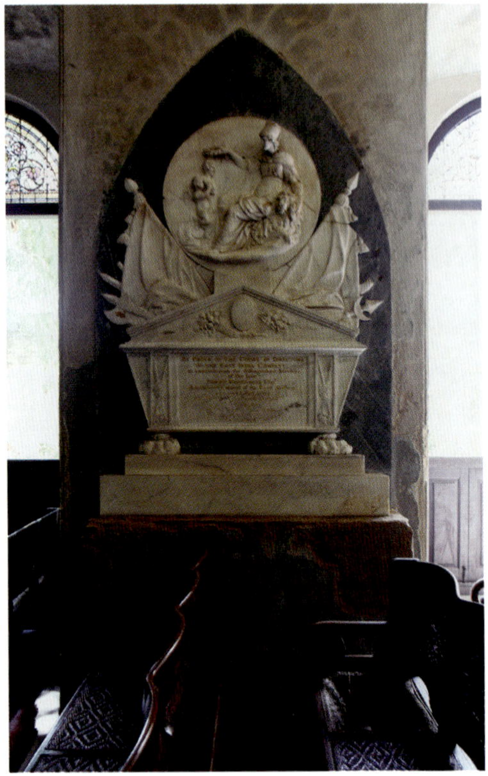

Large marble wall plaque and rattan seats in the foreground

Despite a commemorative plaque to Master Gunner Edward Fowles which has led to him being credited with the building of the church it was most likely to be William Dixon, Master Gunner and Engineer who was the man charged by Master to construct St. Mary's. True to the church's status as the place of worship in the fort St. Mary's was not only solid but bomb proof. With walls over 1.5 metres thick it is little wonder the church withstood the French bombardment of 1746, the only building in the fort to remain unscathed. The barrel shaped roof decorated with roses in relief was cleverly designed to cause bullets to ricochet. The parapet was castellated like an English watch tower. No wood was used in its construction in case of fire from bombing. It was a near impenetrable little fortress.

The altar piece is a large oil painting of the Last Supper thought to have come from Puducherry when the British took the town from the French in 1761 in retaliation for the French attack on Fort St. George. Interestingly the painting covers a large stained glass window with an extract from the bible, 'If Ye Love Me Keep My Commandments.' At some time the painting with its dark background was placed over the window blocking light from the east and giving the church a rather gloomy atmosphere.

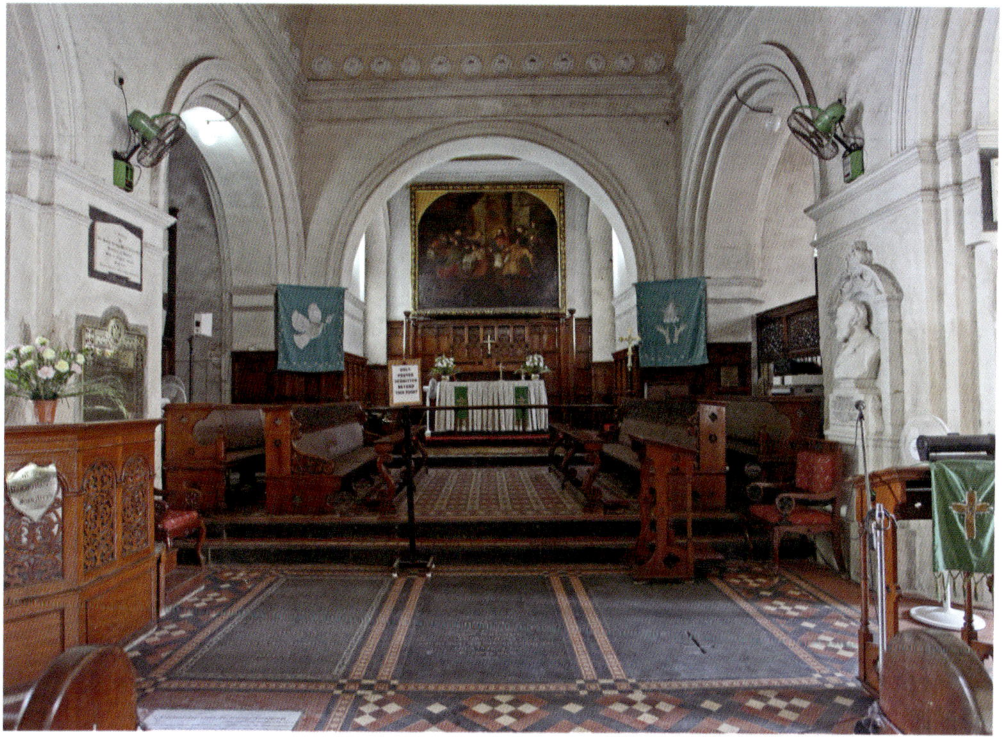

The altar and the painting, 'The Last Supper'

The painting is thought to be a work by a student of Raphael, with the chalice painted by Raphael himself; however it is more likely to be the work of Scottish artist George Willison (1741-1797) who lived in Chennai and painted a version of 'The Last Supper' based on Raphael's original masterpiece. As the painting is not signed the artist must remain a mystery.

The many tombs within the church include Sir George Ward, who died just two weeks after becoming the Governor of Madras in 1860. Another Governor, Lord Hobart, died from typhoid in 1872. There was certainly a high mortality rate for the British in India and many reasons for that. A minister of the church died from fright 'brought about from monkeys' while a brigadier died of sunstroke in Burma.

St. Mary's beautiful spire was added at the beginning of the 18th century. Old prints of the church show the tower without

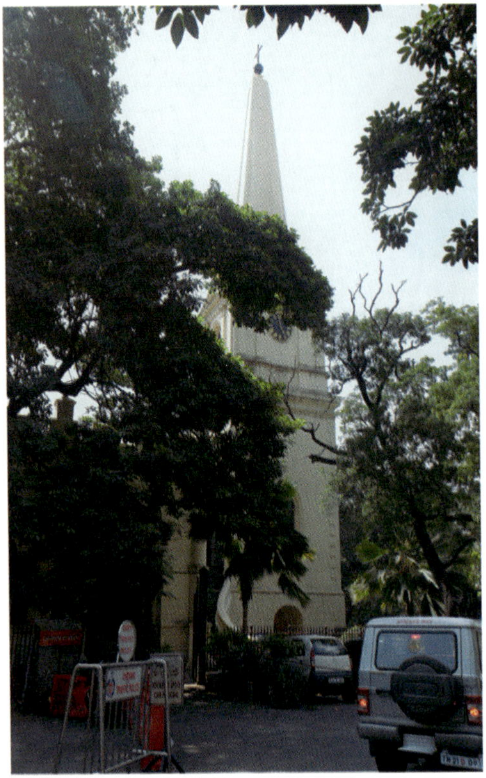

The entrance to St. Mary's Church

the spire. Governor Master added an unusual feature to the church in the form of an exterior staircase which reached a large gallery supported by teak pillars at the far end of the altar. It was from this vantage point that Master could look down on the congregation

A visitor to the fort in the late 17 century describes the governor's progress to church on Sunday:

> Twixt eight and nine the bell tells us the hour of devotion draws near. A whole company of above two hundred soldiers is drawn out from the inner Fort to the church door for a guard to the passing President. Ladies throng to their pews, and the gentlemen take a serious walk in the yard if it be not too hot. On the Governor's approach the organs strike up and continue a welcome till he is seated; when the minister discharges the duty of his function, according to the forms appointed by our prudent ancestors of the Church of England.

The first entry in the church's records is the marriage of Elihu Yale to Catherine Hynmers in 1680. Yale became Governor of Madras from 1687 to 1692 during which time he amassed a fortune through 'dubious' trading which was against Company regulations. He donated funds to a college in Connecticut, America which later became Yale University named after him. Elihu Yale was removed as Governor in 1692 on charges of corruption.

Job Charnock known for his role in Kolkata's early history had his three daughters, Mary, Elizabeth and Catherine baptised in St. Mary's Church in 1689. Robert Clive known as Clive of India, lived in Fort St. George. His marriage to Margaret Maskelyne in St. Mary's Church in 1753 is the

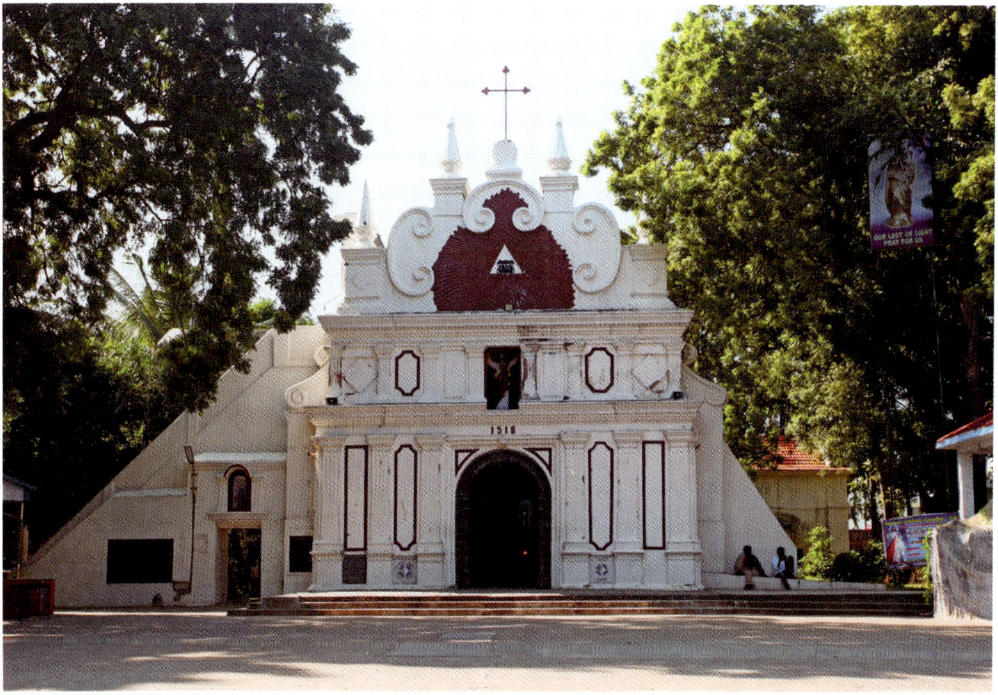

The Church of Our Lady of Light

most famous marriage held there and Arthur Wellesley who later became the Duke of Wellington and triumphed at Waterloo also lived in Fort St. George and worshipped at St. Mary's. Wellesley House and Clive House are situated across from the Church; sadly both are in need of repair.

This sturdy little church in the fort has weathered the years well. Though there is some damage to the plaster, on the whole it is well preserved, and full of history and of fascinating people now gone but not forgotten. The church still holds regular services and today the people who attend are from all religions, Christians, Hindus and Muslims alike.

The Church of Our Lady of Light, 1582

Roman Catholic

'Luz Church' as it is known lies hidden away on a quiet street in the suburb of Luz, west of Mylapore. Locals still call it Kattu Koil or Kattu Kovil, which means 'Temple in the Forest' in Tamil but its full name is Nossa

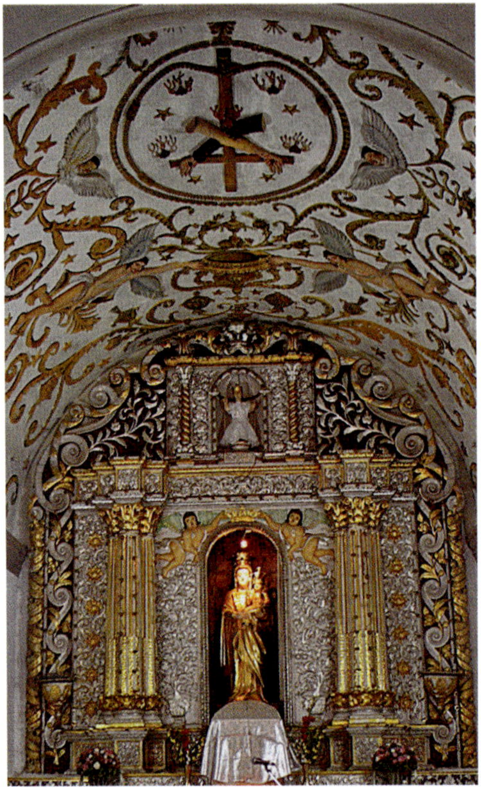

A detail of the ornate gilded altar with the symbolic hands of Jesus above

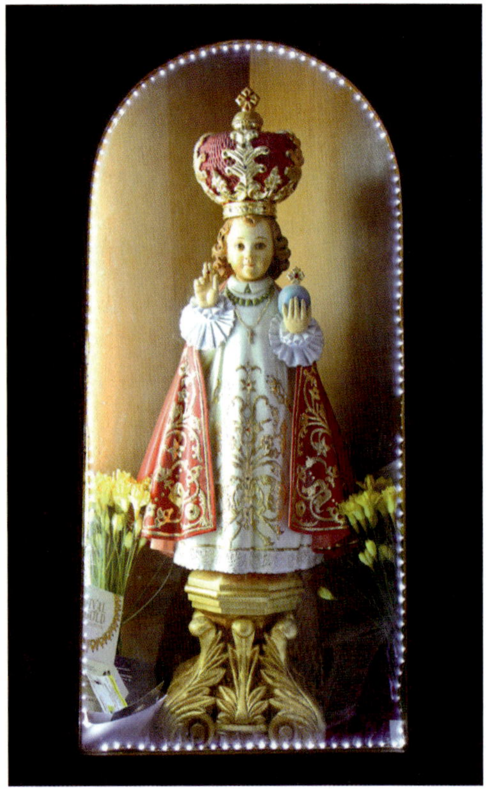

Statue of the 'Infant of Prague' in Luz Church

Senhora da Luz, Our Lady of Light. It is a link in the legend of St. Thomas believed to be the site where the saint stopped to rest on his way from Little Mount to the beach at Mylapore. The church is set back from the road in a garden filled with mature trees and shrubs. It is a quiet, peaceful churchyard and it is hard to believe busy Mylapore is just a few streets away.

Architecturally Luz Church is very much a Portuguese colonial style church. It has a simple Baroque façade and Gothic finials and buttresses on each side. Four steps lead up to the arched entrance with the date inscribed '1516.' In the wall of the church is a stone inscribed in Portuguese, *'Friar Pedro of the Observance of St. Francis built this church of Our Lady of Light in 1516'*.

However the church we see today is believed to have been built between 1547 and 1582. These dates are confirmed by East India Company records. The 1516 date more likely refers to an earlier small chapel or oratory. The church was damaged twice during the 17th century, first by the Golconda forces (1662-1673) and second during a siege by Hyder Ali (1780-1782). When the British began administering from Fort St. George it was repaired a number of times and today it is one of the best preserved churches in Chennai.

The exterior has three embedded columns either side of the entrance above which is a statue of Jesus. On either side are four identical though much shorter columns. The top of the facade displays curving volutes which frame a pleated sunburst motif. Conical finials and a cross decorate the top of the facade. Like St. Mary's in the fort, tombstones are set in the pavement of the churchyard. Inside the church the nave is barrel vaulted without decoration. The vaulted ceiling of the apse however is highly decorative with frescoes showing images of entwined gold and silver leaves, angels and the crossed arms and bleeding hands of Jesus. The main altar is wonderfully impressive with an abundance of gilding in gold and silver leaf. Bright gold columns flank the centrepiece of the altar; an image of the Madonna and Child crowned by angels.

A charming legend tells of a group of priests lost at sea off the coast of Chennai. As they prayed for help a mysterious light appeared and began to move towards the west. They followed the light and reached land safely and then worked their way inland searching in the forest for the source of the light. The light promptly disappeared when they found it. To give thanks the grateful priests are said to have built the church and dedicated it to 'Our Lady of Light'.

Blessed Sacrament Chapel, Little Mount, 1551

Roman Catholic

Little Mount is an intriguing religious site and an integral part of the legend of St. Thomas. After spending ten years in Kerala the apostle crossed the Deccan Plateau to reach Mylapore in 68 CE. The small Portuguese church at the summit of the Mount is above a small cave believed to be the place where St. Thomas led a simple prayerful life, faced death and hid to escape persecution.

The Portuguese named the church the Blessed Sacrament Chapel and dated it 1551. Inside the chapel is cool and quiet. A small number of pews face eight steps which lead up to a shrine of the Virgin Mary. At the base of the steps is the tiny entrance to the cave

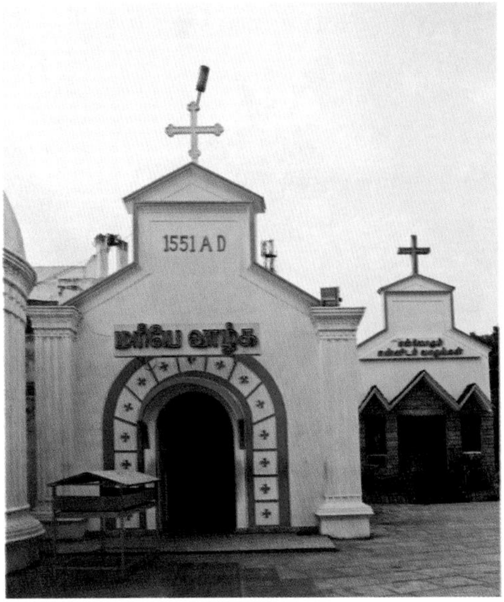

The Portuguese shrine built in 1551

through a crevasse in the rock. It is barely large enough to enter easily. On the left is a cross carved into the rock wall, believed to be the work of St. Thomas but more probably carved by the Portuguese. Inside the 4 metre by 7 metre cave is a small altar with an image of St. Thomas holding a scroll which reads 'My Lord and My God.' Imprints can be seen on a rock in the cave believed to be the apostle's fingers where he leant to pray, worn into the rock over the years. A sign nearby explains everything:

The cave where lay hid persecuted just before being martyred by Rajah Mahadevan, king of Mylapore, AD *68, Thomas, one of the twelve, the great Apostle of India, the very one who put his finger into the wounds of his Lord and God. Drop your penny for this great historical and archaeological monument.*

The next part of the legend has a number of variations. One of the most common is that sometime around 72 CE St. Thomas left the cave in fear of his life. Though he was a favourite with the local king his ministers and Hindu priests were jealous of his influence and intent on destroying him. On hearing they were approaching the cave and afraid of being captured Thomas escaped through a long underground tunnel which led directly to Big Mount, now St. Thomas Mount three kilometres away where he met his fate. There is a second church on Little Mount called Our Lady of Good Health. It is large and modern and built in a circular design. It was consecrated in 1971 and built to commemorate the 19th century of St. Thomas' martyrdom.

An interesting Hindu legend tells that Little Mount was also a sacred site for Hindus, a place where the god Muruga, 'Lord of the Tamil People' was worshipped. Long after the Portuguese had removed any evidence that a Hindu site had ever existed on Little Mount, Hindu women continued to pray there.

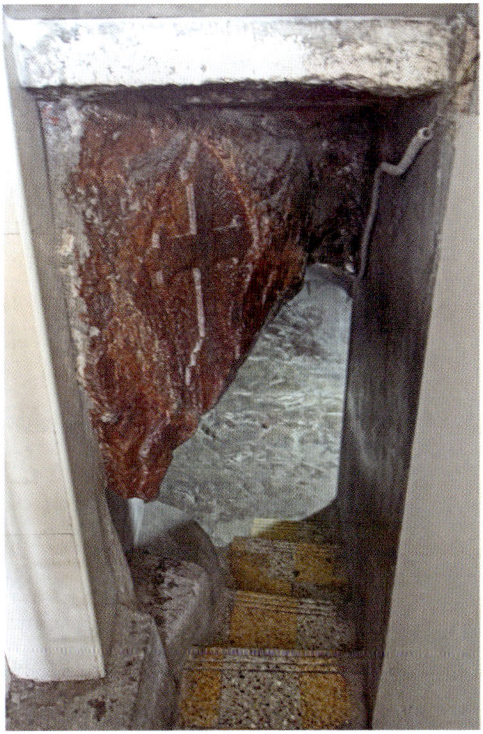

The entrance to the cave

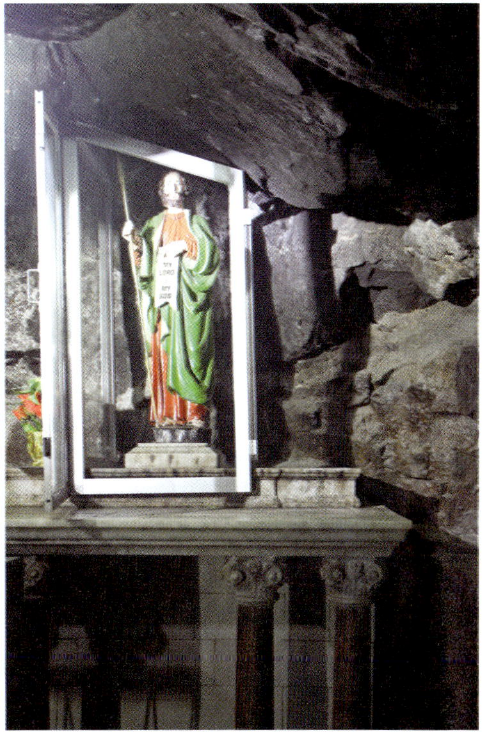

The cave of St. Thomas

St. Thomas Mount, 1547

Roman Catholic

St. Thomas Mount was known to locals as 'Parangimalai' or 'Europeans Hill', those Europeans being the Portuguese who began to settle in the area between 1514 and 1523. They discovered what they believed to be the tomb of St. Thomas and built a small chapel. As word spread more and more pilgrims began arriving so a larger church was built around 1547, the building we see today. It is dedicated to Our Lady of the Mount and inside is a statue of Senhora da Expectacao, the Mother of Expectation.

The chapel is reached by climbing 134 steps passing brightly painted life sized religious images and the Fourteen Stations of the Cross. At the summit an impressive viewing terrace offers a wonderful view of the city of Chennai. The entrance to the site is inscribed in granite with the Portuguese coat of arms.

The chapel has a piece of the bone of St. Thomas enshrined in a Chinese casket placed on the altar. It is believed that by being close to this holy relic miracles can happen. A stone plaque carved with a cross and topped with a dove with extended wings was also discovered by the Portuguese. It is thought to be from the 8th century and is very famous having 'bled' on occasions. It is in pride of place in the centre of the altar.

On the chancel walls are paintings of the twelve apostles. On the right side of the altar is a small painting of the Madonna and Child believed to be almost 2000 years old and brought to India by St. Thomas himself. According to Christian tradition the painting is by St. Luke, one of seven in various churches throughout Europe. This painting preserved at St. Thomas Mount is believed to be the oldest.

For Christians St. Thomas Mount is one of India's most important religious sites and a part of the ancient tradition of the apostle's life on India's Coromandel Coast where he met his death at this mount which now bears his name. The story has continued for 2000 years.

St. Andrew's Church, 1821

Presbyterian

It is not widely known that there was a large Scottish presence in India, in fact by 1792 approximately one in nine Scots were employed by the British East India Company, a third of its officers in India were Scots and one in eleven of its soldiers too. During the 18th and 19th centuries Scots were also deeply involved in many ways including trade, manufacturing, and the founding of the railways throughout India.

St. Andrew's, the Scotch National Church, or simply 'The Kirk' is known as the Queen of Scottish Churches in the East. It is based on the design of St. Martin-in-the-Fields, an enduring and popular model used for many British churches in India though in St. Andrews the designers Major Thomas Fort de Havilland and Colonel James Caldwell added side porches and temple fronts below the steeple. The church was also altered due to the marshy site. Ingeniously the foundations were made of deep wells of brick and pottery cylinders so that ground water would not cause the foundations to sink or allow rising damp to damage the building.

De Havilland was employed by the army and had achieved success in Mysore, building a large banquet hall unsupported by columns. In 1816 Presbyterian Church elders agreed on a circular plan with a dome for St. Andrews thus a plan was drawn up by engineer Lieutenant Grant based on an earlier unused design by James Gibbs for St. Martin-in-the-Fields. The building of domes was unfamiliar to Grant who recommended a wooden dome

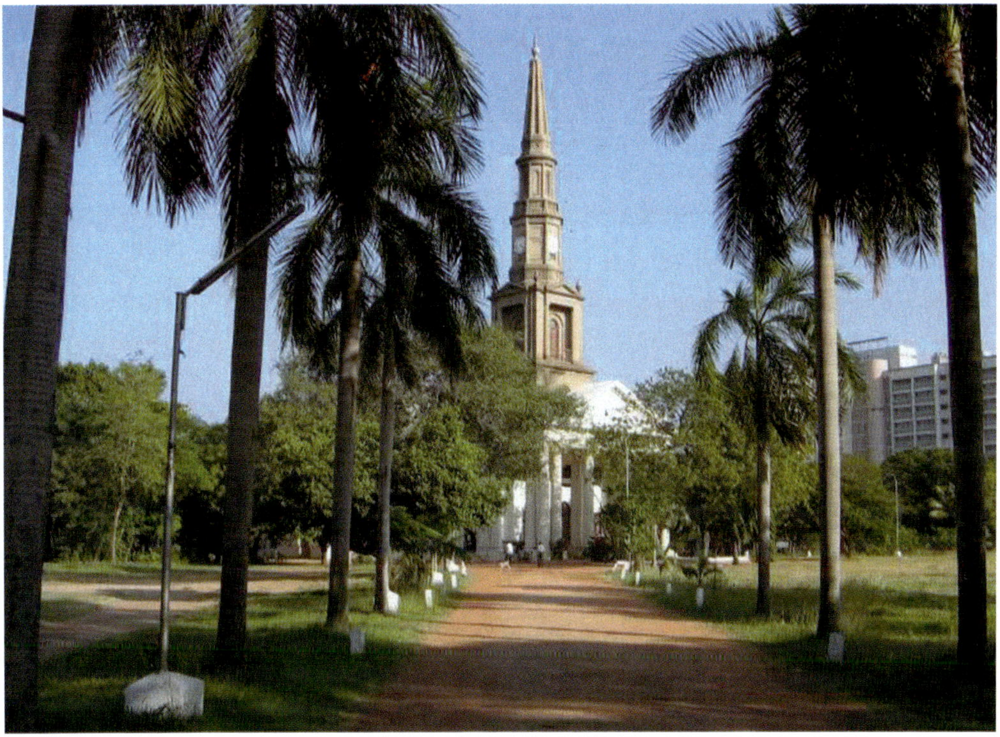

St. Andrew's Church

covered in metal. De Havilland argued that a timber structure would not last in the harsh climate, instead suggesting a brick dome built by Indian master masons, the *sthapati*s. A model of the dome though shallower and smaller in circumference, was built in his garden following Gibbs original design.

The dome was finally constructed using bamboo laid over wooden trusses supported by sun-burnt bricks packed together on the bamboo and then earth thrown over them. Wet mud made into a plaster was then applied and rendered to make the dome smooth. Ninety years after the church was built British architect Robert Fellowes Chisolm who initiated the Indo-Saracenic architectural style in Chennai said that, 'If a dome was turned on true Hindoo principles without a centre, the cost of doming was very little more than the cost of walling.'

The belfry tower sits between the portico and the dome, its striking steeple rising fifty

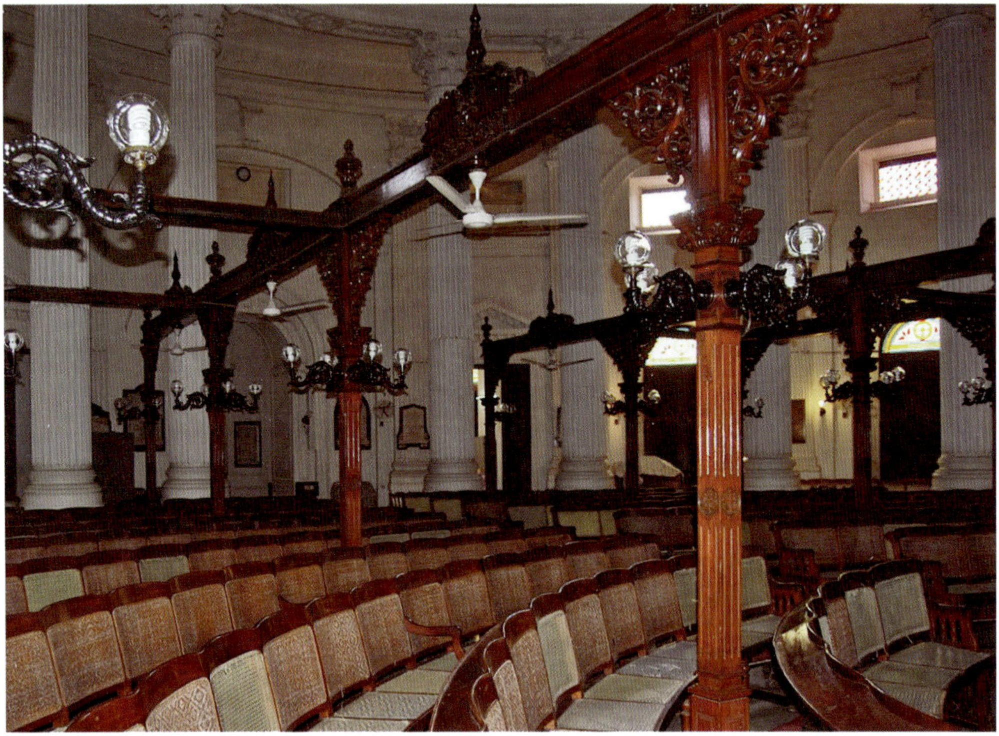

The timber and rattan pews, the Corinthian columns, the fluted mahogany pillars and the lights

two metres above the ground. It is topped with a weather-cock. The masonry used is unique to India and can be found in many buildings in other cities, particularly in Kolkata. It involves the application of ground lime mortar made on site by grinding organic additives such as gallnut (a swelling on a branch that looks like a nut) *kadukkai* and a brown sugar (jaggery), solution. It is applied in layers over several days. The final layers are a mixture of egg-white and quartz sand. Coarse sand is applied in the beginning, then layers of very fine grains of sand are applied up to four times depending on the area. Sometimes the layers were cured for at least ten days before the final finish was applied. When polished it gives the effect of marble.

The interior of the church is elegant. A black-and-white tiled marble floor and fine white Doric columns is the backdrop for decorative mahogany pillars on which are attached ornate lamps. Stained glass windows portray religious scenes. Concessions were made to the tropical climate of Chennai by incorporating woven cane pews and louvered doors. On the inner surface of the dome are painted gold stars which replicate the constellations seen in the far away sky of Scotland. The rich blue of the dome is achieved by crushed shells with lapis lazuli. Sixteen columns support the dome and outside the entry porch is supported by a double colonnade of twelve huge Ionic columns topped with a pediment. Another façade has a pediment with the British East India Company motto engraved on it.

With its impressive spire, stately columns and the dome St. Andrews is a well-known colonial landmark in Chennai. In de Havilland's words;

'*...a handsome building, and is of peculiar construction, being entirely of masonry...and the pews divided by arms into single sittings, all ranged concentrically to the pulpit...*' As beautiful as the church is, the acoustics were a failure and the service could not be heard clearly. Major de Havilland simply blamed it on the age of the reverend!

The Santhome Basilica, 1896

Roman Catholic

Near Chennai's endless Marina Beach sits the city's most recognised church, the Santhome Basilica in the suburb of Mylapore. It is another important Christian location in Chennai associated with the apostle St. Thomas.

In the 10th century CE Nestorian Christians from Persia founded a little Christian settlement on the beach at Mylapore. It was known as *Betumah*, or 'The Town of Thomas'. Marco Polo visited in the 13th century and Bishops from Baghdad came in 1504 and wrote '*... as to the monastery of St. Thomas the Apostle, it is on the shore of the sea in a town called Mailapore*'. Further, in 1515 the Portuguese writer and officer Duarte Barbosa wrote that Mylapore was '*an ancient city, a deserted city, near the sea and there, in a little church, lay the body of the blessed Saint Thomas*'.

When the Portuguese arrived they found the church in ruins. They built a modest church inland to safely house the remains of St. Thomas. Over the centuries the church has been replaced numerous times, either due to the nature of the structure or the lack of funds needed to maintain it.

By the early 18th century Portuguese power had begun to weaken on India's east coast which cleared the way for the British who were enjoying great economic success. In 1740 the British took the church from the Portuguese and by 1893 the foundation stone was laid for a grand cathedral to commemorate the consecration of Pope

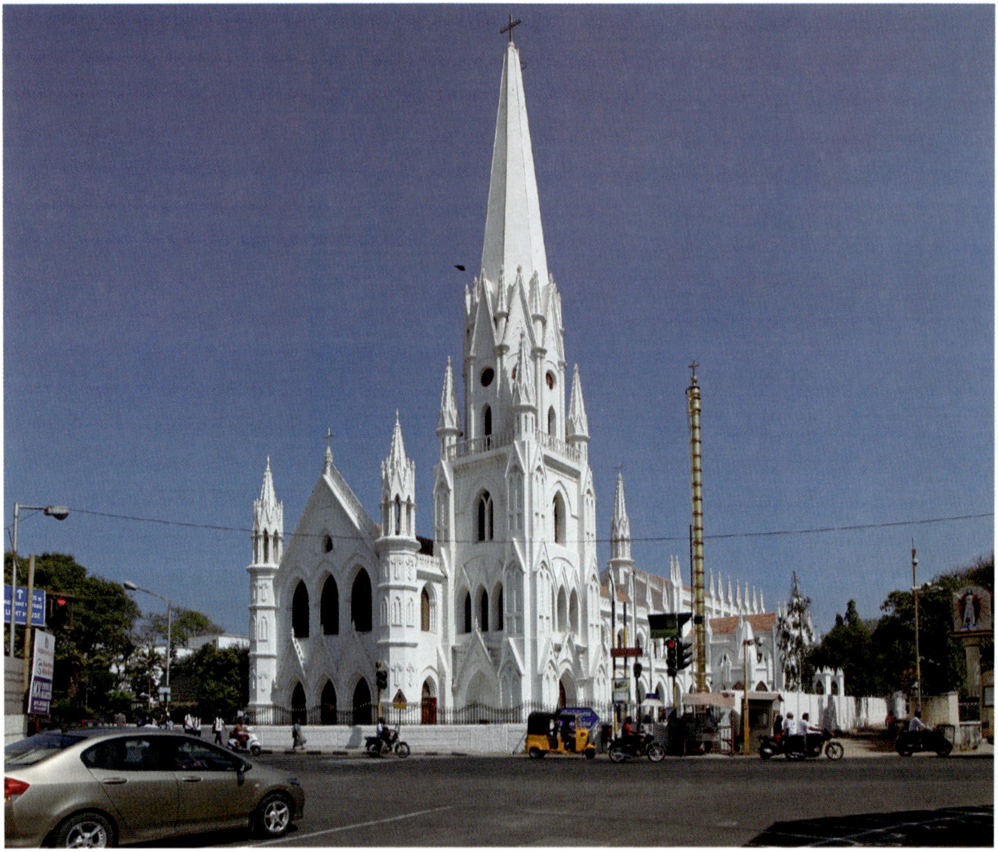

Leo XIII. It was completed in 1896 and consecrated by the first Bishop of the diocese Rt. Rev. Dom da Silva. This is the church we see today, built over what is believed to be the tomb of St. Thomas. In 1956 the church was elevated to a Minor Basilica then elevated again in 2004 to a Cathedral Basilica.

It is a grand Gothic edifice with a towering steeple above the entrance and a smaller steeple built directly over a small chapel below which contains a relic of St. Thomas. This underground chapel is reached by a tunnel with an entrance at the back of the church. In this way church services above are not disturbed. The chapel houses a casket

ABOVE: *"The citie of Saint Thomas is so called of the Reliques of the Saint, which are kept here with great veneration..." Gasparo Balbi, 1582*

FACING PAGE TOP: *The interior*

FACING PAGE BELOW: *The underground chapel and effigy of St. Thomas*

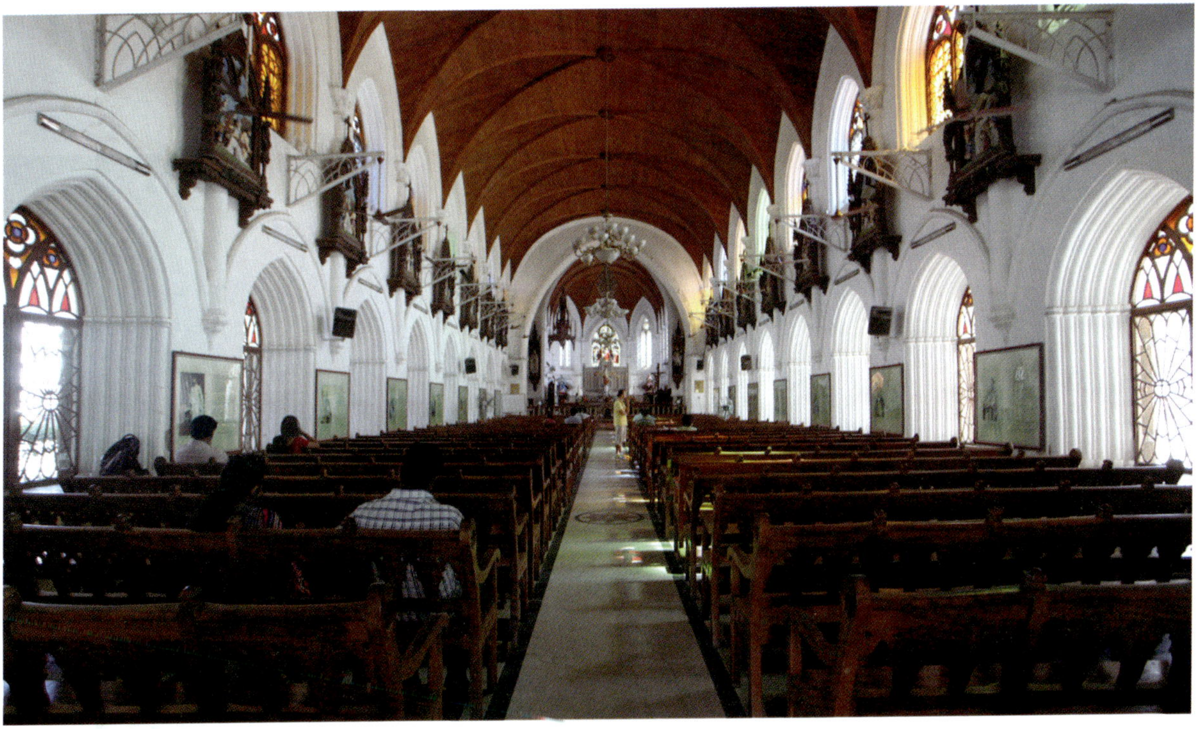

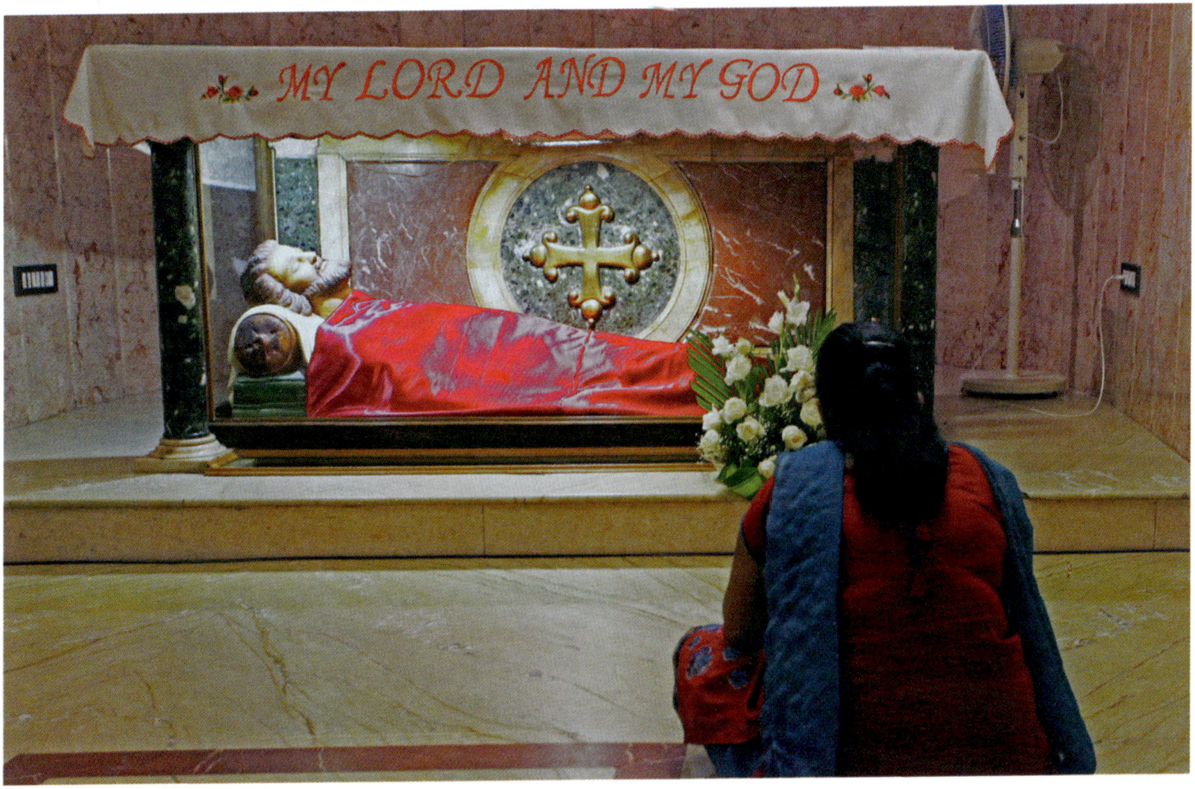
MY LORD AND MY GOD

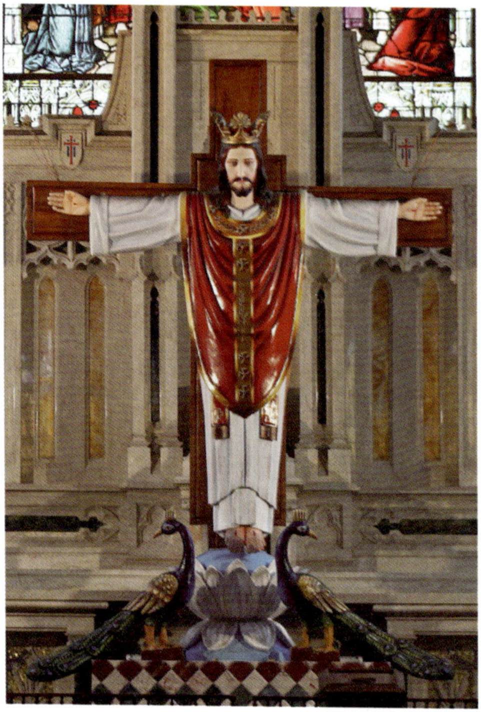

The statue of Jesus as a king with a lotus below his feet and a peacock on either side

which holds an effigy of the saint. A small cross on the wall contains a fragment of a bone labelled 'Relic of St. Thomas'.

The chapel is simply decorated and completely silent. Windowless and soundproof it has all the qualities needed for quiet contemplation and prayer. Pilgrims patiently wait their turn to kneel in front of the casket and offer their prayers to St. Thomas. It is believed that over the centuries the majority of the saint's remains have been taken from place to place and are now finally entombed in the Basilica di San Tommaso Apostolo in Ortona Italy.

The Basilica is a famous Christian place of worship and hundreds flock to the church on Sundays. The most faithful buy a little card with some grains of sand from the saint's tomb embedded in it. It is believed that sand gathered from the tomb of St. Thomas has great healing powers.

The interior of the church is enormous and highly decorative. Marble floors, a teak vaulted ceiling and intricate stone work cover walls. Murals adorn the interior and paintings depicting the Fourteen Stations of the Cross line the side walls. The ancient statue of Our Lady of Mylapore is enthroned in the church. It is famous as St. Francis Xavier prayed before the statue during his time in Chennai.

Gothic shaped stained glass windows have stone tracery surrounding them. The most beautiful are the three windows behind the altar showing Jesus appearing to St. Thomas with the words above 'Be not faithless, but believe', a reference to St. Thomas doubting that Jesus had appeared to the apostles after death. In front of these windows is the figure of Jesus on the cross portrayed with interesting indigenous symbols rather than the traditional image. Here Jesus stands hovering above a lotus at his feet and peacocks either side, both symbols of eastern mythology and used frequently in Hindu temples. He wears a gold crown rather than the usual crown of thorns. Jesus is depicted as a king.

Churches of Bengaluru: A Hint of England

The city of Bengaluru has been called 'The City of Churches' but today is better known as the 'Silicon Valley of India' for its position as India's leading information technology exporter. It is a cosmopolitan city yet it has a distinctly English appearance which dates back to 1809 when the British Cantonment was established and the city's churches began to develop. Many of these colonial era churches appear to have been plucked from the English countryside and placed carefully on the ground in India with their rose gardens still intact.

In contrast the city has had a turbulent past. From the 6th century on a series of South Indian rulers claimed the area as part of their domain; the Ganga Dynasty, the Cholas and later the Hoysalas. In the 12th century the Marathas, the Mughals and the Delhi Sultanates from the north were drawn to the area. The great Hindu empire of Vijayanagar rose in 1336 and ruled over southern India for more than two centuries.

Kempe Gowda was a chieftain under the feudal rule of the Vijayanagar kings and is widely known as the founder of Bengaluru. For his loyalty he received a piece of land and in 1532 it is said that he marked off the first streets of the future city with a plough drawn by two white bullocks. By 1537 he had built a mud fort and in this fort grew the little markets of Cottonpet, Chickpet and Balepet which still survive as market towns today.

The Vijayanagar rule came to an end in 1638 when the Marathas captured the city for the Sultans of Bijapur who ruled for the next sixty years. A succession of events and various rulers followed until 1761 when Wodeyar chief Hyder Ali became the de-facto ruler of the Mysore Kingdom which included Bengaluru. Ali transformed it into a military town where mercenaries from French Pondicherry, gunsmiths and sword makers soon arrived and the city began to resemble a vast military camp.

During the rule of Hyder Ali and his son Tipu Sultan known as the 'Tiger of Mysore,' and an inveterate enemy of the British, the city reached its height but clashes with the British and their Indian allies such as the Marathas and the Nizam of Hyderabad were ongoing, eventually leading to the first of the four Anglo-Mysore Wars. Hyder Ali and his son triumphed in the first (1767-1769) and the second war (1780-1784) but Hyder died suddenly of cancer in 1782.

Like his father Tipu Sultan became the de facto ruler of Mysore and proclaimed himself the Emperor. He protected his empire until the end of the 18th century when he was killed in 1799 defending Seringapatam during the fourth Anglo-Mysore war. The British along with their ally the Nizam of Hyderabad, broke through the walls of the fortress at Seringapatam and stormed the citadel capturing the city and gaining large parts of Tipu's kingdom. The British returned the Wodeyars to the throne of the Kingdom of Mysore as figureheads. It remained as an autonomous region of the British Raj until Indian independence in 1947.

During the Anglo-Mysore wars Britain's Indian allies were 'more like small nations on the move' than armies. Scottish born Major Alexander Dirom wrote a fascinating account; *'...it was highly entertaining to see them in motion the whole day; the chiefs in different group...themselves and their principal attendants mounted on elephants, distinguished by their state flags and nagars, also borne on elephants. They were surrounded by cavalry, with their various standards, and preceded by their bards, and bands of music, who sung the praises of their masters and the heroes of their nation...a spectacle so wild and irregular, yet so grand and interesting, resembled more the visions of romance than any assemblage that can be supposed to have existence in real life'.*

In 1807 a malaria plague broke out in Seringapatam where the British were based. This time they turned their sights to Bengaluru with its cool, healthy climate. Consequently they moved and Bengaluru became their administrative capital. A military cantonment was established with all the trappings of Empire building; engineers, surveyors, cartographers and the Indian Army. By 1827 it had expanded to include twenty villages. Barracks and hospitals were built and churches rose to provide places of worship for the British regiment. Eight thousand men were stationed at Bengaluru. William Arthur, a Wesleyan minister gives a description of the city in 1830 after a difficult journey from Madras;

'About an hour after night, hedgerows skirting the broad, regular roads, English-looking gates, lights shining from between clumps of trees, the white fronts of houses glistening in the brilliant moonlight and the stir of buggies hurrying hither and thither, told us that the merciful care of our heavenly Father had conducted us to the English capital of Mysore.'

One of the most unique features of Bengaluru's colonial architecture was the high pointed hood or tiled canopy over the windows and entrances of bungalows and some churches. They are known as 'monkey tops.' They were a practical design, keeping the sun at bay and preventing rain from entering the house in winter. The windows often had vertical timber slates and were inscribed with a crest. Classical buildings can be found in Bengaluru with the addition of one or many Gothic style 'monkey tops.'

After independence Bengaluru has become one of India's fastest growing cities and home to over two hundred churches, some of which are from the colonial era and as such is an important part of the city's heritage. One of the finest examples is certainly St. Mark's Cathedral, an important part of the British Cantonment in Bengaluru and once the largest garrison in Southern India.

St.Mark's Cathedral, 1808

Anglican

In a quiet area of Bengaluru this beautiful colonial church can be found set in a peaceful garden of rain trees, silver oaks and jacarandas. Apart from a few small cars there is not a soul to be seen so I have the churchyard to myself. It is hard to believe the church was once described as 'one of the ugliest buildings ever erected' but that was in 1812 when the church was a simple rectangular building with a low roof built to cater to the British regiment stationed in Bengaluru. The lovely Classical church we see today with its graceful dome dates from 1927. It is the result of a series of disasters.

The church's history begins with its foundation in 1808, its completion in 1812 and its consecration in 1816 by the Bishop of Calcutta. It accommodated around 400 soldiers at that time and its architecture was described as looking like 'a matchbox'. In just a few years the British population had grown so much that the congregation increased to two thousand but it wasn't until 1901 that a much larger church was built. In that same year the east side of the building collapsed. It was restored in 1906. For the next 17 years the church remained unscathed. However a fire broke out in 1923, destroying much of the building. It was completely rebuilt in 1927 to what stands today.

St. Mark's is the oldest Anglican Church in Bengaluru and is said to be modelled on the 17th century St. Paul's in London. Along with the lovely dome, the rows of Roman arches along the external walls are the church's most striking features. The arched windows have red painted timber shutters with decorative fanlights above each. Wedge shaped panes of glass are separated by vertical timber mullions which give support to the arches.

The main entrance on the south has a large portico to protect the congregation from the sun, and the rain during monsoon. The portico is supported by twelve Corinthian columns in sets of threes, above which is a flat roof surrounded by a parapet.

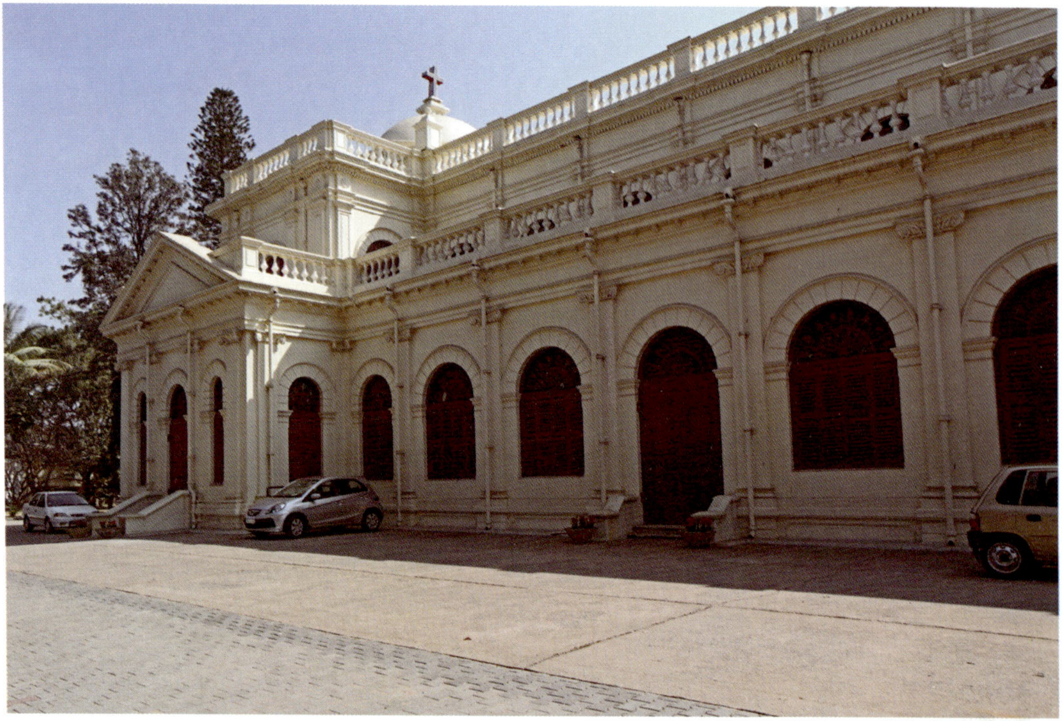

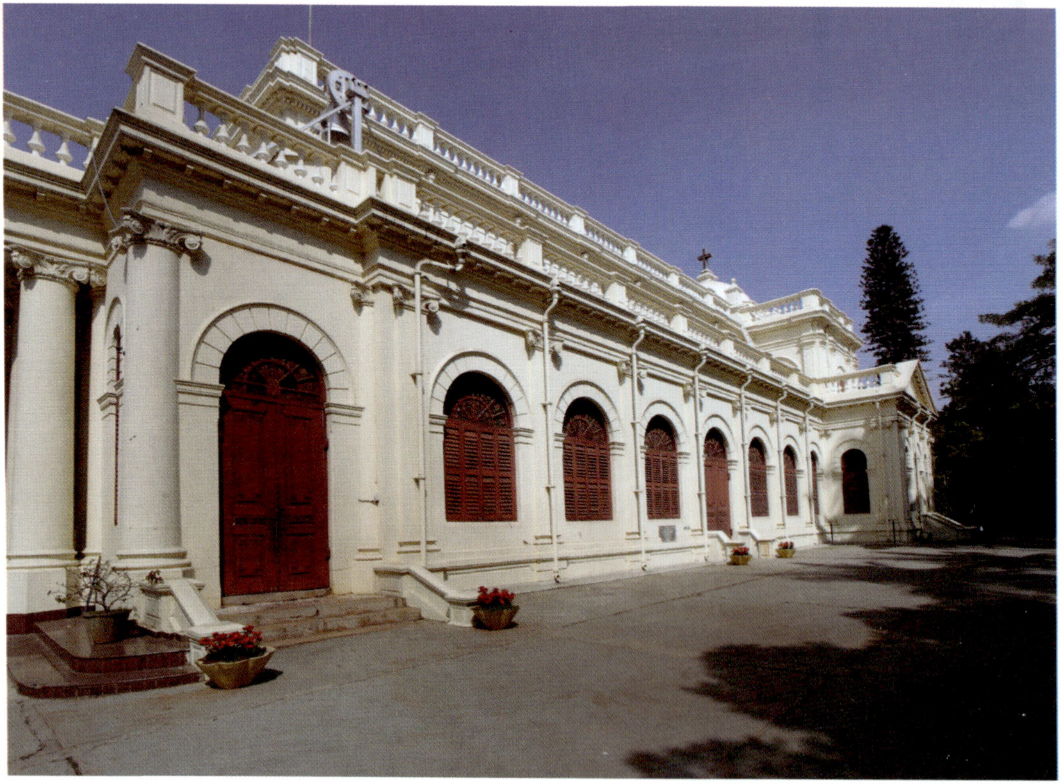

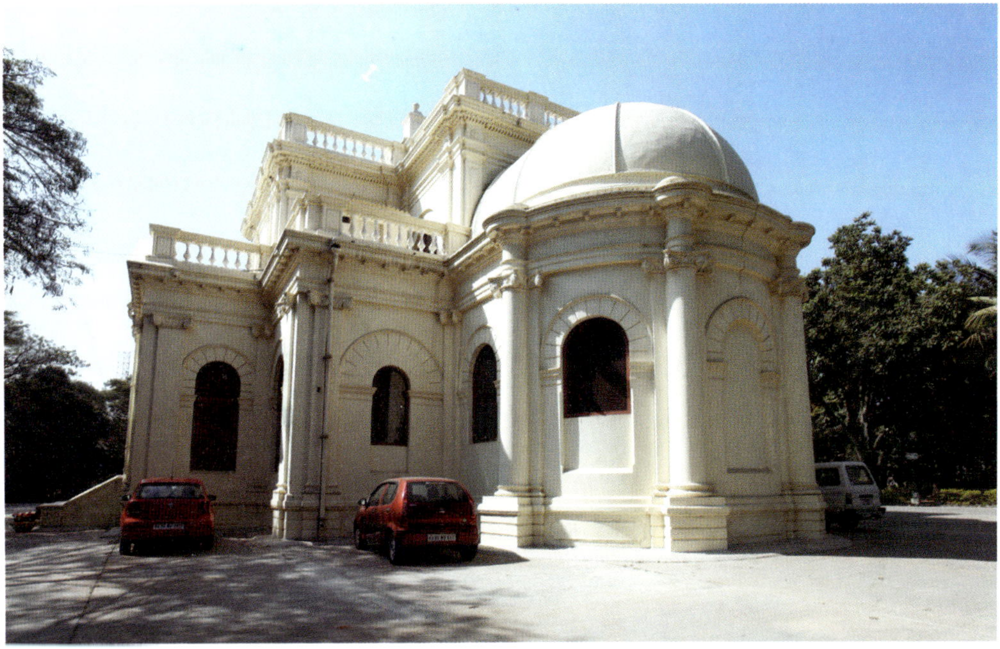

ABOVE: *St. Mark's Cathedral in Bengaluru, a side view*
FACING PAGE TOP AND BELOW: *Facade of St. Mark's Cathedral*

A side entrance is reached via a small set of steps with solid balustrades on each side. It has a double door which opens outwards and a Roman arch above. On either side are narrower arched windows, also with shutters. Above the three openings is a parapet with small dentils

There is also a well maintained bell which was cast in London in 1847. The church and gardens are well kept, making it a lovely spot. On hot days the gardeners of St. Mark's pour buckets of water along the outside walls of the church to reduce the temperature inside; one of the many ingenious ways India keeps cool.

Passing through the entrance with its carved woodwork the interior is delightful with beautiful ceilings, interior domes and massive pillars. A lovely semicircular chancel has a magnificent white dome above, decorated with gold stars. The marble pulpit with its inlay work and the font were both made in Genoa. The lectern is decorated with a brass eagle, its wings spread atop a globe of the world, a gift from a group of planters from Mysore in 1903. Another gift is the magnificent pipe organ encased in Burmese teak which arrived in 1929. However the

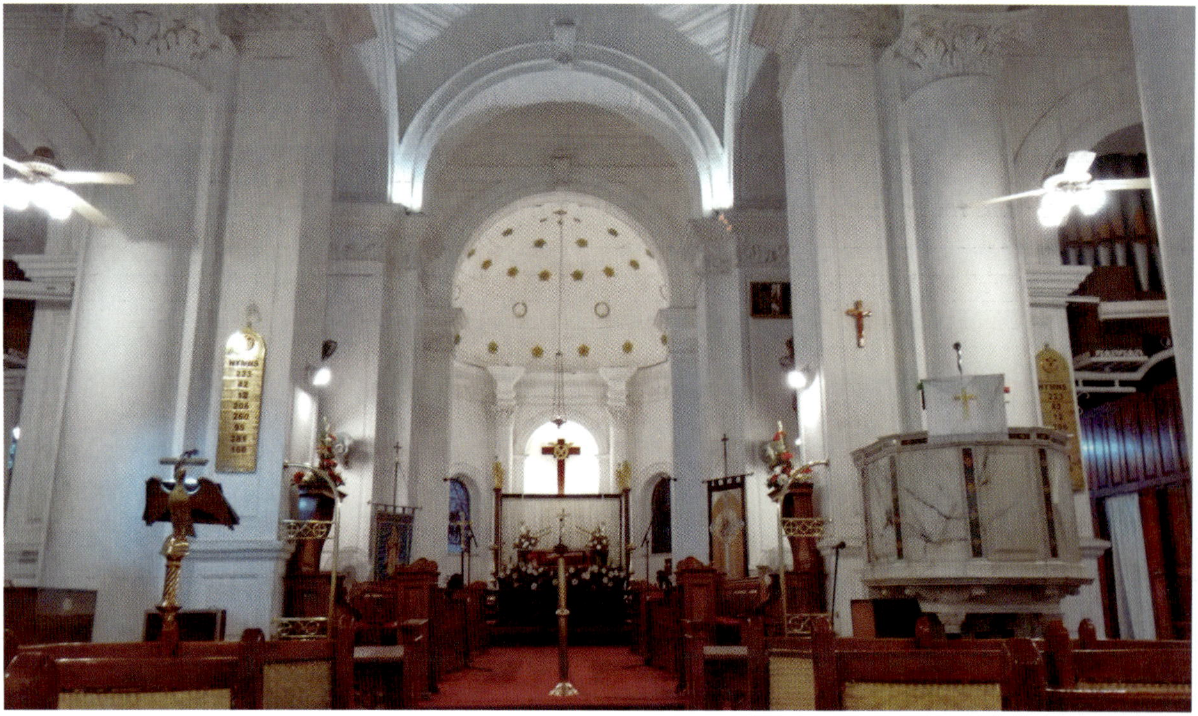
HYMNS

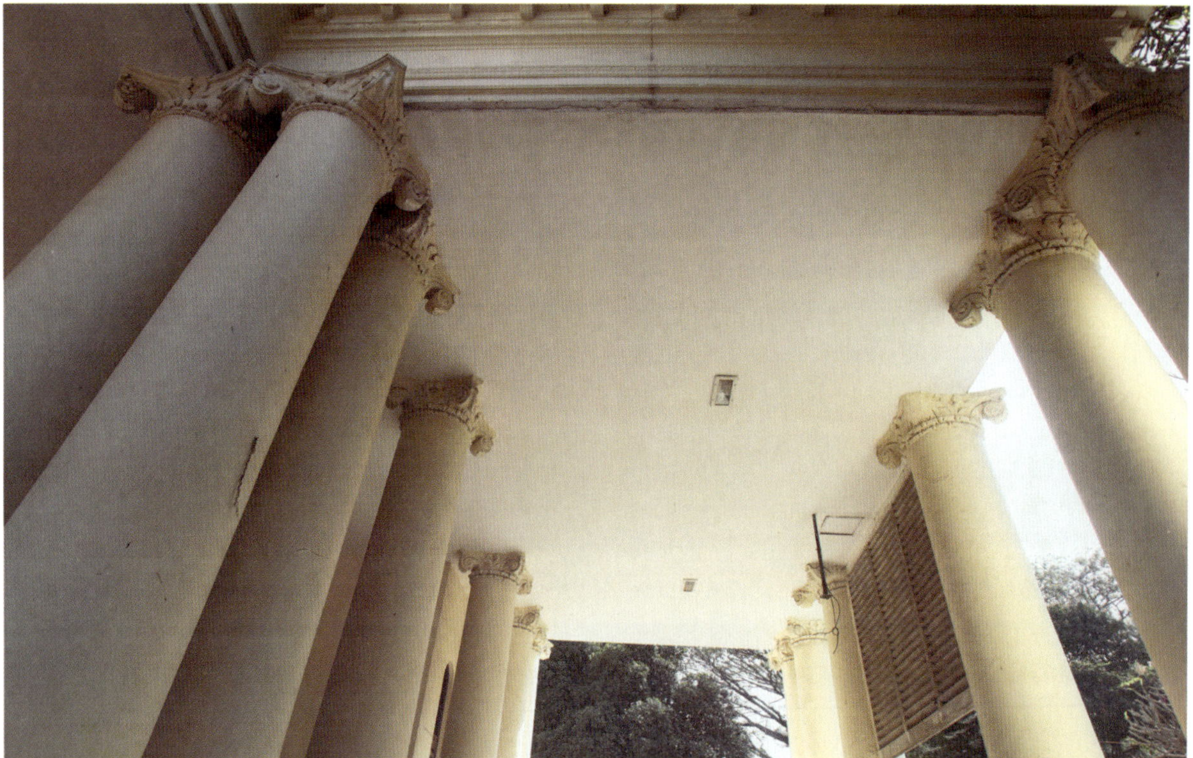

church is best known for its stained glass windows, the most famous being the depiction of the Holy Communion. The large columns are decorated with memorial tablets, typical in a garrison church. One such tablet is dedicated to Lt. Col. Sir Walter Scott of Abbotsford who died off the coast of Chennai (formerly Madras). He was the nephew of the famous Scottish writer Sir Walter Scott whose son fought in the fourth Anglo-Mysore war against Tipu Sultan in 1799.

In 1947, the year India finally gained independence, the church was raised to the status of a cathedral and in the same year the CSI, the Anglican Church of South India was formed.

St. Francis Xavier's Cathedral, 1851

Roman Catholic

St. Francis Xavier's was first built in 1851 then enlarged in 1911. Today it is an imposing cathedral which dominates the surrounding area. The most obvious features of the building are the unusual blue grey

FACING PAGE TOP: *The interiors of St. Mark's*

FACING PAGE BELOW: *The soaring Corinthian columns and timber shutters of the portico*

BELOW: *St. Francis Xavier's Cathedral*

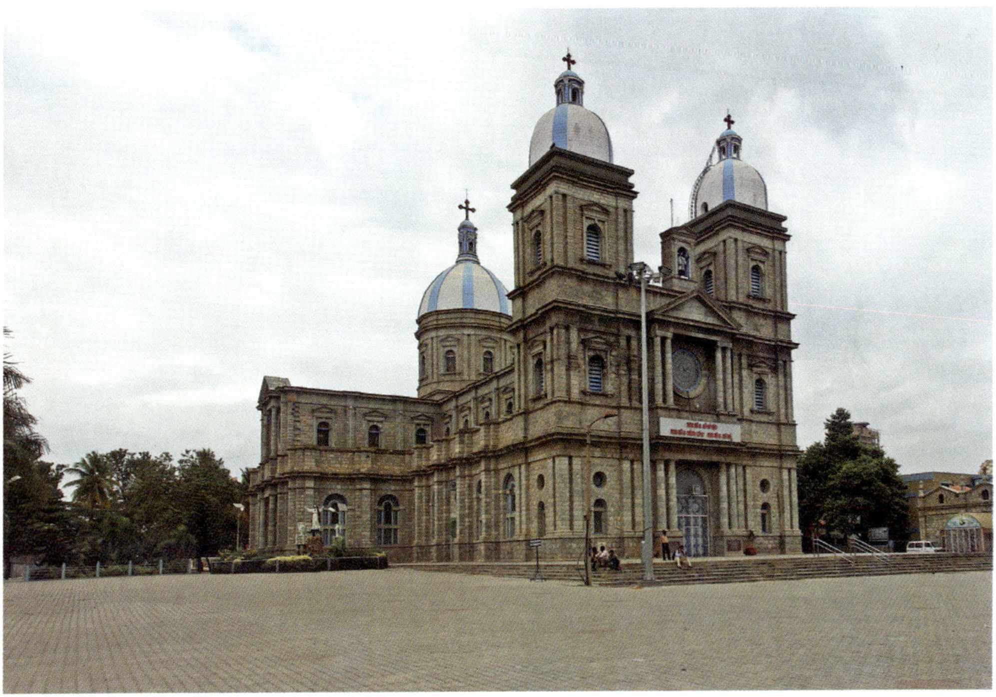

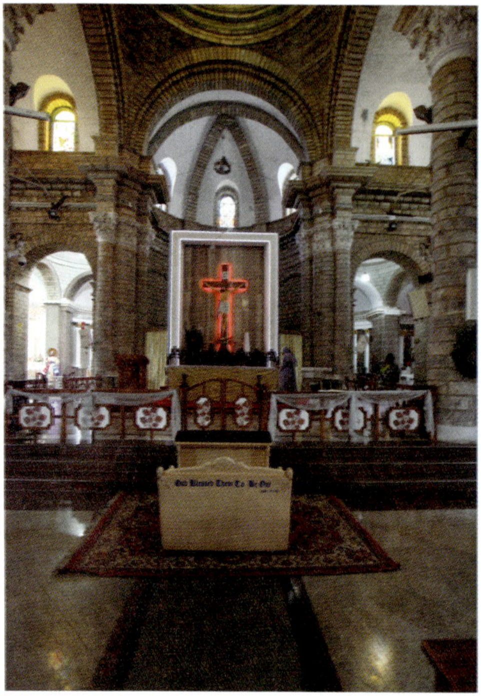

The altar, the brick arches, columns and the cross

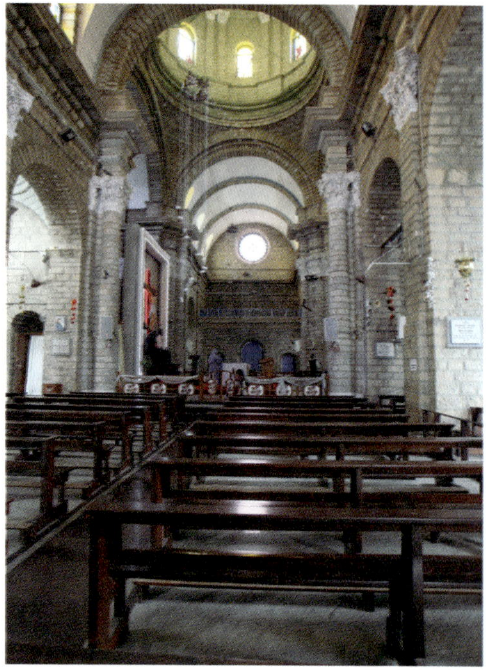

Side chapel with light from a dome, St. Francis Xavier's Cathetral

domes, the towering steeples and spires and the arched windows. The whole structure is built of granite and is cruciform in plan. The largest dome sits above the sanctuary and the other two sit atop the twin belfries. Each dome is topped with a lantern and a cross. It is the light from the lanterns that create the extraordinary numinous light and mystical atmosphere inside the church. This light is created intentionally by church architects and builders and many believe it is essential for a place of worship. It was Gothic churches that introduced ideas of the numinous and created as much interior light as possible. It was seen as 'the light of God.'

The facade of the church features classical columns. A large round window on the second level has twin columns on both sides and a parapet above. On one side of the church is a grotto with a large statue of Jesus placed high above a pretty garden.

The church owes its origins to French religious orders who built many beautiful churches during colonial times. The original

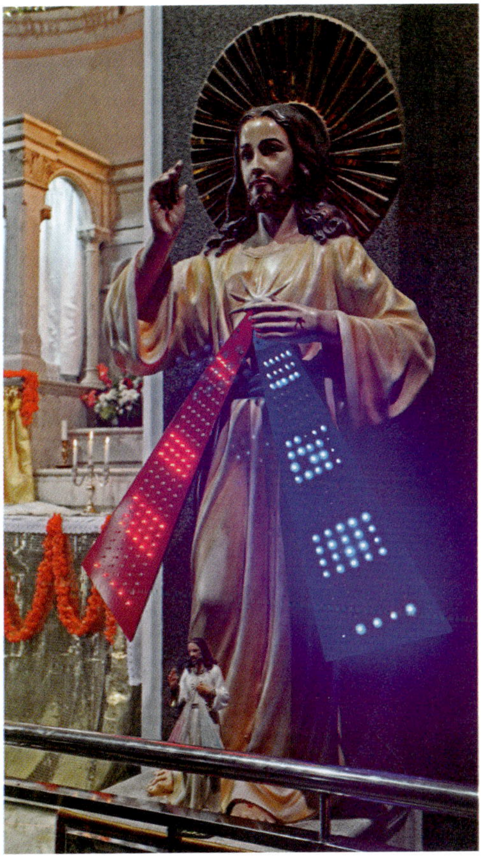

Christ's bleeding heart in neon lights

church was built by Father Chevalier who later became the first parish priest and later the Bishop of Mysore. Friar J.B. Servanton arrived in Bengaluru in 1898 and became the driving force behind the rebuilding of the church. On completion the parish had grown into 15,000 Catholics but it had taken Friar Servanton 20 years of fund raising to complete the church. In 1940 the church became the Cathedral of the Roman Catholic Archdiocese of Bangalore

Due to the exposed brick work the church's interior is rather sombre. There are numerous archways and brick columns with cream painted Corinthian capitals that support other archways. In the chancel decorative pilasters, again with Corinthian capitals sit between archways. A striking life-size figure of Jesus is central to the interior. Red and blue ribbons of flashing neon lights emanating from the Christ's body represent the 'bleeding heart of Jesus'. A red neon cross is on the wall behind the altar. Despite these dazzling effects the altar, the multiple domes, archways and brickwork manage to create a serious, somewhat archaic quality to the church's interior. Father Servanton stayed on in India and is buried in the church he devoted his life to.

Church of the Holy Trinity, 1852

Anglican

The British rule was 'one church one station' however when St. Mark's Church had become too small for the growing population so many protests were staged that the British changed their policy for Bengaluru and a second garrison church was built; the Holy Trinity Church. It could hold a larger congregation and could also cater to non-English speakers.

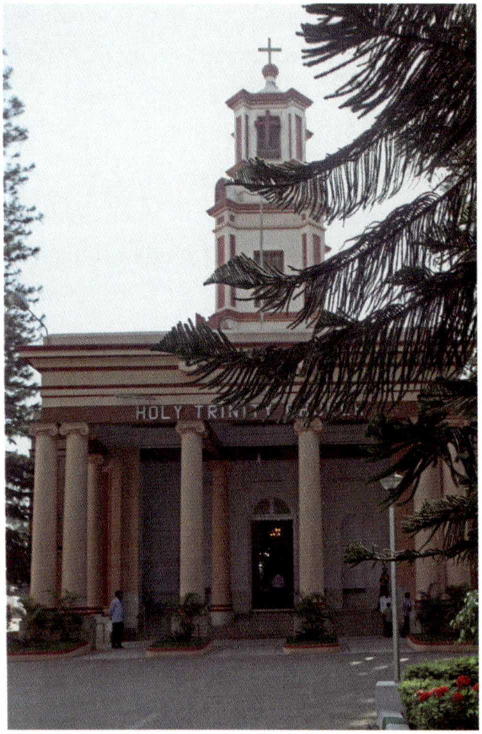

Church of the Holy Trinity

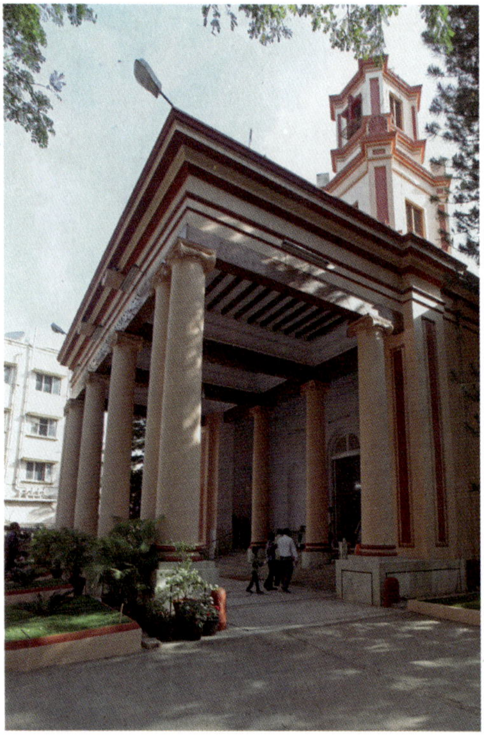

The grand portico

The foundation stone was laid in 1848 near the Military Parade grounds in the very centre of Trinity Circle, now one of Bengaluru's busiest areas. The church is surrounded by whirling traffic but in its little island of plane trees and English firs it is surprisingly peaceful and time seems to stand still.

The church was consecrated in 1852 and opened the same year. Its architecture is typical of a British colonial garrison church with rows of timber shuttered Roman arches similar to St. Mark's. The designer, Engineer Major Pears decided on a large portico, similar to St. Mark's but more weighty in appearance. The portico is supported by ten ionic columns. The cross above the elegant bell tower was a gift from Queen Victoria's Own West Kent Regiment in memory of their soldiers who died while stationed in Bengalaru between 1928 and 1932. The church bell was cast in 1847 by the famous Mears Foundry of London. Other monuments in the church

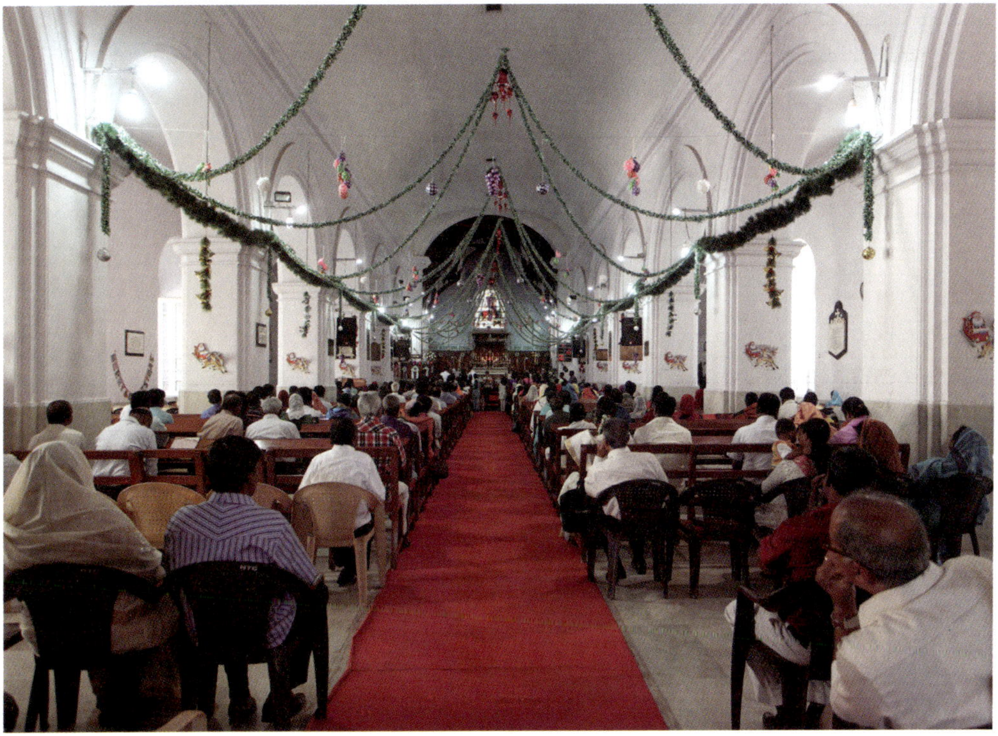

The interiors of Holy Trinity

were also made in London, including a beautiful statue of a young soldier in memory of Lieutenant Augustus Croft Dobree who died in 1867 at just twenty two.

Round archways lead to the altar, the focal point of which is the large stained glass window depicting the baptism of Christ. As a garrison church there are statues and stone tablets on the walls in memory of British officers who made their mark by dying in battle in India or other parts of South East Asia.

After India gained independence in 1947 the church experienced great changes. The large congregation of British soldiers and their families had left; in fact the church was left without a chaplain as there was no one to pay wages or contribute to the funds to maintain the church. Gradually a congregation of Indian Military and their families developed and three Indian chaplains were appointed; Reverend Easterraj, Reverend Pushpanathan and Reverend Joseph. Other changes followed including the Tamil language being used in services which meant remaining English parishioners slowly drifted away. Today the church remains the same and is well attended and maintained by mainly Indian Christians. It is a well-loved landmark in the city.

St. Andrew's Church, 1866

Anglican

The Scottish church of Bengaluru was completed in 1866 and was entirely Scottish with a congregation of Scottish soldiers and officers, their families and some civilians with a Scottish Presbyterian upbringing. It was often a transient congregation owing to regimental transfers and Scots returning home after their time stationed in India was over. The many plaques on the interior of the church are in memory of Scottish soldiers and others who either died during war or were important during their time.

The church has been witness to many lively Scottish events; Robbie Burns Nights, Scottish dancing, and St. Andrew's Day

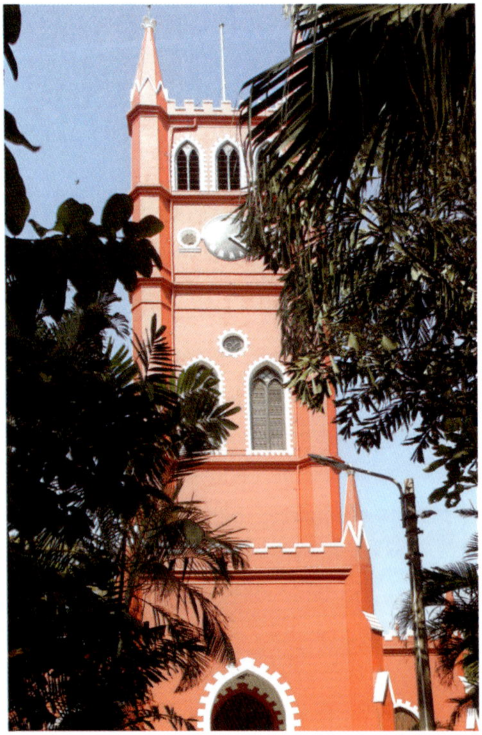

St. Andrew's Church

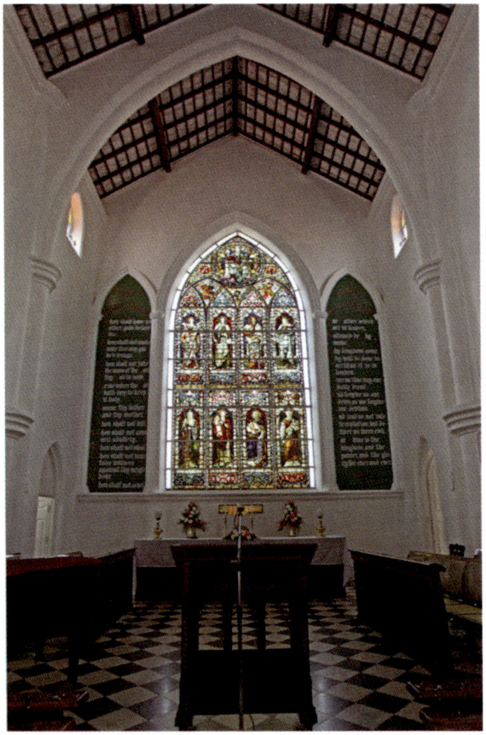

Beautiful stained glass window painted by Alex Ballantine

celebrations. During colonial times Scottish soldiers in kilts would march around the church to the sound of bagpipes every Sunday, a scene which must have fascinated local children. Once inside they would store their weapons and take the central pews 'with military bearing'. The side pews were often used by Indians who could speak English and who were eager to worship in the church. They received a warm welcome and soon became part of the churches community.

Named after Scotland's patron saint, Saint Andrews is Gothic in style and painted a bright red with contrasting white trim. It is a striking building with a twenty-seven-metre-high tower embedded with a chiming clock on each side so that the time can be seen from every aspect far and wide.

Behind the altar is a beautiful stained glass window commemorating the diamond jubilee of Queen Victoria in 1897 painted by master glass artist Alex Ballantine. Gothic arches define the side aisles otherwise the interior is relatively simple in keeping with most Presbyterian churches. In the extensive garden are over thirty one species of trees including the Ashoka and the Nile Tulip.

Despite the large Scottish presence in India most Scots began returning home after independence. Church numbers improved in the 1960s when the ancient Dravidian language, Kannada was introduced and services in both languages began. St. Andrew's joined the Church of South India in 1959 and the first Indian Minister of St. Andrews Reverend G. Hari was appointed in 1969. Over the years St. Andrews has evolved from a traditional Scottish church into a modern Indian version while managing to preserve the original denomination and many of the traditions.

All Saints Church, 1870

Anglican

In Richmond Town is the charming All Saints Church that harks back to colonial times. It seems more suitable to an English country village. However here it sits in India in the middle of a little wood surrounded by a flower garden. The church is built of stone with a steeply pitched double-gabled roof. On each side of the entrance porch is a lancet window above which is a large rose window. A small church bell hangs at a side entrance to the garden beyond which can be seen the length of the church and the dormer windows.

The founder of the church and founder of Bishop Cotton's School was Reverend Samuel Thomas Pettigrew who was born in London in 1827, a Cambridge graduate and ordained in 1848. He loved nature and his interests included botany, entomology (the study of insects) and church building. The

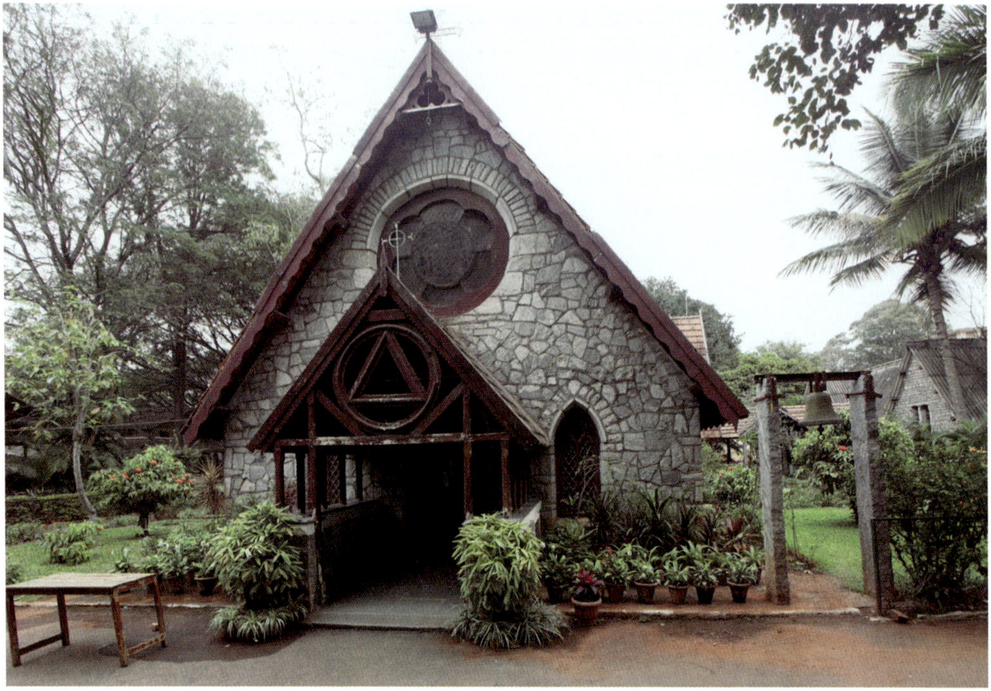

ABOVE: *Front view of All Saint's Church*

FACING PAGE TOP: *Sprawling grounds outside All Saint's Church*

FACING PAGE BELOW: *Side view of the church*

reverend designed the gardens around All Saints church. He was also an author who anonymously wrote *Episodes in the Life of an Indian Chaplain*. The designer was the famous Robert Fellowes Chisholm, the consulting architect for the Madras Government.

The foundation stone was laid in 1869 though not without a number of financial obstacles. In Reverend Pettigrew's notes; '*A few hundred rupees had been collected and placed in a bank, but all interest seemed to have died out*'. The building came to a standstill when Reverend Pettigrew worked in the Nilgiri Mountains for two years. His shock on returning to Bengalaru and seeing the church had not progressed instigated the buildings completion. The foundation stone was finally laid in 1869 and the church was consecrated in 1870.

The altar, pulpit, font, and altar cross were donations and the rose window was presented from the principal of Cooper's Hill College in memory of a much loved child.

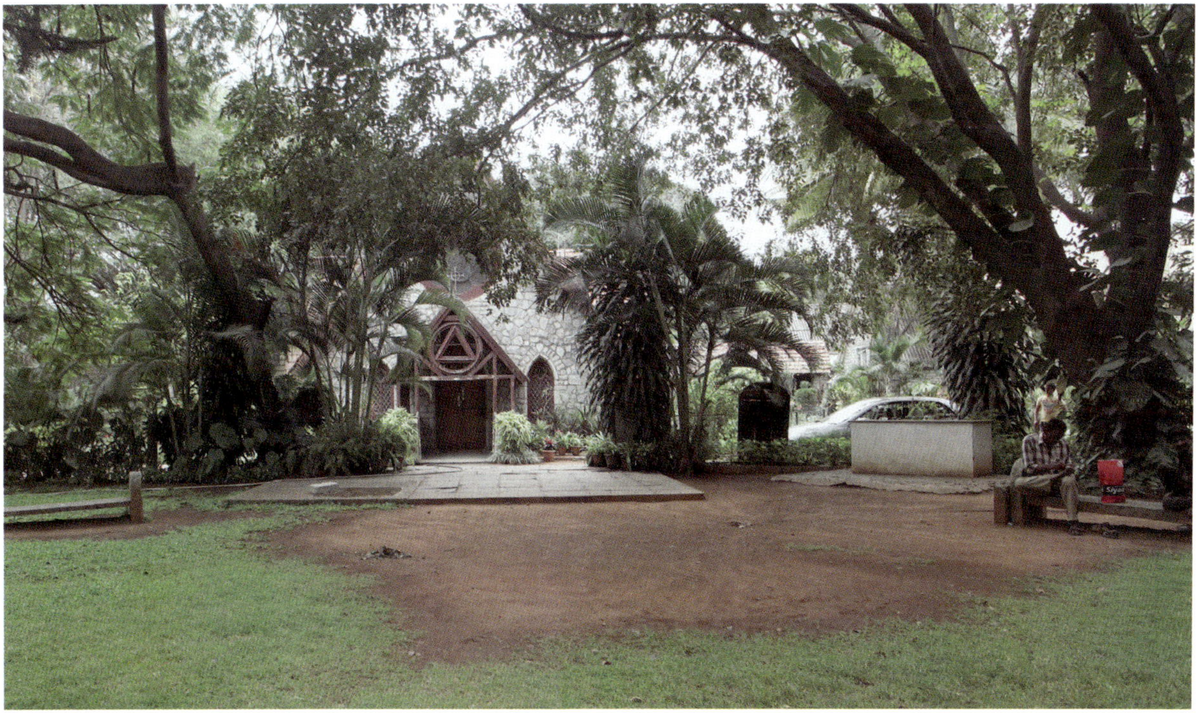

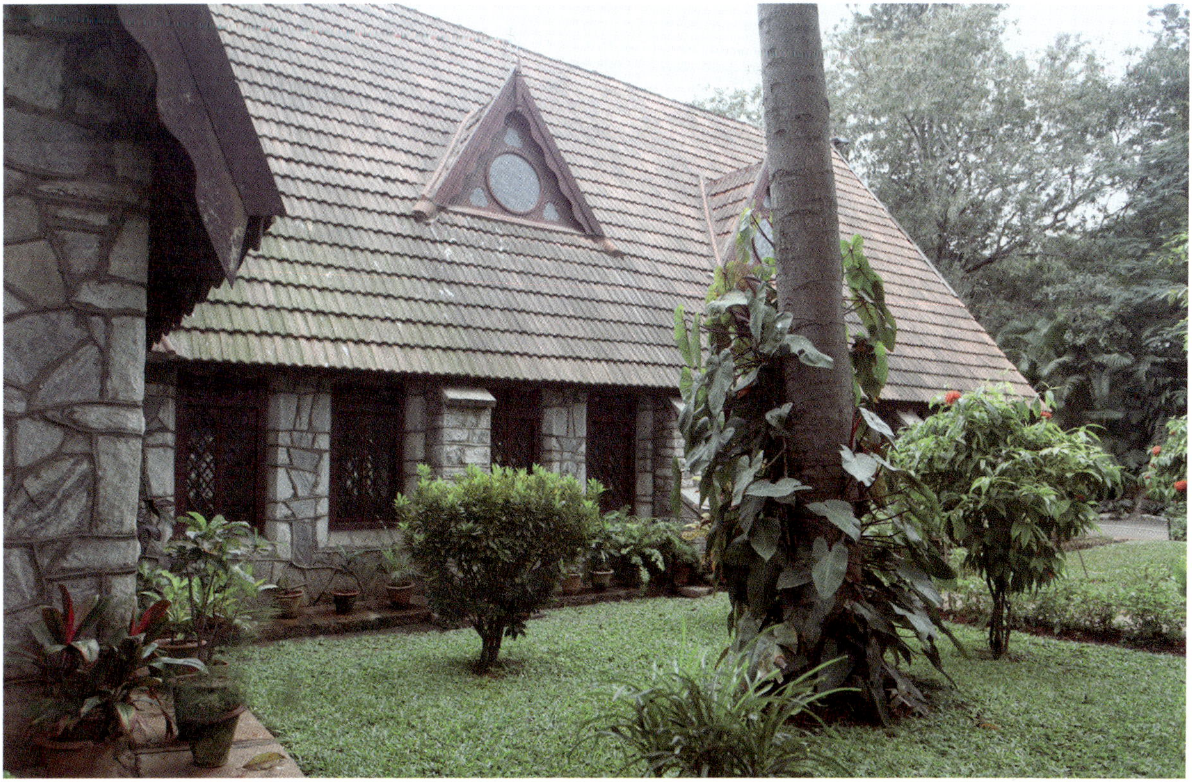

The Royal College of Engineering began at Cooper's Hill in 1872 to train civil engineers for the Indian Public Works Department. It is this window that lets afternoon sun enter the nave of the church with its dark wood pews and altar above which is a lovely trio of stained glass windows.

During British rule Richmond Town was populated by Anglo Indians, the British who lived in India and who had built bungalows around the church and in Richmond Town. Muslim merchants from Persia and Parsis were also part of the population. These colonial bungalows were set in large blocks of land, sometimes with a tennis court. They were indeed lovely houses and some of these well maintained bungalows can still be found today.

St. Mary's Basilica, 1892

Roman Catholic

St. Mary's Basilica had humble beginnings as a simple thatched hut built by Christians from Tamil Nadu who settled in the area in the 17th century. At the turn of the 18th century the famous Abbe Jean-Antoine Dubois arrived from France and replaced the hut with a small chapel and housing for priests. Dubois is renowned for re-establishing the Catholic religion in and around Bengaluru and introducing vaccination in India, one of the first to do so. He also wrote the well-known book *Hindu Manners, Customs and Ceremonies*.

The basilica plan of St. Mary's was later extended into a cruciform shape by Friar Andreas, an Indian priest from Puducherry. During communal riots in 1832 the building was pillaged and destroyed and the army was called in to protect the settlement for months.

Much has changed over the centuries. The building of the impressive Neo-Gothic church we see today began in 1875, completed in 1882 and consecrated the same year. The building is credited to Friar L. E. Kleiner who later became the Bishop of Mysore. It is a large church but appears confined due to its lack of outdoor space and its location within the grounds of Russell Market, one of Bengaluru's busiest areas. The car park between the covered fruit and vegetable market and the church is congested with traffic and a myriad of stalls selling everything imaginable. At the gates of the church are stalls selling offerings of flower and religious souvenirs both Christian and Hindu. This muddle of an Indian market has to be negotiated before getting to the iron gates of the church after which the church soars above.

An enormous statue of Mary, a copy of the Pieta by Michelangelo, holding a dying

FACING PAGE: *St. Mary's Basilica*

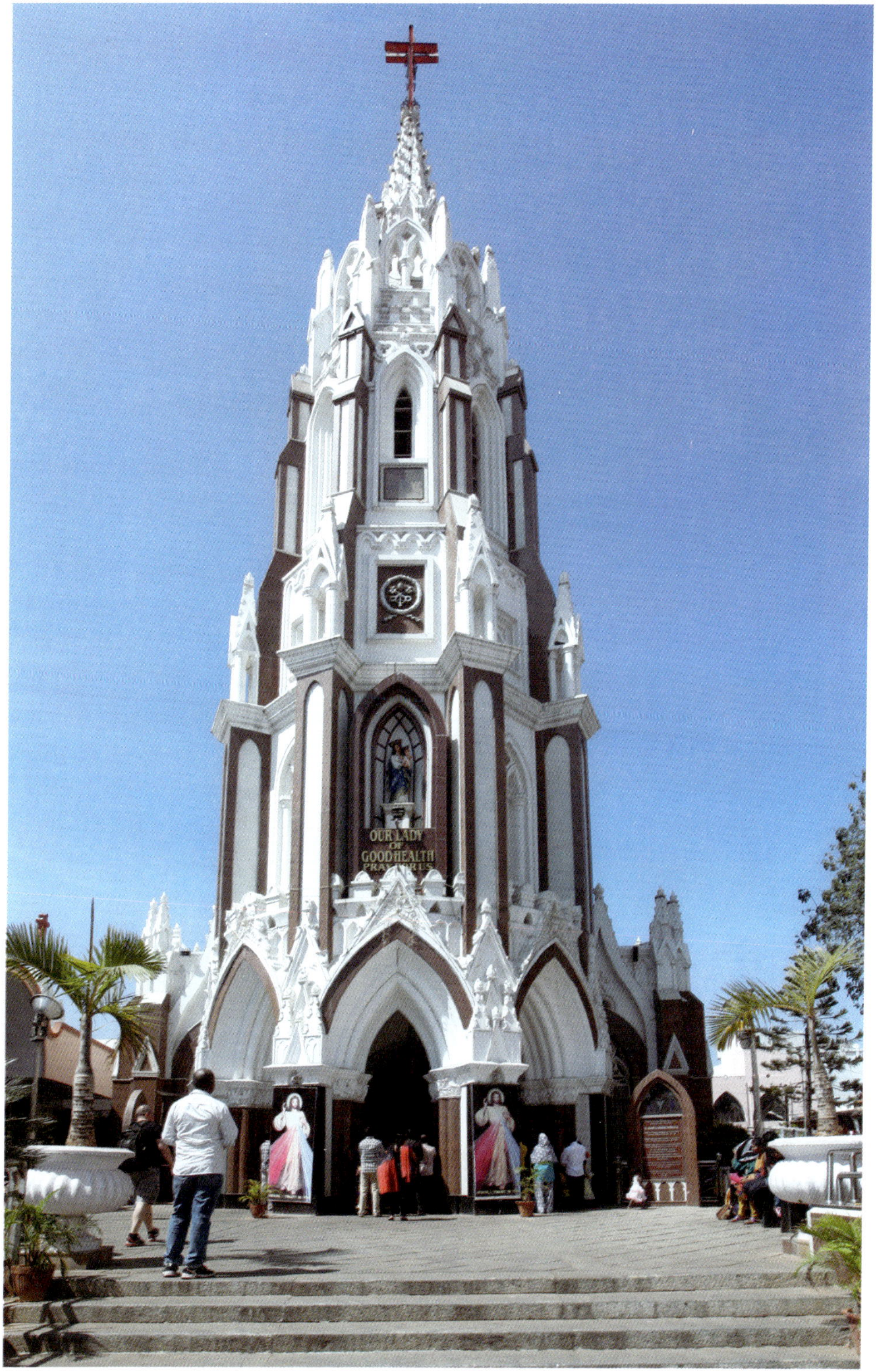
OUR LADY
OF
GOOD HEALTH

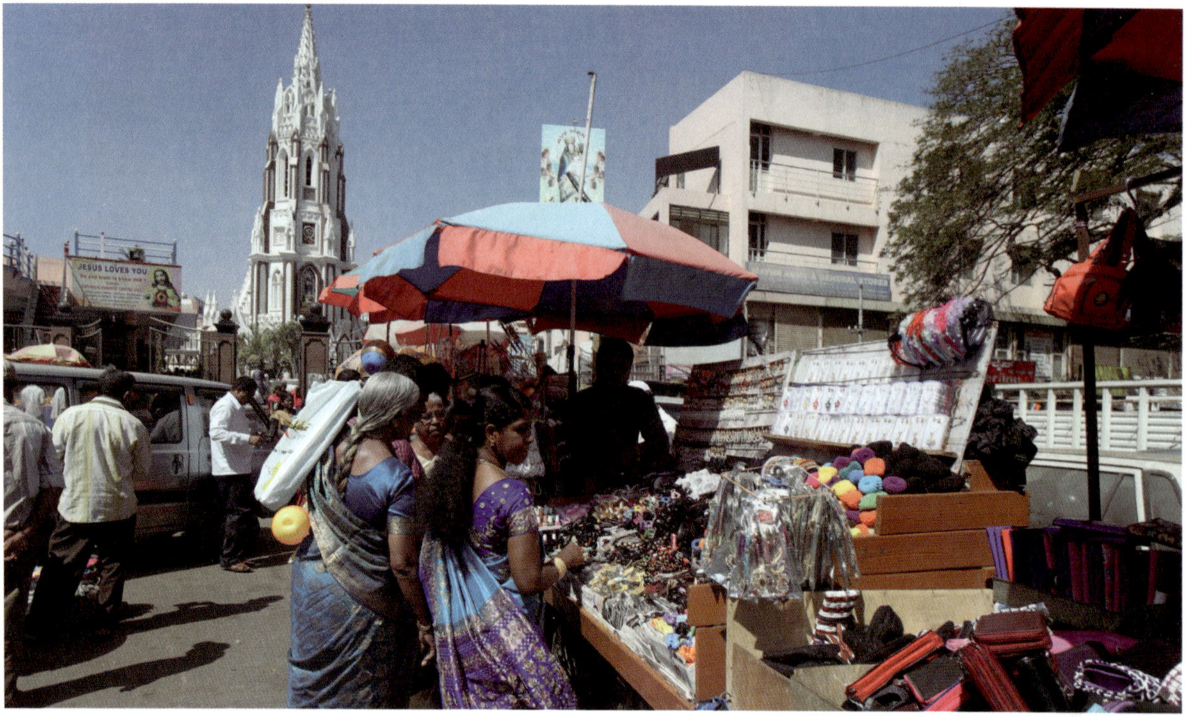
JESUS LOVES YOU

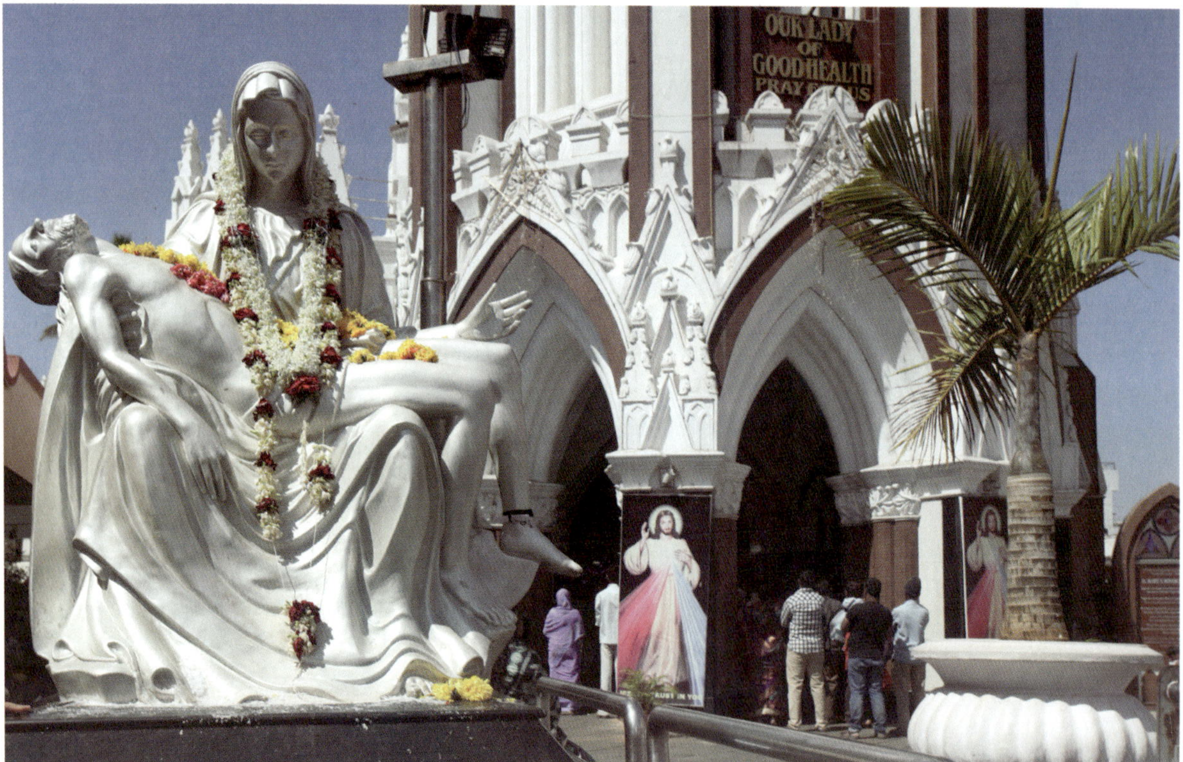
OUR LADY
OF
GOODHEALTH

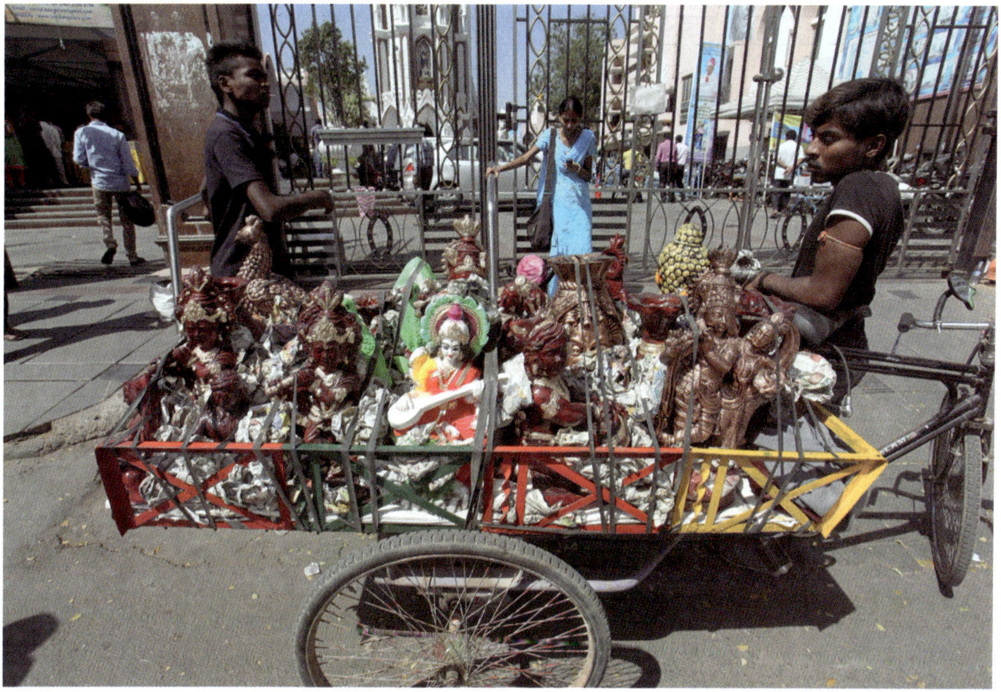

Above: *Hindu gods for sale at the gates of St. Mary's*

Facing page top: *Russell Market with St. Mary's spire in the background*

Facing page below: *The replica of Michelangelo's Pieta*

Jesus in her arms is covered with necklaces of fresh saffron coloured marigolds. Close to the entrance of the church is a six foot high statue of Mary holding the Baby Jesus. It is housed in a shrine and Mary is dressed in an Indian sari, which is changed every day. This statue is considered to be wondrous and the object of much worship. When the church was built the statue was to be installed inside the church but all efforts failed and the statue couldn't be moved, thought to be a sign of Mary's miraculous power.

The church tower rises to a substantial cross above. It is an imposing sight. Behind is the 23-metre-long nave with many stained glass windows all brought from Paris. During World War II they were removed for safety but finally re-installed in 1947, the year of India's independence. Beautifully ornate Corinthian columns support the arches of the church.

In 1973 the church was raised to the status of a minor basilica through an edict issued by Pope Paul VI. It was officially announced in 1974 to much celebration. Each September

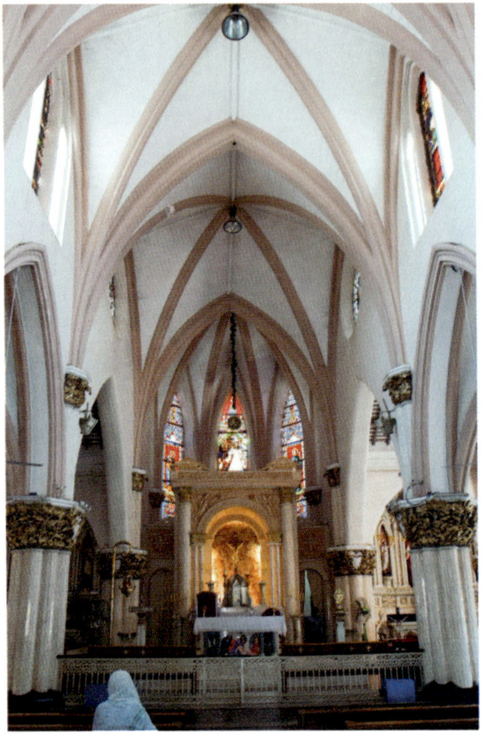

The interior of St. Mary's Church

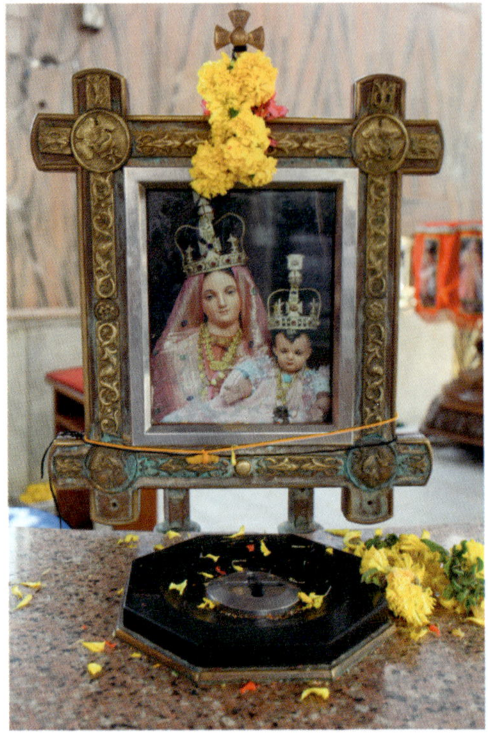

St. Mary with floral offerings

the holy flag is hoisted to announce the beginning of the ten day feast of the birth of Mary. Thousands of worshippers, Christians, Hindus and Muslims all dressed in saffron coloured clothes come from far and wide for the celebrations which come to a close only when a huge decorated chariot holding a huge statue of Mary dressed in a beautiful gold sari is carried through the streets. Like all such celebrations in India it is a truly grand spectacle.

The Joshua Hudson Memorial Church, 1904

Kannada Protestant

This Gothic style stone church with its pretty English garden and row of Ashoka trees is a landmark in the heart of Bengaluru. It is dedicated to British born Reverend Josiah Hudson who arrived in India in 1865 and stayed for thirty two years. He is remembered for his services to the church and his encouragement of the Kannada language

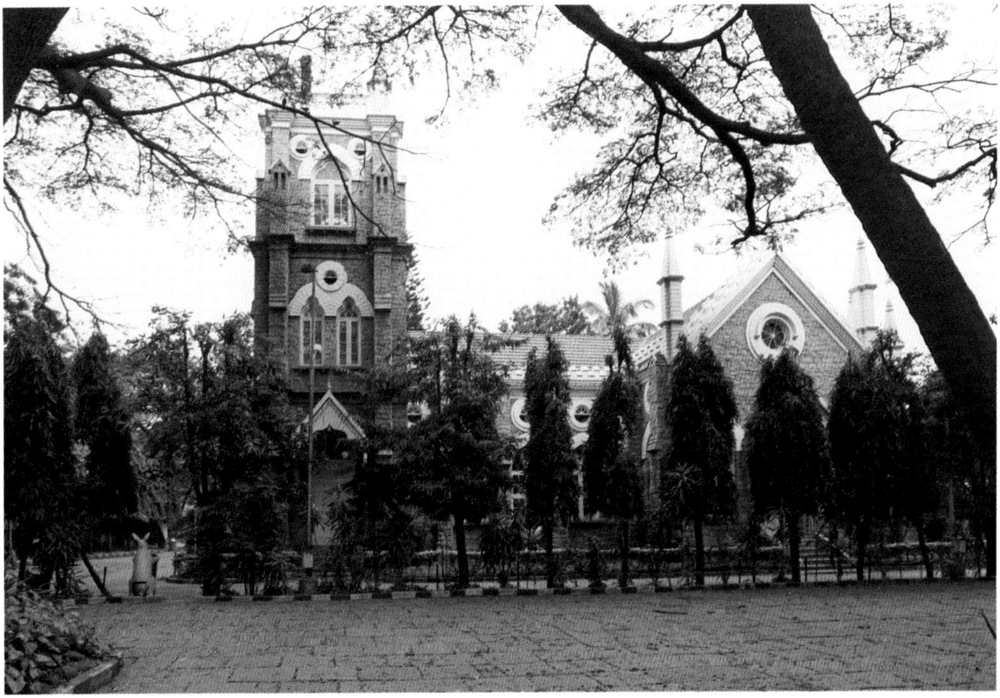

The Joshua Hudson Memorial Church

by founding a number of Kannada schools. Kannada is the official language of the state of Karnataka.

Like so many of Bengalaru's churches the Hudson Memorial church is full of history, since colonial times. It was originally called the Wesleyan Mission Canarese Chapel and was located in Nagarathpet. It was moved to its present location in 1904.

Designed by architect J.H. Stephan the building has nine facades with an entrance at each so that the altar seems to face the congregation from all positions. The large church can accommodate 2500 people and there are no internal columns to obscure their view. The architect donated the circular stained glass window over the main entrance and the pulpit and communion table were carved from teak. Many parts of the churches interior were donations including the marble floor of the chancel, the organ, the church bell, hymn books and so on. In those early days the land around the church consisted of fields and ponds.

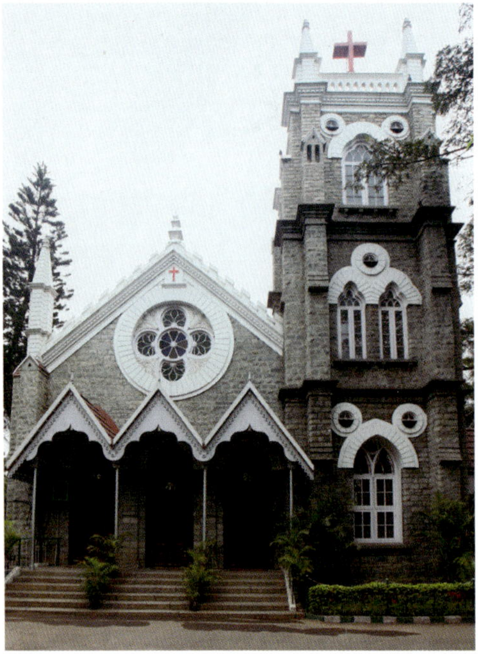

The round stained glass window, the tower and three 'monkey tops'

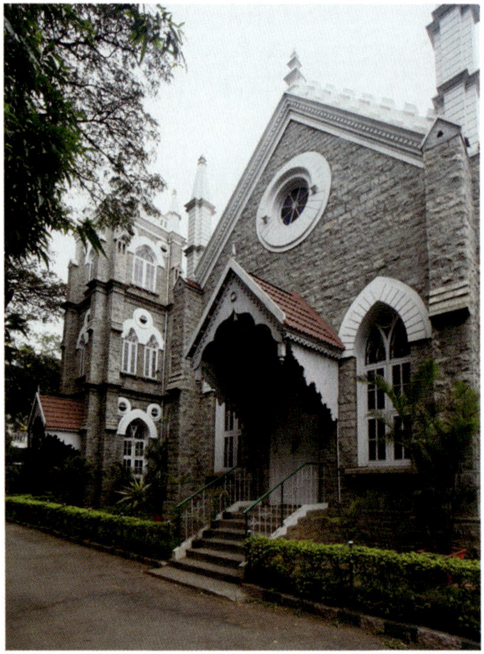

Side view of the stone church

The rise of this Gothic styled church must have been striking.

Typical of Gothic architecture are the church tower and the lancet windows. The little pointed canopies over the windows and doors are a Gothic feature but mainly characteristic of Bengaluru's architecture. They are called 'monkey tops' and can be found throughout the city particularly on remaining colonial bungalows. In India the monkey top is unique to Bengaluru.

September 1904 was a memorable day in the history of the church. At 4 pm Josiah Hudson's daughter dedicated the church for worship to all Christians in the name of her late father. A dedication service was carried out in the Kannada language to 600 people.

The Infant Jesus Church and Shrine, 1971

Catholic

This striking blue and white church is in Viveknagar, approximately six kilometres from central Bengaluru. It is the largest church in Karnataka and a place of pilgrimage as it commemorates the famous Infant of

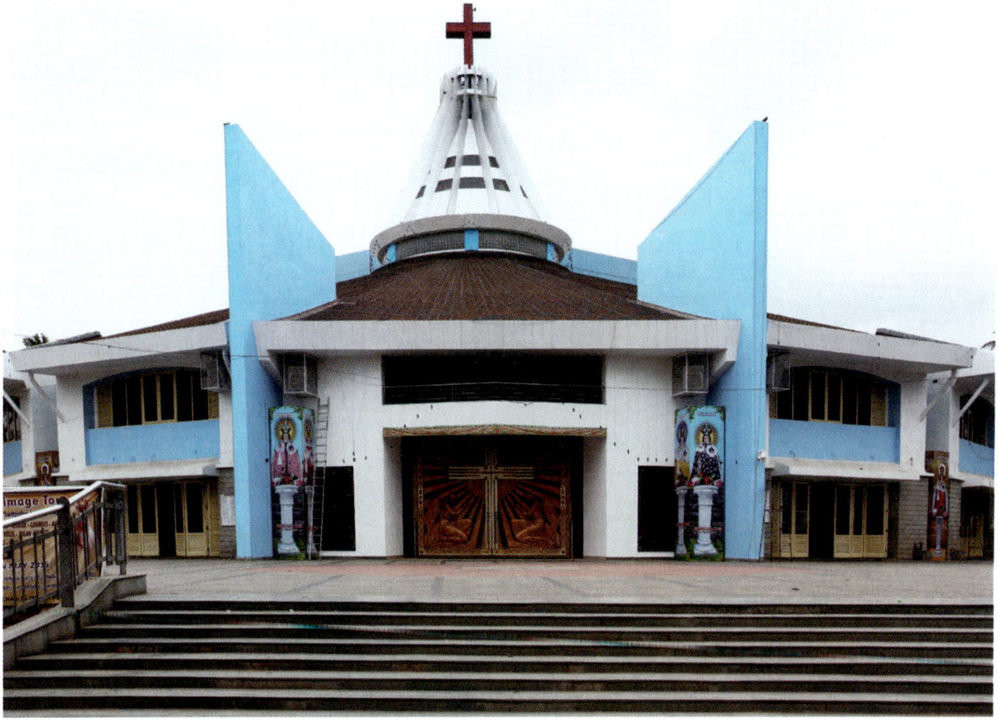

The Infant Jesus Church

Prague. It was designed by the architectural firm K. Thomas and Associates in Bengaluru. Though it is a modern construction it also references Hindu temple designs and incorporates elements that suit India's climate such as the overhanging roof on both levels of the structure.

There are nine entrances around the church and the space inside is fan shaped, accommodating 2,500 worshippers, all of whom feel that the altar is facing them. There is an enormous 6 x 9 metre mural of the nativity scene, a copy of the original in the Nativity Church in Jerusalem. The foundation of the Church was laid in 1969 by the then Archbishop of Bangalore Reverend Duraisamy Simon Lourdusamy and was opened in 1971.

The original statue of the Infant of Prague is a 16th century Spanish wax-coated wooden figure of the Child Jesus holding a globe topped with a cross, a symbol from

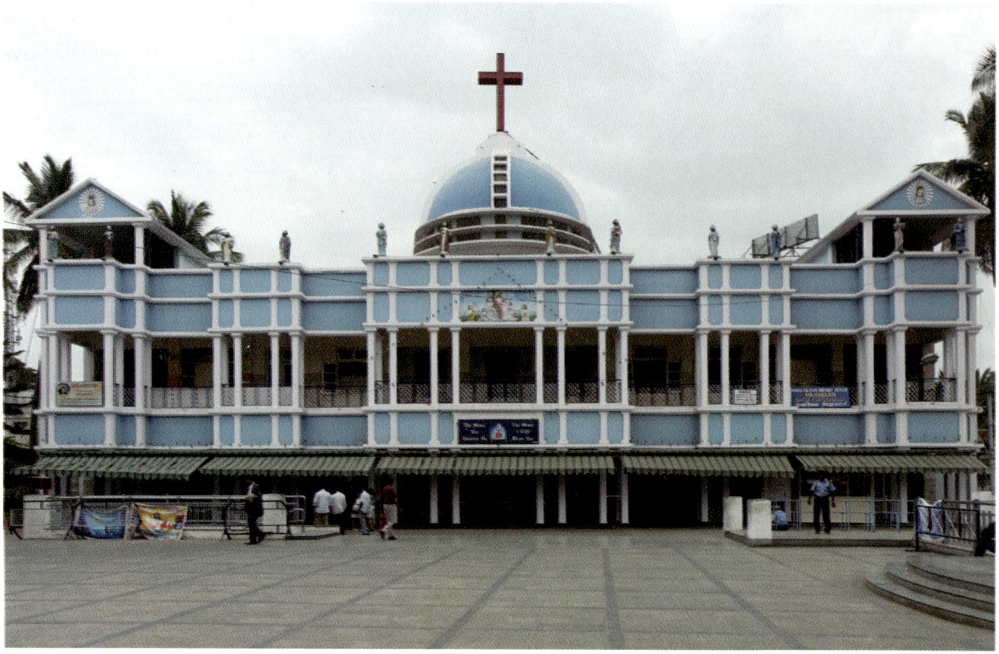

The enormous shrine to the Infant Jesus

the Middle Ages representing the dominion of Christianity over the world. It is installed in the Church of Our Lady Victorious in Prague, in the Czech Republic and was donated to the church in 1628. The Infant's right hand is raised with the palm out, giving a blessing and He wears a gold crown studded with jewels and magnificent clothes including a special robe for each part of the ecclesiastical year. It is thought to have miraculous healing powers and to have protected the city of Prague against plague and destruction during war.

A new building adjacent to the church was built in 2005 which is used as a shrine to the Infant Jesus. The church, the additional building and the large forecourt are big enough to welcome up to 10,000 people of all religions who flock to the church each year on January 14th, the annual feast day of the church. Behind the church is a metal grid where people have tied locks and strips of cloth as a way to leave a prayer or ask for a miracle. Small statues are placed about too, perhaps to give thanks that prayers were answered.

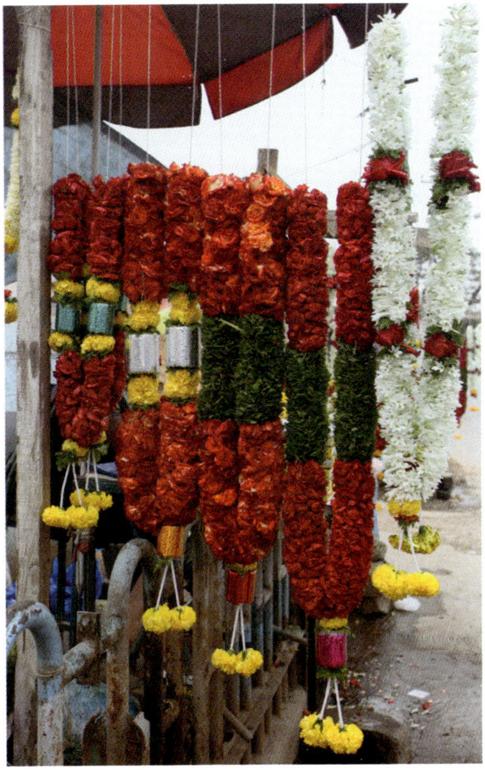

A small street stall sells offerings for the Infant Jesus

Kolkata: A City Above Pretence

By the late 18th century Kolkata had surpassed Chennai and become the site of the East India Company's headquarters. As the centre of British India the city began to resemble a grand European capital and every new building made it clear that the British intended to stay. Kolkata became known as the 'Jewel of the East' and the 'City of Palaces.'

As the capital of West Bengal it is the most important city on India's east coast. It displays all the characteristics of Victorian England in its architecture, however crumbling the old colonial era buildings may be. It has created its own unique identity. Kolkata's story is as fascinating as the city itself.

In 1685 Job Charnock, an agent of the British East India Company had set up a factory in Bengal but after a falling out with the Mughal ruler in 1690 he was forced to move the trading post down the Hooghly river to settle at a village called Sutanuti or 'thread market.' This was one of three villages (the other two were Gobindapur and Kolikata) which would later grow into the city of Kolkata.

A fort was completed in 1696 and named after King William III of England. Wherever there was a British fort in India there would be a church and so the first English church in Kolkata was St. Anne's built in 1704 and situated near the main gateway of Fort William.

H.E. Busteed's *Echoes of Old Calcutta* published in 1908 describes a visit to St. Anne's on a typical Sunday in the early 18th century;

> 'I have been at church in my new palanquin (the mode of genteel conveyance) where all ladies are approached by sanction

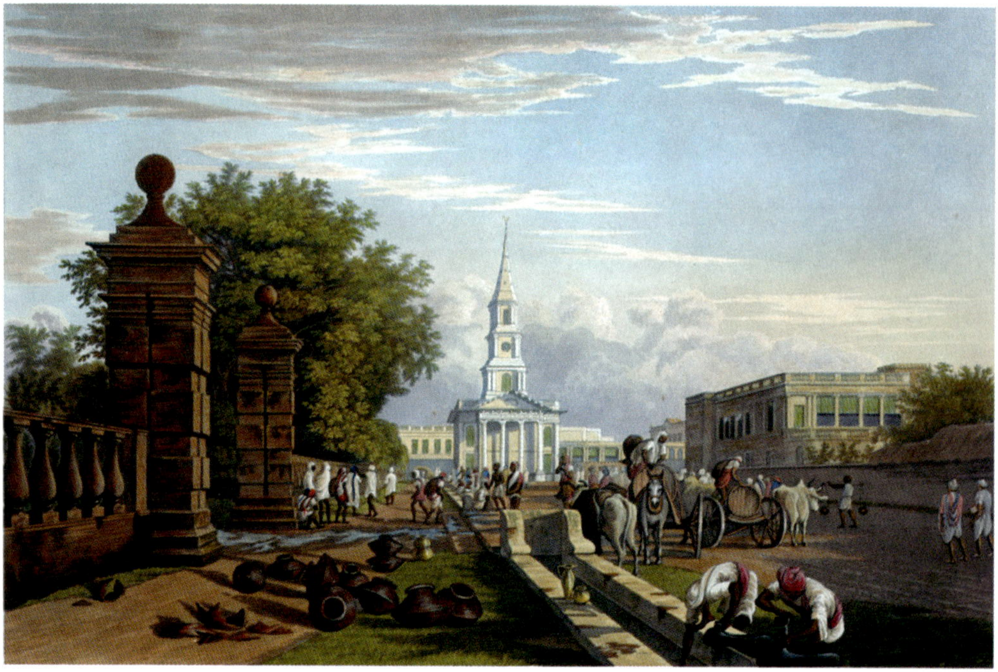

'View of the Scotch Church from the Gates of Tank Square,' aquatint by James Baillie Fraser, 1826 (Courtesy: Thesis by Amanda Sciampacone, 2008)

> of ancient custom by all gentlemen indiscriminately, known or unknown, with offers of their hands to conduct them to their seat. Accordingly those gentlemen who wish to charge their condition (which between ourselves are chiefly old fellows) on hearing of a ship's arrival make a point of repairing to this holy dome and eager tend their services to the fair strangers'.

Regrettably St. Anne's no longer exists. In 1756 the twenty-three-year-old ruler of Bengal, Siraj-ud-Daulah heard that Fort William's fortifications were being increased without his permission, he was enraged. Aware of Britain's global colonial ambitions the Nawab resented their presence in Bengal. Therefore when the British ignored his request to stop militarising their 'trading post', Siraj-ud-Daulah sent his forces from Murshidabad to attack Kolkata and capture the fort. In the process St. Anne's was completely destroyed.

It was during the siege that British captives were imprisoned in a small cell the

British soldiers had named 'the Black Hole'. There was much confusion and the prisoners were forgotten and left in the Black Hole overnight. Many died from lack of ventilation and water. Despite varying accounts of what happened it was a great tragedy for the victims and resulted in the city of Kolkata becoming synonymous with the 'Black Hole' incident ever since.

Retaliation came in the guise of Lieutenant Colonel Robert Clive, 'Clive of India' to the British, who was sent from Chennai to recapture the fort and the city which the Nawab had renamed Alinagar. In June 1757 in a small village between Kolkata and Murshidabad 2,800 soldiers of the East India Company under Robert Clive attacked 50,000 Bengalis and allies under Siraj-ud-Daulah at the Battle of Plassey. Though more a skirmish than a battle the Nawab's army had no chance of winning as Siraj-ud-Daulah's army chief Mir Jafar had secretly aligned himself with Clive, bribing the Nawab's men to side with the British during the battle. The Nawab was defeated. Later Jawaharlal Nehru wrote that Clive had won the battle 'by promoting treason and forgery.'

The Battle of Plassey was a turning point for Kolkata as it confirmed the East India Company's presence in Bengal and marked the beginning of the Company's rule in India. It also foreshadowed the birth of the British Raj even though direct control by the British Government would not take place until 1858. It bears some thought about the outcome if Siraj-ud-Daulah's enormous army had remained loyal.

The traitor Mir Jafar had his former ruler tortured and killed in Murshidabad where his corpse was paraded through the streets on an elephant. Mir Jafar then became the Nawab of Bengal, Orissa and Bihar, a puppet ruler of the British and Robert Clive was given a peerage, Baron Clive of Plassey.

With the British triumph and their trading success, Kolkata and its people began to rise. Hindu moneylenders, merchants, tradesmen, boatmen and even courtesans realised they could become rich by serving the increasing number of British, mainly Scotsmen, who arrived to facilitate the running of the Company. It was a time of great confidence. Europeans made huge fortunes and Indian merchants aspired to be like them. By 1772 Kolkata became the capital of British India and a new Fort William was completed. Later the Neo-Gothic St. Peters church was built inside the fort. Today it is used as a library for the Eastern Command of the Indian Army. Yet by the late 19th century Kolkata began to brew with anti-British defiance. The British became fearful of another uprising similar to the Mutiny of 1857 when Hindus and Muslims fought side by side against the British. In response the Viceroy of India Lord Curzon partitioned Bengal in 1905 to 'ease administration.' The eastern areas of Bengal were separated from the rest of the state creating two provinces; simply put, West Bengal and East Bengal. West Bengal was predominantly Hindu while the eastern part was mainly Muslim. The result was more unrest; in fact almost the entire state of West Bengal rose in protest and joined or supported the Swadeshi Movement that boycotted foreign goods and encouraged domestic production with a view towards independence. Kolkata was now the centre of the national movement of independence. Irrespective the British continued their 'divide and rule' policy, provoking a separate consciousness between Hindus and Muslims.

In 1911 Delhi staged a spectacular *durbar* to celebrate the coronation of King George V and Queen Mary, the Emperor and Empress of India. An empty plain was covered in 40 square kilometres of canvas tents which housed 300,000 dignitaries including the princes of different states whose tents were ornate, even sumptuous. As many as 750,000 people swarmed into the city which according to architectural historian Robert Irving the population of Delhi at that time was a little over 400,000. The durbar cost a spectacular one million pounds, the equivalent of 600 million today. India paid.

At the very end of the durbar King George made a surprise announcement that Kolkata, the seat of the Government of India would be transferred to Delhi. This well- kept secret was a shock to both cities but for Kolkata it was the beginning of the end. No longer was it the capital. Business people rejected the city and moved to Delhi. Trade diminished and jobs were lost. Revolutionary activity increased and the British tried to placate Kolkata by reunifying east and west Bengal which only inflamed anti-colonial sentiments further. In 1939 the British Viceroy Lord Linlithgow declared India would take part in World War II without consulting the newly elected India Congress leaders. By 1946 the Indian independence movement against the British began spreading across India accompanied by widespread violence. India had reached a crucial stage.

On the brink of midnight, on August 15th 1947 India gained independence from British rule, 'a fateful moment' as Jawaharlal Nehru described it in his famous independence speech. The celebrations and joy that ensued were short lived as India was plunged into the nightmare that was Partition. The country was divided into two separate states, India and Pakistan, a disastrous last minute decision over how independence would transpire and how quickly the British could leave. Few really understood the ramifications of Partition and the price India would pay for freedom.

People who were profoundly attached to their religious identity and their land were traumatised, reacting with fear and violence. The mass displacement was the largest migration of people in recorded history, all desperate to be on the right side of the lines Britain had hastily drawn up with no thought to religious or cultural communities. This triggered a rift between Muslims and Hindus and an estimated two million people died and 17 million were displaced. By creating separate electorates on the lead-up to the vote on Partition the British shrewdly separated the voting process by preventing a united Muslim/Hindu nationalist movement vote that would have overthrown the British and prevented the tragedy that was Partition.

The greatest migrations were in the Punjab in the west and Bengal in the east. Millions of Hindus travelled mostly on foot from what was then East Pakistan to Kolkata and Muslims travelled to the new state of Pakistan. As Britain was unwilling to use its army to maintain law and order chaos and violence ensued. Women in particular were targeted. Over the course of time East Pakistan became independent from Pakistan after a war with India in 1971. This partition was also intensely violent. The result was the birth of a new nation, Bangladesh and another mass of people looking towards Kolkata, a city that had stagnated post-independence and was already bursting at the seams with the poor and the displaced.

Christianity left less of a mark in Kolkata than in India's south but Kolkata's churches are still being used long after the end of British rule. The three most historically important Anglican churches are St. John's church, St. James' church and St. Paul's Cathedral. Inside their doors every marble statue, wall plaque, stained glass and oil painting is a record of the church's history and the people who worshipped there. Their dark wooden pews with rattan seats are shiny from use and cleaning wax. Lancet shaped stained glass filters rays of light showing wear and tear or a missing piece of plaster. Wooden shutters almost keep the heat at bay and outside a tropical garden complete with palms and perhaps a lone neem tree can be seen.

The Church of the Holy Nazareth, 1724, 'Armenian Church'

Armenian Orthodox

Not British but Armenian, the oldest church in Kolkata and also one of the most beautiful. The Church of the Holy Nazareth dates from 1724 and is situated in north Kolkata, an area known for its Armenian and the Portuguese communities in early times. Today the few

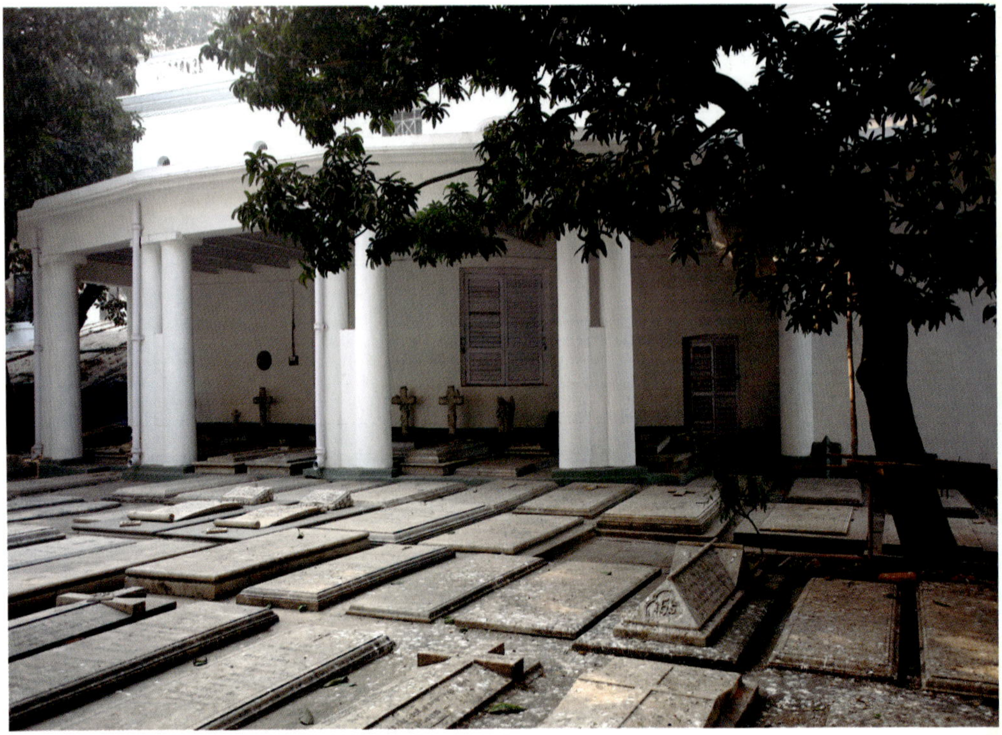

Above: *Entrance to the Church of the Holy Nazareth through the gravestones*

Facing page top: *Looking towards the altar*

Facing page below: *Looking from the altar to the entrance, the curved choir gallery above*

Armenians left in Kolkata prefer to live in the more salubrious areas of south Kolkata.

The exact date of the Armenians arrival in Kolkata is unknown but they were among the first traders, following Job Charnock possibly at the end of the 17th century. They first came to India to escape religious persecution from the Turks and later the Persians. In due course they became well-respected traders in spices, silk and precious stones. They were a thriving vibrant community who traded astutely with both the Indians and the British during the 18th century.

The church is located in a small lane in the chaotic area of Burrabazar. It is hard to locate in the hustle and bustle of hawkers and stalls and it is equally difficult to photograph with just a glimpse of the interesting tower now and then. Once inside the church wall it is a surprising oasis of peace. The original 1707 church was built in wood but after a

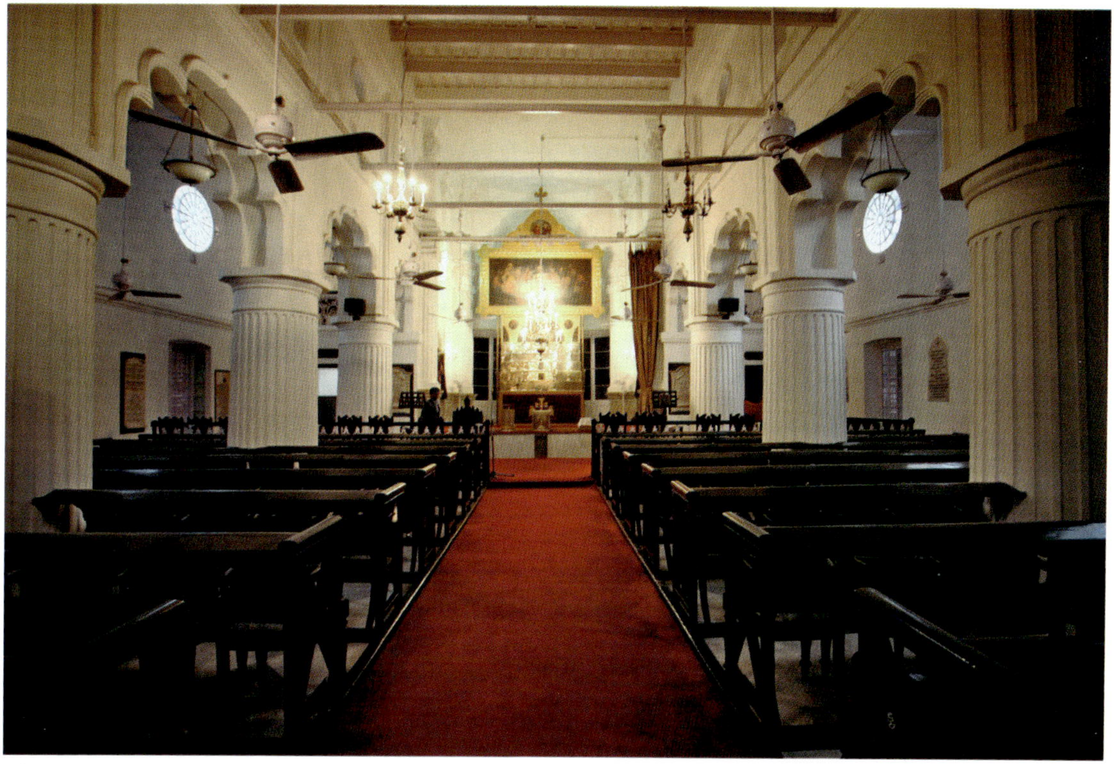

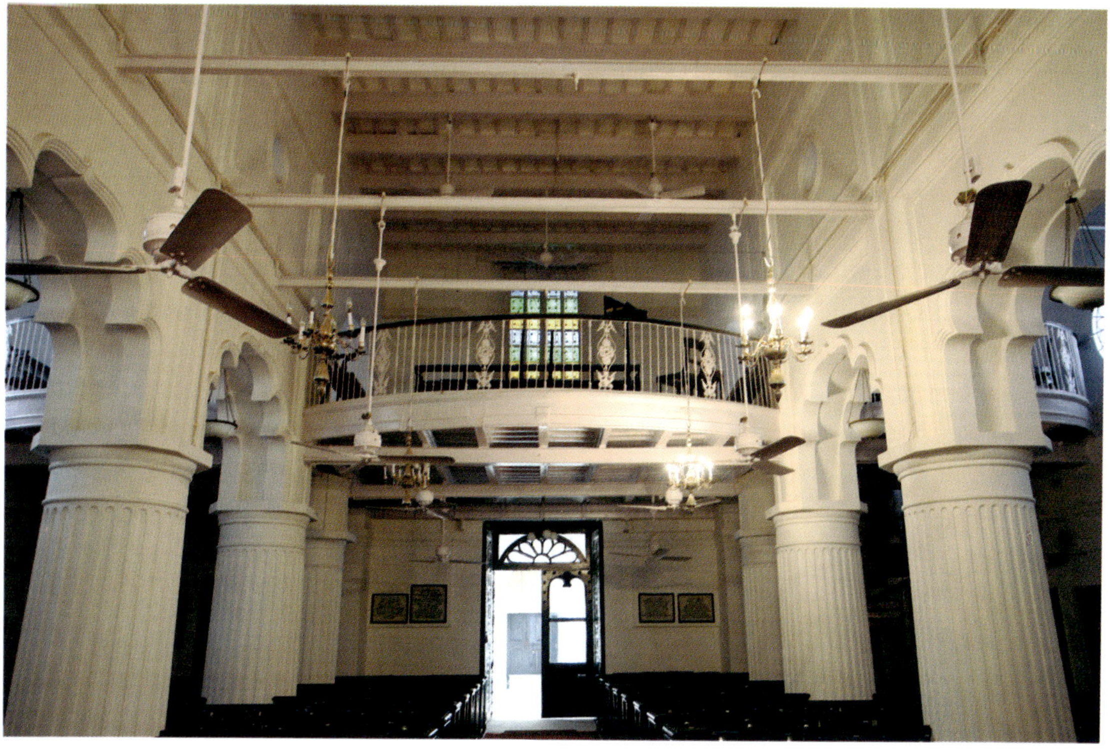

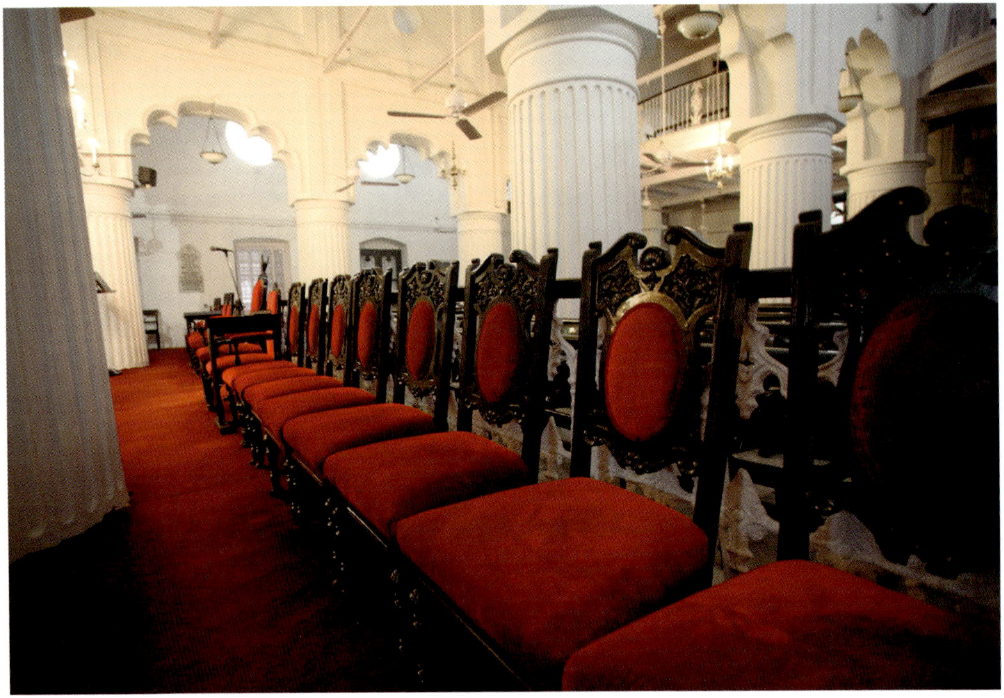

The chairs for church officials

fire today's church was built in 1724, some 60 years before St. Johns was built. An entrance is reached by pathways between tomb stones; the most well-known is that of an Armenian woman, Rezabeebeh, dated 1630. Some mystery surrounds the grave as it is not written in Cyrillic but in English, and if the date is correct it is the oldest grave in Kolkata. Or perhaps the date is a mistake and the grave was installed after the original church was built in 1707. It remains a mystery.

The interior of the church is elegant with whitewashed walls and two rows of Islamic styled arches between enormous columns which form three aisles. At the altar are three paintings by English artist A.E.Harris; 'The Holy Trinity', 'The Last Supper' and 'The Enshrouding of Our Lord'. Twelve ascending candlesticks signify the twelve apostles. Rows of fine wooden chairs with rattan seats fill the church and a row of grand high backed chairs with red velvet seats are reserved for church officials.

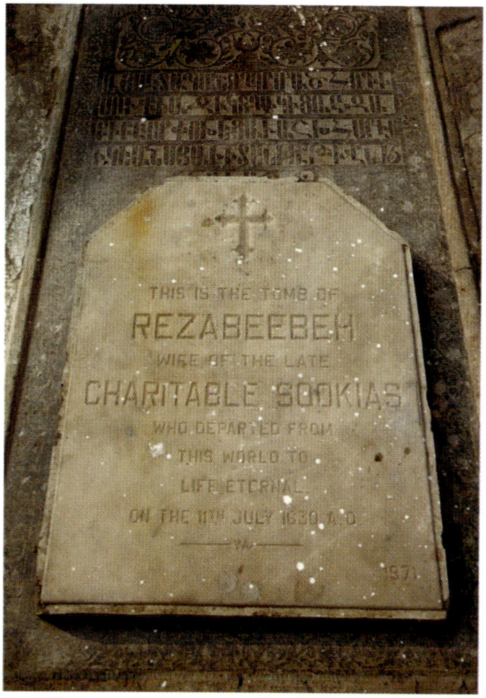

The gravestone of Rezabeebeh

Three Armenians were responsible for building and decorating the church; the architect Levon Ghevond, the builder Aga Nazar and the interior designer Katchik Arfiel. The church had support from wealthy Armenian patrons whose names are also remembered on the church walls. It is a solemn, elegant church. There are a number of marble plaques adorning the walls, most in memory of former parishioners who helped establish the church and who supported the Armenian community

In the same area is a very different church in spirit and architecture; the Portuguese Church, Kolkata's first Catholic Church.

The Old Mission Church, 1770

Protestant

Today this historical church, completed in 1770, is dwarfed by unattractive high-rise buildings. The red brick work has been covered in white plaster with touches of blue on the bases of the still grand Doric columns and the gates.

The church was designed by M. B. Melville who was the first in Kolkata to use St. Martin-in-the-Fields as a model. In 1835 a transept was added on the south and the height of the spire was increased. Sadly the 1897 earthquake damaged the spire so badly that it was never rebuilt. The interior of the

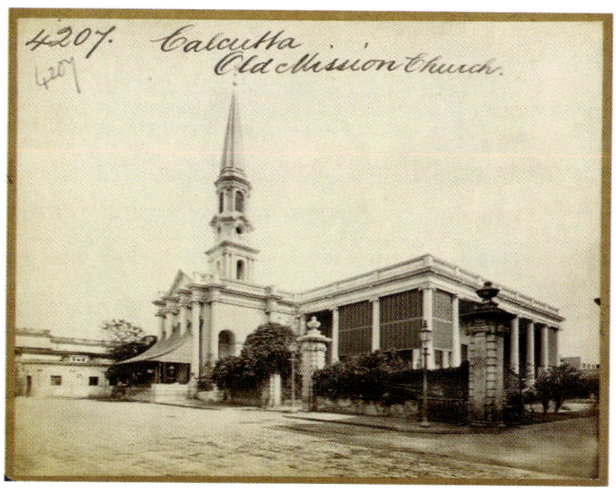

Old Mission Church (courtesy: collection of Joanne Taylor)

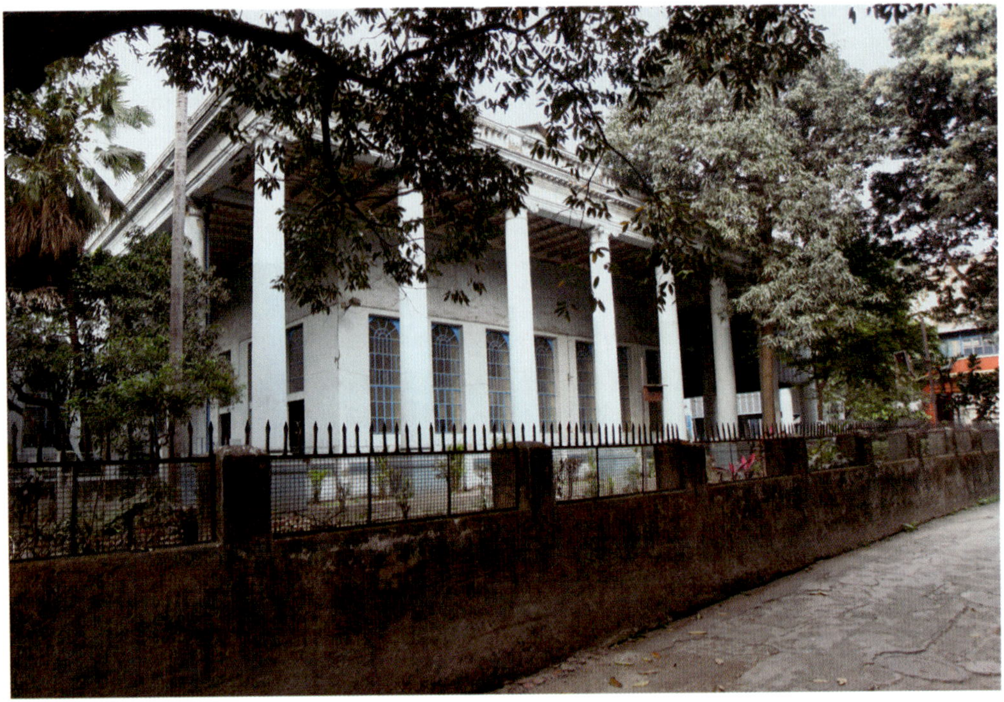

The Old Mission Church now

church is modestly decorated with simple timber planks for pews.

The altar is decorative with three tall arched stained glass windows set into blue surrounds with an inscription 'This Do in Remembrance of Me.' A fine white marble bust of Bishop Thomas Dealtry who became the Archdeacon of Kolkata in 1835 sits in front of a number of marble commemorative plaques. Though there is no commemorative plaque Madhusudan Dutta (later known as Michael Madhusudan Dutt) the iconic poet and playwright was baptised in the old church. Among others his work influenced Bankim Chandra Chatterjee, the Bengali poet, writer and journalist, and later Bengal's much loved Rabindranath Tagore who reshaped Bengali literature and music. Tagore was awarded the Nobel Prize in Literature in 1913.

St. John's Church, 1787

Anglican

Though situated in the heart of busy Kolkata, St. John's churchyard is surprisingly quiet and a lovely place to wander discovering the many historical monuments scattered about. One of the most impressive is the mausoleum of Job Charnock, a domed octagonal structure built sometime in the late 17th century and made from a stone which is named after him, Charnockite. Charnock was an English merchant and administrator of the East India Company and traditionally known as the founder of Kolkata until 2003 when Kolkata High Court ruled that the founding of the city could not be attributed to one man. Indeed markets and trading settlements existed long before Charnock arrived in 1690; subsequently today's Kolkata has no 'date of birth'.

Charnock was certainly an adventurer. With guns blazing he is said to have rescued a beautiful fifteen-year-old Rajput princess from the funeral pyre of her husband. When she died he built his garden house at Barrackpore to be close to her grave and every year on the anniversary of her death would sacrifice a cock on her tomb.

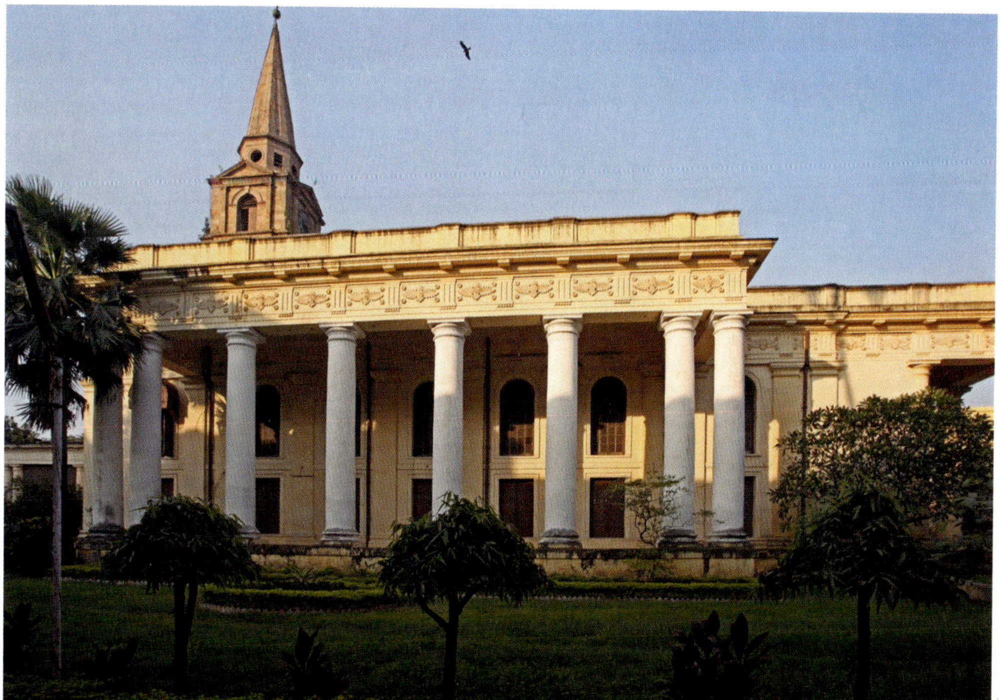

St. John's Church in the glow of the setting sun

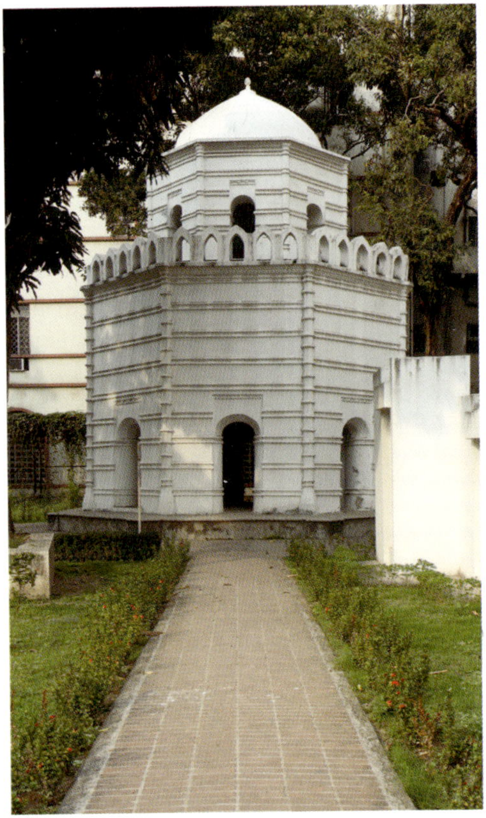

Job Charnock's Mughal influenced tomb

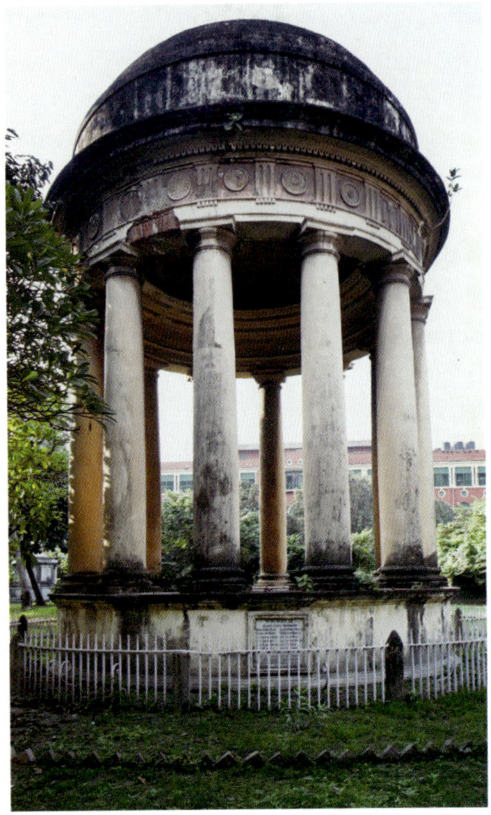

The large Rohilla Monument

Like many Englishmen in those early days Charnock adopted an Indian way of life. He remains a controversial figure in Indian history, admired or denigrated depending on who is doing the telling.

An octagonal structure with an obelisk commemorates the infamous 'Black Hole' tragedy of 1756 mentioned earlier in this work. The incident certainly advanced Britain's expansion in India though it has remained controversial. The rotunda of the Rohilla Memorial with its interesting carvings commemorates the men of the East India Company who died fighting the war between the Rohillas – the Afghan or Pashtun tribes who had settled in the region – and the Nawab of Oudh in the north west of Uttar Pradesh in the 1770s.

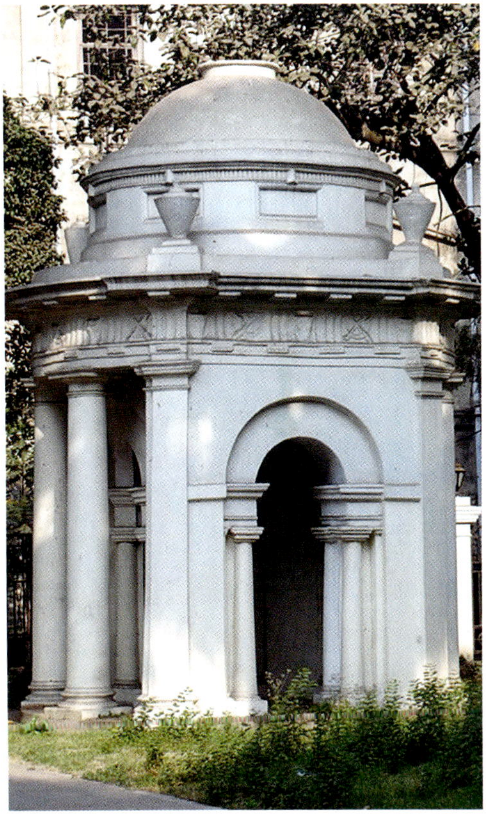

Begum Johnson's Mausoleum

Further is the monument to Begum Johnson (Mrs Frances Johnson 1725-1812) an English woman born in India who became well-respected in Kolkata with friends from both Indian and British society such as Warren Hastings, Lord Cornwallis and Amina Begum, the mother of the Nawab of Bengal. She was married at 13, a widow at 18 and went on to marry three more times, her last husband being the much younger, self-centred Reverend William Johnson, the Chaplain of St. John's Church. The marriage was annulled in 1787 after which Begum Johnson lived a peaceful life to the age of eighty three, one of Kolkata's most beloved British ladies of her time. She was a wealthy woman who outlived all her four husbands. She chose the site in St. John's churchyard where she was to be buried.

The church was completed in 1787, the third oldest church in Kolkata. It is a lovely church built of brick and stone shipped down-river from the ancient city of Gaur, once the capital of Bengal. The entrance is reached through a grand portico where two marble plaques are found. The first commemorates St. John's earlier status as Kolkata's Anglican Cathedral and the second commemorates the donation of the land by Rajah Nabakrishna, a famous Calcutta merchant who rose in fame and fortune due to his association with the British and his friendship with Robert Clive. The land had previously been the old gunpowder magazine yard which the government had sold to the rajah some seven years earlier. When Governor General Warren Hastings suggested Nabakrishna gift the land as a site for the church the rajah consented, presenting it to Hastings who laid the foundation stone in 1784. The architect was Lieutenant James Agg of the Bengal

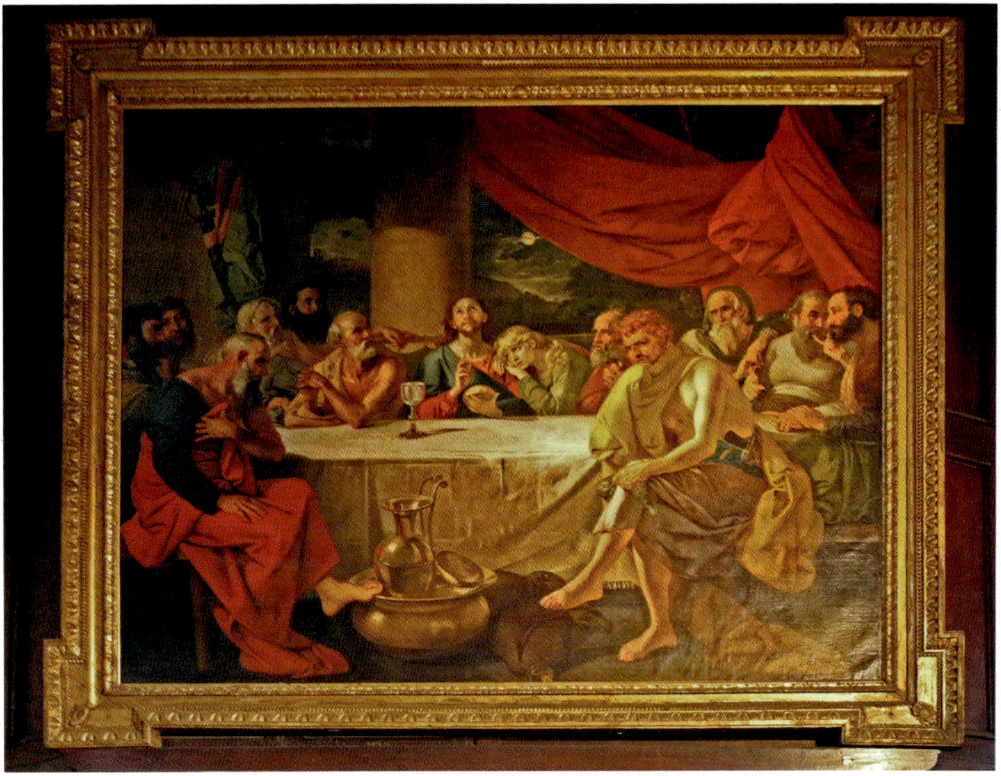

Zoffany's controversial painting of 'The Last Supper'

Engineers and again London's St. Martin-in-the-Fields was used as a model.

St. John's is built in the shape of a square with tall classical columns on each side. Rising up 53 metres is a stone spire embedded with a clock which is wound every day. Inside the floor is paved with beautiful blue-gray marble, also taken from Gaur where much of it covered the ancient tombs of the Mughal kings of Gaur. In the church office the minute's book details how the ruins of Gaur were plundered by the British.

Above the west gallery to the left of the altar is the huge painting of 'The Last Supper' painted by Johann Zoffany, a German born artist who spent six years in India. He was an expert in the peculiarly British School of painting called the 'conversation piece,' or the 'theatrical conversation piece' a genre using informal group portraits which satirised contemporary life and manners. It became very fashionable in the 18th century but later the term took on a different meaning and referred to the subjects and objects being interesting enough to trigger a conversation.

Zoffany's painting certainly evoked conversation. A scandal ensued when it was unveiled in 1787. Calcutta society was shocked to see the models Zoffany used to portray Jesus and the apostles were in fact members of their own congregation, well known Kolkata residents and people from the East India Company. Zoffany also included Indian articles such as a spittoon in place of a water ewer. The artist's sense of humour prevailed as today the painting is considered a masterpiece.

On the right of the main altar is Lady Chapel, a small altar with three beautifully coloured stained glass windows illustrating the life of Jesus. The chapel entrance is guarded by two winged golden angels on tall wooden pedestals. On the left wall is a mesmerising painting of Leonardo da

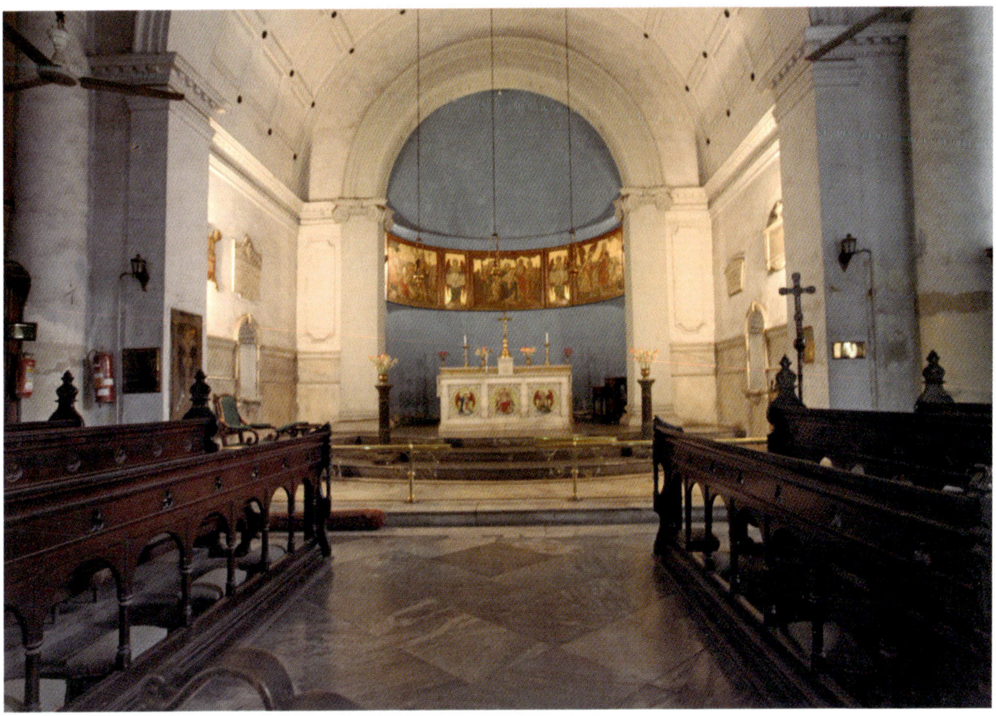

The interior and the altar with the three mosaic works

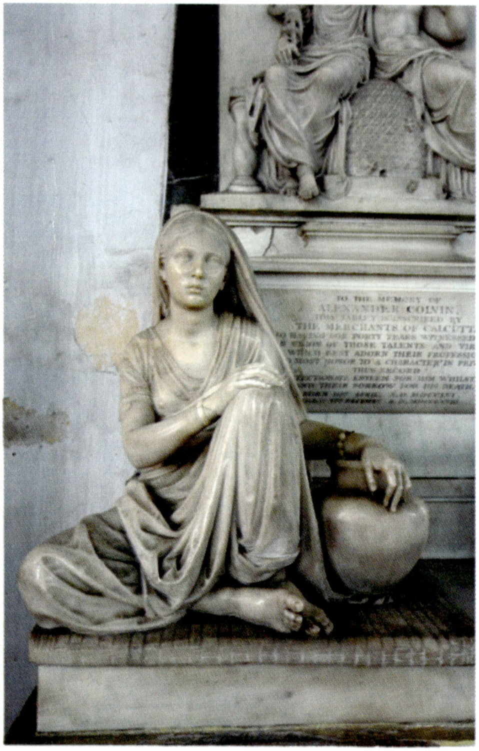

Part of the Colvin Memorial by Richard Westacott in memory of Alexander Colvin, an eminent merchant

Vinci's Jesus titled 'Salvator Mundi', 'Saviour of the World.'

The roof of the nave is supported by fourteen Corinthian columns which create two aisles. In early times parishioners were seated according to their rank in society; the Governor General, his family and other members of the council had the most prestigious seats with a clear view to the altar. The women would sit behind them. Judges of the Supreme Court and gentlemen of society came next, and last the community's poor would sit on simple benches.

The main altar is simple and elegant in white marble decorated with three mosaic works. Behind is a semi-circular blue dome decorated with three beautiful paintings illustrating the important phases in the life of Jesus; His birth, His work and His Resurrection. Around the walls of the church are a number of marble and brass memorial plaques, cenotaphs and coats of arms in memory of those long gone. Many died from tropical disease or from battle but one memorial celebrates the safe return of a mother's son.

St. John's position as Kolkata's cathedral was superseded in 1847 with the consecration of St. Paul's, the first Episcopal Church of the Orient. Today St. John's is often called 'the old Cathedral.'

The Cathedral of the Most Holy Rosary, 1799

Roman Catholic

The 'Portuguese Church' is in north Kolkata where crowded streets teem with people selling everything imaginable. Rickshaws block ones path and merchandise teeter-totters on the back of carts. Men sit on dirt floors selling plastic buckets and wig makers vie for customers on one street while the next sells coloured dye or wedding invitations.

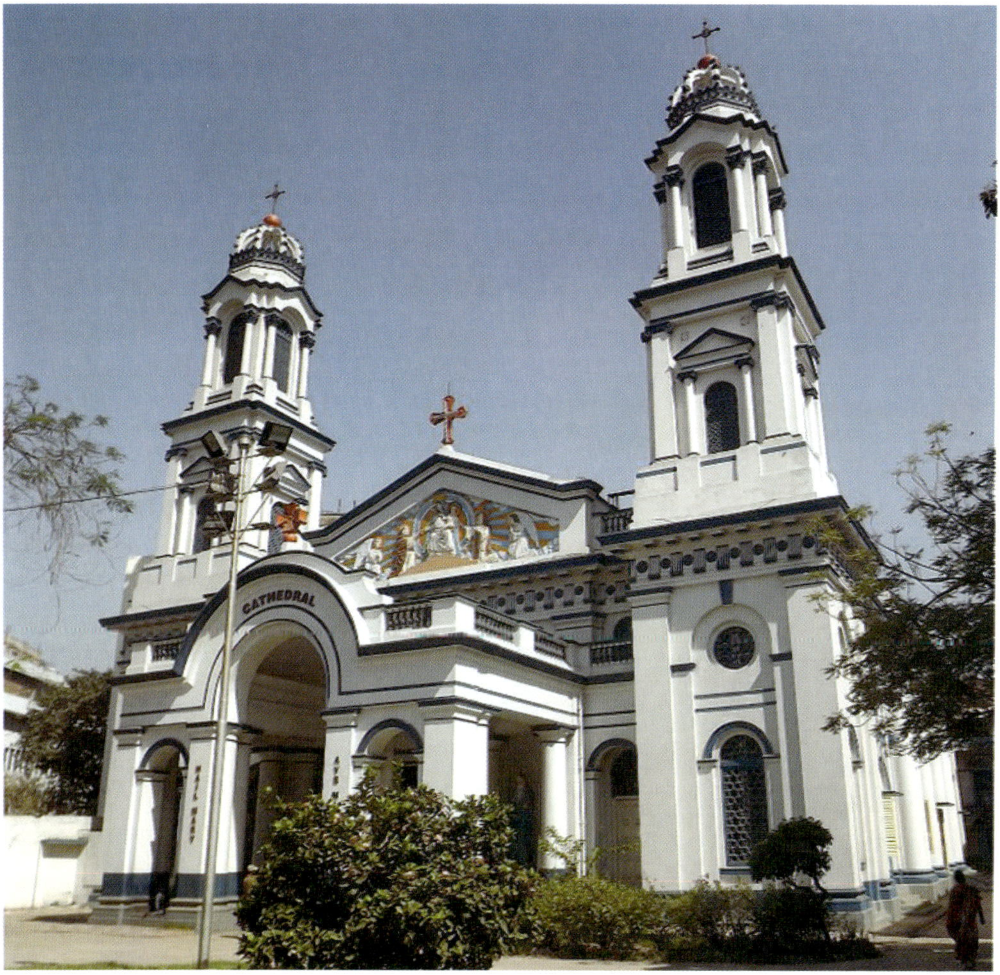

The Cathedral of the Most Holy Rosary (collection of Joanne Taylor)

In the midst of this confusion the blue and white twin towers of Kolkata's Portuguese Church can be glimpsed.

Portuguese traders had established settlements in Bengal, at Chittagong and Satgaon as early as 1530. When they settled in Kolkata around 1797 they founded the church. Like many early Indian churches it has had many incarnations. The present building was designed by James Driver. The

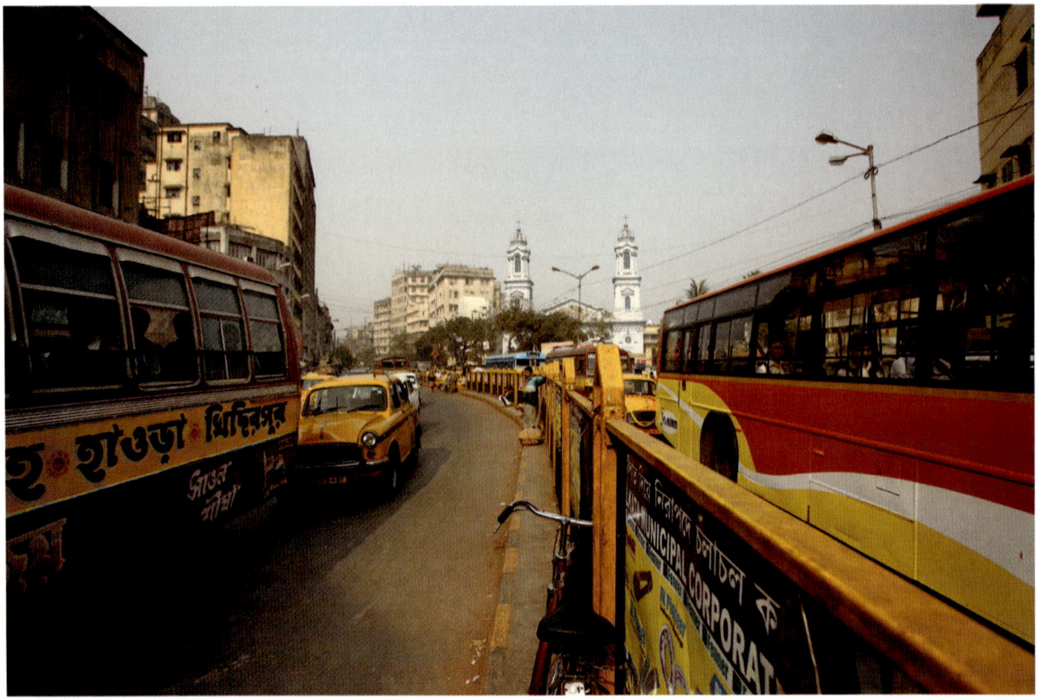
হাওড়া খিদিরপুর

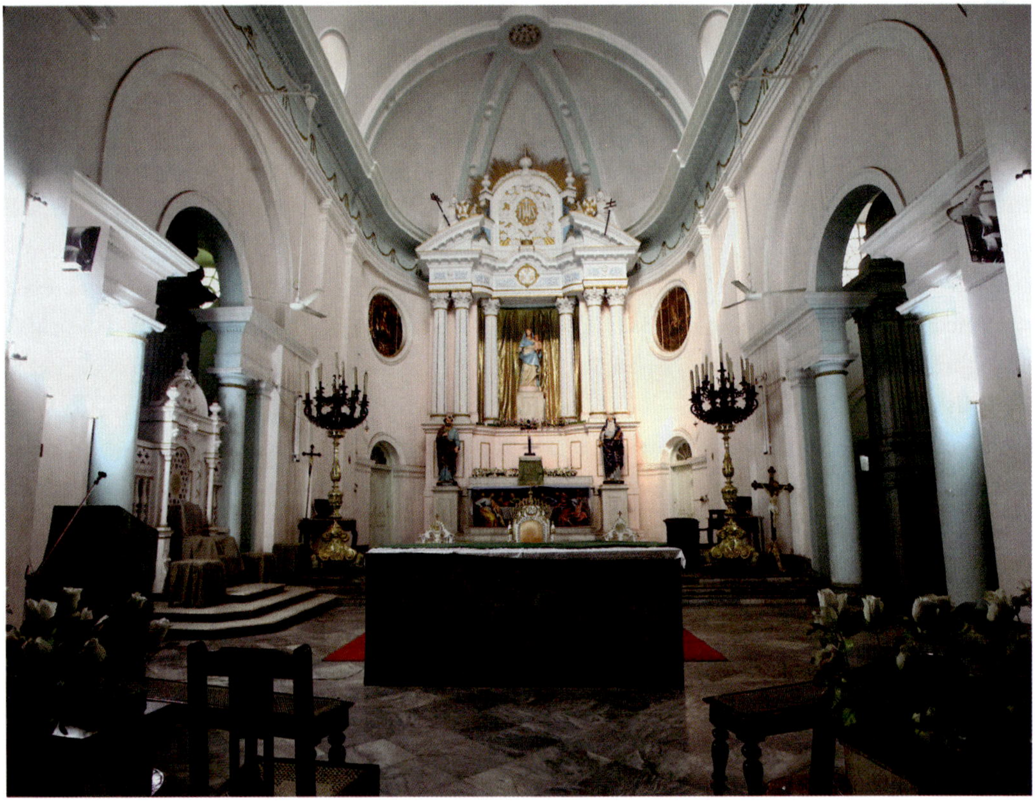

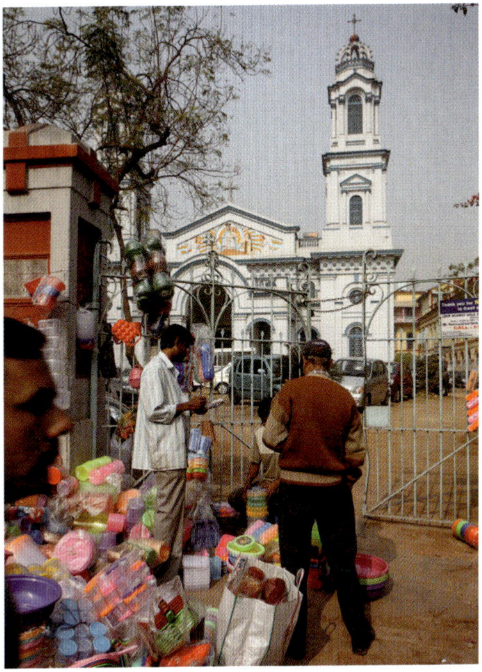

ABOVE: *Everyday chaos at the church entrance*
FACING PAGE TOP: *The church towers in the background*

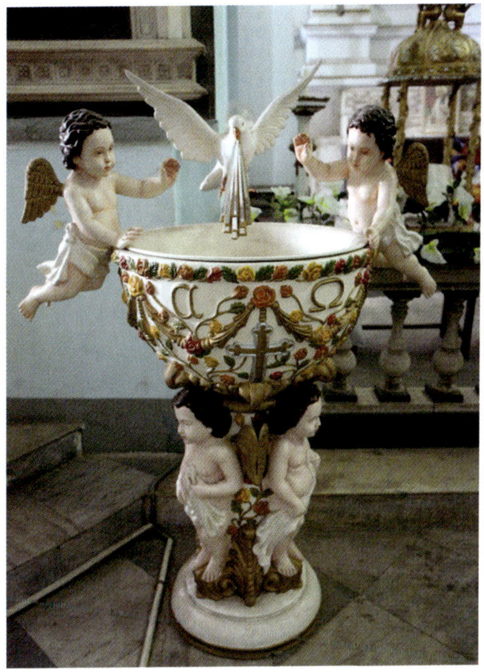

ABOVE: *The baptismal font*
FACING PAGE BELOW: *The interior with floor candelabras*

towers are intricately designed and topped with cupolas in the shape of crowns. A wide portico with an arched entrance gives shade to parishioners entering the church. Above this is a pediment decorated with a brightly colored bas-relief of a biblical scene. Larger than life Biblical figures flank the entrance. Overall the church is more exuberant in style and colour than the elegant simplicity of the nearby Armenian church.

There is much to see in this Portuguese church. The interior is painted white with blue details on the pillars and arches and a there are a number of decorative objects, the most important of which are the wooden panels depicting the Fourteen Stations of the Cross. Marble commemorative plaques adorn the pillars and the Madonna and Child stand behind the altar in a decorative temple supported by Corinthian columns. Above is a half dome set into the curve of the chancel. On each side of the altar are smaller versions of the Biblical figures that seem to guard the entrance and a painting of the Last Supper

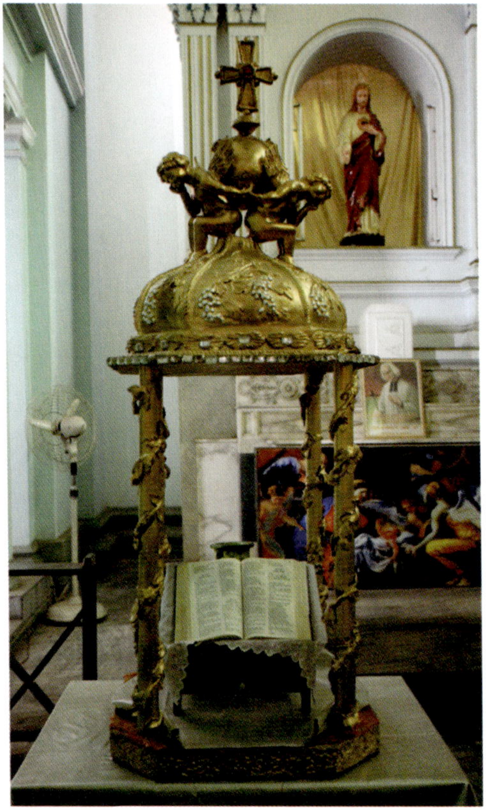

The brass bible stand

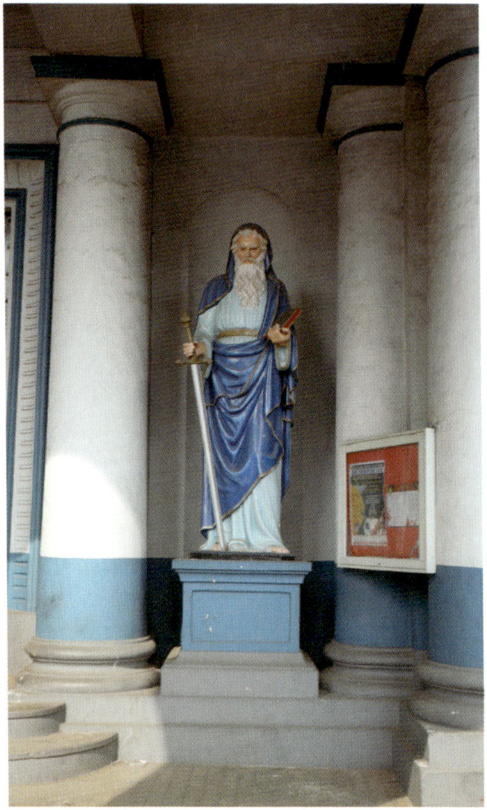

One of the life sized biblical figures at the entrance

stands between. Tall floor candelabras grace each side of the altar and beneath a rounded arch is the throne of the Archbishop. A brass bible stand is unusual and beautiful. Four narrow posts covered in winding ivy support a Mughal style canopy and an elaborate baptismal font decorated with hovering cupids and a dove in flight is striking and cannot be missed.

St. Andrew's Church, 1818

Protestant

Like St. Andrew's in Chennai (1818) St. Andrew's in Kolkata is another Scottish Kirk modelled on the popular St. Martin-in-the-Fields. Architectural pattern books from London were readily available in 18th century India and church designs were either drawn up in England or designed

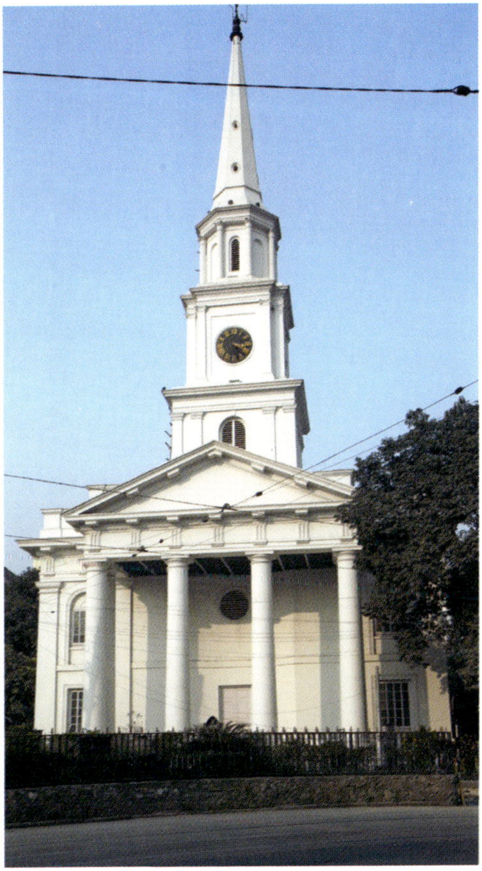

St. Andrew's Church (collection of Joanne Taylor)

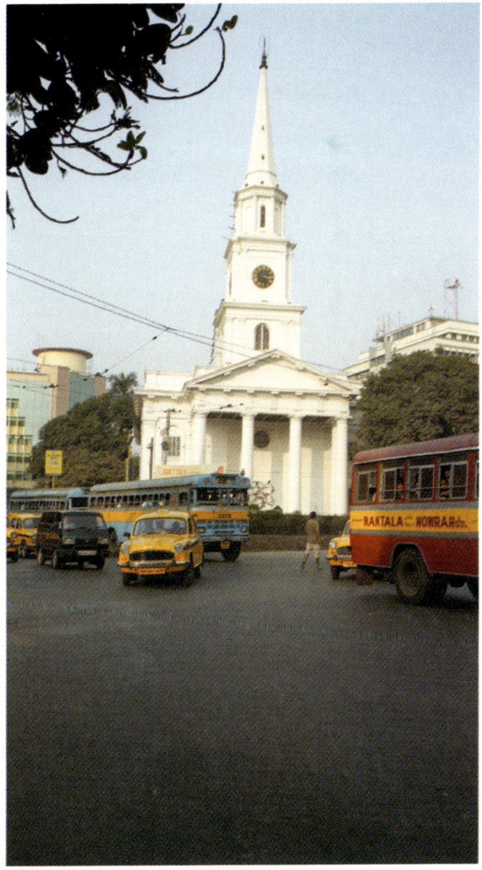

A photograph of the church taken on a busy day at this writer's peril

by surveyors and engineers in India. It was simple and straightforward, particularly as trained architects rarely ventured out to India at that time.

St. Andrew's sits in B.B.D. Bag (formerly Dalhousie Square) once the centre of British administration in Kolkata. The church was completed in 1818 when Kolkata was a much quieter city. Today the traffic swirls relentlessly around the lovely colonial church which is bordered on two sides by Brabourne Street creating an island on which the church stands looking a little stranded and lonely.

The church was built over three years by the building company of Burns, Currie and Co. and dedicated to Scotland's Patron Saint Andrew. The union of Scotland with England in 1707 created the United Kingdom which gave wealthier Scots access to the East India Company. Consequently Scottish engineers, traders, tea planters, teachers and others poured into India. The Scottish were also instrumental in the success of the British Raj. Three Governor-Generals and almost half of the 'writers' or clerks of the East India Company were Scots.

As the number of Presbyterians (a denomination that has its origins mainly in Scotland) grew in Kolkata so did the demand for a Presbyterian minister. The Reverend Dr. James Bryce sailed to India on the 'Warren Hastings,' the same voyage that carried Bishop Middleton, the first Bishop of the Indian Episcopate. They arrived in 1814 but it is recorded that during the long journey the two men enjoyed both pleasant conversation and some unpleasant debate, particularly on the height of their prospective church towers. The Bishop was adamant that the Church of England was the only church entitled to a spire but the Scottish Reverend Bryce disagreed, vowing that he would build a spire for his kirk that would be higher than the steeple of St. Johns and that he would crown it with a weather-cock in order to crow at the Bishop, who was mortified. The cock was installed and can still be seen, a little battered but intact after so many centuries, surely a symbol of the nature and tenacity of the Scots. The foundation stone was laid on St. Andrew's Day, 30th November 1815 in the presence of Lady Moira the wife of the Governor General, other dignitaries and members of the Scottish community.

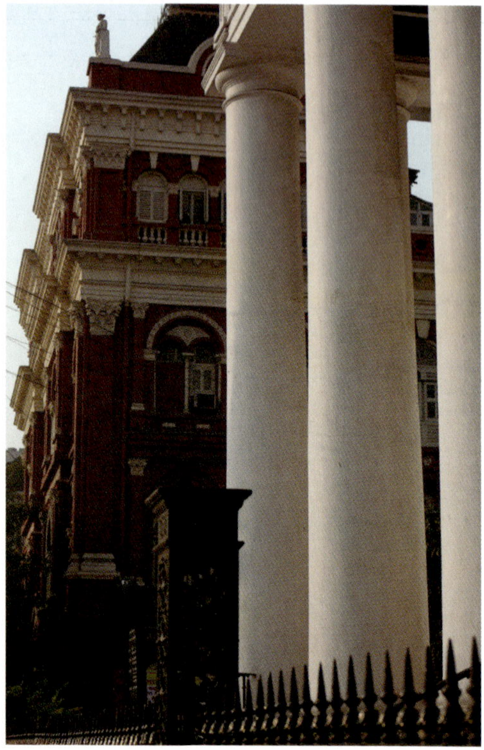

Columns of the church with the Gothic styled Writers Building in the background, BBD Bag

The design features graceful porticoes on both north and south ends of the church with Classical temple fronts supported by enormous Doric columns. The interior is very simple, typical of many Presbyterian churches in Scotland. Ionic columns, an organ loft above the dark wooden altar and a pulpit also in dark wood is reached by a set of steps. The area is painted white with blue/green touches. There are a series of low hanging lights. The atmosphere is stern in keeping with Scottish sensibilities, however it is air-conditioned and that makes up for a lot on a hot day in Kolkata.

Many Scots stayed on in India and are buried in the decaying Scottish Cemetery. As was usual in those days most were very young. Others did not settle but returned to Scotland after which younger family members replaced them. By the early 20th century volunteers of Scottish descent raised the Calcutta Scottish infantry regiment of the British Indian Army. Their dress uniform was Hunting Stewart tartan. However after India's independence the regiment was disbanded.

St. Paul's Cathedral, 1847

Anglican

At the southern end of the Maidan–Kolkata's vast parkland–is the great Neo-Gothic St. Paul's Cathedral. It stands between Cathedral Road and Chowringhee Road (now Jawaharlal Nehru Road) on the quaintly named 'island of attractions' which includes the Victoria Memorial Museum, the Nandan Theatre Complex and the Birla Planetarium. The cathedral is surrounded by a garden with groups of palms and a large number of ancient trees.

In 1819 the Governor-General of Bengal Warren Hastings requested a design for a cathedral which was drawn up by military engineer Major William Nairn Forbes. However it was rejected as being too expensive. Later Bishop Middleton suggested a site (where the cathedral stands today) but that was also rejected. It wasn't until Bishop Daniel Wilson arrived in Kolkata in 1832 to officiate at St. John's Cathedral that the plan was re-considered. From the beginning Bishop Wilson realised the city's growing European population needed a larger cathedral.

Again Major William Nairn Forbes was asked to design the building. He used neo-Gothic elements such as thin vertical piers, buttresses, vaulting, pointed arches and spires creating an imposing cathedral with a graceful central steeple modelled on Norwich and Canterbury cathedrals and Yorkminster. Through perseverance and passion Bishop Wilson's vision of an accurate Neo-Gothic styled Cathedral for

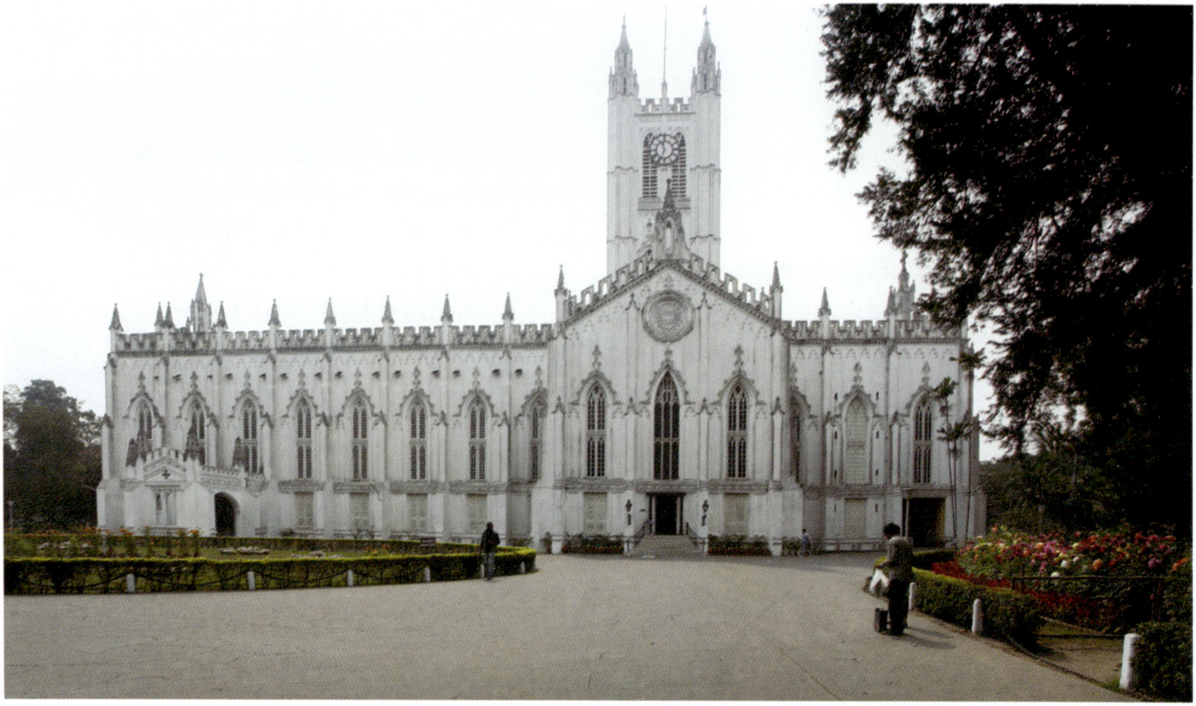

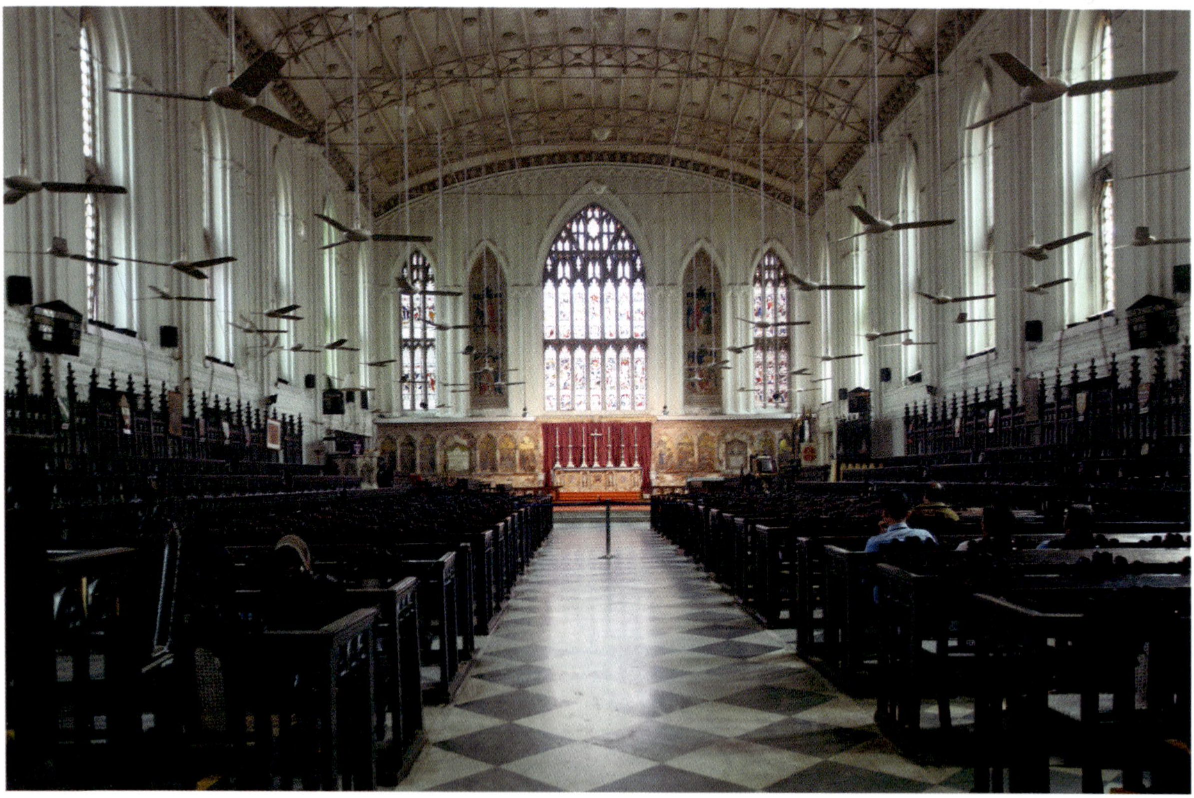

Kolkata finally came to fruition. He laid the cornerstone in 1839 and saw the completion of the building in 1847.

A great earthquake struck in 1897 damaging the city and the upper section of the Cathedral's steeple. It was later restored but in 1934 another serious earthquake struck, this time destroying the entire steeple. This time it was not restored but replaced with the sixty metre tall central tower we see today, a tower reminiscent of the Bell Harry Tower of Canterbury Cathedral. Indeed the cathedral itself was reconstructed with adjustments made to suit the extreme climatic conditions of India. The cathedral became more 'Indo-Gothic' in style with louvered windows replacing stained glass to permit more ventilation and the addition of iron trusses to support the vast shallow-curved span of the roof due to concerns that the soil, as part of the lower Ganges Delta would not bear the weight of heavy pillars. Hence the nave of the cathedral has no Gothic side aisles, just one basilica-like great hall.

Like most early buildings in Kolkata the cathedral is constructed of bricks and a mixture of lime and brick dust for mortar. A mixture called *chunam* was used to plaster the interior and exterior. When polished the effect in some lights is pearly and mystical. Skilled indigenous craftsmen were responsible for most of the decorative wrought iron and wood work.

Without side aisles the exceptionally large interior (75 metres long and 25 metres wide) is seen as a whole; a vast serene space with beautifully carved wooden pews. The stained glass west window is by Pre-Raphaelite British artist Sir Edward Coley Burne-Jones. It is a memorial to Lord Mayo, the fourth Viceroy of India. The large gold communion plate presented by Queen Victoria is also a treasured object. A series of paintings illustrate the life and works of St. Paul.

Churches such as St. Paul's Cathedral are visible reminders of Britain's colonisation of India. However they also speak of young military engineers with no architectural training, and of the indigenous craftsmen who created beautiful, delicate details. They also speak of the design, not architecturally correct in many cases, nor ecclesiastically correct in many others but still treasured as historical monuments by Indian Christians and non-Christians alike, long after the British left India's shores.

FACING PAGE ABOVE: *The St. Paul's Cathedral*
FACING PAGE BELOW: *Looking toward the altar*

The Bishop's House

Opposite the Cathedral is the Bishop's House, once the home of Governor General William Wilberforce Bird who signed the act abolishing slavery in India in 1844. It is a robust building close to the busy road with massive ionic columns. At the entrance is a large cast iron Chinese bell hanging from a bracket carved in the shape of a dragon. There is some mystery to the bell's origin and the meaning of its inscriptions.

Bishop Wilson lived at 5 Russell Street in what was then known as the Bishop's Palace. Two years after the completion of St. Paul's, Bishop Wilson relocated to the Bishop's House on Chowringhee Road where he enjoyed hearing the pleasing chimes of St. Paul's Cathedral clock. From a small courtyard a creaky teak staircase leads up to the administrative offices and further on to the large veranda where the massive size of the Ionic columns are revealed. Simple in design with no fluting, their great bases take up much of the verandas space. While standing under the columns feeling quite small I can't help thinking that the sign on

FACING PAGE TOP: *The teak staircase with decorative wrought iron balustrades and timber handrails*

FACING PAGE BELOW: *Entrance to the Bishop's room*

BELOW: *St. James' Church 1864*

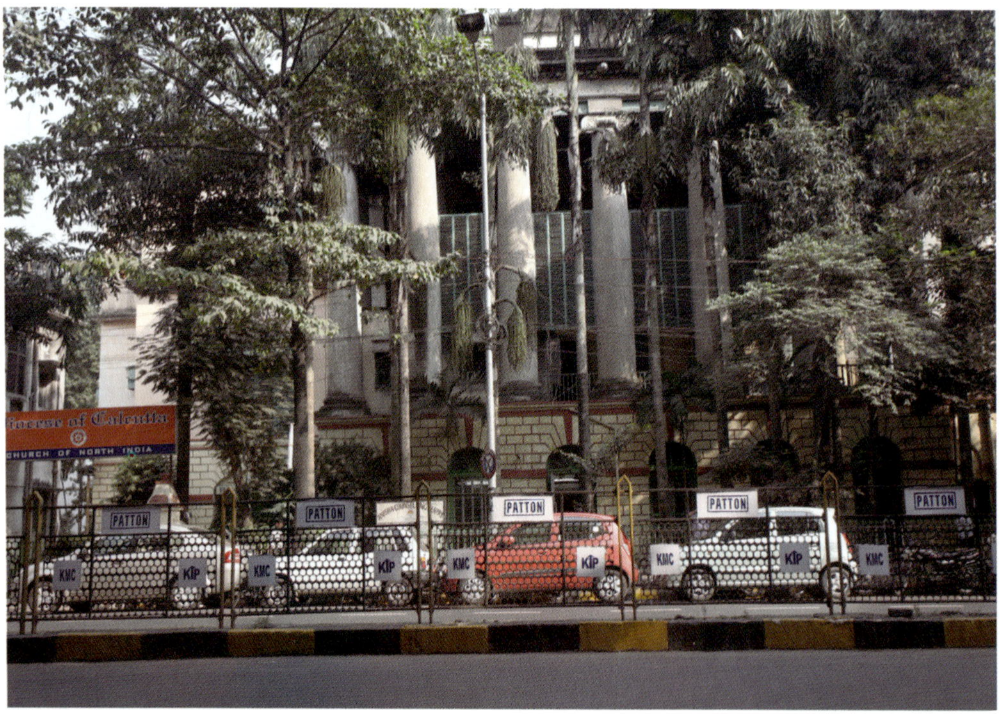

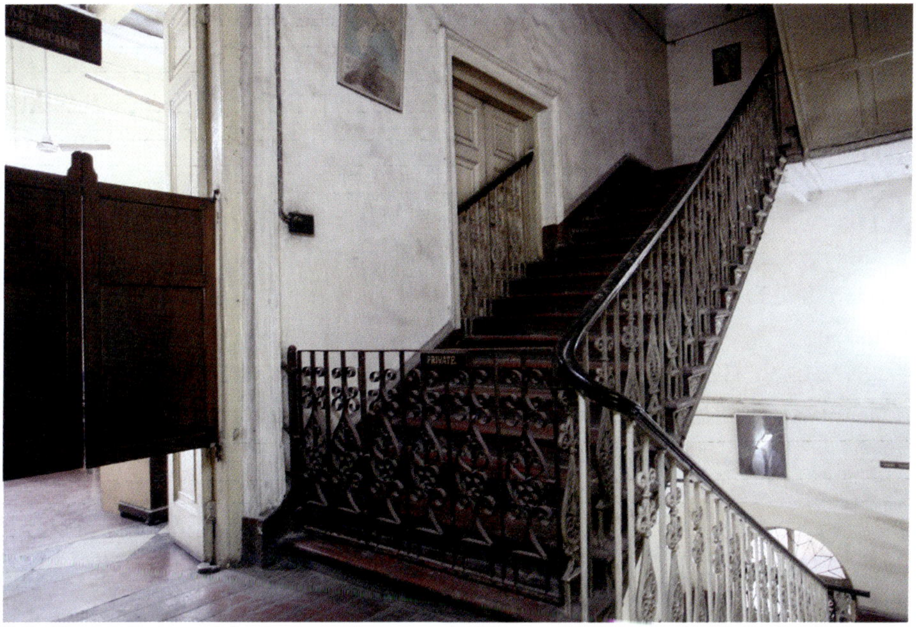
PRIVATE.

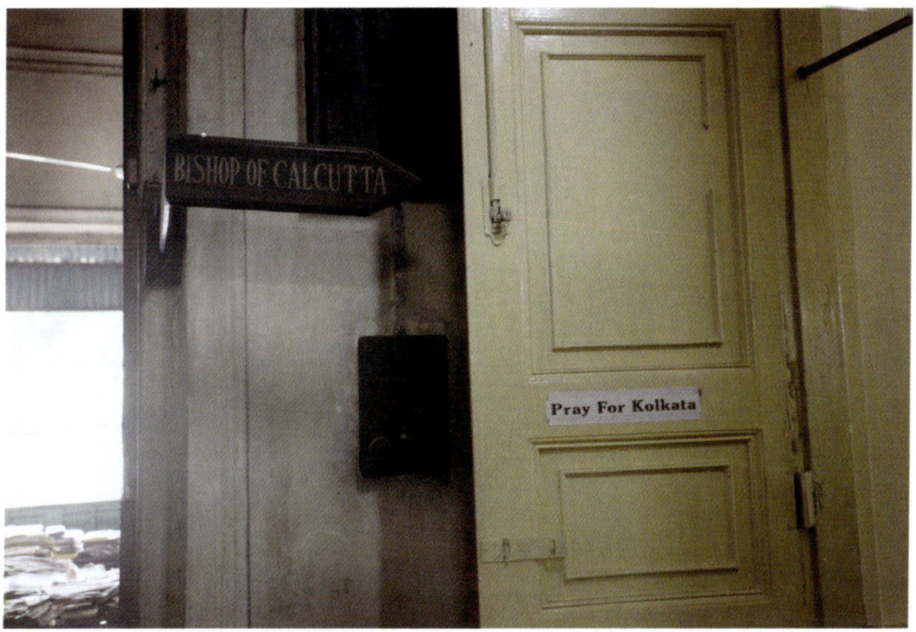
BISHOP OF CALCUTTA
Pray For Kolkata

the Bishop's office door will long stay with me; 'Pray for Calcutta'.

St. James' Church 1864

Protestant

Walter B. Granville designed St. James' Church along with a number of other important buildings in Kolkata, the most celebrated of which is the splendid Government Post Office. His appointment as Consultant Architect to the Government of India was to design and construct the major public buildings for the British Raj. Granville lived mainly in Kolkata for twelve years and is renowned as one of the most talented British architects to work in India.

Granville used thirty nine metre high spires topped with metal crosses above double-tiered towers for St. James' Church resulting in the church being known locally as Jora Girja, 'the twin church.' They give the church its most distinctive feature and

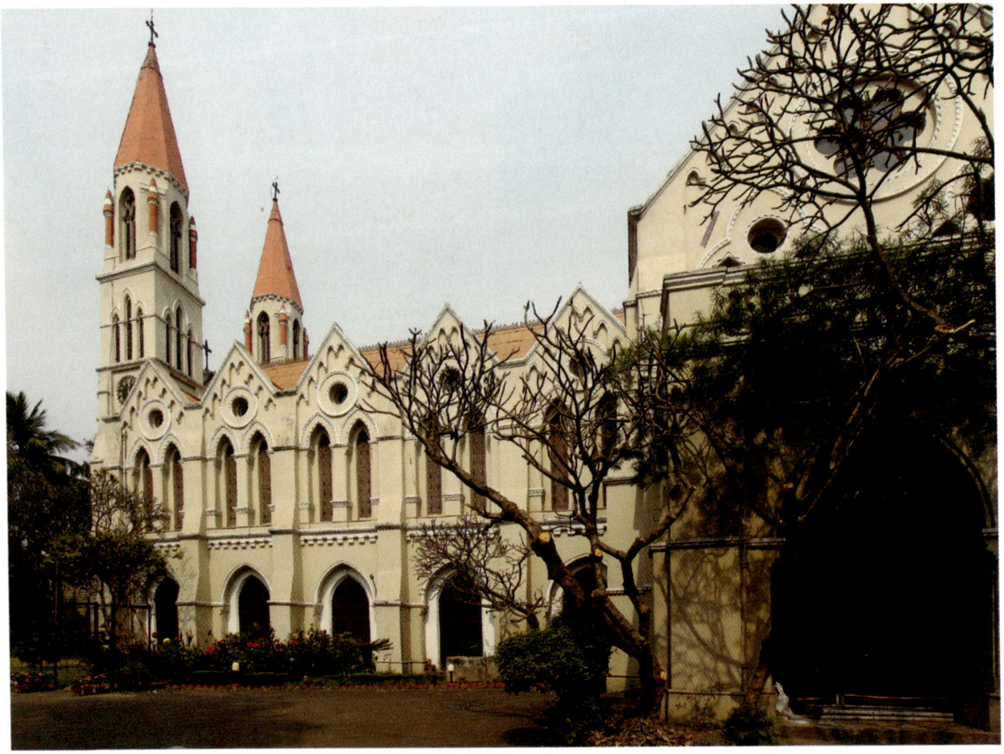

St. James' Church still stands tall

suggest a fortified Norman castle. The outer walls of the English Gothic styled church are supported by buttresses, and along the length of the church are a row of doors with pointed arches, both distinctly Gothic but with a distinct advantage. These doors can be opened, which is important for India's climate.

The large *porte-cochere* has pointed arches on the eastern and western sides and is topped with a cross. A gable above is decorated with stained glass and other exterior elements include a double-dialled black faced clock on the lower section of one of the towers. Above the clock are eight bells which produce a wonderful sound.

The interior is spacious with a high black mahogany ceiling. Both sides of the nave are lined with Gothic arches on the lower level and the gallery. From the black and white marble floor the white marble altar is reached by three steps and decorated with a bas-relief panel portraying 'The Last Supper.' The Tabernacle sits atop the altar and shelves each side display sheaves of wheat and clusters of grapes. The apse is covered by an arched and ribbed semicircular roof at the eastern end of the church.

The church was consecrated by Bishop Cotton in 1864 and today it is a beautifully restored and maintained building much loved by a community of young and old parishioners.

Park Street Cemetery, Kolkata

After the British success in the Battle of Plassey the British no longer needed to be protected by the confines of Fort William. One of the first changes to take place was the development of a new burial ground. 'Burying Ground Road' (now Park Street or officially Mother Theresa Sarani) leads to the cemetery which at that time was surrounded by fields. Today it is one of the city's busiest roads.

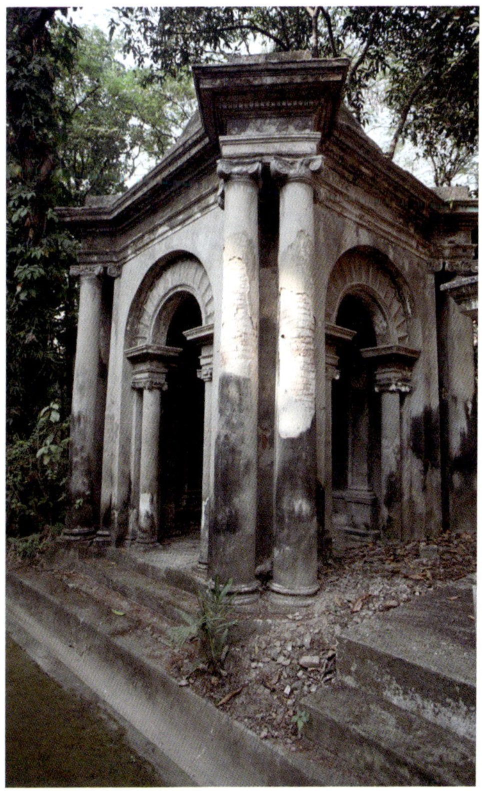

Classical stone embellishments, now in dilapidation

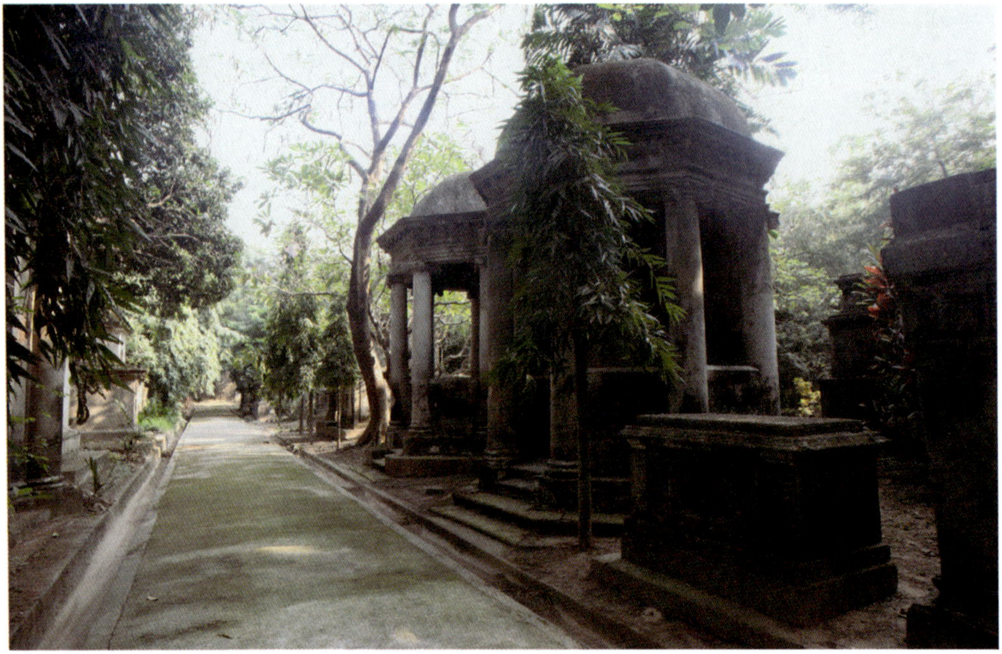

Park Street Cemetery, Kolkata, in a mix of splendour and decay, is a tourist attraction

Park Street Cemetery is wonderfully atmospheric and eerie with a mix of Kolkata splendour and decay. It certainly feels like an ancient resting place, the quiet only interrupted by the squawk of a crow alighting on a tomb or the rustling of stray dogs. Narrow pathways are lined with elaborate moss covered tombs decorated with classical details such as Corinthian columns, festoons of flowers or angels. Others are designed as obelisks, sarcophagi, tombs and vaults, all shaded by tall trees and palms. It is a classical city in miniature. Some 1600 tombs are dotted across eight acres of land, many with touching epitaphs. The earliest tell us of the lives they experienced in colonial Kolkata. Many died at a young age.

One of the most revered graves in the cemetery is the tomb of Sir William Jones, the founder of the Royal Asiatic Society and admired by the British and Indians alike. 'Asiatic Jones' as he was known is one of Kolkata's most important figures. He arrived in India in 1783 and became a judge in the Supreme Court of Kolkata. He spoke several European and Asian languages. His works on

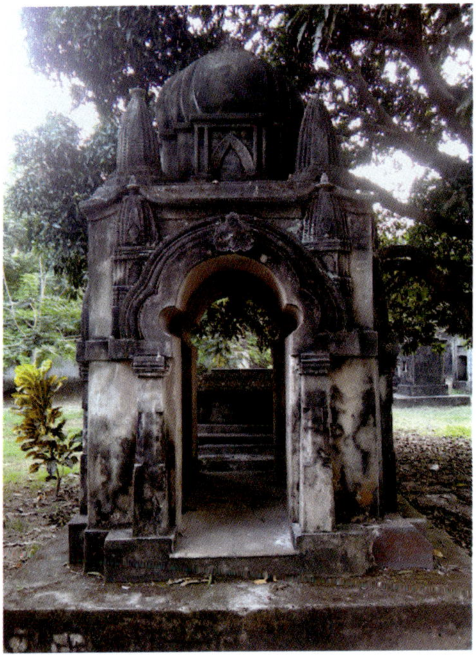

Charles 'Hindoo' Stuart's unique temple styled tomb

India include the first English translations of Indian literature. He died in 1794.

Many buried in Park Street Cemetery have famous descendants. The sons of Captain James Cook and Charles Dickens can be found as well as the radical young Anglo-Indian poet Henry Vivian Louis Derozio who was born in 1809 and who influenced the Young Bengal Movement of the early 19th century. He was one of the first teachers to spread western learning and science but died of cholera at just twenty two years leaving a lasting impact on Bengali society.

Richmond Thackeray was only 34 when he died. His son was the writer William Makepeace Thackeray, born in Kolkata and placed second only to Charles Dickens during the Victorian era.

One tomb is different to the rest. Built in the shape of a Hindu temple and topped with stone carvings of the Goddess Ganga, it is the tomb of Major-General Charles Stuart of the East India Company, known as 'Hindoo Stuart'. He embraced local customs and an Indian way of life, becoming a Hindu just a year after he arrived in Kolkata. He died in 1828 with images of his favourite Indian gods alongside him.

Many ordinary people came to India for various reasons and made it their home but for British and Indians alike, death came too soon in Kolkata as a result of tropical illnesses. Young women who came to India in search of a husband or perhaps the families of merchants trading in the city or stationed there were all equally at risk. It is difficult to imagine Kolkata in those days to the noisy mega city of today. Park Street was named after a deer park that existed there in the middle of unhealthy marshland and jungle and Warren Hastings, Britain's first and most famous Governor General of India would hunt Bengal tigers in the jungles that are now the peaceful, safe parklands of the Maidan.

Mumbai: Gothic Splendour

In medieval times on India's west coast lay seven islands surrounded by swamps and steamy jungle. The inhabitants were the Koli, a tribe of fisher folk. These islands were part of the famous Indian emperor Ashoka's kingdom. He was born around 304 BC and when he died the islands passed into the hands of various Buddhist and Hindu rulers. Then in 1343 the Islamic Sultanate of Gujarat took possession and ruled the islands for the next two centuries. These islands were the beginning of Mumbai, one of India's most important and busiest city.

In 1534 the islands were captured by the Portuguese. That same year aboard the Portuguese galleon *Sao Mateus* the Kingdom of Portugal and the Sultan of Gujarat signed the Treaty of Bassein, which relinquished the main islands and other territories to the Portuguese Empire. This resulted in significant social and religious changes including the building of Roman Catholic churches.

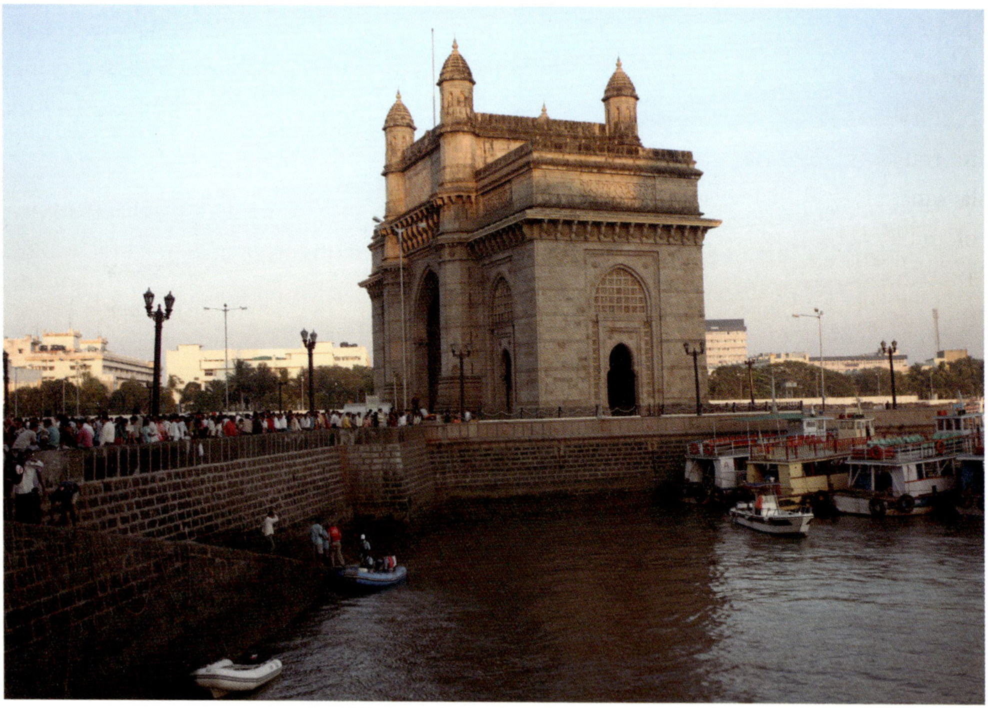

The Indo-Gothic Gateway of India in Mumbai attracts throngs of visitors every day (collection of Joanne Taylor)

In 1662 when Princess Catherine of Portugal married Charles II of England she brought an enormous dowry to the union, part of which included the seven islands of Bombay. Despite having a protected harbour King Charles was not interested. The Portuguese had done nothing to improve them and they were covered in jungle and unhealthy. In 1668 he rented the islands to the British East India Company who set about transforming the islands.

By 1708 they had established their headquarters and the deep water port was busy docking large vessels from India and other parts of the world. Trade began to increase significantly and by the late 18th century a huge reclamation of land began to transform the seven islands into one landmass. When Britain took direct control of India from the East India Company in 1857 Europe's first port of call in India was the exciting, prosperous city of Mumbai.

Architecturally Mumbai embraced the Victorian neo-Gothic style of architecture in the second half of the 19th century. It was seen as the only 'true' architectural style for Christian churches. For the English in India a pointy church steeple was a reminder of 'home'. For the Indians Gothic architecture was seen as 'modern'. A number of other architectural styles were used in Mumbai but it was the Gothic that triumphed. Later Indian architects combined the fundamentals of Victorian Gothic with contemporary elements to produce what is known as 'Bombay Gothic', a style that took into account India's climate and culture.

Historian Thomas R. Metcalfe suggests two reasons for the choice of Gothic architecture for Mumbai. First, the city's position facing Europe on the west coast of India and the second the opening of the Suez Canal in 1869 which reinforced Bombay's prominence as an international port. For a European arriving in India for the first time, seeing Mumbai's Gothic architecture would have been reassuring. This familiarity enhanced trading opportunities. For church building, the Gothic style was ideal as it was a symbol of a Christian culture. Its dramatic verticality, pointed arches, pinnacles and spires pointed upward to heaven, and god. Walls and windows overlaid with fine tracery and of course stained glass symbolised the mysticism of religion, and it was cheaper to build than the Classical. Mount Mary's Basilica (1760) is an early example of Gothic architecture as is the more beautiful Afghan Memorial Church (1847-58). The enormous Victoria Terminus, now Chhatrapati Shivaji Terminus, 1888, was the first major Gothic building in Mumbai. Apart from England, the city has one of the largest collections of Gothic buildings in the world.

As one of the three great port cities of India the Bombay Presidency was far-reaching. Between 1843 and 1936 it encompassed the states of today's Gujarat, Karnataka, and the Sind province of Pakistan, the city of Aden in the Yemen, the western area of Maharashta and some princely states. With independence in 1947 the British began to leave. The last were the British officials who sailed from the great port of Mumbai.

The last moments of the British Raj reads:

> The Somerset Light Infantry marched their colours past the Governor to the sound of their regimental band. The Indian guard of honour then gave the Royal Salute and God Save The King was played. To this The Somerset Light Infantry replied with a Royal Salute and the Indian National anthem. Then the escort trooped the colours to the tune of Auld Lang Syne down the centre of the parade ground and out through the Gateway of India. The whole maneuver was carried out with the utmost precision and proved to be a very moving sight. Finally, the Somerset CO and General Whistler said their good-byes and passed through the Gateway to a launch where the colours had already embarked. As the launch pulled away towards the troopship 'The Empress of Australia', the crowds were shouting, waving and in some cases weeping. It was the end of the Raj.

The Cathedral of St. Thomas, 1837

Protestant

The Cathedral Church of St. Thomas began as the garrison church inside the walls of Fort George. Building began in 1672 at a time when Mumbai was just a British

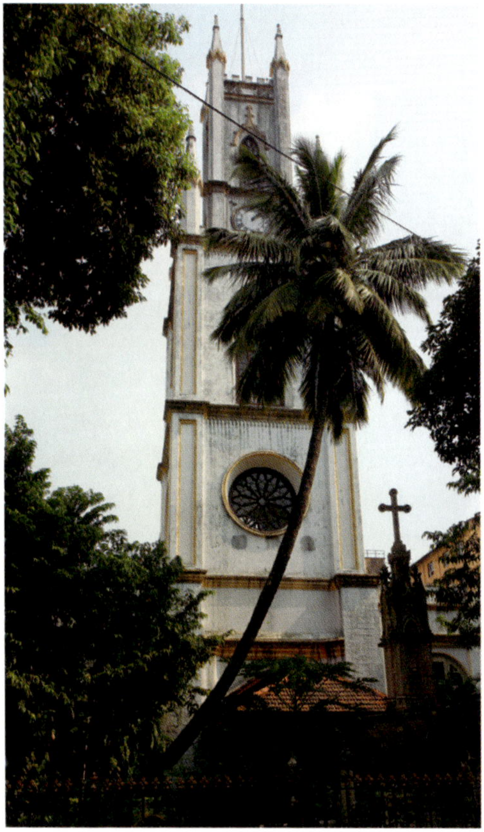

The Cathedral of St. Thomas in the 'Fort' area

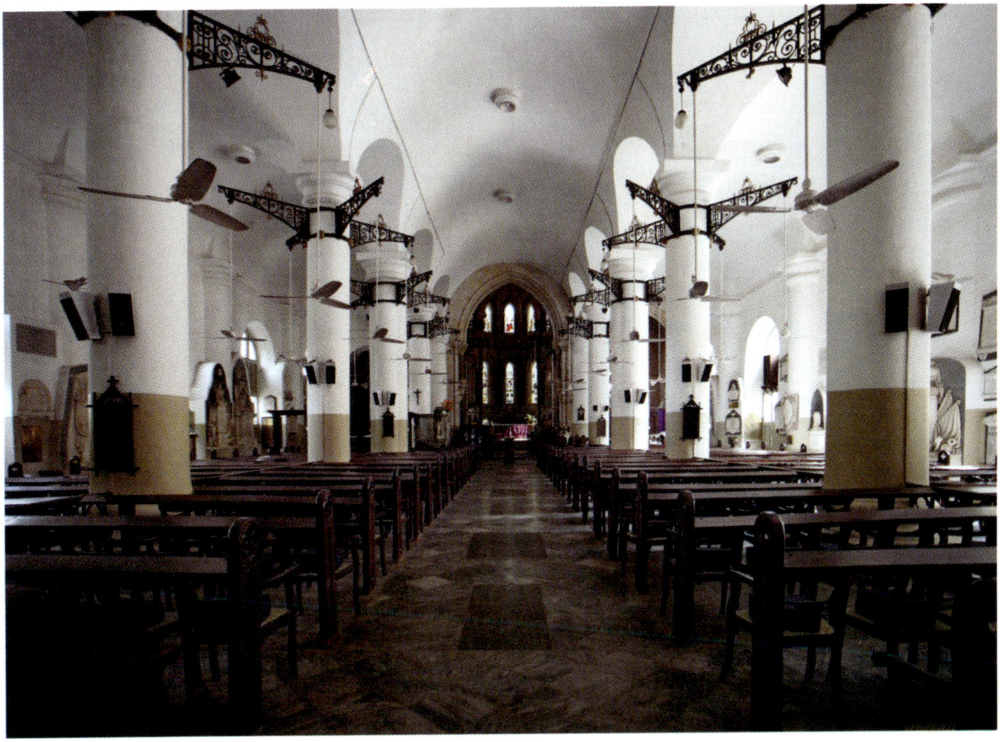

The interior of the Cathedral of St. Thomas

controlled spot on India's map surrounded by a vast Indian controlled territory. It remained unfinished and neglected for forty years until a young chaplain arrived and took on the task of completing the church. Today the walls of the fort have long gone but the area is still called 'Fort', now the business district of Mumbai and the area to the west of the church is still known as 'Churchgate'.

A marble plaque at the entrance reads:

'Let all who enter this church remember. Richard Cobbe, chaplain to the Honorable East India Company 1715 to 1719, sometime vicar of Whitechurch Dorset. The walls of this church had risen to the height of 15 feet when the building ceased and the site lay desolate for 33 years. At length the devoted energy of Mr Cobbe stirred up his countrymen to complete the church which was opened for divine worship on Christmas day 1718...'

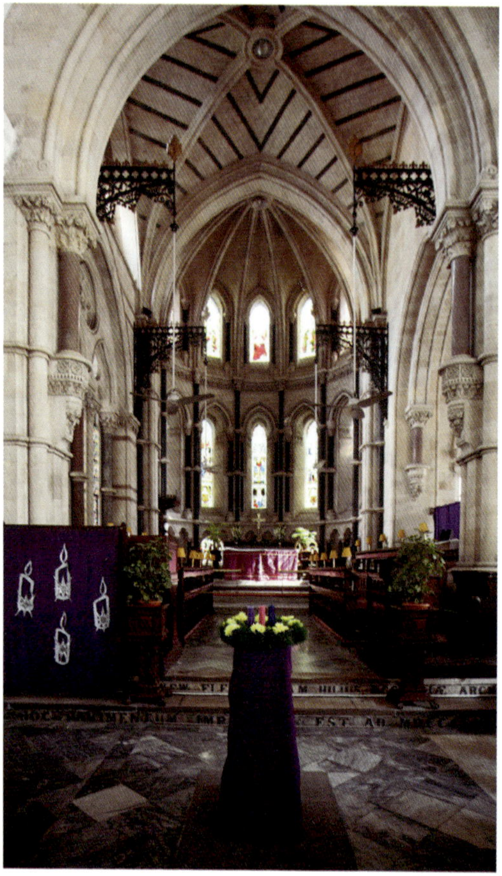

The sanctuary, altar, ribbed vaulted ceiling and iron fixtures supporting fans in the Cathedral of St. Thomas

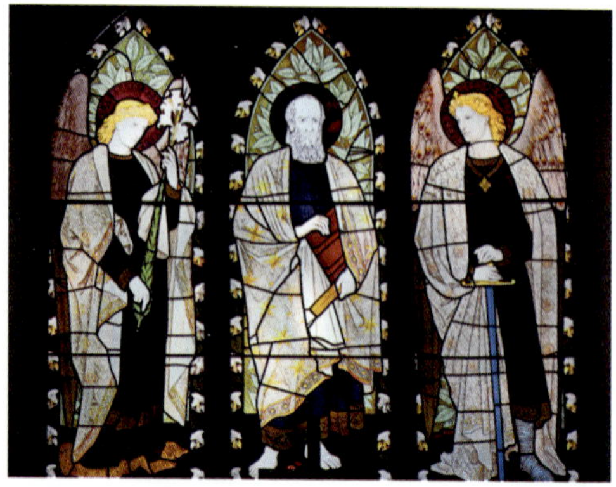

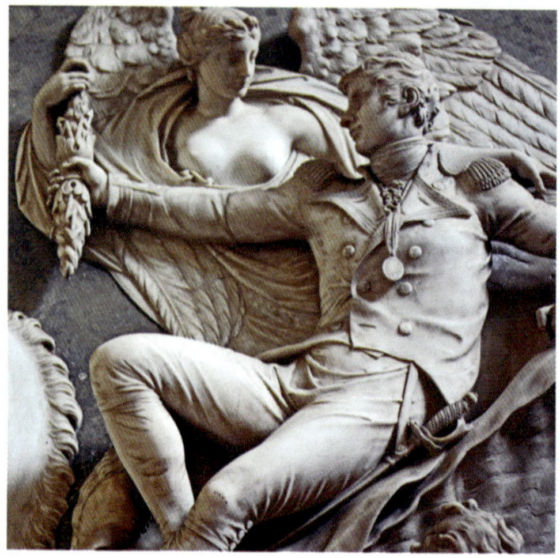

TOP AND BELOW: *Part of a beautiful stained glass window and a marble carving of a soldier and angel*

In 1837 the church was made a cathedral and a year later the Gothic styled tower and the clock were added creating a fine combination of Classical and Gothic elements. The church is well preserved despite being the oldest Protestant church and the oldest English building in Mumbai. In the garden is a beautifully ornate Gothic cross surrounded by a pond but the cemetery reveals the large number of young people who came to India and died there from malaria.

Inside the walls of the church are one hundred and fifty memorials, most from the 19th century, to British parishioners

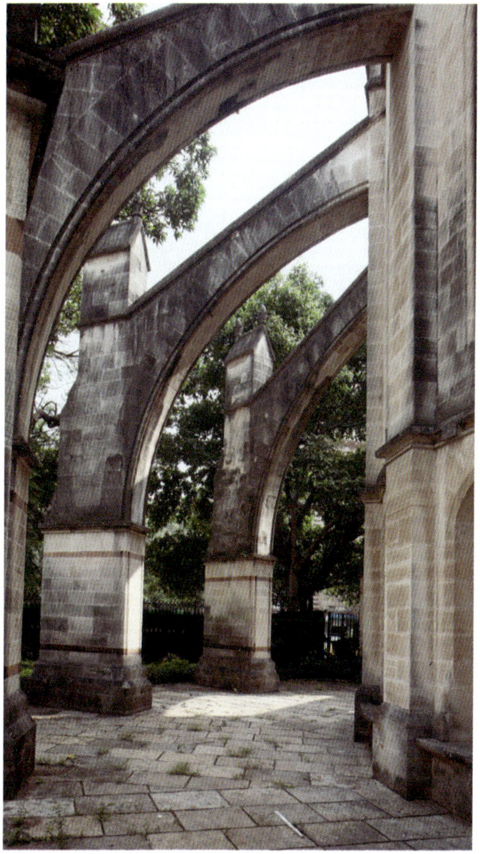

Flying buttresses at the entrance

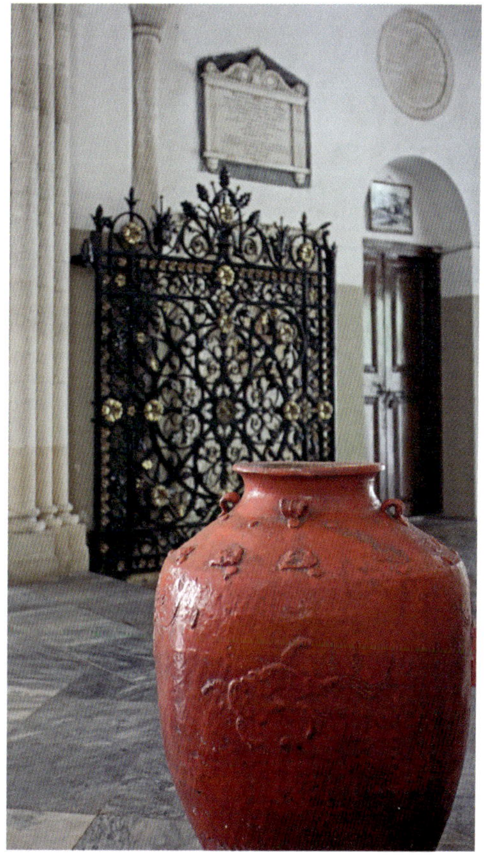

A Chinese jar, classical columns and decorative iron work

long gone, either from battle or disease. As the major church of the Bombay Presidency these historic memorials are beautifully carved in marble and it is touching to read the names of people from all walks of life; rulers of India, adventurers, young women, merchants, sailors, officers, husbands and wives who helped raise Mumbai to be the great port city. Foremost are memorials to Jonathan Duncan, Governor of Bombay from 1795 to 1811 and Captain Hardinge who was killed in the naval battle against the French off the coast of Ceylon, now Sri Lanka.

The famous stained glass windows of the church are beautiful as are the polished brass brackets and decorative Victorian iron work

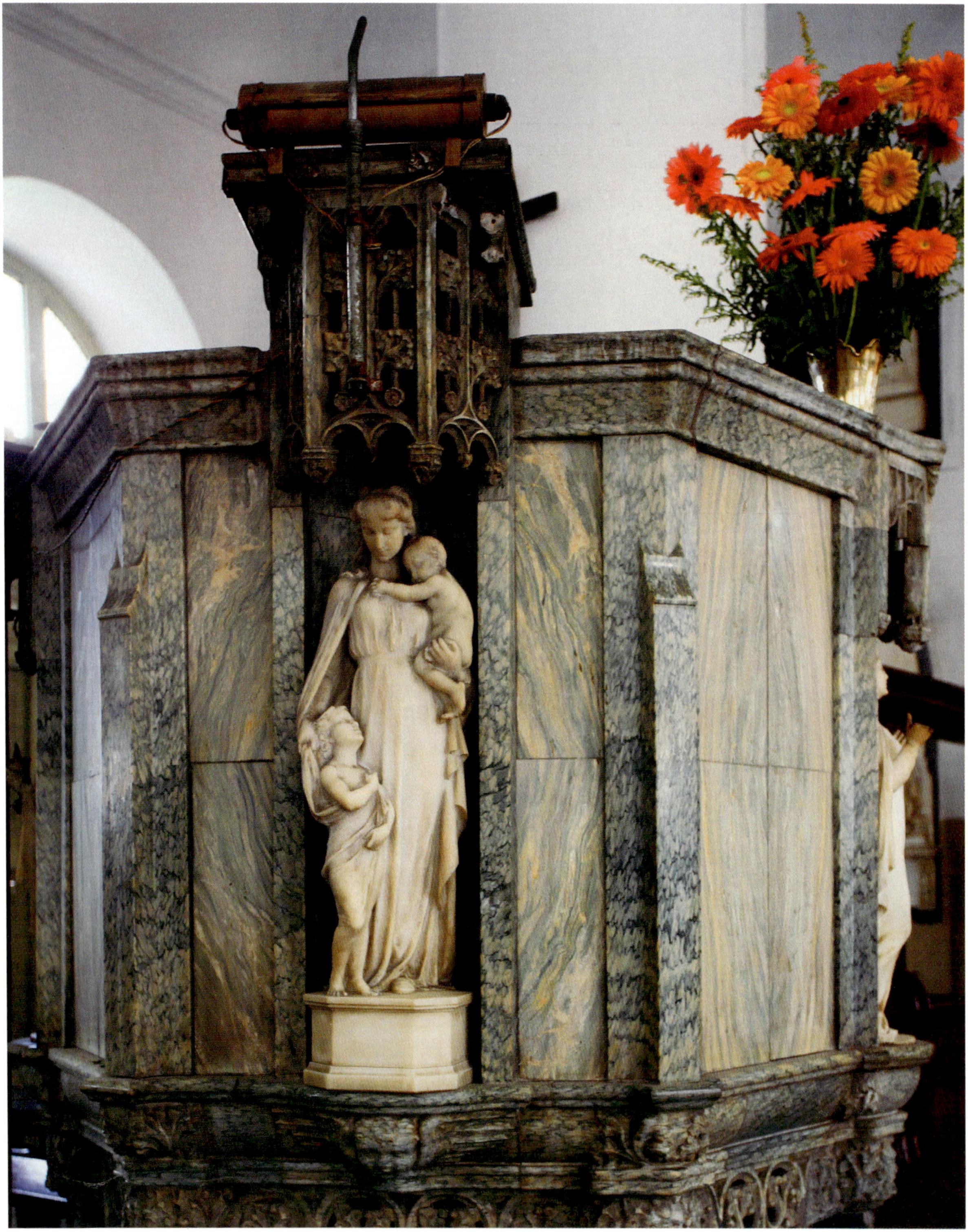

throughout. Being a Protestant church there are no images of saints or the Madonna. This beautiful cathedral is an example of how the British left permanent marks in a country so far from their own. The many memorials to a people who never saw 'home' again it allows a glimpse into Mumbai's colonial past and as such is an important part of the city, a credit to the Indian people who maintain it and of great importance to Mumbai's Christian population.

St. Stephan's Church, 1853

Protestant

The charming 'Little Church on the Hill' is one of Mumbai's earliest Anglican places of worship. It was built for the British Protestants who settled in Bandra after 1775 when the

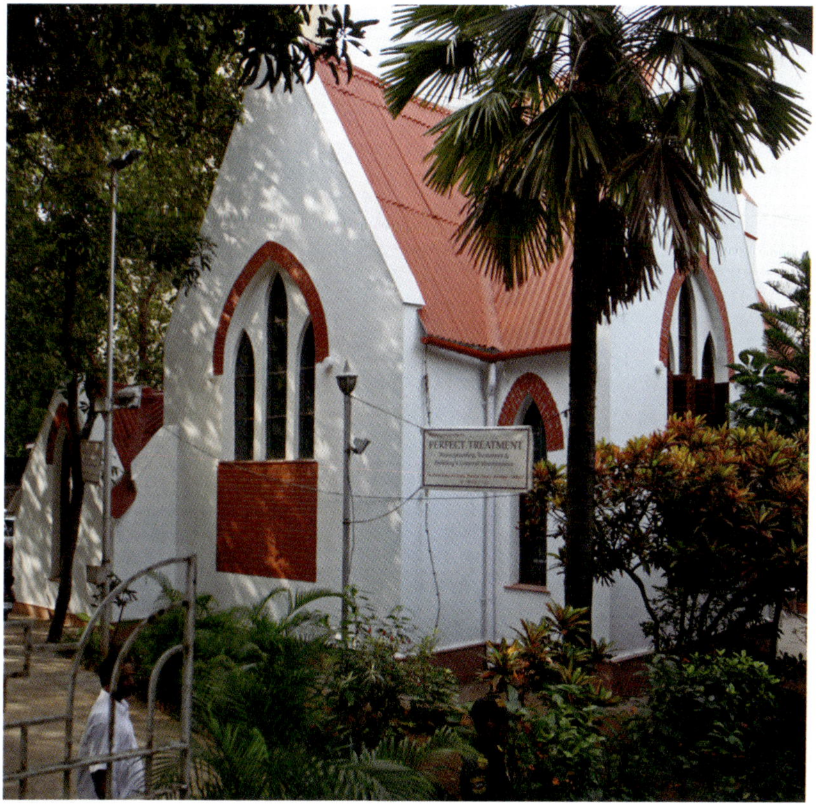

ABOVE: *St. Stephan's Church*

FACING PAGE: *The marble pulpit*

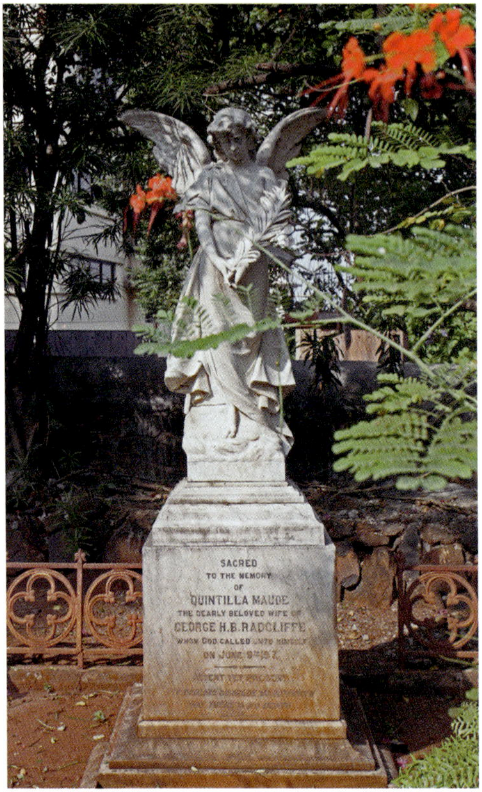

An angel in the cemetery

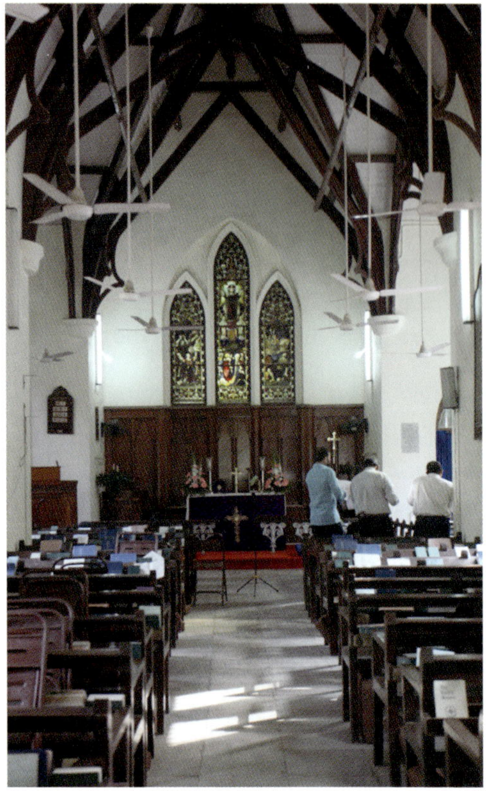

The simple interior and stained glass windows of St. Stephan's Church

island of Salsette and Bandra became part of the British domain. Before that time the area was made up primarily of Roman Catholics. Today the church is no longer a specifically Anglican church but has changed with the times and the nature of cosmopolitan Mumbai to become a church which is open to everyone across all denominations.

This 'story-book' church has whitewashed walls, a bright red high pitched roof and Gothic styled arched windows outlined in red and fitted with shutters. Around the church is a well-maintained garden with a cemetery and a home for the minister. The interior is lovely, filled with a gentle light from beautiful stained glass windows that depict scenes from the Bible. Like many churches in India St. Stephan's manages a centre for poor children. The simple appeal of St. Stephan's makes it one of the prettiest churches in Bandra.

The Church of St. John the Evangelist, 1886

Presbyterian

This beautiful church in Colaba, the southernmost point of Mumbai, is known as the 'Afghan Church' as it was built to commemorate those who died during the battles of the first Afghan War (1837-1843). A large plaque in the church reads;

> *'This church was built in memory of the officers whose names are written on the wall of the Chancel and the non-commissioned officers and private soldiers, too many to be recorded, who fell mindful of their duty, by sickness or by the sword in the campaign of the Sind and Afghanistan,* AD *1837-1843'.*

The church is important as it is the first religious monument to have been built in India to commemorate a military event. As such it is also an important Anglo-Indian monument. Like other military churches

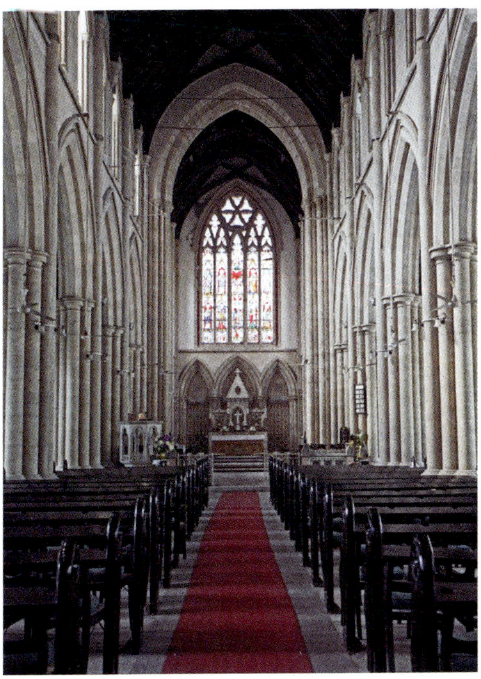

The Church of St. John the Evangelist 1886

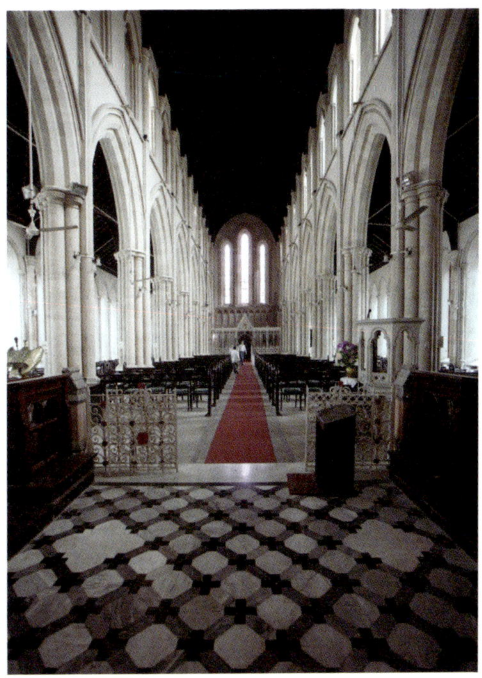

The interior, looking from the altar

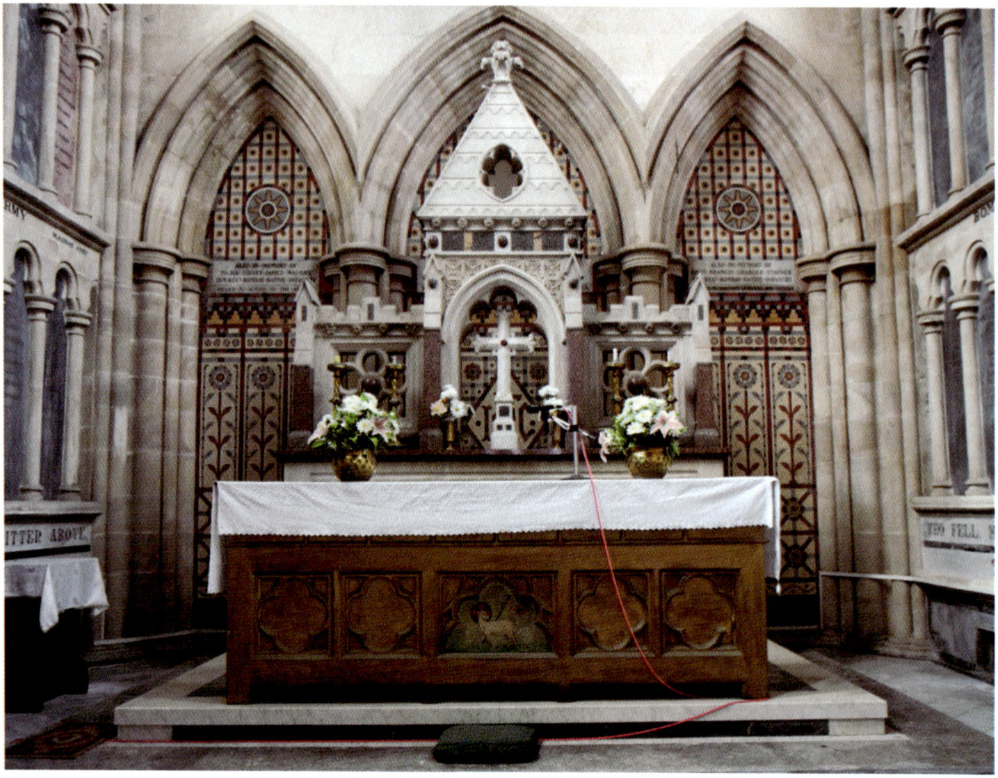

The altar

there are many commemorative plaques to officers and members of the British Army who died in the Second Afghan War of 1879-1887. The plaques also commemorate various Indian regiments such as the Bombay Army, the Madras Army and Ranjit Singh's army from Lahore.

The city's engineer Henry Conybeare was an English engineer who came to India in his twenties to work on the Great Indian Railway System. While there he became interested in Gothic Revival architecture and submitted a design for the construction of the church. It was accepted by the government on the condition that the church's steeple is high enough to guide ships into Mumbai harbour. British sailors who saw the steeple from afar said it reminded them of home. Today the 60 metre steeple can still be seen from the harbour.

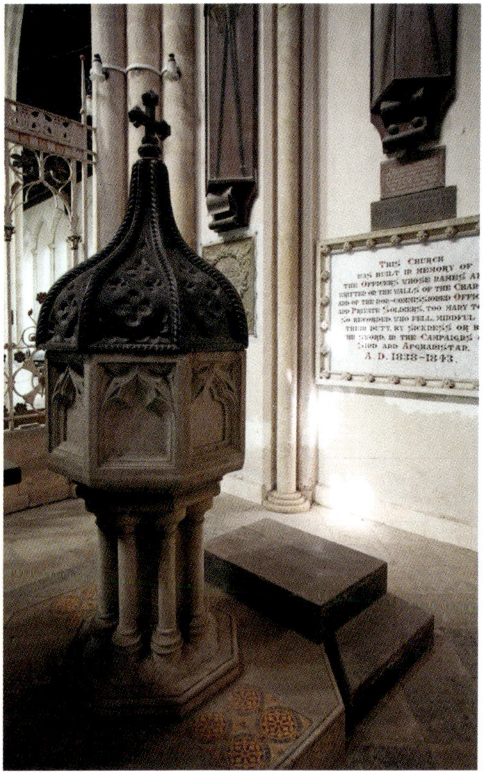

Gothic styled baptismal font

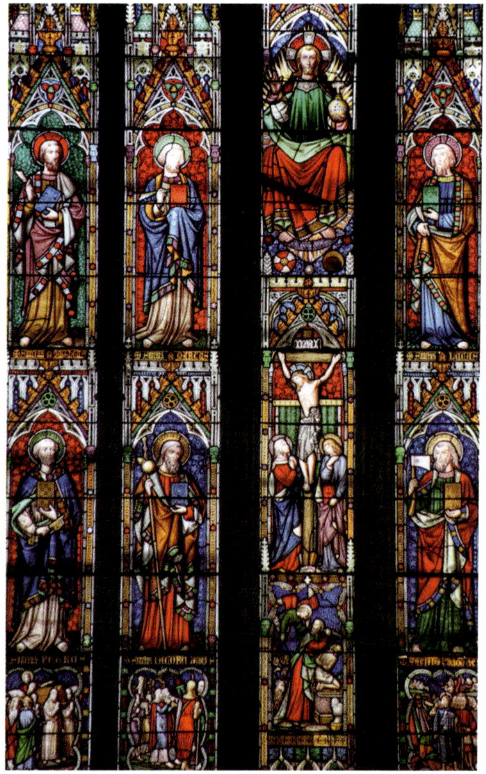

Beautiful stained glass window to trap the sunlight

The foundation stone was laid in 1847 but in 1850 Conybeare stood down as town engineer and Captain Tremenheere of the Royal Engineers undertook the role of supervising the design. He reduced the pitch of the roof and the height of the tower. The church was consecrated in 1858 by John Harding, the Bishop of Bombay.

The graceful steeple which rises some 64 metres was not completed until 1865. The walls of the church are made of rubble faced with Kurla stone, beige-coloured basalt, with arches, piers and finishes in cream coloured Porbunder stone. The high pitched roof is made of varnished teakwood with hammerbeam style ribbing common to English Gothic architecture. Hammer beams are short but when supported by curved braces from the wall a hammerbeam roof can span a far greater distance than an

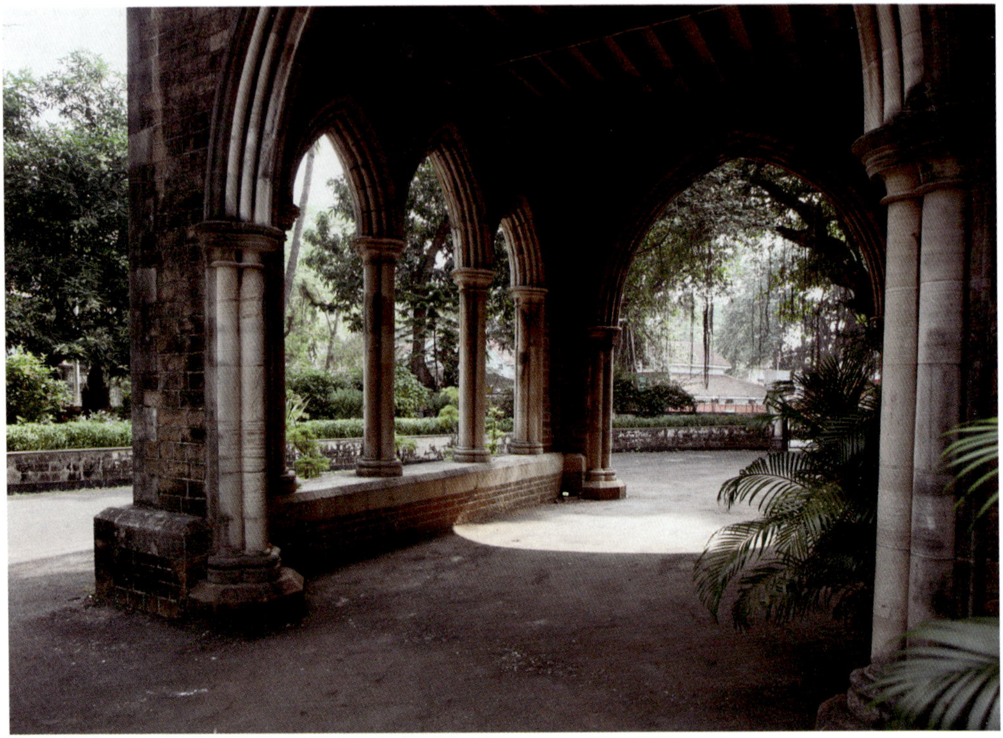

The Gothic styled portico set in a lovely lush green garden

individual piece of timber. These rooves are often highly decorative.

The Gothic portico and entrance is reached by a driveway running through a pretty garden. There is a Celtic style memorial cross in the garden, a rarity in Mumbai, which has four panels inscribed with a list of British soldiers who died in battle. Inside the church is understated and elegant with fluted columns topped with Doric styled capitals. The long red-carpeted nave with side aisles draw the eye to the beautiful stained glass window above the altar designed by William Wailes, the English artist who was known for his English Gothic Revival glass work.

Stained glass was introduced to India by the British and though beautiful it was designed to trap the sun, perfect for cold winter days in Britain but not for the searing heat of an Indian summer. When the Gothic was chosen for Mumbai however, stained glass followed, whether suitable or not. It was

William Butterfield, the famous 19th century British ecclesiastical designer who was commissioned to design much of the interior including the beautiful tiled *reredos*, the choir stall, the Afghan War Memorial mosaics, the geometric floor tiles and the teak wood pews, some of which feature niches for the placement of guns. Sir Cowasji Jehangir, a Cambridge educated Parsi merchant and philanthropist contributed a large sum to help complete the church.

The foundation stone was laid in 1847 by Sir George Clerk, Governor of Mumbai. The beautiful altar is carved in wood with a painted image of the Lamb of God, a name for Jesus that appears in the Gospel of St. John; 'Behold the lamb of God who takes away the sin of the world'. The Afghan Church is known as one of the most beautiful churches in India.

The Basilica of Our Lady of the Mount, 1904

Roman Catholic

The Gothic style Basilica of Our Lady of the Mount sits on a quiet hill overlooking the Arabian Sea in Bandra, a suburb of Mumbai once populated mainly by Christian residents. Today it is home to a variety of religions, Bollywood stars and fashionable boutiques. The Basilica has an interesting history. In the late 1500s on the site of today's church was a small mud and thatch church used as a place of worship by Portuguese settlers. A wooden stature of Mary brought from Portugal by Jesuit priests sat on the altar. In 1640 the thatched church was replaced by a larger wooden chapel and slowly news of the interesting Portuguese statue spread. In 1700 Arab pirates from Muscat pillaged the chapel looking for treasure but finding none they cut off the right arm of the statue looking for anything of value. The ruined statue remained in the church until Maratha warriors desecrated it in 1738 and threw the now famous statue of Mary into the sea. A fisherman dreamt he would find a statue in the sea and on a voyage years later he miraculously did, finding the one armed statue of Mary floating in the sea. The statue was restored in 1761 and placed in the church amidst great rejoicing and a tiny statue of the Baby Jesus was placed carefully to hide Mary's missing arm. This legend made the chapel a place of pilgrimage for Christians and non-Christians alike.

When the chapel needed to be rebuilt it was on a much grander scale. In 1902 the foundation stone was blessed by the Bishop of Damaun and plans were undertaken by architect S.N. Chandabhoy. The church was built in Neo-Gothic style, blessed and opened for public worship towards the end of 1904. The statue of Mary had fulfilled the prayers of her devotees.

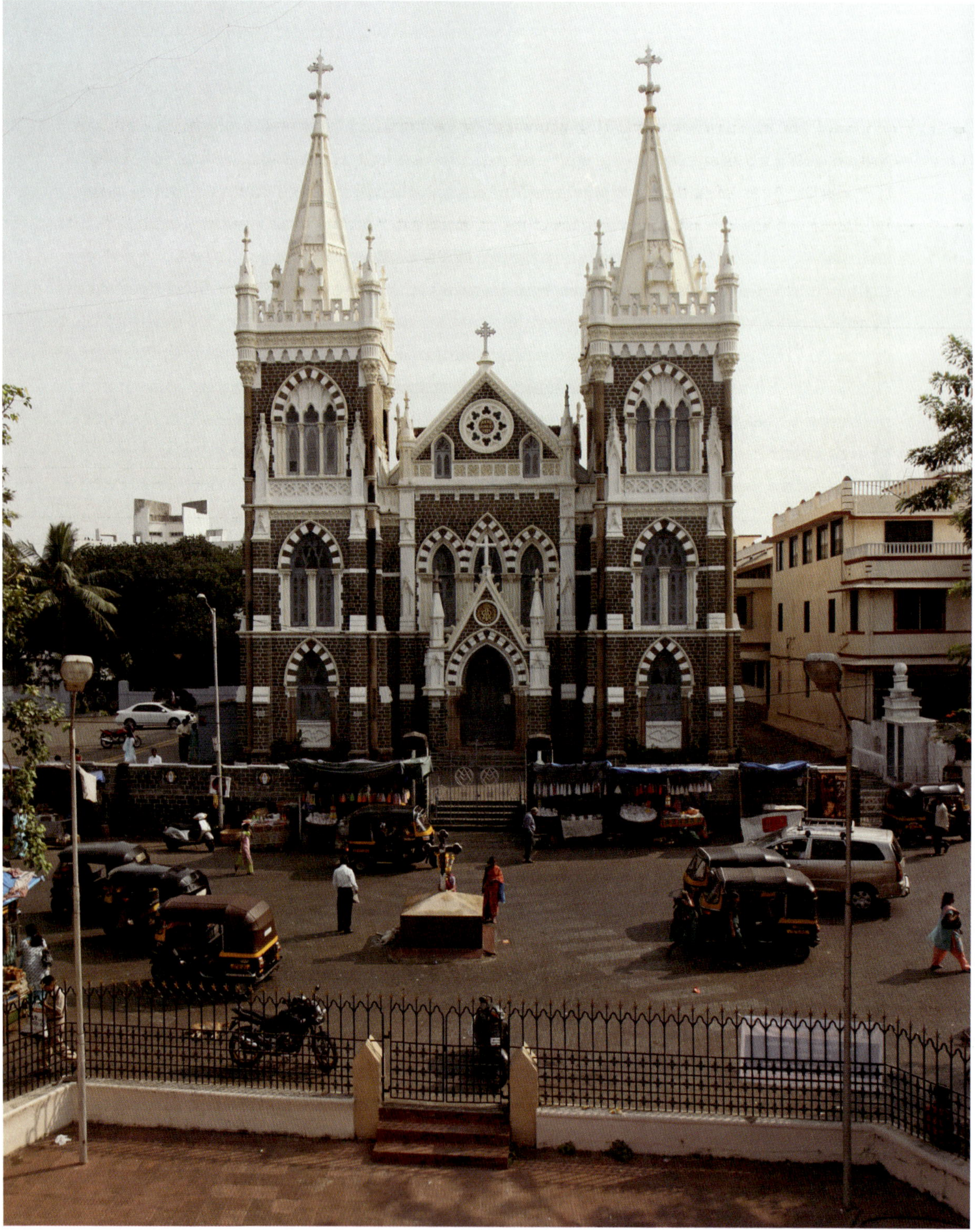

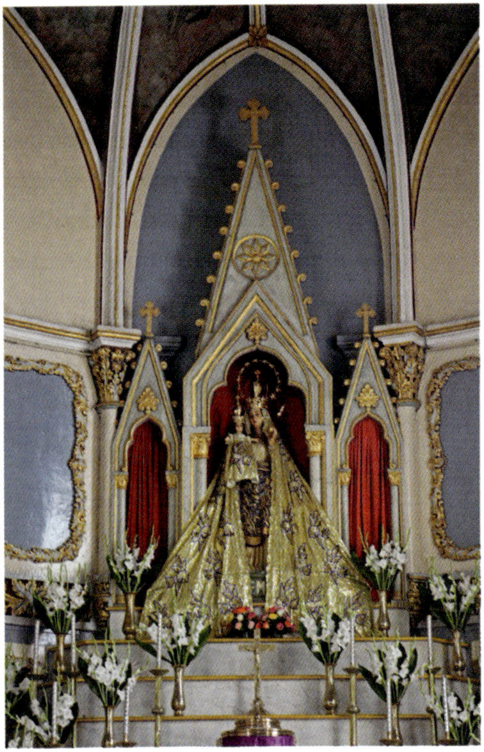

The one armed statue of Mary holding Baby Jesus

FACING PAGE: *Basilica of Our Lady of the Mount in Bandra*

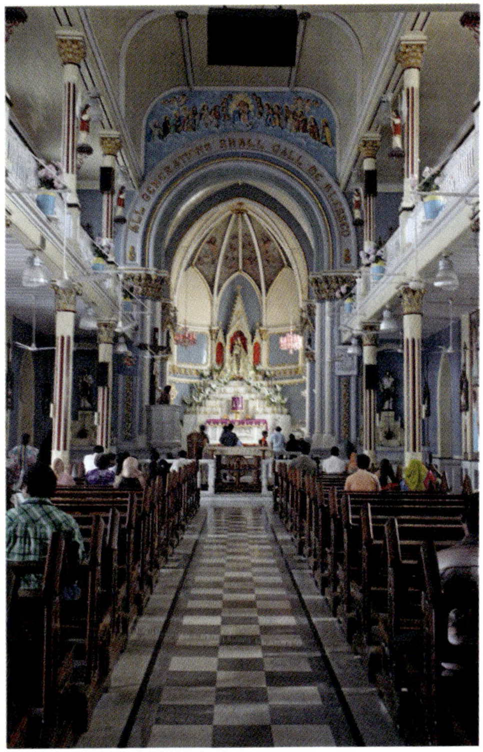

The interior in pastel blue and cream with gilt embellishments

The miraculous statue was the beginning of what is now the famous Bandra Fair celebrated at the Basilica each September to celebrate the birth of the Virgin Mary. During the festival thousands of people of all faiths visit the church which is surrounded by stalls offering images of Mary and curious wax candles in the shape of heads, limbs, babies, aeroplanes and houses. After finding a candle that matches an ailment or a desire, devotees light it inside the church in the hope their prayers will be answered. Many strongly believe that the church has great healing powers. During the fair Christian, Hindu, Muslim and Parsi devotees bring gifts of jewellery, crowns and garlands.

On the facade of the Basilica is a circular plaque bearing the emblem of the Basilica, A.M. the initials for Ave Maria, the Angel Gabriel's greeting to Mary of Nazareth before

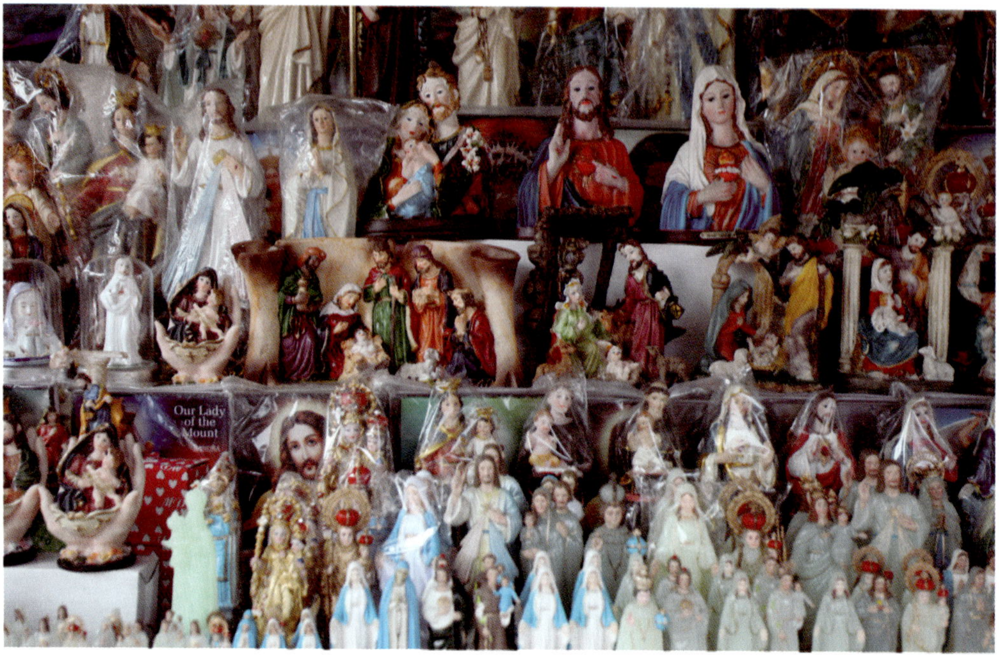

ABOVE: *Religious souvenirs*

FACING PAGE TOP AND BELOW: *Candles, and below wax* tokris *used for wishes*

announcing that she had been chosen to be the mother of Jesus Christ. The letters are on a crown with lilies to symbolise Mary's elevated position and her purity.

The Basilica is an impressive twenty metres wide, the facade of which is dark brick with tall white spires and borders. The main feature of the Basilica is the twin towers crenulations and the tall spires each topped with a cross.

The main entrance has Gothic styled stone arches each side in front of which are delicate round stone columns. Three connecting windows on the first level are for ventilation inside the church and each of the twin towers has a window. The third level has four windows with a large circle in the middle inscribed with the words; 'Anno Jubilaei 1904' which signifies the golden jubilee year of the announcement of the creed of the Immaculate Conception, and the year of the new Basilica's inauguration. Surrounding this large circle is a triangular elevation above which sits a cross. The twin towers have ribbed spires topped with distinctive crosses.

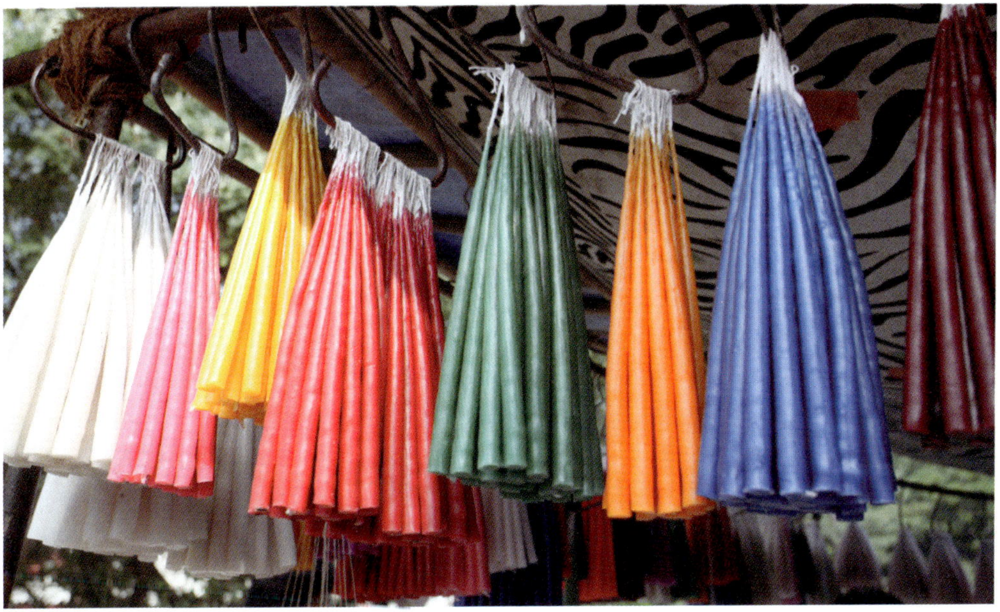

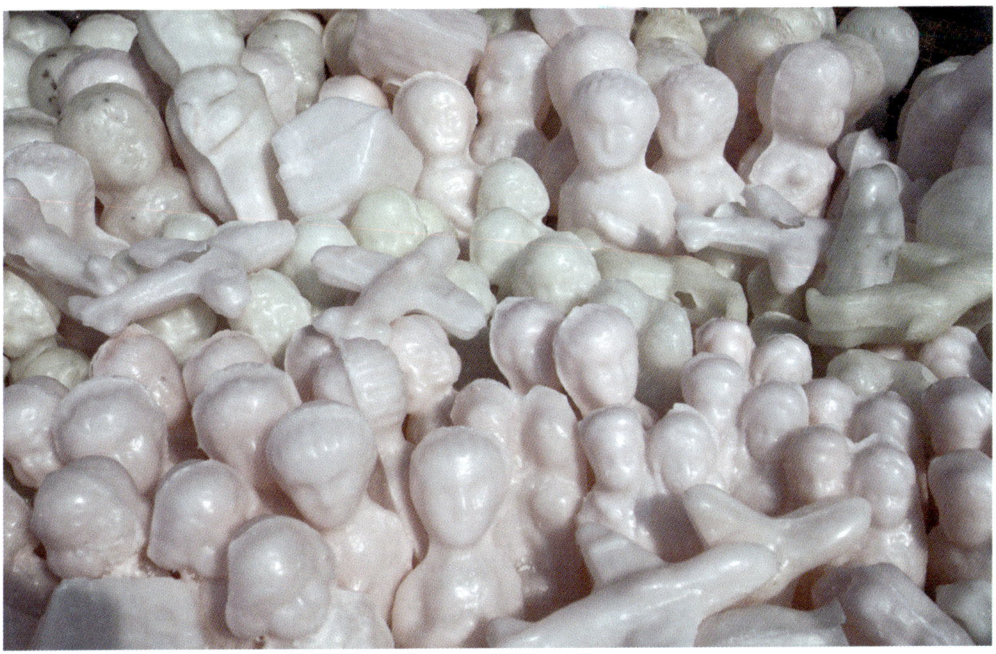

The interior is painted pastel blue and cream with gilt embellishments including the capitals of the fluted Corinthian columns which support an upper gallery. Taller Corinthian columns support a large round arch that separates the nave from the sanctuary, on which are the words in gold, 'All generations shall call me blessed.'

On the high ceiling of the sanctuary is the image of a gold dove, the symbol of the Holy Spirit. Seven rays radiate from the dove symbolising the seven gifts of the Holy Spirit. Murals adorn the walls but it is the famous statue of Mary holding the baby Jesus that is the centrepiece of the main altar. The church was granted the status of a Basilica in 1954.

Opposite the Basilica set on the western slope of the hill is the interesting Oratory of Our Lady of Fatima crowned by a two metre high statue of Our Lady of Fatima.

The Oratory of Our Lady of Fatima

The Oratory is directly opposite the Basilica of Our Lady of the Mount. It was erected to commemorate the Marian Congress held in Mumbai in 1954. It is a shallow stepped building with a wide curved facade. Thirty

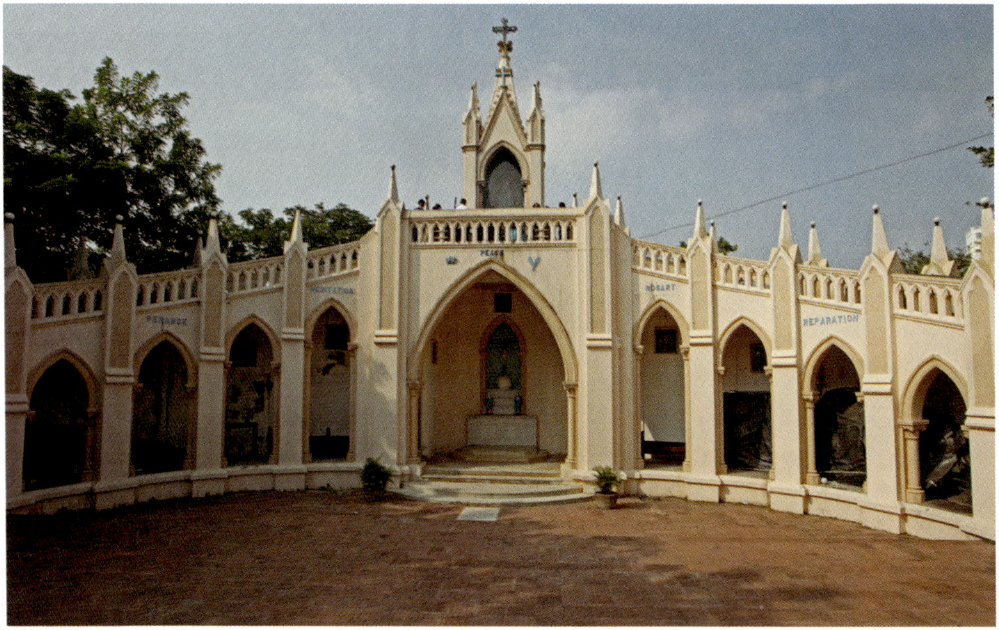

The Oratory of Our Lady of Fatima

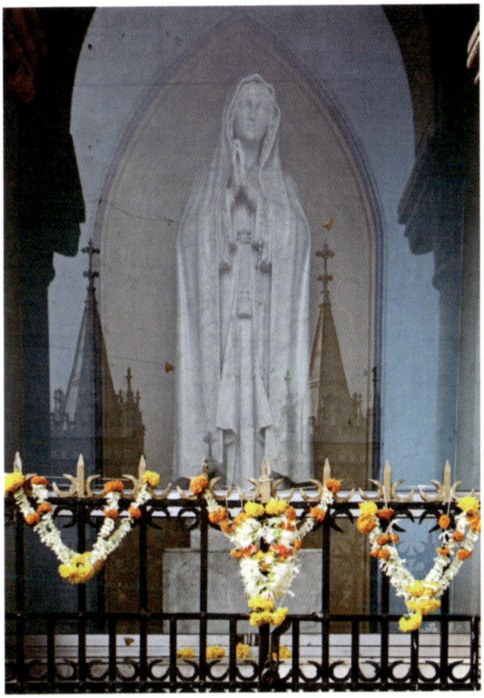

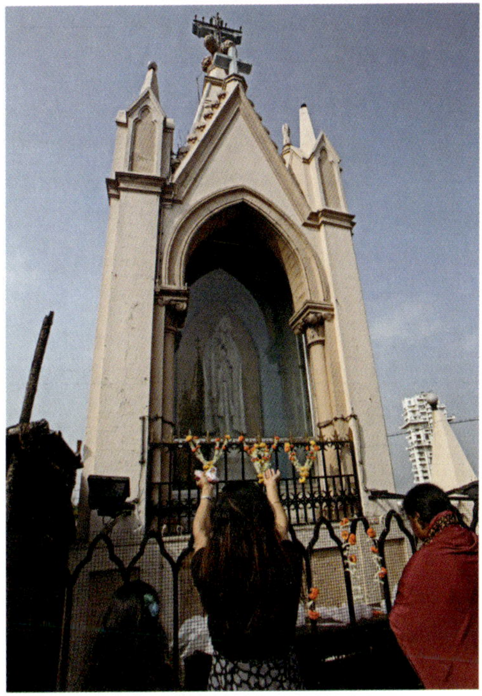

ABOVE (L & R): *The statue of Our Lady of Fatima at the top the Oratory*

eight steps lead to a landing where a little Gothic chapel holds an important marble statue of Our Lady of Fatima holding a rosary. This statue is a replica of the famous 'Pilgrims Virgin' the origin of which is based on an image of the Virgin who appeared above an oak tree before three children in Fatima, Portugal in 1917. From a description given by one of the children a statue was carved in Portugal in 1947 and soon after 150,000 pilgrims saw the statue blessed in Fatima as 'the pilgrim, the traveller' and to this day the statue travels the world as the International Pilgrim Virgin Statue of Our lady of Fatima, an 'Ambassador of Peace' for the Catholic Church. In 1950 the Oratory was built to commemorate the statues visit to Mumbai. H.M. Patel was the architect and the devout Monsignor Eddie planned the building and is buried at the foot of the Oratory, now a Minor Basilica. Words on the walls of the Oratory read; Prayer, Penance, Meditation, Peace, Rosary, Reparation and Sacrifice.

Salvacao Church, Our Lady of Salvation Church, 1977

Roman Catholic

In Dadar, a bustling suburb of Mumbai is the Nossa Senhora da Salvação known by locals as the Salvacao or the 'Portuguese Church.' Originally built in 1596 by Portuguese Franciscans today it is a modern church designed by famous Indian architect Charles Correa based on original church designs being the three major stages of Christ's life;

FACING PAGE TOP: *The entrance to Correa's modern version of the 'Portuguese Church' in Dadar*

FACING PAGE BELOW: *The pulpit is a single piece of granite*

BELOW: *The skylight in the baptistery by M. F. Husain*

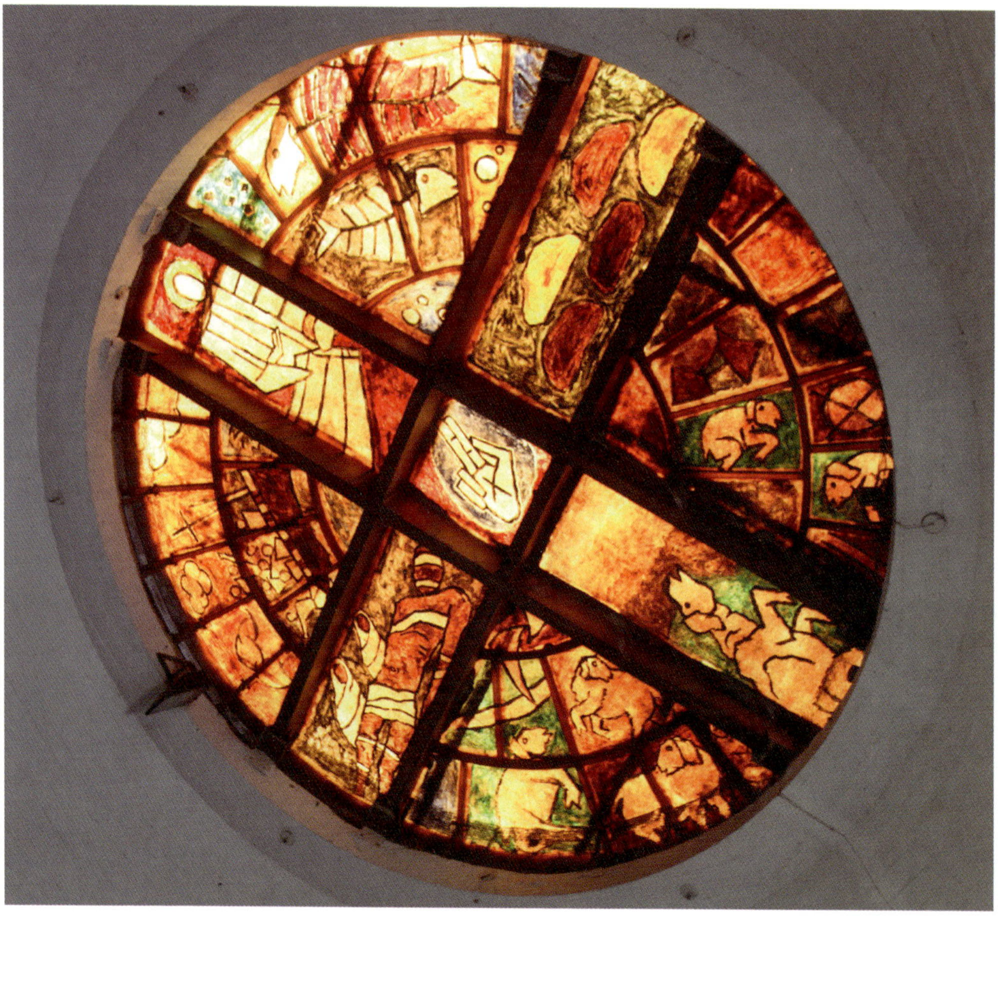

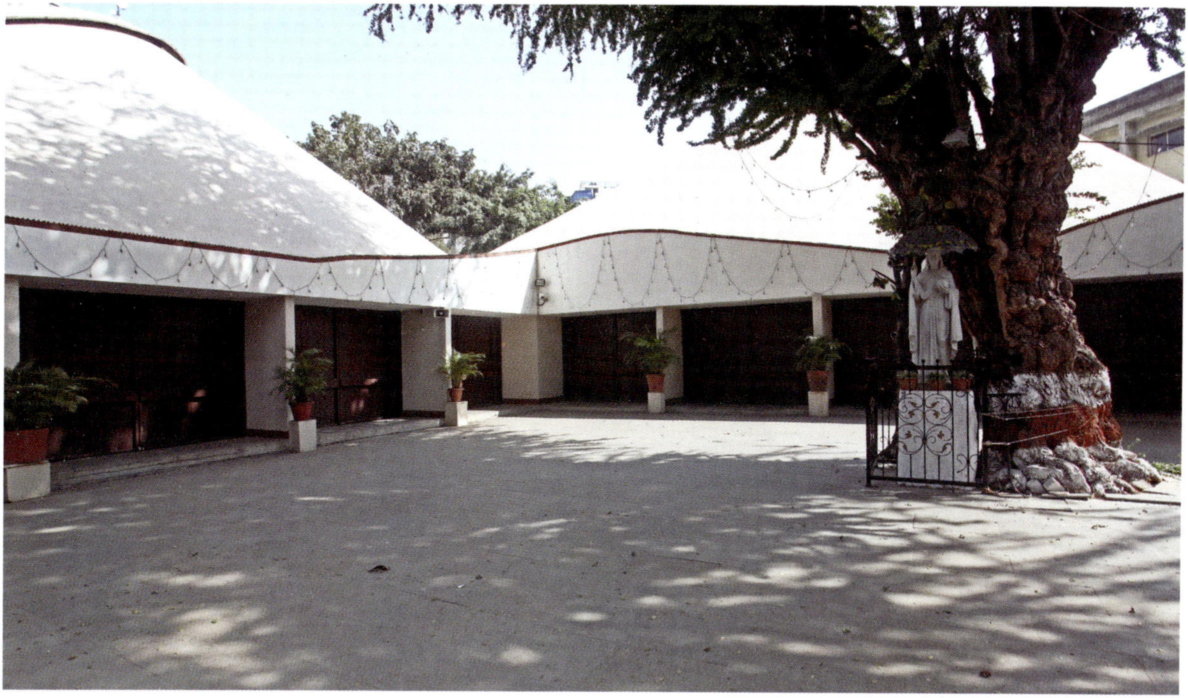

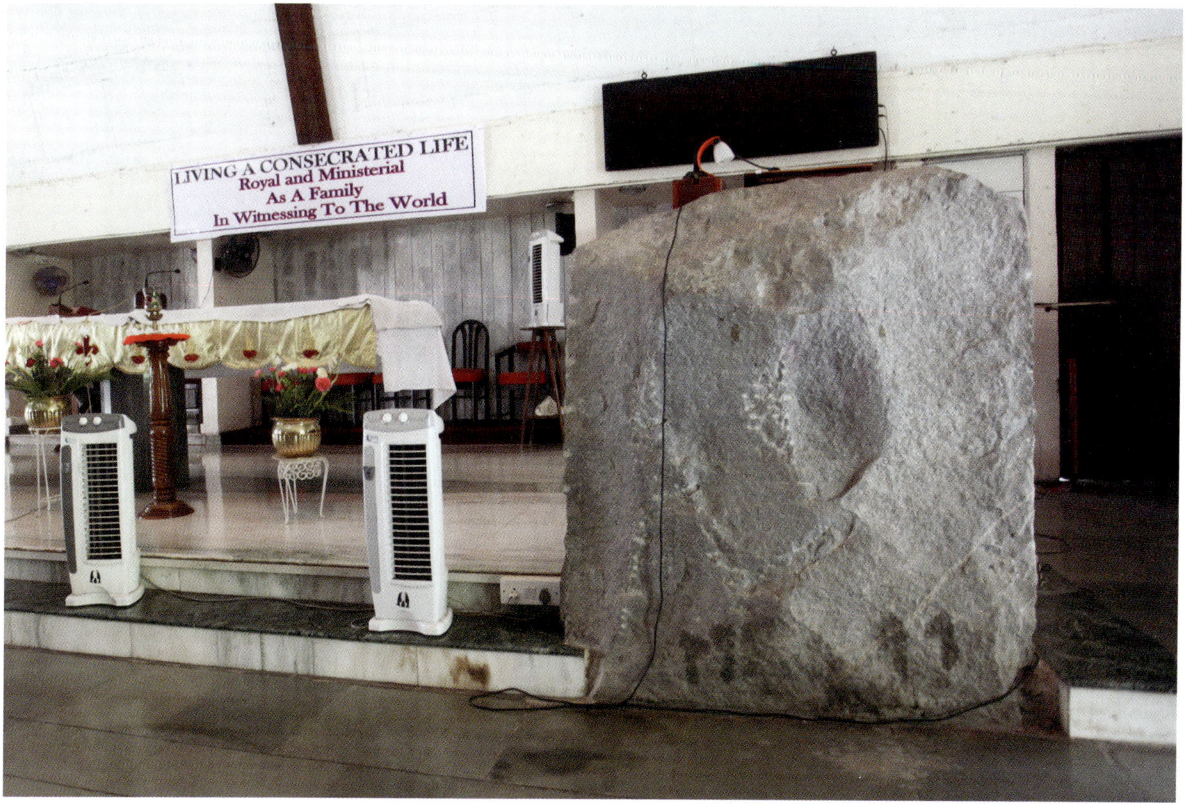
LIVING A CONSECRATED LIFE
Royal and Ministerial
As A Family
In Witnessing To The World

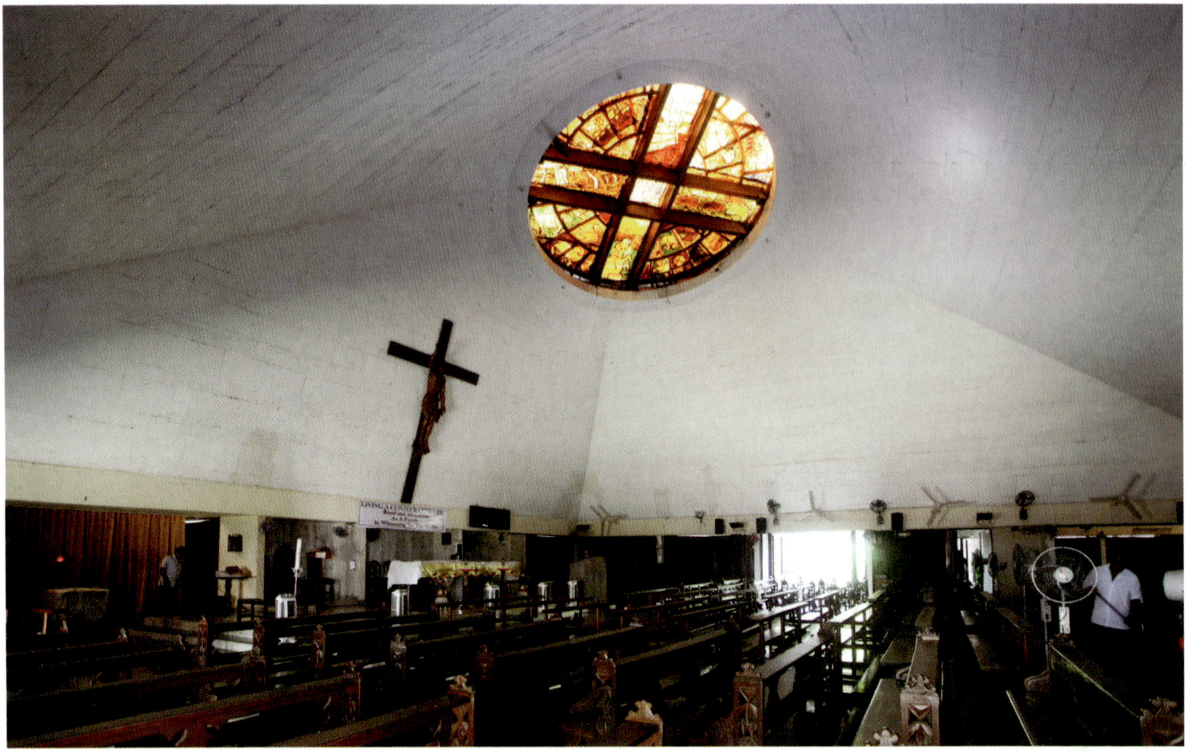

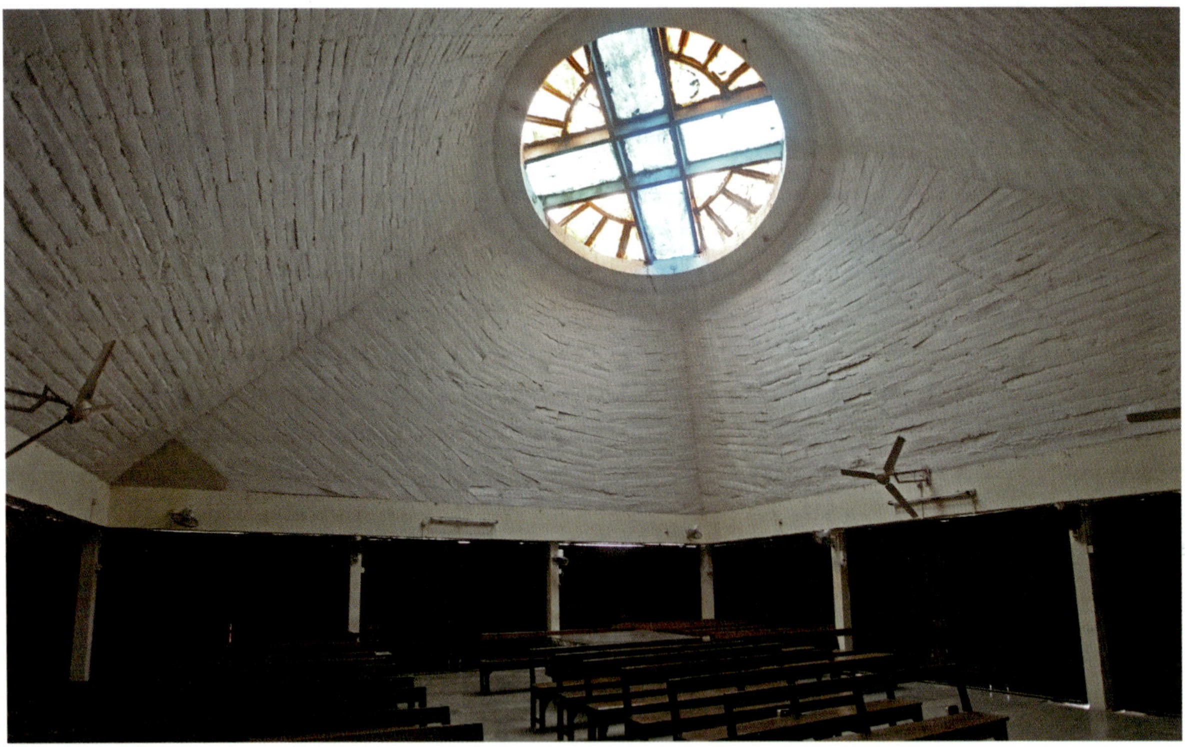

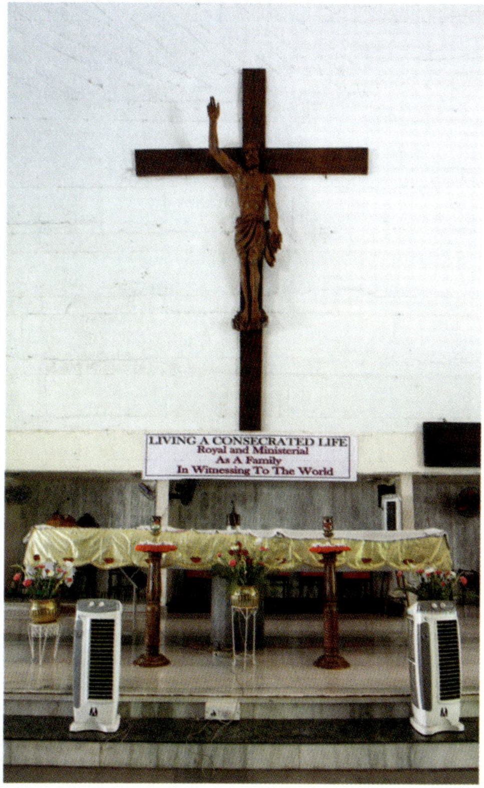

ABOVE: *The simple carved wooden crucifix and the altar*
FACING PAGE TOP AND BELOW: *Interior spaces*

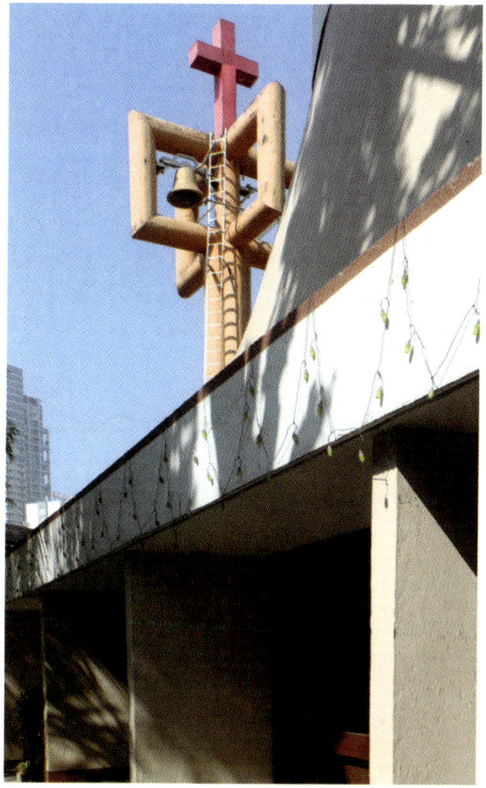

Though secular in design the church is clearly a Christian place of worship

the baptism, public life and the crucifixion. Physically these three stages are manifested by the baptismal font, the pulpit and the altar. By returning to fundamental church principles Correa wanted to combine traditional Christian themes with modern concepts such as environmental concerns and the demands of a modern society. Enclosed by a high wall Correa has created interior and exterior spaces that flow together harmoniously, described by architect Jon Lang as a 'walled island of architectural forms.'

The building is an interesting arrangement of horizontally connected square spaces. Some are courtyards open-to-the-sky and others are closed with huge shell shaped concrete roofs, like flues, with vents to draw out warm air and covered with round skylights of stained glass.

The church reflects Correa's principle that 'breathing buildings' are best suited to India's warm climate where open to the sky spaces are a part of India's culture. In many ways the church is similar to India's courtyard houses.

The main areas, the baptistery, the congregational area, the oratory and the sacristy are linked and covered resulting in what seems to be a series of intimate spaces and yet over a thousand people can be accommodated, able to flow from one space to another, to courtyards and a garden with grottos and the Fourteen Stations of the Cross. Correa has said "Architecture is not an object to be looked at but an energy field to be moved through."

The interiors are simple, with plain timber pews and little decoration. The altar is a large single piece of rough-hewn granite. Behind the altar is a wooden crucifix with Christ's hand raised in the sign of a blessing. Correa's use of stained glass windows in the apex of the shells create the mysterious numinous light that falls from a great height, a device seen in Gothic churches in particular. It is these shafts of light that create a dramatic mood to the interior. The most beautiful is the painted glass window over the nave by prominent artist Maqbool Fida Husain. The painting is divided into sections similar to stained glass. The subject is the biblical 'Loaves and Fishes' story.

The late Charles Correa was asked to design the new church which was built between 1974 and 1977. P.G. Nair was the engineer and Abbas Jasdenwalla was the builder. Externally the Salvacao Church appears secular in design yet it is clearly a Christian place of worship. Internally its moulded concrete linked spaces and low light invoke a silent retreat from the outside world, a place of prayer and contemplation.

Delhi Old and New: The Ancient and the Modern

Over centuries the capital of India has been occupied by a succession of dynasties and empires that came to plunder it or rule India from it. It is one of the oldest surviving cities in the world and the site of many earlier people who once thrived, were destroyed after which others rose again,, thrived and were also destroyed…

A brief history of Delhi can begin in the 7th century with the emergence of the Rajputs, a Hindu warrior clan from northern India who ruled until the early 12th century. When the Muslim sultans who ruled much of northern India captured Delhi, it was the beginning of a succession of different Muslim dynasties who ruled during different periods

FACING PAGE: *The aerial view of the city of Delhi before the Siege* - The Illustrated London News, January 16, 1858 (Wikipedia public domain)

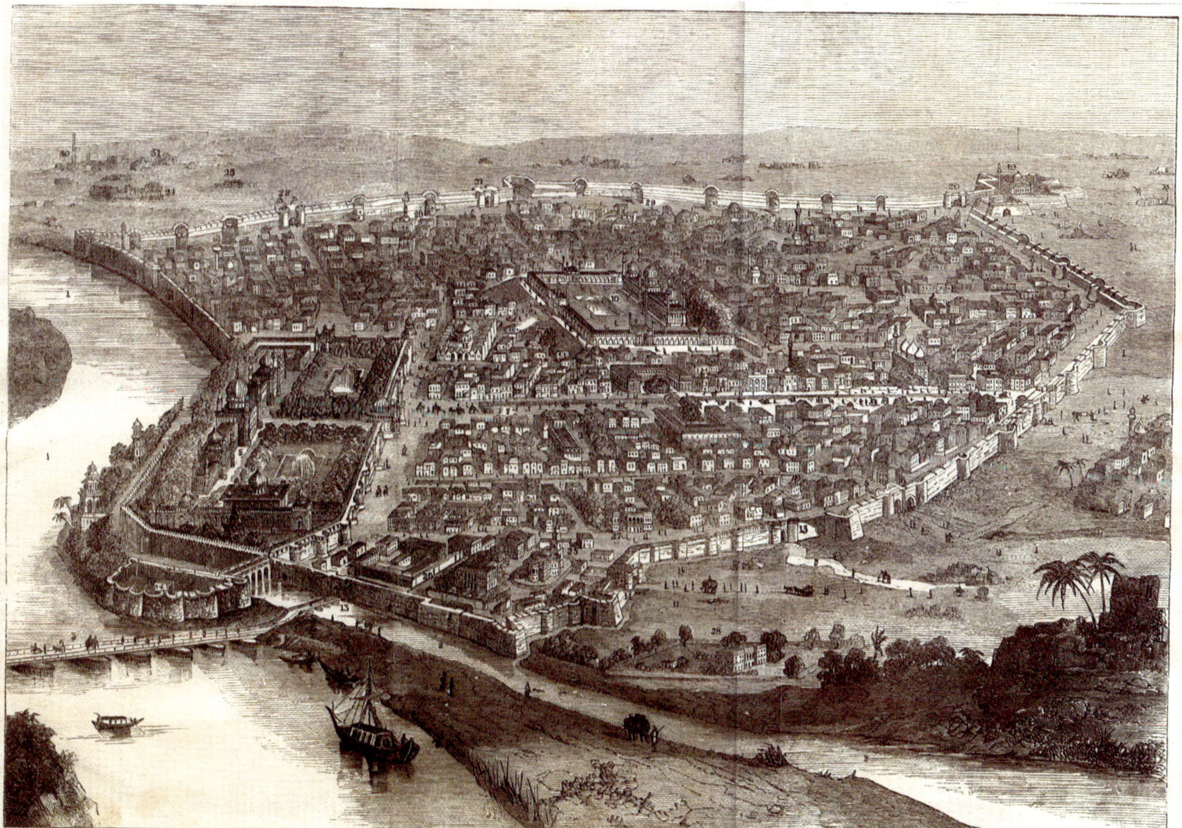

1. The Jumna. 2. Offshoot of the Jumna. 3. Pontoon Bridge. 4. Selimghur, an ancient fort. 5. Palace and Gardens. 6. The Marble Hall, or Throne-room. 7. Main street of Delhi, Chandni Chauk. 8. Canal-street. 9. The Banking-house. 10. The Jumma Musjid. 11. The Sadoola Khan. 12. The Musjid Fetipore. 13. Negum Bod Gate. 14. Cashmere Gate.
15. Moree Gate. 16. Cabul Gate and Water Gate. 17. The Canal. 18. Lahore Gate. 19. Hindoo College. 20. Ajmere Gate. 21. Turkoman Gate. 22. Delhi Gate. 23. Gaol. 24. Lunatic Asylum. 25. English Church. 26. Magazine and Store Houses. 27. Skinner's House. 28. Custom House. 29. Martello Towers. 30. Kotub Minar. 31. Ruins of Ancient Delhi.

THE CITY OF DELHI BEFORE THE SIEGE

from the 13th century on. They became known as the Delhi Sultanates.

In 1398 the ruthless Turko-Mongol warlord Tamerlane pillaged Delhi and left it in ruins. Much of the city's population was executed. With the rise of the Lodhi Dynasty around 1451 the Delhi Sultanate regained some control. However Babur, a descendent of Tamerlane, was the next Muslim warlord to destroy Delhi at the Battle of Panipat in 1526. In just a few years the Delhi Sultanate rose again but fell in 1555 to Babur's son Humayun. A year later Humayun died and the same year his son Akbar defeated the Hindu army lead by General Hemu. The Sultanate was then swallowed up by the mighty Mughal Empire.

The Mughal Empire reached its peak in the 17th century and Delhi was known as the capital of Islamic India. The ruler Shah Jahan, best known for building the Taj Mahal, created a beautiful walled city and called it Shahjahanabad after himself. It was filled with mansions and mosques, vast gardens, fountains and arcaded shops where artisans and merchants traded in precious stones, embroidered cloth and gold and silver jewellery. Thick walls surrounded the city and people came and went through fourteen splendid gates, including grand royal processions complete with decorated elephants. It was known as 'heaven on earth.' Writer William Dalrymple describes Delhi at that time as being 'decadent and sophisticated.' Christian churches also existed in Shahjahanabad built by Armenians but are no longer standing, having been destroyed by warlord Nadir Shah of Persia who was eager to attack India after learning of the country's wealth. He attacked Delhi in 1739 in a battle that lasted just three hours. Nadir Shah's massive army was simply too strong for the Mughals.

Shah's Persian soldiers clashed with the people of Delhi. When a rumour spread of Shah's death many Persian soldiers were killed, prompting Shah to order a complete massacre of Delhi. It was brutal and the city was destroyed, leaving the Mughal Empire weak and depleted, unable to rise and fight future invaders.

Things changed for Delhi In 1757 when the city was captured by the Marathas, a Hindu warrior race, originally mercenaries, who collected revenue for the Muslim rulers. They transferred their loyalties from one ruler to another when it suited as was customary during feudal times. By 1771 Delhi was ruled by Maratha ruler Mahadji Shinde.

More change ensued when the British East India Company's army disrupted the Marathas rule in 1803 by defeating them in the Battle of Delhi. When peace was restored the British moved into the walled city of Shahjahanabad where they lived amongst the wealthier Indian population. They integrated well even learning Persian, the language spoken in those days. It was very different to the way the Presidency cities of Chennai, Kolkata and Mumbai later developed, where Europeans and Indians lived in well-defined areas.

This pleasant arrangement changed after India's First War of Independence in 1857, the first united rebellion against British colonial rule. Delhi had experienced a four month long siege after which there was a shift in British thinking. They were intent on revenge, executing the rebels and punishing the Muslim population who were widely seen as being the main instigators even though many important Hindus also played a part. Mosques were destroyed and the area around the fort cleared for protection. The western walls of Shahjahanabad were pulled down to allow for the railway and by the 1870's the British were living further north in an area called the Civil Lines (White Town in earlier times) that was developed for senior officers and their families.

The British were now intent on eradicating Delhi's Mughal past but they were also aware of Delhi's symbolic importance to the people. Grand events were staged in Delhi to showcase Britain's power and a durbar was planned to announce Queen Victoria as the Empress of India in 1877, even though Kolkata was the capital of British India. Delhi, once ruled for centuries by Mughal emperors, was being flaunted to the world as the centre of British power.

The most important durbar was certainly the crowning of King George V in 1911. It was an astonishing spectacle, a gathering of Indian princes and attended by over 200,000 people. At this Imperial durbar King George made the surprising announcement that the capital of India would shift from Kolkata to Delhi, a fateful declaration for the people of Kolkata.

Today Shahjahanabad is known as 'Old Delhi'. It is a faint shadow of its former glory. No longer is the city a majestic wonder, instead it is a frenzied, fascinating place of narrow winding lanes, ancient mosques and some crumbling mansions. Monkeys scamper about bustling bazaars while cows wander at will and beggars jostle. Women sell mounds of colourful spices and now and then a snake charmer can be seen. Chandni Chowk or 'Moonlit Square', once India's richest street and famous for its silver merchants still survives. In many ways the city has retained many of its ancient traditions.

South-west of Shahjahanabad is a slope called Raisina Hill which rises up from the Yamuna River. It is here that the British created their own Delhi in the early 20th century. British architects Sir Edwin Lutyens and Sir Herbert Baker were called on to design an imperial city, vastly different from the old both in architecture, space and ways of life.

As a planned city New Delhi developed into an orderly place of wide tree lined avenues which radiated out from major imperial landmarks. The most impressive avenue is the Rajpath which leads west from the National Stadium, through the India Gate to the Rashtrapati Bhavan or the Presidential House, which stands in a 330 acre estate. In this new, open city the British also built their churches and elegant bungalows complete with gardens, gates and walls.

There is no boundary between Old and New Delhi but the contrast between the two is clear, like an invisible line more noticeable in some places than others. For the British New Delhi needed to look orderly, clean and law abiding compared to the chaos of the old city which the British now saw as unhygienic and disease ridden.

It took almost twenty years to build New Delhi however it was the British capital for just 16 years. With independence in 1947 it became the seat of the Government of India. It is an impressive, cosmopolitan city scattered about with ancient Mughal monuments, some famous and others forgotten over time. They are a reminder of the city's history. In the more recent past are the churches, mainly Anglican and Protestant with a small number of Catholic churches as well. The most famous are the colonial churches; the Church of the Redemption and the Church of the Sacred Heart. The most remarkable and most overlooked is St. Martin's, the garrison church. In this chapter we begin with the oldest, a well preserved church in Old Delhi at Kashmere Gate, St. James' Church built in 1836 by Colonel James Skinner, the son of a Scottish officer and a Rajput mother.

St. James' Church, 1836

Anglican

St. James' Church or 'Skinner's Church,' as it is known is named after Colonel James Skinner, one of India's most famous soldiers and adventurers. Set in peaceful gardens at Kashmiri Gate, a relatively quiet area of Old Delhi, it is a beautiful Protestant church steeped in history.

James Skinner was born in Kolkata in 1778 of parents from two very different cultures; his father was a Christian, a Scottish Lieutenant-Colonel of the East India Company and his mother was a Rajput princess and a devout Hindu. Skinner longed to serve as an officer in the British East India Company's Army but as a child of a mixed marriage he was rejected. He was offered the rank of ensign in the Maratha Army of Maharaja Daulat Rao Sindhia of Gwalior in 1795. It was not

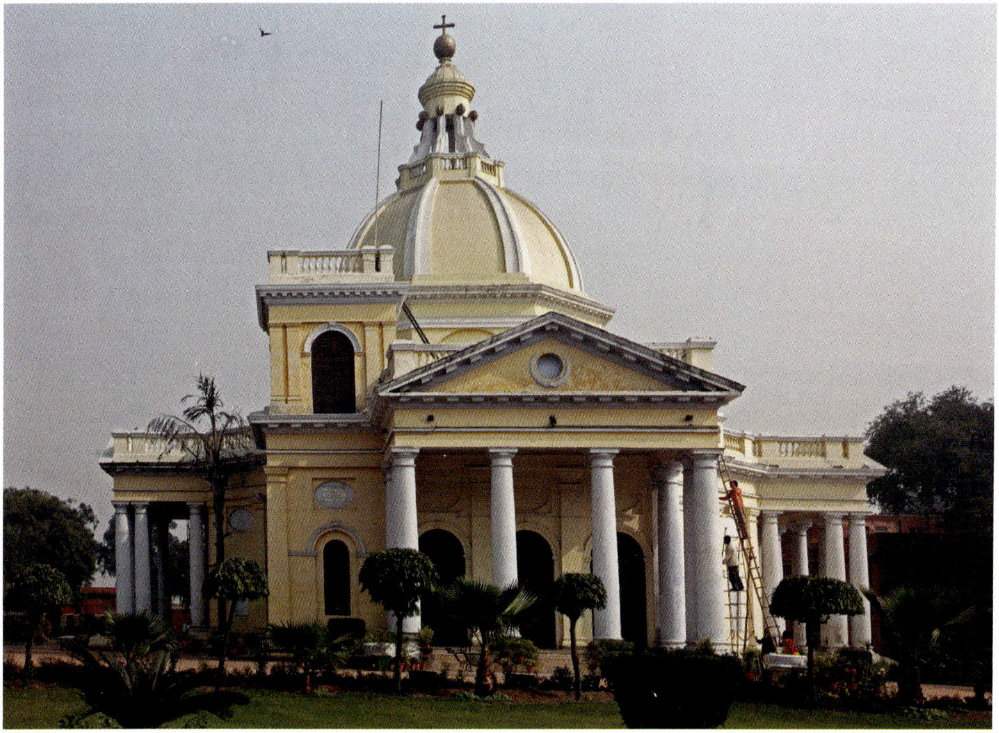

St. James' Church or 'Skinner's Church'

uncommon for Anglo-Indians to join the armies of Indian princes. At just 22, he was commanding three battalions. After eight years in the Maharaja's army he experienced a life changing moment during a battle in eastern Rajasthan in 1800. A near-death experience while on the battlefield of Uniara was what spurred him to swear that if he lived, he would build a church. St. James' Chruch in Kashmiri Gate, Delhi, where Skinner lies buried, was the result of the oath. Fighting men of a defeated state rode out for a final, suicidal battle dressed in yellow. That antiquated Rajput code has survived in the yellow ceremonial uniform of one of Indian Army's oldest cavalry regiments, the 1st Horse of Skinner's Horse. Wounded and left for dead Skinner made a vow that he would build a church if he survived. Remarkably he was rescued by a Dalit (an untouchable) woman who took him to the enemy's camp where he was nursed back to health and released. He never forgot his rescuer, later sending her 1000 rupees.

When war broke out between the Marathas and the British (the second Anglo-Maratha War in 1803) Skinner and many other Anglo-Indians refused to fight and subsequently all were dismissed. When the Marathas seized Delhi the British convinced Skinner, now known as a courageous soldier, to join the British Indian Army. He was invited to raise a regiment of Irregular Cavalry for the East India Company. He accepted on the condition he would not be asked to fight against Maharajah Sindhia, his former employer.

Skinner was able to form his own regiment. Eight hundred horsemen deserted the Maratha Army to serve under Skinner in his Irregular Cavalry Regiment, 'Skinner's Horse' or the 'Yellow Boys' as they were known. Irregular regiments were appealing to the adventurous as they were less disciplined than regular cavalry regiments. Soon 'Skinner's Horse' became famous. With their yellow uniforms and dashing patterned turbans they were a striking lot. Skinner became known as 'Sikander Sahib', the reincarnation of Alexander the Great as his cavalry never lost a battle. Despite the regiment's success it was later disbanded due to economic reasons. James Skinner became disillusioned with the British. He wrote; "*I imagined myself to be serving a people who had no prejudices against caste or colour. But I find myself mistaken.*"

James Skinner's church is his legacy. It is the physical embodiment of the promise he made on the battlefield in Rajasthan and the place where he is laid to rest. It is said that he also built a temple and a mosque somewhere in Delhi but to this day their location remains unknown. He was always attached to the Indian way of life; however the architecture he chose for his church (and his house in Delhi) classical in design. Originally painted pink the church today is pale yellow and a splendid example of Renaissance architecture.

Built in a cruciform shape it has three porticos, each supported by six huge Doric columns. The fourth arm of the church on the east contains the altar. The main entrance consists of three archways with a pediment atop and a round window within the apex. The octagonal dome is the most striking feature of the church. Begum Samru's 1822 church in Sardhana which Skinner knew and admired would seem to be the model for St. James'.

The dome of St. James' is topped with a striking copper ball and cross. Next to it is a small square tower with a parapet. Inside the exterior dome is a smaller dome which creates a lower ceiling in keeping with the reduced scale of the interior. Though not as grand as other churches in Delhi the design of

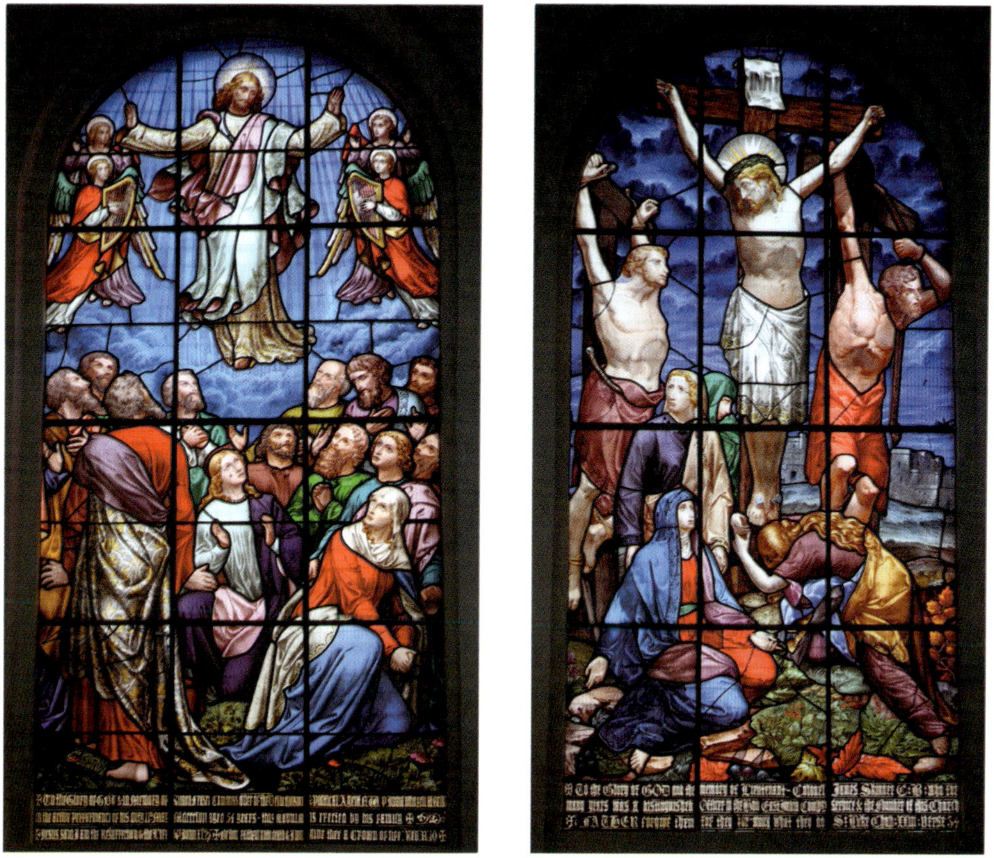

The stained glass windows of St. James' Church

St. James' is complex. The blue painted dome sits in the centre of the church supported by a substantial octagonal arcade. The circular shape it creates circumscribes the area below where the congregation sit. On either side of the altar are two beautiful 19th century stained glass windows depicting scenes from Christ's last days; the Crucifixion and the Resurrection. They create a soft glow which changes according to the time of day.

A third window is in the vestry. It illustrates the terror of soldiers witnessing the Ascension of Jesus, a fitting image in a church linked to battle and a reminder of a greater power. The pulpit is made of wood and inlaid with carved marble panels. The interesting font was designed by Colonel Samuel Swinton Jacob (1841-1917), the architect who championed the Saracenic architectural style in India, often called Indo-Gothic.

During India's First War of Independence in 1857 St. James' Church was seen as a symbol of British domination and the area of Kashmere Gate was the setting for much fighting. The ball and cross topping the dome were used as target practice by the rebels and the church itself was peppered with cannon balls. Men lay dying inside the church and hundreds of British were killed in the streets of Delhi.

The church was designed by engineers Major Robert Smith and Captain De Bude and commenced in 1826. The Bishop of Kolkata Reverend Wilson consecrated the church on its completion in 1836. The church's memorials, monuments and cemetery best show its poignant history, much of which relates to battles won and lost and soldiers and families long gone. To the north of the church are the graves of James Skinner's family and Scotsman William Fraser, the British Commissioner of Delhi, a popular colourful character and a close friend of Skinner. Fraser's grand tomb was destroyed during the fighting but a small section of beautiful inlaid marble work still survives. A slab outside the church is inscribed with Skinner's words, expressing his shock at Fraser's assassination and describing him as being "as dear to him as life." Many graves were desecrated by the rebels though the tomb of 'Sikander Sahib' was respectfully left intact.

The East India Company acquired great stretches of Northern India for Britain with the help of Skinner's Horse, "reckoned to be the most useful and trusty, as well as the boldest body of men in India." In gratitude the British gave him land in Hansi, where he built a mansion in the classical style even though he was always more aligned with the Indian world. He received the Jagir of Hansi which consisted of 194 villages and other properties and businesses. Now owning a great fortune he lived a Mughal life style in Hansi surrounded by beautiful gardens and dressed in the finest muslins and silks. His favourite wife (it is said he had fourteen) was Muslim but Skinner remained Christian his entire life. His fluent Persian was an important asset as he could bridge the gap between the Mughal Court and the British.

James Skinner was awarded the rank of lieutenant-colonel by King George IV in 1828 and later became a Colonel of British India. In India however he still held the lower rank of Brigadier. Major-General Sir John Malcolm said of Skinner; "I do not mean to flatter when I say you are as good

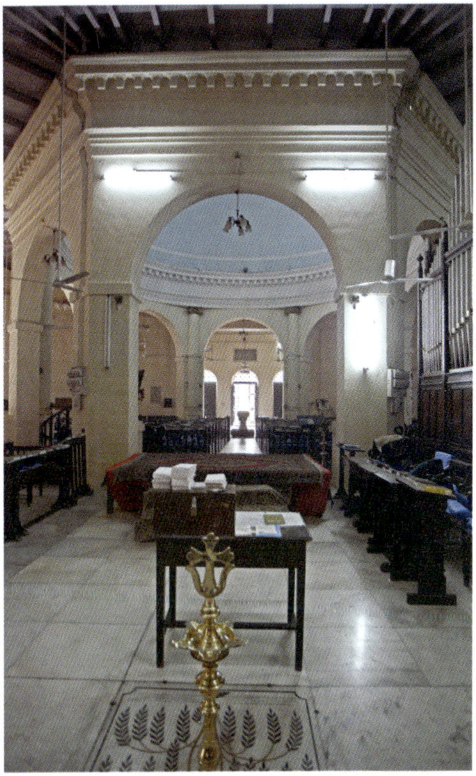

View towards the entrance

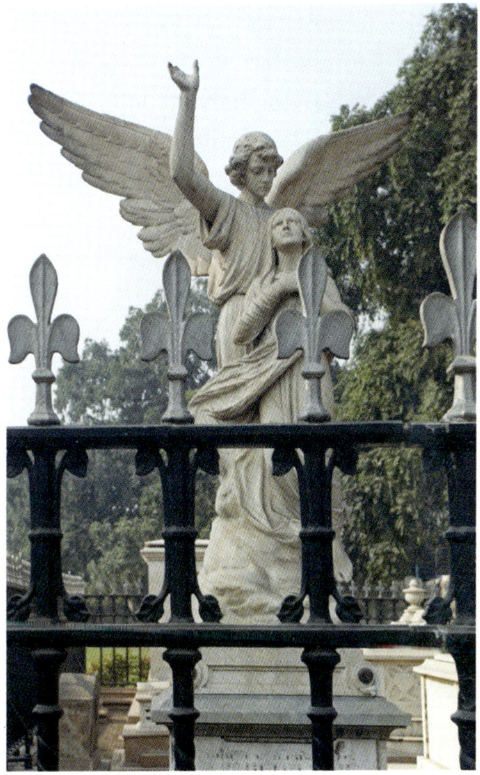

Marble sculpture of an angel

an Englishman as I know; but you are also a native irregular, half born and fully bred; you armed them, understand their characters, enter into their prejudices; can encourage them without spoiling them; know what they can and, what is more important, what they cannot do. The superiority of your corps rests upon a foundation that no others have."

James Skinner's Church was the Viceroy's church in Delhi until the Cathedral of the Redemption was built in Lutyens's Delhi in 1931, the year New Delhi was inaugurated as the new Capital of India. St. James' continued to be used as a revered place of worship by the British until 1947. Skinners regiment is still part of the Indian Army though from 1859 it has been called the 1st (Duke of York's Own) Bengal Lancers.

James Skinner died in December 1841 at the age of 63 and was buried at Hansi with full military honours. His 'Yellow Boys' formed a long funeral cortege. Later his coffin was conveyed in state to Delhi for a British style funeral. Finally he was buried in his own church where his tomb lies in a white marble vault just below the communion altar table. For a man once shunned by both his parents' faith and who became a military hero to both, it is a fine resting place.

The Cathedral Church of the Redemption, 1931

Roman Catholic

This beautiful Cathedral Church is dedicated to Christianity's great lesson; that Jesus on the cross redeemed our sins for us. It sits in a large garden in Church Lane, a quiet street in New Delhi. Adjacent to the church was the home of Lord Irwin, the Viceroy of India between 1926 and 1931. As a religious man he was interested in the plans of the church, discussing them with the architect Henry Medd as well as helping to raise funds for the building. Indeed, he took so much interest and was so impressed with the design that it became known as 'The Viceroy's Church'.

Henry Alexander Nesbitt Medd was an English architect who began working with Sir Edwin Lutyens in 1915, three years after Luytens and Baker began designing New Delhi. Medd was part of an eminent team which included Arthur Gordon Shoosmith who designed St. Martin's Garrison Church in Delhi. Medd's design for the Church of the Redemption is similar to Luytens Free Church at Hampstead Garden Suburb in London. Both have similar domes. St. Paul's Cathedral in London also has a similar dome but the greatest influence is certainly Palladio's II Redentore in Venice. Henry Medd returned to England before the church was completed. It was Lutyens who later added the dome.

The exterior of the church is classical in style and appears as a solid massing of blocks that rise vertically from a broad base. The central tower is striking and draws the eye upwards to the beautiful dome topped with a cupola which carries a cross. With advice from Luytens, Medd designed the church for the Indian climate with roofs of split red sandstone and walls of coarse untreated stone. Arched doorways, horizontal bands and the dome bring to mind the Duomo in Florence. With few windows the interior of the church remains cool and comfortable, even in Delhi's summer. Three classical orders are incorporated in the church's elevation; Doric on the lower lever, Ionic on the middle level and Corinthian on the top. Despite the many classical elements the overall design of the church suits the Indian landscape.

FACING PAGE: *The Cathedral Church of the Redemption*

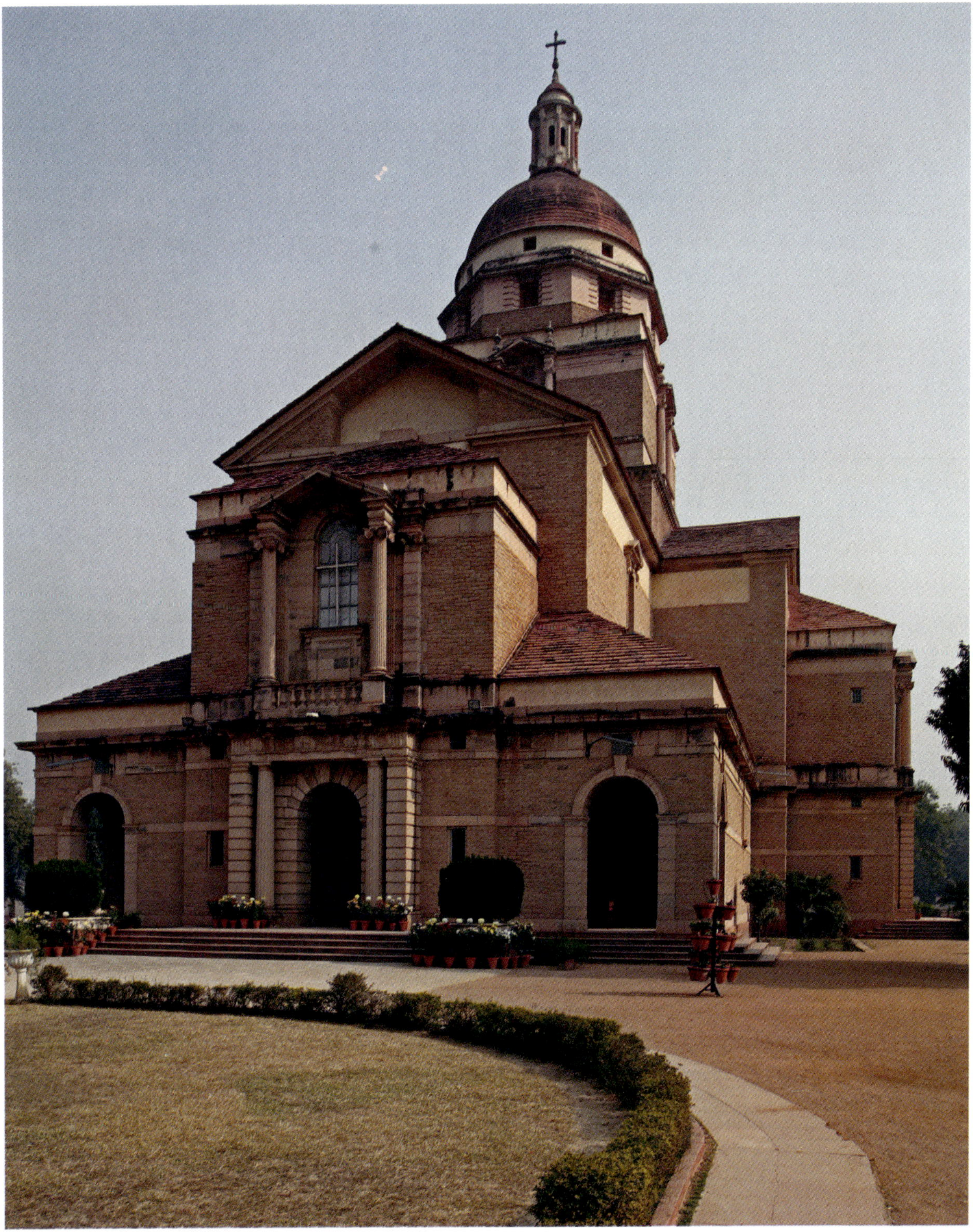

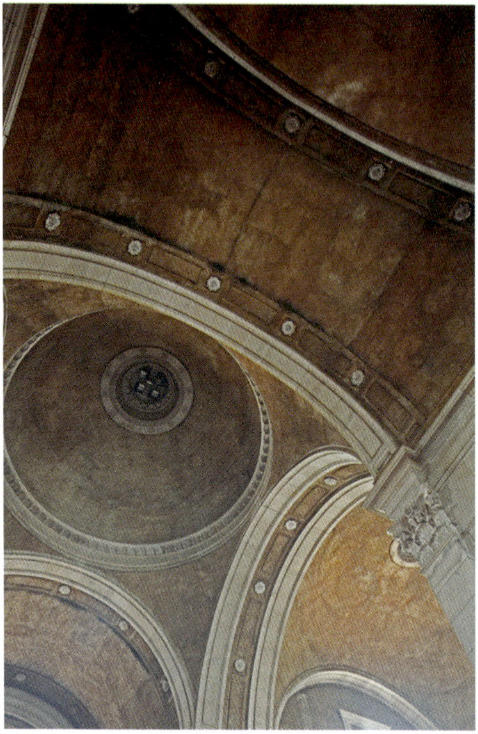

Inside the dome of Cathedral Church of the Redemption

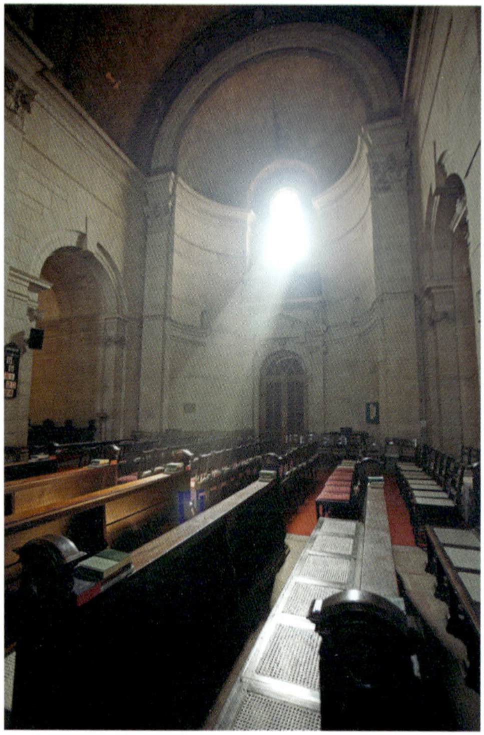

The sacred light signifying the risen Jesus

The Cathedral Church of the Redemption runs from east to west, with the entry on the west. This plan is in accordance with the Christian practice of building churches facing the rising sun signifying the risen Jesus. The church is designed to focus on the altar decorated with six tall silver candlesticks. At the opposite end is a gallery for the organist and the choir. The interior of the Cathedral is magnificent. The long chancel gives distance between the altar and the congregation. Dark wood panelling features in the elegant pulpit and surround the white marble altar. The curves, high arches and domes that form the ceiling enhance the sacred space. Furthermore high recessed windows of tinted glass allow rays of light to descend into the church creating the numinous mystical light, something beyond the material world.

Dignitaries who have attended ceremonies in the Cathedral include the Duke of

Edinburgh in 1950, India's First President Dr. Rajendra Prasad and President Eisenhower. Her Majesty the Queen of England visited in 1961 as well as the Archbishops of York and Canterbury. The Prime Minister of Canada came in 1964 and in June of the same year the memorial for the late Pandit Jawaharlal Nehru was held in the cathedral. In 1965 Sir Winston Churchill attended and in 1966 were two memorial services, the first for India's late Prime Minister Shri Lal Bahadur Shastri and the second for Australia's Prime Minister Sir Harold Holt.

There have been many interesting and historical items gifted to the church over the years. Lord Irwin donated a silver cross and a painting, said to be in thanks for escaping an attack to blow up his train in 1929. The silver cross on the high altar was a gift from King George V, the only ruling monarch to visit India before independence. At the great Durbar in Delhi in 1911 it was this king who announced that the capital of India was to be moved from Kolkata to Delhi.

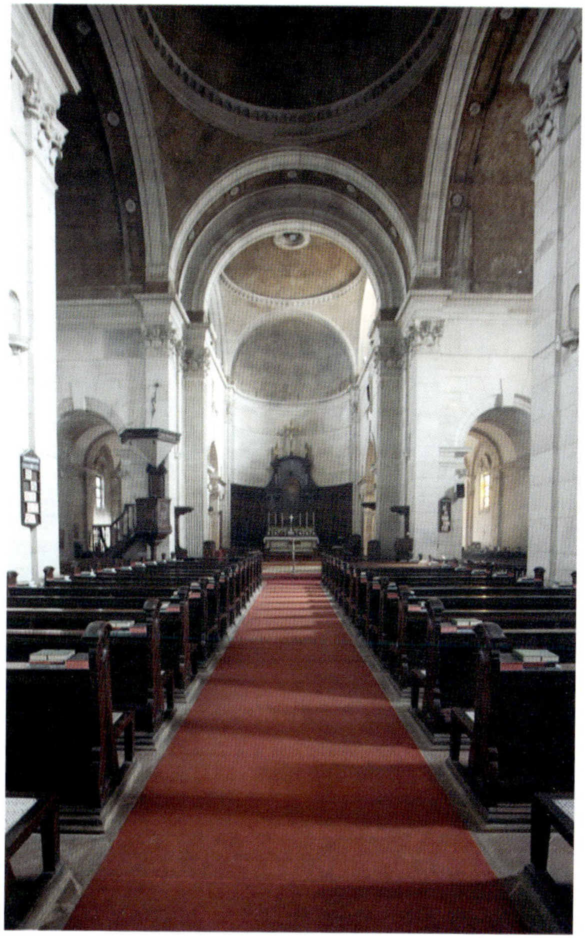

The interior

The Santa Maria Gloriosa dei Frari of 1330, one of the greatest churches in Venice donated the reproduction of Bellini's 'Madonna and Cherubs' above the altar. The Dean and Chapter of York Minster, the seat of the Archbishop of York and the second highest office of the Church of England gave the Cathedral three figures carved in Italy to celebrate the city of York's thirteenth centenary. The first is of Christ on the cross which can be seen atop the carved wooden screen behind the altar. The second is the Virgin Mary on one side and St. John on the other. Lord Irwin was a landowner in York, which formed the connection between the cities and their cathedrals.

The foundation stone of the parsonage, the future residence of Delhi's bishops, was laid by Lady Willingdon in 1933. She used a silver trowel and buried the day's Hindustan Times and the Statesman with some 'coins of the realm' in a time capsule.

In 1948 the Cathedral held the moving ceremony for Mohandas Karamchand Gandhi. The congregation, which included Governor General and Lady Mountbatten, asked to 'commend the Father of the Nation into God's hands' and the biblical line was read 'The souls of the righteous are in the hands of God'. Aurobindo Nath Mukherjee, Delhi's first Indian bishop said "Nothing would have pleased Bapu more than our resolve to be ambassadors of healing and reconciliation."

The Cathedral of the Sacred Heart, 1935

Roman Catholic

This striking Italianate Cathedral was designed by Henry Medd in 1927. It is in the heart of New Delhi close to Connaught Place. The Cathedral along with St. Columba's School and the Jesus and Mary Convent School are all set in fourteen acres of peaceful green lawns and gardens. Medd declared that he designed the Church of the Redemption for the Anglicans and the Church of the Sacred Heart to please the Catholics.

Medd's plans were chosen from eight competing architects invited to submit plans for the Sacred Heart. One of the judges was Sir Edward Lutyens and another was Father Luke, Capuchin priest from Tuscany who had arrived in Delhi in 1919. It was Father Luke who became the driving force for the building of the Cathedral.

Despite many setbacks and the constant seeking of funds the foundation stone was finally laid in 1929 by the Archbishop of Agra. Construction started the following year though it was not completed until 1935. Today it is Delhi's most important Roman Catholic Church. In 1999 the Church was consecrated to become a Cathedral in celebration of the newly-formed Archdiocese of Delhi.

The Cathedral is situated in the area known as the Lutyen's Bungalow Zone, a prestigious area of over 2,800 hectares of bungalows and administrative buildings built for the British during their colonial rule. The ornate red brick Cathedral with crisp white borders is eye-catching. It rises up from the ground floor with just two simple arched openings and windows either side to the first level where white pillars support a pediment. The top

Facing page: *The Cathedral of the Sacred Heart*

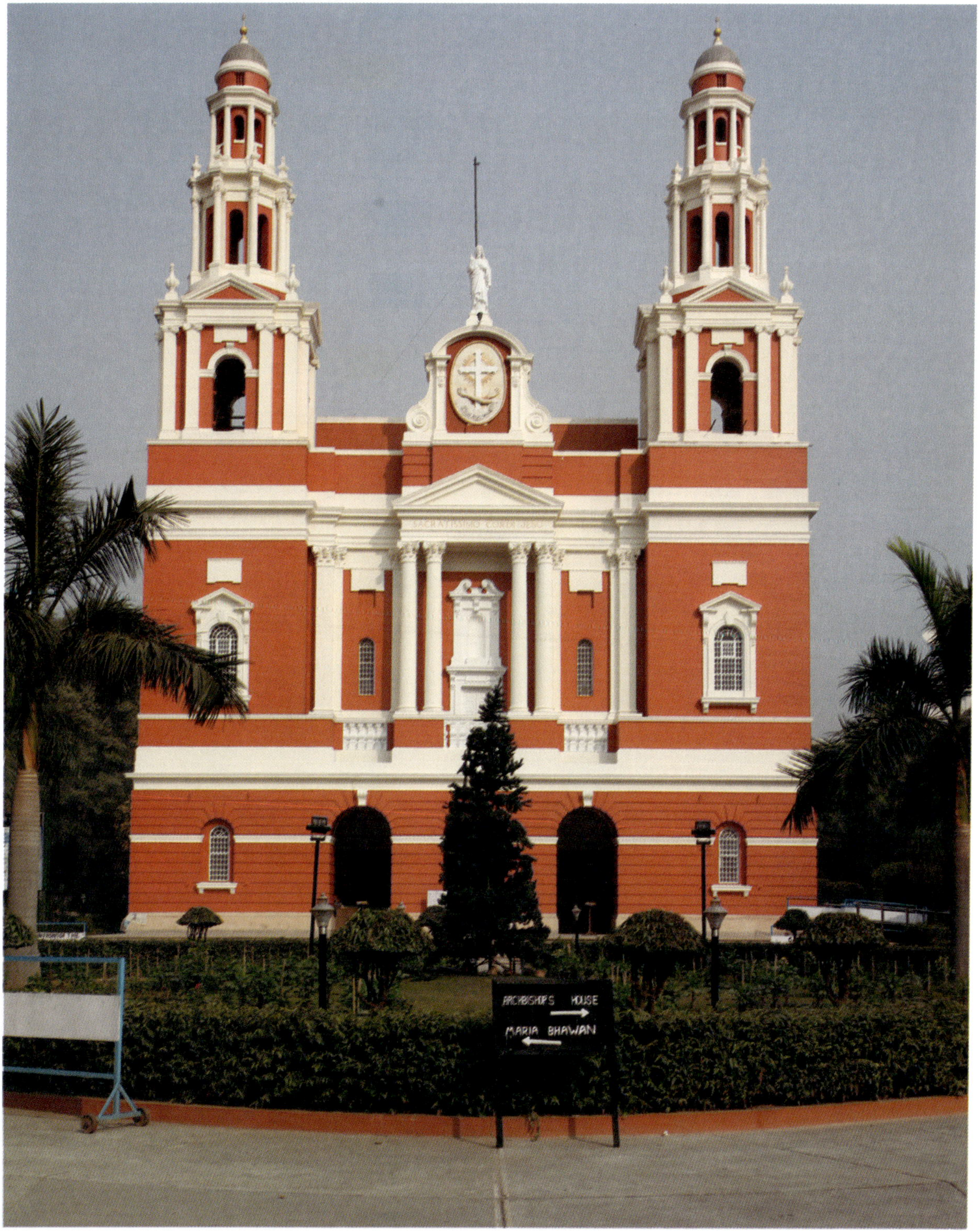
ARCHBISHOP'S HOUSE
MARIA BHAWAN

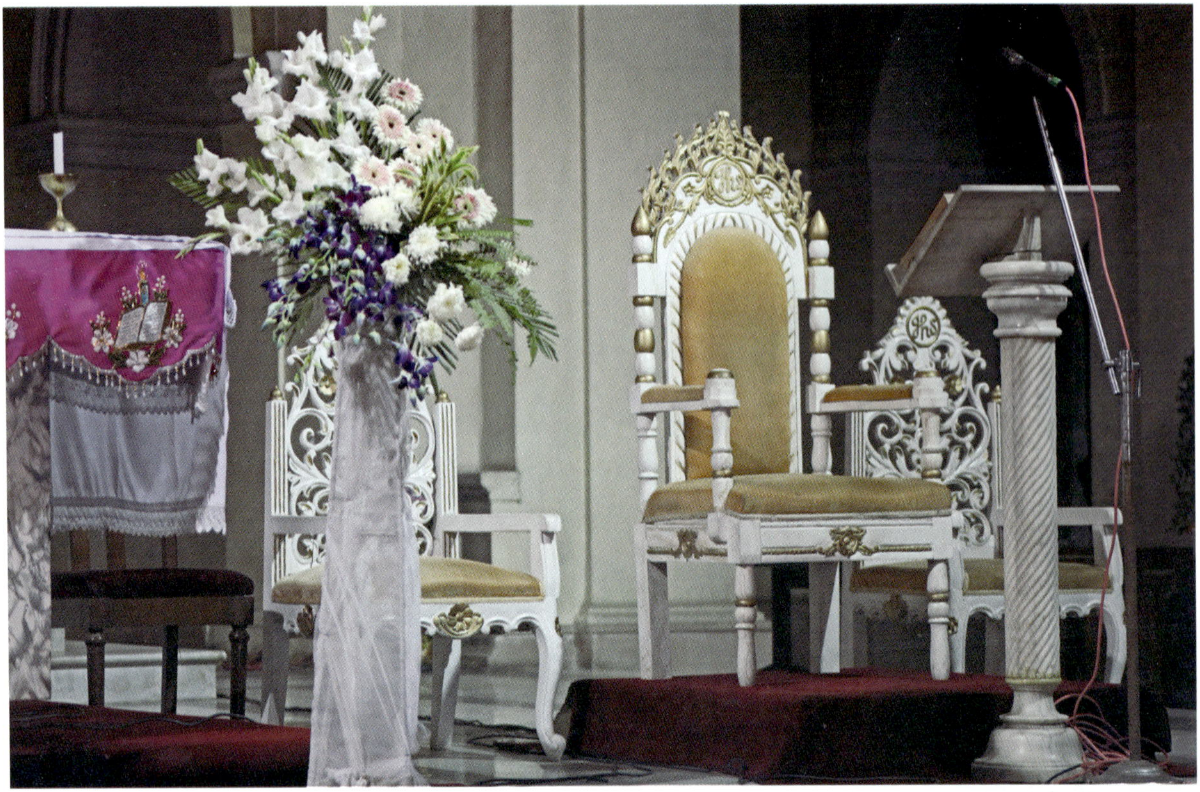

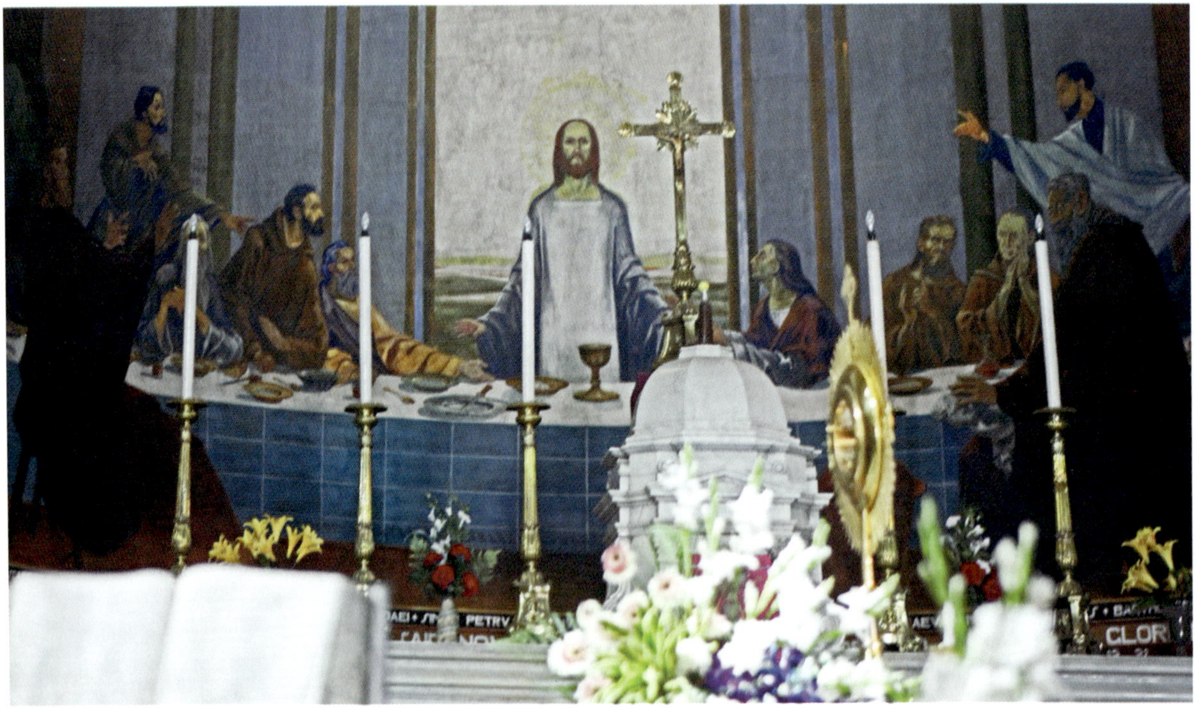

level consists of twin towers or steeples in a square form above which are circular arcaded turrets adorned with finials. In the centre of the towers is a statue of Jesus atop a curved pediment which supports a cross.

The interior of the church is decorated in pastels and gold with a lofty roof and broad arches. Polished stone floors are set with marble mosaics and a large Carrara marble altar and lectern take pride of place. Above the altar hangs a painting of the Last Supper. The walls of the church are decorated with other biblical scenes including the Fourteen Stations of the Cross.

Most architects involved with the design of Lutyens New Delhi left India for home after the city's inauguration. However Henry Medd stayed on in the country that had given him his remarkable career. He continued to design and was given the position of Chief Architect to the Government of India from 1939 to 1947.

Like many before him by the time he eventually returned to England his work in India had gone out of fashion subsequently he was largely ignored however his architectural skills evident in both the impressive Cathedral Church of the Redemption and the Sacred Heart Cathedral are his lasting legacy.

FACING PAGE TOP AND BELOW: *The ornate Carrara marble lectern; The painting of the Last Supper*

St. Martin's Garrison Church, 1930

Anglican

'It is without question one of the great buildings of the 20th century'

–Gavin Stamp writer and architectural historian

Many architects share this view of St. Martin's and yet the church is not well known. Designed by Arthur Gordon Shoosmith in 1928 it is strikingly different to the church architecture being built in India at the time. Shoosmith was a Russian born English architect who went to India in 1920 as Edwin Lutyens' permanent representative in New Delhi. He was part of the brilliant team that worked with Lutyens in designing the new city. Shoosmith supervised the building of the Viceroy's House and several other prominent buildings however his design for the unique St. Martin's Church was the high point of his career.

Taking advice from Lutyens, Shoosmith rejected the more usual ecclesiastical, decorative style of architecture and went for 'the Roman wall' in his design of a new garrison church in the military cantonments west of Delhi. Architect Jon Lang suggests that Shoosmith may have drawn his design from European Expressionism. It is often called the 'the Cubist Church' and is certainly remarkable.

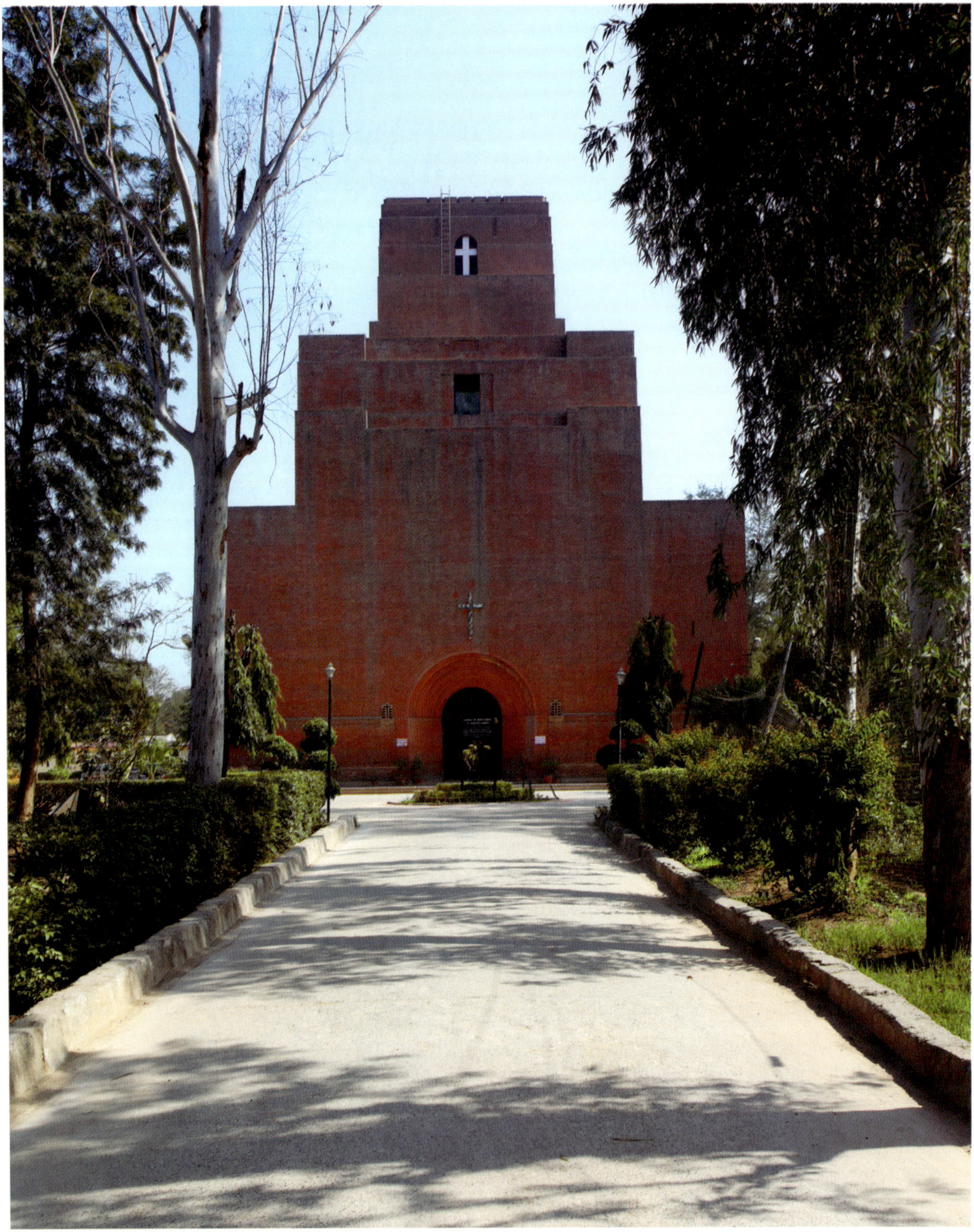

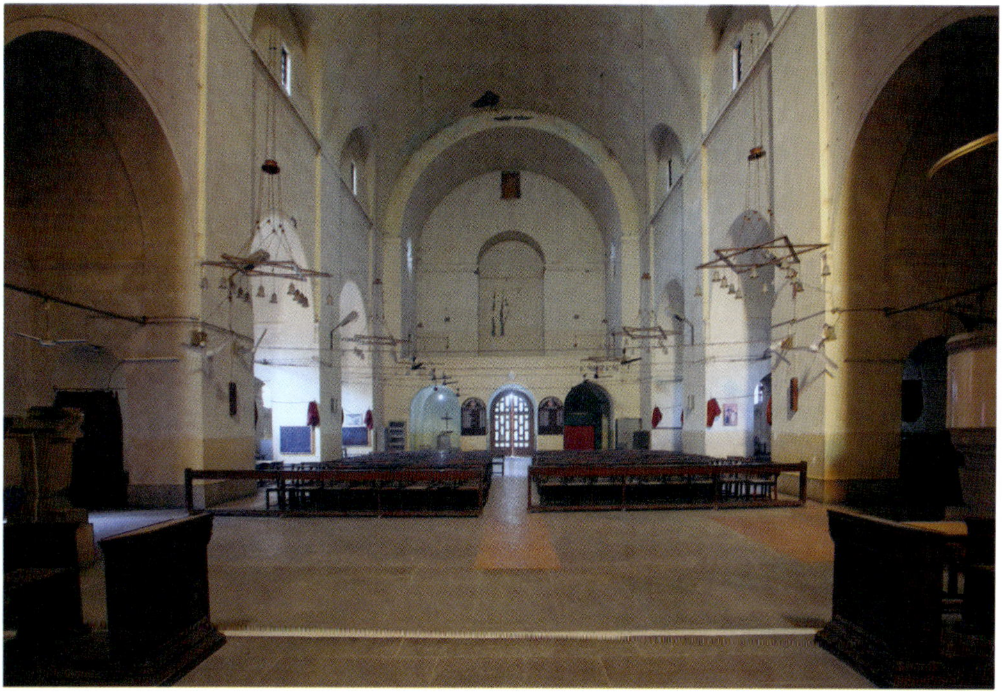

ABOVE: *St. Martin's Garrison Church, a view from the altar*
FACING PAGE: *The impressive façade of St Martin's*

The church is massive. From a stone base sloping walls rise into an enormous tower adorned with a simple white cross. 'Fortress-like' and 'austere' are often words used to describe the church. A shallow parapet on top of the tower reinforces the notion of a fortress. It seems part of the ancient, dry red earth of northern India.

Built in brick with reinforced concrete and faced with red brick its design belongs to India both environmentally, climatically, materially and visually. The few windows are small with deep ledges to keep out the bright light of Delhi's summer and the harsh winds of winter. Three and a half million locally made two inch thick bricks with tiny recessed joints were used to face the church. As it was built for the British troops it was their Garrison Church and as such the soldiers appreciated the fortress like exterior. It could be easily defended in an emergency. Field Marshal Sir William Birdwood, the Commander-in-Chief in India who had commanded Australian forces in Gallipoli in 1915 laid the foundation stone of the church in 1929.

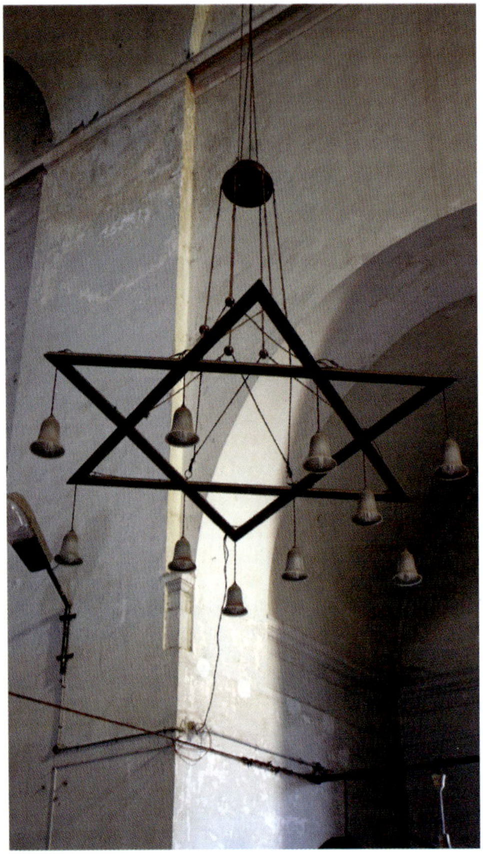

Star shaped wooden frame with small lights attached

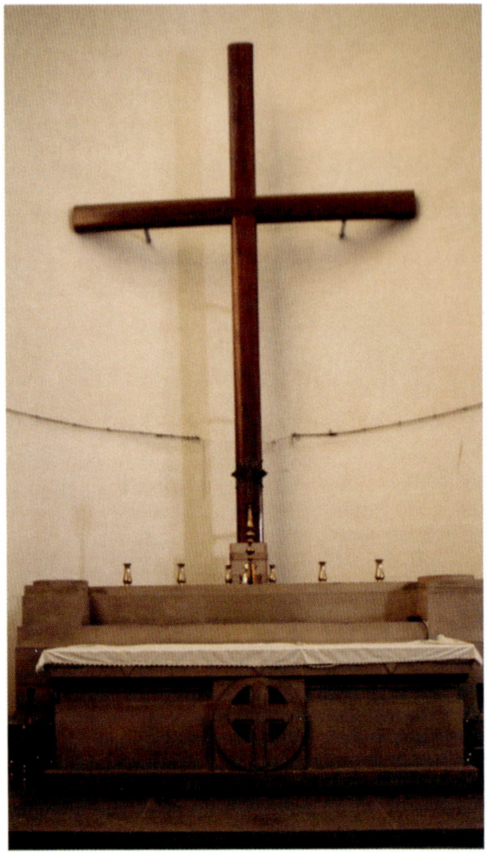

The simple wooden cross

On the ground the building's plan is a rectangle but as the walls rise they step back, reminiscent of an ancient temple. Inside the massive brick dome over the chancel keeps the church remarkably cool no matter what the temperature. The interior is sombre, with a simple large unadorned wooden cross above the altar and a series of simple star shaped wooden frames with small lights attached which hang from the ceiling by ropes. The height of the interior is an astonishing 37 metres high and the nave is around 18 metres at its highest point. Shoosmith, like many other young British architects in India at the time idolised Lutyens. In the cool atmosphere

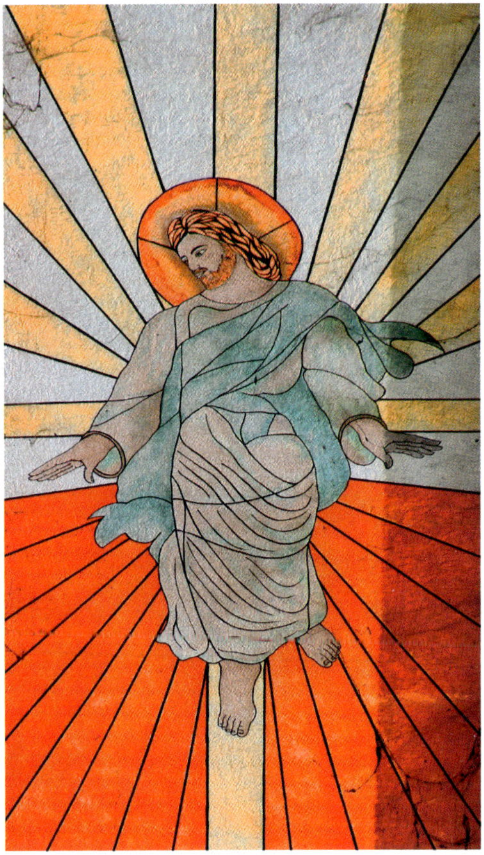

The stained glass

of the church's interior there is an element of Lutyens style. However Shoosmith was searching for ways to keep simplifying his design, 'brickwork unadorned...stark and vital forms...a new conception of beauty.'

The only other building Shoosmith designed was a simple inn for travellers, the Lady Hardinge Serai in Delhi. It was to be his last. He left India for Britain in 1931 to find his country in the midst of the Depression and demoralised. Like Medd's experience there was no interest in his work or the architecture of the British in India. Shoosmith's Garrison Church is today recognised as being a masterpiece of the 20th century and a high point of Britain's architectural undertakings in India. When his work was exhibited at the Royal Academy George Gordon Byron (Lord Byron) told Shoosmith 'It is superb'.

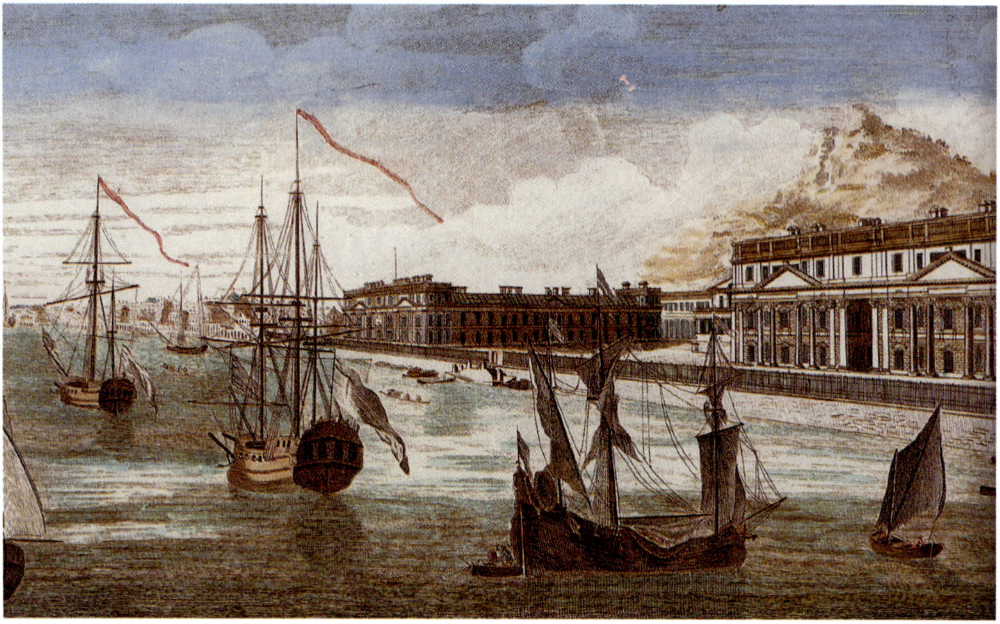

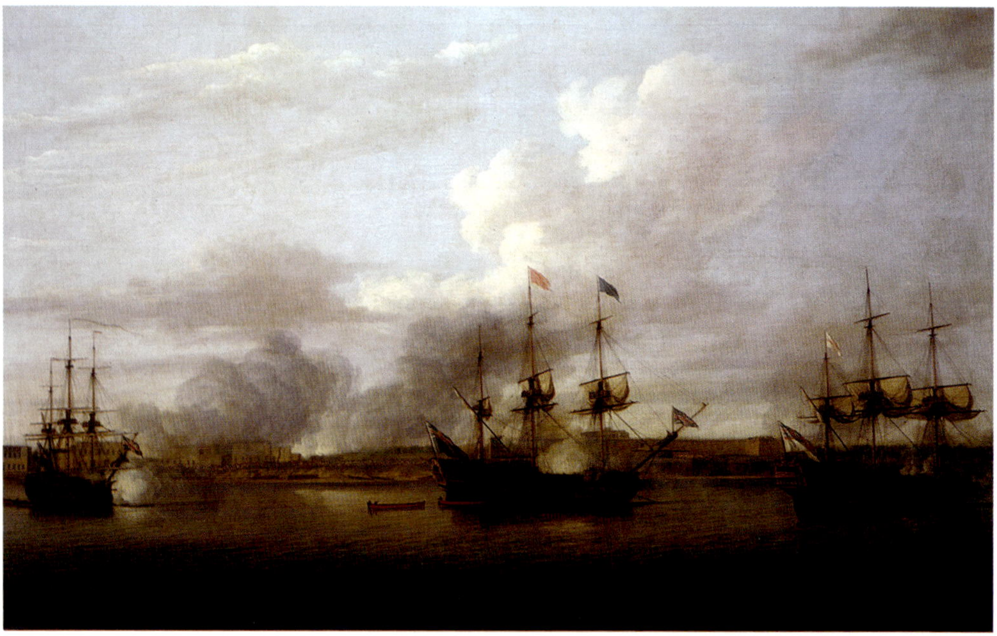

FRENCH FRAGMENTS
Puducherry and Chandannagar

The idea of a French town in the tropical south of India is irresistible to many including this author. Quite different to anywhere else on the Subcontinent Puducherry has a relaxed charm with a blend of Indian and French culture. The best time to explore is during the afternoon siesta when the French Quarter seems suspended in time. Many beautiful old French villas have been converted into hotels and charming bungalows are painted in bright yellows and blues. The French flag flies from administrative buildings that are set in large gated grounds and policemen wear bright white uniforms and 'kepis', the French military cap. Though buildings have been adapted to India's hot climate there is a lingering atmosphere of colonial France. Many locals speak French or Tamil with a slight French accent. Many are the descendants of the French colonisers.

Facing page above: *View of Pondicherry in the late 18th century (Wikipedia public domain)*

Facing page below: *The capture of Chandernagore in 1757 by the Royal Navy (Wikipedia public domain)*

Archeologists have found the remains of a Roman settlement at Arikemedu, an ancient port just south of Puducherry confirming that the area was settled from the 1st century. The Romans traded gold coins for semi-precious stones, textiles and glass beads from various Hindu rulers. In the 14th century it became part of the great Vijayanagar Empire. This was followed by Islamic rule. When the Portuguese arrived in 1521 Puducherry was a town of fisher folk and weavers who were well known for creating fine textiles. This drew the French to the area. It was French governor Francois Martin Puducherry who developed the trade and soon fine organdies and French style toile were being exported to Europe.

The French were the last of the European maritime powers to arrive in India during the 17th century. They had established the Compagnie des Indes Orientales in 1664 to seek out the spices, trade and riches of the Orient. A decade later they had secured their trading post in the port town of Puducherry, 'new settlement' in Tamil.

When wars between the French and the British broke out in Europe the conflict travelled all the way to the Puducherry. Like pieces on a chessboard Puducherry changed hands repeatedly until finally in 1816 French Puducherry became secure. The city remained in French hands after India's independence in 1947 however in 1954 the French handed it back to India. Today it remains a Union Territory of India. Before the French left India they offered the Tamil people French citizenship and many took up the offer. This resulted in the establishment of French government schools and language colleges in Puducherry

Today there are two distinct areas that make up Puducherry, the Indian or Tamil Quarter and the French Quarter. They are divided by a partially covered drain known as 'the canal', running north to south. In contrast with the French architecture the buildings in the Indian Quarter are in the vernacular style of Tamil Nadu; small scale back-to-back attached houses each with a veranda, talvaram, offering shade. Raised masonry benches on the street offer places for locals sit and chat. In fact the streets are called 'talking streets'. As Britain did not achieve any lasting occupation in Puducherry it was the French who shaped the city and who built a number of interesting and ornate Roman Catholic churches in both the French and Tamil quarters. Thankfully the population of Puducherry is dedicated to keeping their heritage alive and consequently the churches are all well maintained.

The Cathedral of Our Lady of the Immaculate Conception, 1791

Roman Catholic

Though more flamboyant this cathedral is similar in style to Luz Church in Chennai. The Baroque style is known for its embellishments and the Immaculate Conception Cathedral is certainly decorative. The white façade has yellow painted volutes and finials along with horizontal and vertical stripes on paired embedded columns, Doric below and Ionic above. A statue of Our Lady resides in a niche in the centre of the upper level of the facade and angels in white stucco hover above. There are three blue painted entrance doors, the two at each side feature more volutes above. In front of the church stands a large statue of Jesus dressed in saffron coloured robes. The statue is protected by a metal fence painted blue and white where flowers and offerings are placed.

The interior has a central nave and two side aisles with archways dividing the spaces. The archways are hung with painted terracotta plaques illustrating the Fourteen

FACING PAGE: *The cathedral in the afternoon sun*

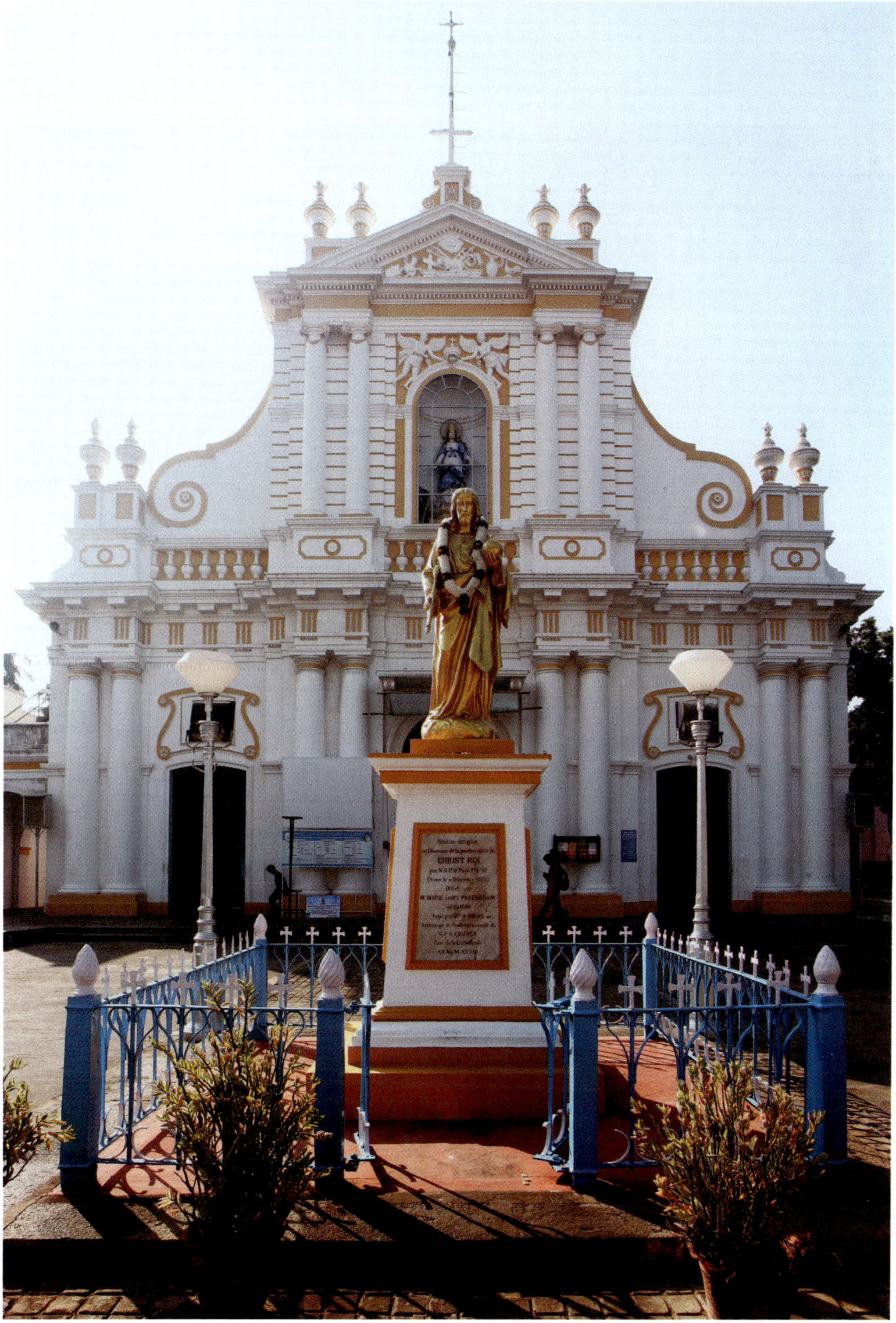
CHRIST ROI

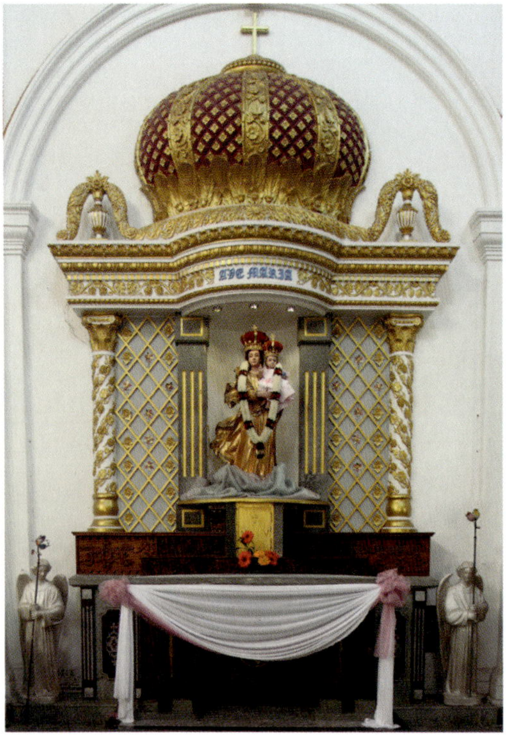
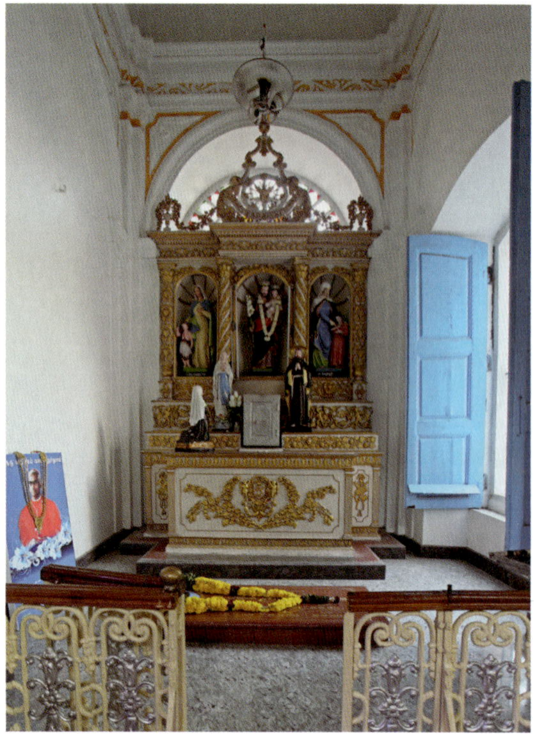
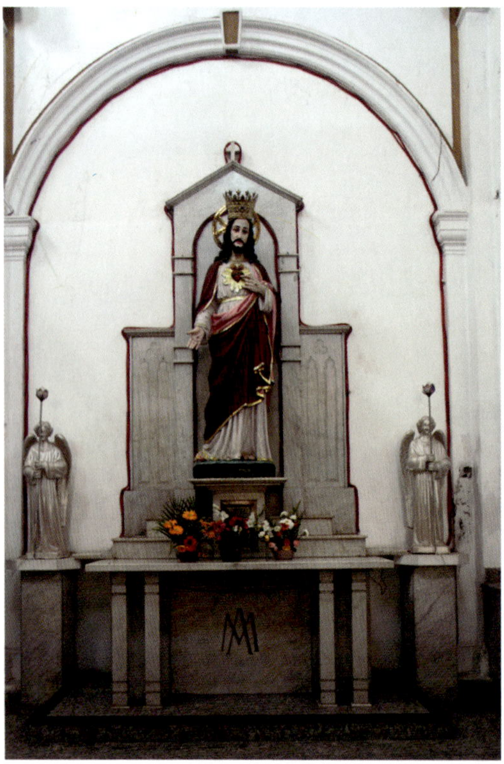
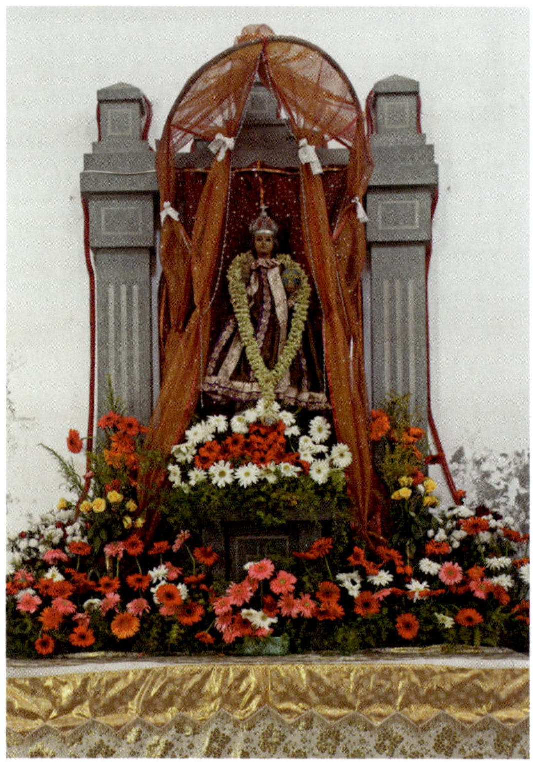

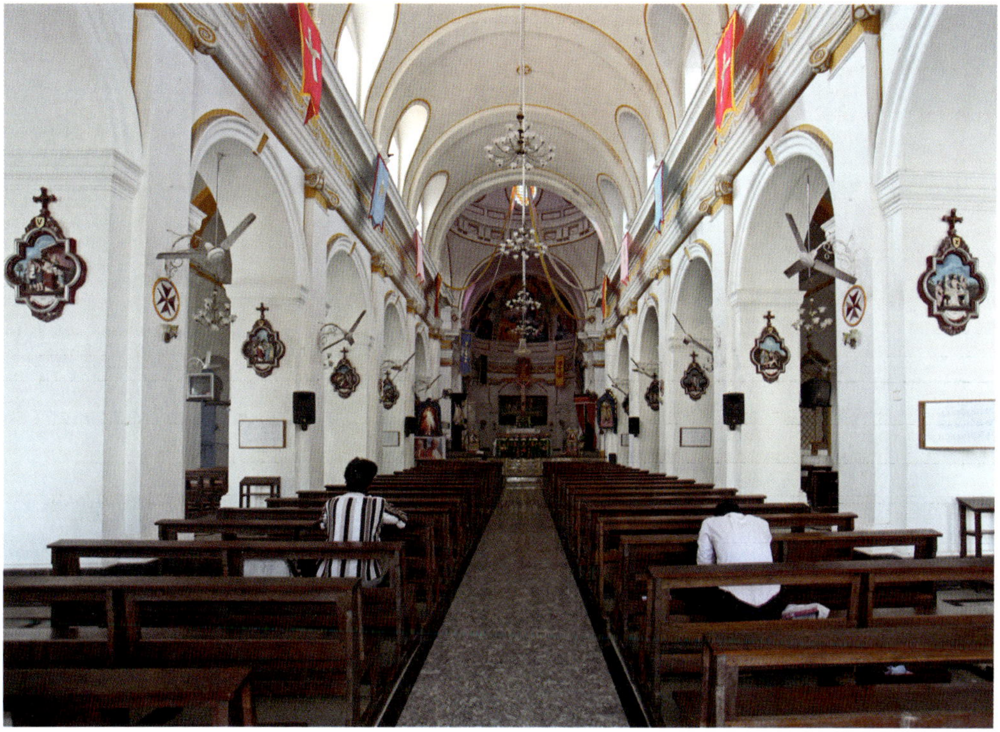

ABOVE: *The interior of the cathedral with the Stations of the Cross on the pillars*

FACING PAGE ALL: *Four side altars*

Stations of the Cross. The ceiling has plain barrel vaults with round windows allowing light to fill the interior space. There is a lower dome behind the altar which has three murals illustrating biblical stories. A classical frieze runs around the upper walls of the cathedral and a large crucifix stands on the left of the altar. An image of Jesus wearing a crown is close by. On the right of the altar is a highly decorative dome in red, gold and white sheltering velvet crowned images of the Madonna and Child.

The Immaculate Conception Cathedral has had a turbulent past with three other churches built on the site even before the French colonised Puducherry. Dutch and British attacks saw these churches destroyed. However it was the Jesuits who bought the land and with funds from King Louis XIV of France they were able to begin building the church in 1779. It was completed in 1791 and consecrated by French Bishop Nicolas Champenois. The bell tower and

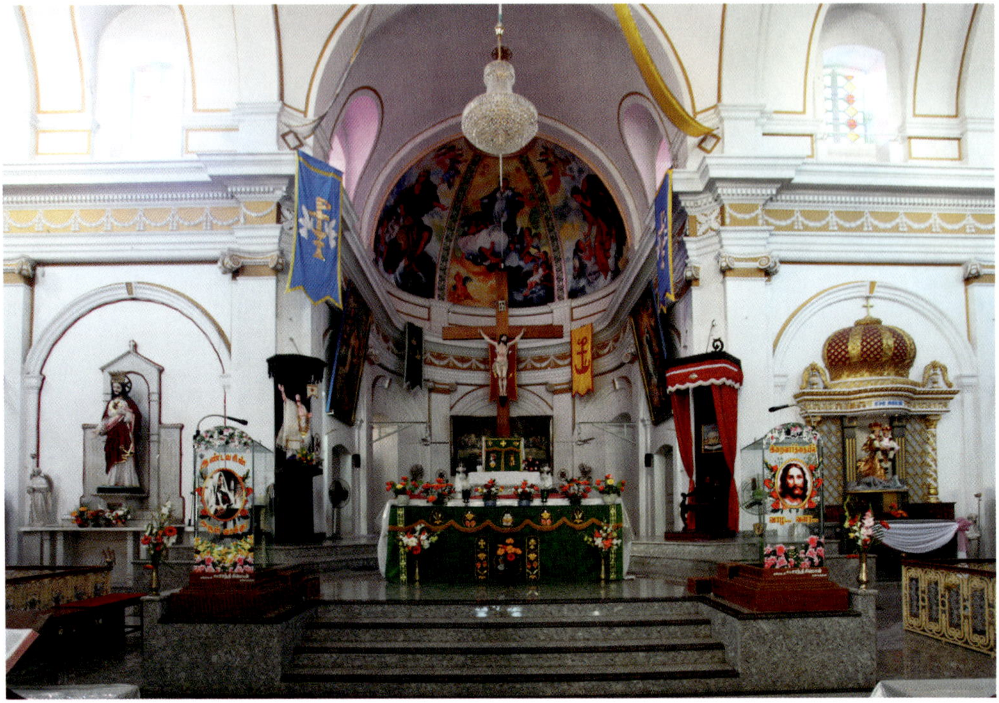

The altar and the dome

choir loft were later additions and in 1970 the sanctuary was updated. Outside the cathedral is a large courtyard used for ceremonies and gatherings, particularly at Christmas and on the first week of December when the annual feast is celebrated.

Our Lady of Lourdes Chapel, 1877

Roman Catholic

This church is situated in the small town of Villianur, eleven kilometres from Puducherry. The church is said to be modelled on the famous Basilica of Our Lady of Lourdes in France and though there are similarities they are more alike in spirit than in architecture. There are however a number of important links to the church in France.

In 1858 in France an apparition of Mary appeared 18 times before a young girl, Bernadette Soubirous in the grotto of a church. Mary told the girl her name was 'The Immaculate Conception.' This amazing story inspired Bernadette's cousin, Friar Tarbes to build the church. Construction began in 1866

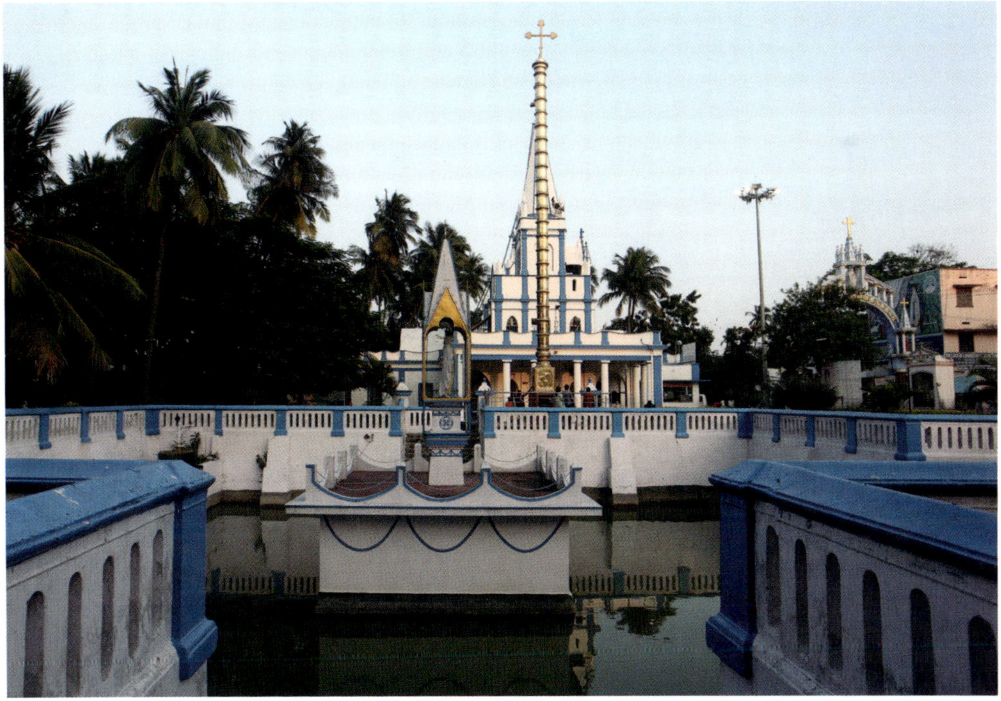

Our Lady of Lourdes Chapel

and was completed in 1877. Over the next ten years the church reported an increase in miracles and was given the status of The Shrine of Our Lady of Lourdes.

A six foot high statue of Our Lady of Lourdes, known for its miracles, was a gift from the French church in the late 19th century. The statue was crowned in the name of the Pope at a huge mass in Rome after which it was sent to India, arriving in Puducherry. Though it had been dropped a number of times it arrived in perfect condition. Today the statue stands in a grotto inside the church and is adored by locals and visitors alike.

A Christian church with a large pond is intriguing as ponds are usually found in or near most Hindu temples and used for ritual bathing. The Lady of Lourdes pond was used for irrigating the surrounding lands in earlier times, now a statue of the Madonna brought from Lourdes in 1924 stands in the centre of the pond. A formal ceremony took place when the statue was installed and consecrated. It is known for its healing powers. The church in

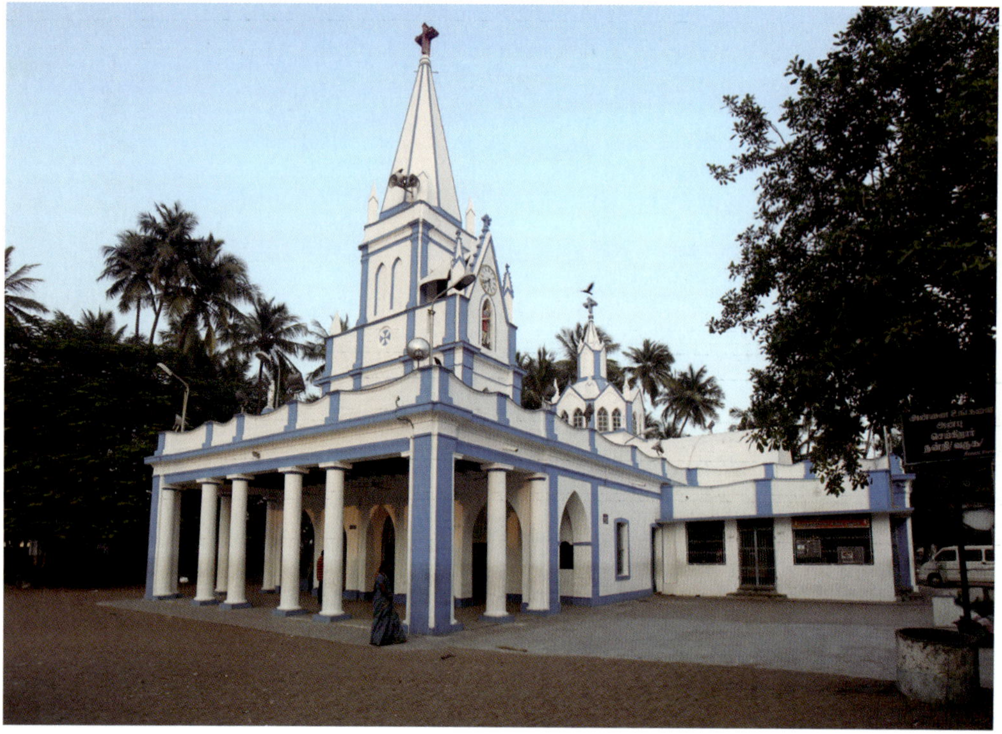

ABOVE: *The exterior of the church*
FACING PAGE TOP: *The Hindu practice of circumambulation*
FACING PAGE BELOW: *The Fourteen Stations of the Cross*

France also has a sacred spring and its water is brought to India once a year and mixed into the sacred pond of Our Lady of Lourdes Chapel. Many parishioners like to take the water back to their homes.

The church itself was constructed between 1866 and 1877. It has been well restored over the years and today it is a bright white and blue Indo-Gothic church with a tall delicate steeple at the front and a shorter, more robust steeple behind. Columns form a portico above which is a wide veranda. The church, the pond and the Fourteen Stations of the Cross form a compound bordered by a stone wall. Between the church and the pond is the flagpole seen outside many South Indian Christian churches and Hindu temples.

The Lady of Lourdes Church is an important religious site. The feast day is a Puducherry State Christian festival and takes place after Easter beginning with raising the flag and continues for nine days during which

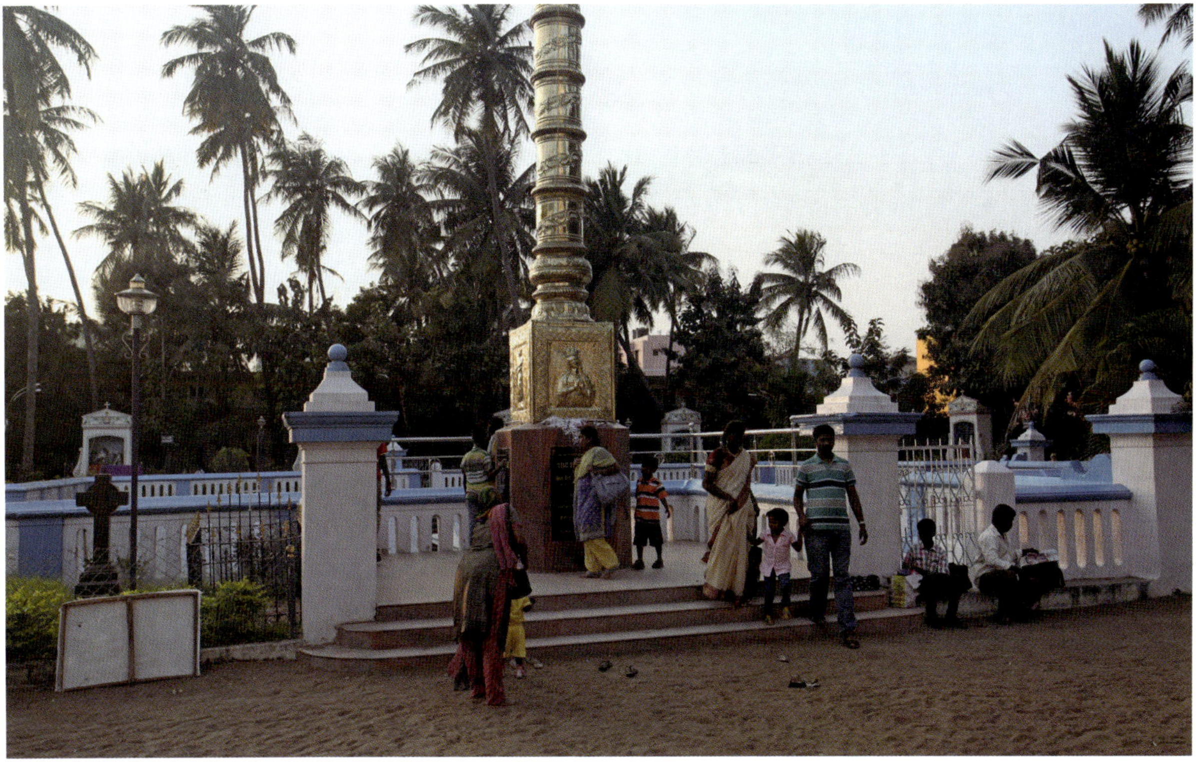

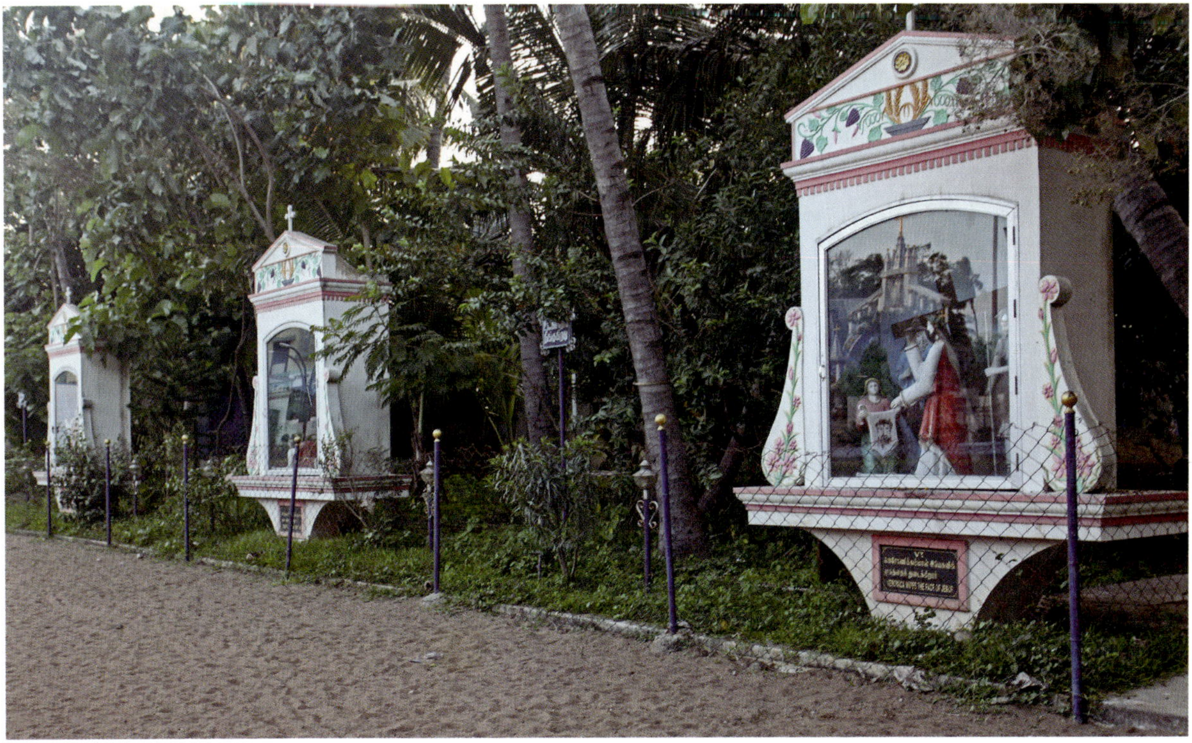

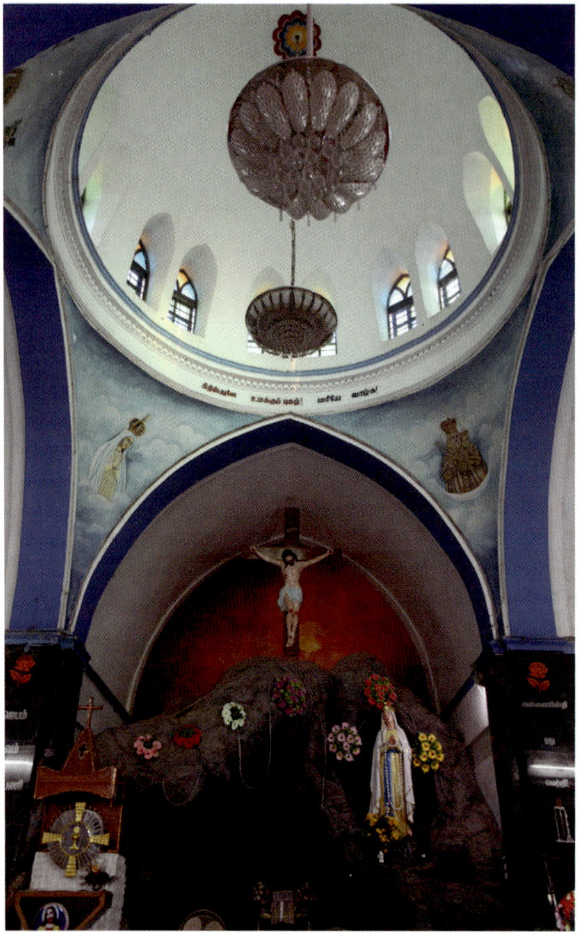

ABOVE: *The grotto and the famous statue of the Madonna*
FACING PAGE: *Church of the Sacred Heart Basilica 1907*

the wonderful 'car procession' takes place. A statue of the Madonna adorned with a diamond crown is placed in a colourful, highly decorated 'car'. The almost unrecognisable vehicle is then taken through the streets in a procession. It attracts thousands of people of all denominations, many of whom carry mats to sleep on and some conduct a special penance or prayer by going around the pond on their knees each day of the nine day festival. On the last day fireworks light up the sky. It is at this festival that the pond at the church is used for ritual bathing. An important Hindu practice at Our Lady of Lourdes Church is *pradakshina*, the circumambulation or meditation which involves walking clockwise around highly sacred objects, perhaps a deity, a sacred fire, a Peepal tree or a Tulsi plant. In this case it is the flagpole.

The links joining the Puducherry Lady of Lourdes Church to the world famous French church of the same name are significant in the way this Christian church has embraced local Hindu customs and traditions. It is understandable that all the people of Pondicherry have a great fondness for this lovely church.

Church of the Sacred Heart Basilica, 1907

Roman Catholic

The Church of the Sacred Heart of Jesus began in 1895. Bishop Monsignor Gandhi had dreamt of a building as magnificent as the Church of Sacre Coeur on the hill of Montmartre in Paris. Though the church has very little in common with the Sacre

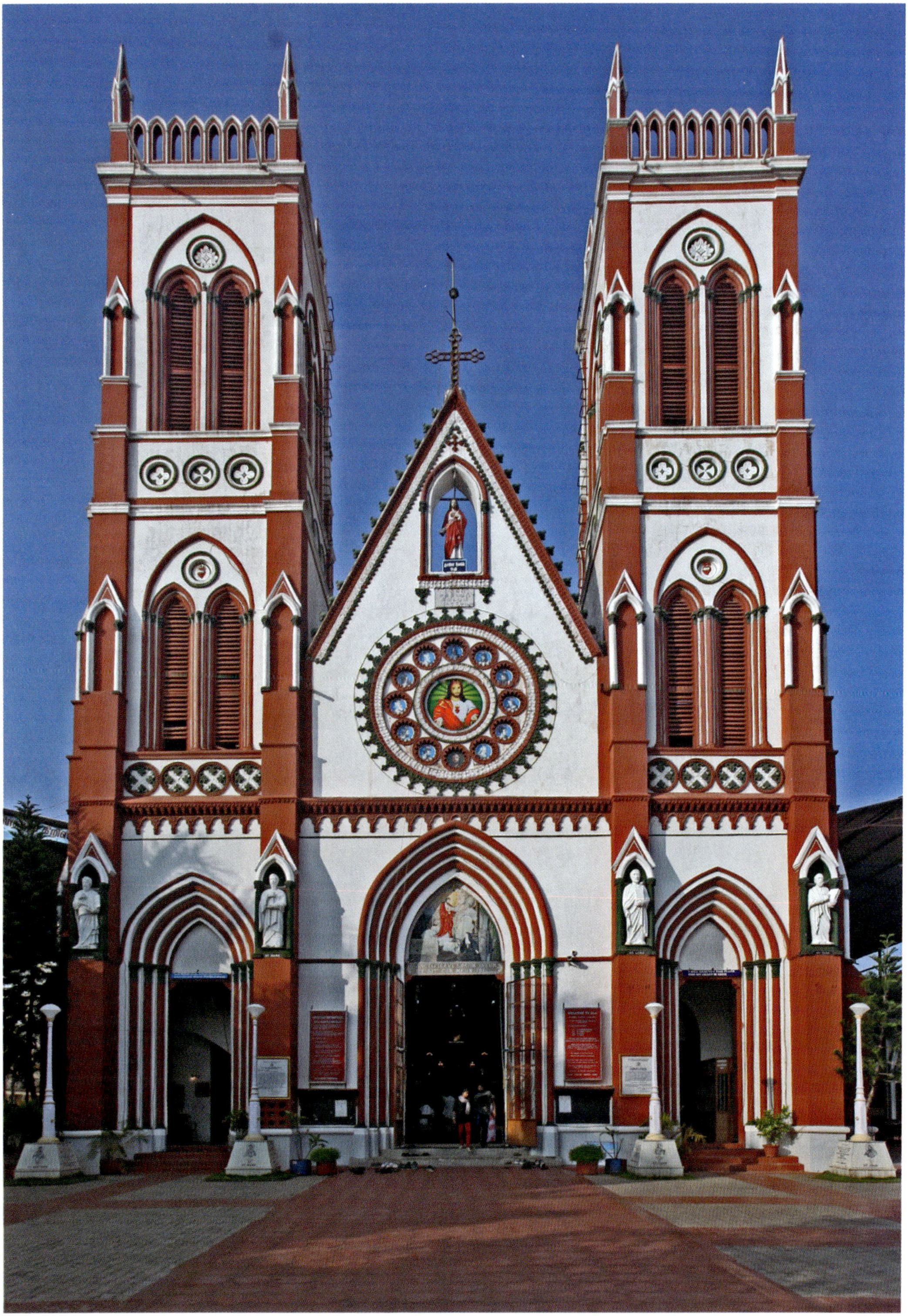

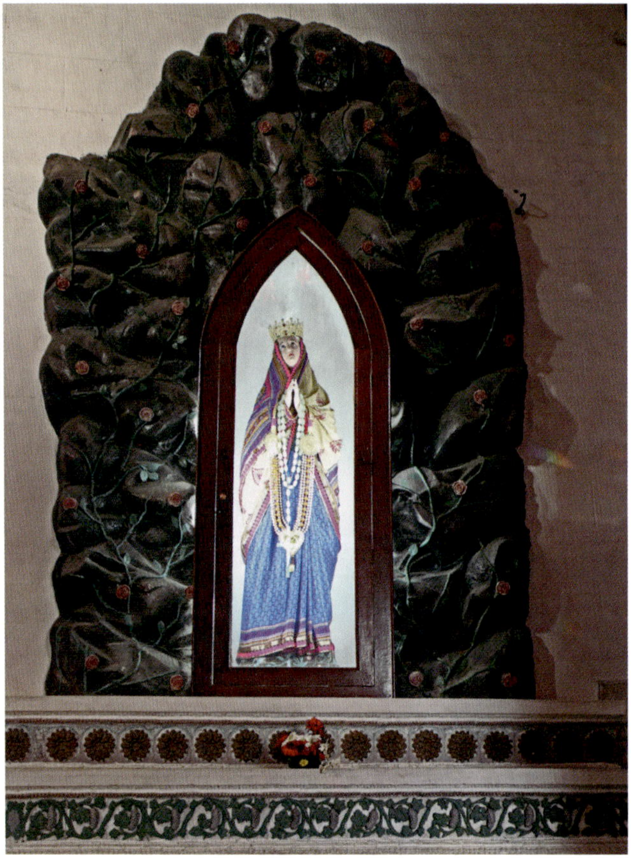

The Madonna in a blue sari

Coeur, it is striking and one of the most well-known churches in Puducherry. The Bishop's dream came to reality in 1907 when the church was completed.

Built in an Indo-Gothic style and painted a striking reddish brown and white the building is located in the Tamil Quarter of Puducherry and known to locals as the 'Jesus Church.' Twin towers flank a central gable which features a large round window with twelve smaller round windows within. At the centre is an image of Jesus and above a statue of Jesus sits in a niche at the apex of the gable. Overall the church is similar in style to the Notre Dame in Paris with its famous rose window. Three Gothic arched entrances lead

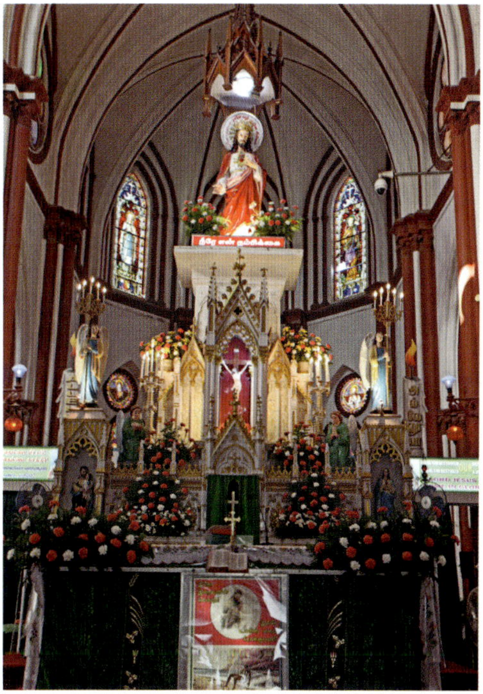

The ornate altar with gold leaf tracery

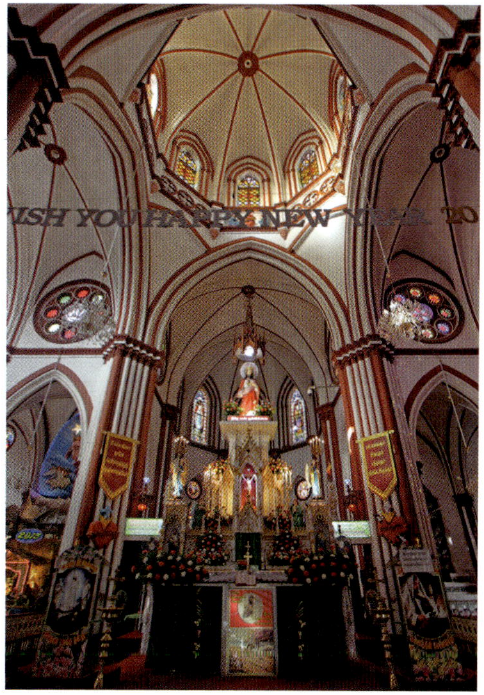

A wider view of the altar

into the church. The main door is ornately carved with images of Mary and the Sacred Heart of Jesus. The windows of the twin towers are fitted with louvres, a necessity for a French church built on Indian soil.

The interior is large and impressive. The white walls decorated with terracotta tracery and columns create a bright atmosphere. Stained glass windows depict twenty eight saints, all of whom focus their devotion on the Heart of Jesus. One of these is Joan of Arc. Other windows illustrate events from the life of Jesus. The altar is ornately decorated with gold leaf tracery and various levels on which sit Gothic niches, like small tabernacles, with images of Jesus and Mary inside. Two angels hold candelabras and another two are portrayed as praying. At the top of the altar is a crowned and haloed Christ who looks down on the congregation. Above the altar is the domed ceiling with stained glass windows and chandeliers. A statue of the Madonna wearing a blue sari stands at the side of the altar.

'l'Eglise du Sacré Cœur'
Church of the Sacred Heart 1884, Chandannagar (Chandernagore)

Roman Catholic

Another French colony can be found in Bengal forty kilometres north of Kolkata. It was established in 1673 when Bengal was a province of the Mughal Empire. The French gained permission from the ruler Ibrahim Khan to establish a trading post and by 1688 it had become a permanent French settlement. Joseph Francis Dupleix became governor in 1730 and maritime trade developed rapidly, exceeding even Kolkata at one time.

A series of wars between France and Britain began in 1756 during which Robert Clive of the British East India Company along with the British navy attacked and destroyed much of Chandannagar resulting in a great fall in trade and a subsequent rise of trade in Kolkata. The French regained the city in 1763 but once again the British captured it during the Napoleonic Wars. It was returned in 1816 and governed as part of French India until the governor-general of Puducherry took over politically in 1850. In just fifty years the town had collapsed commercially, becoming a sleepy quiet place with wide French boulevards and more pushbikes than cars, quite unlike the chaos that is Kolkata.

The Strand is the wide riverside promenade along the Hooghly. Lined with shady trees it is ideal for strolling European style in the cool of the afternoon. Many buildings show the French architectural style and there are a number of remaining French mansions built along the river. The Church of the Sacred Heart established in 1884 is one of the most prominent buildings. Situated at the fork of two main roads the church can't be

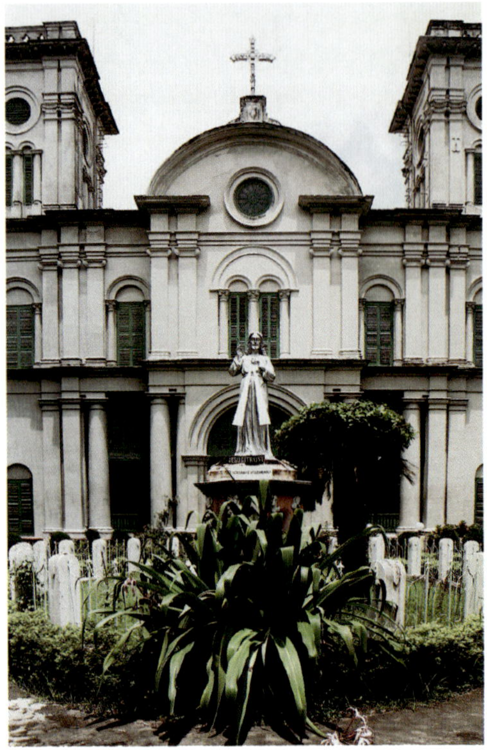

The church with statues in the garden

FACING PAGE TOP LEFT: *The statue of Joan of Arc*

FACING PAGE TOP RIGHT: *The pavilion on the Hooghly*

FACING PAGE BELOW: *Lone walker passes by the church*

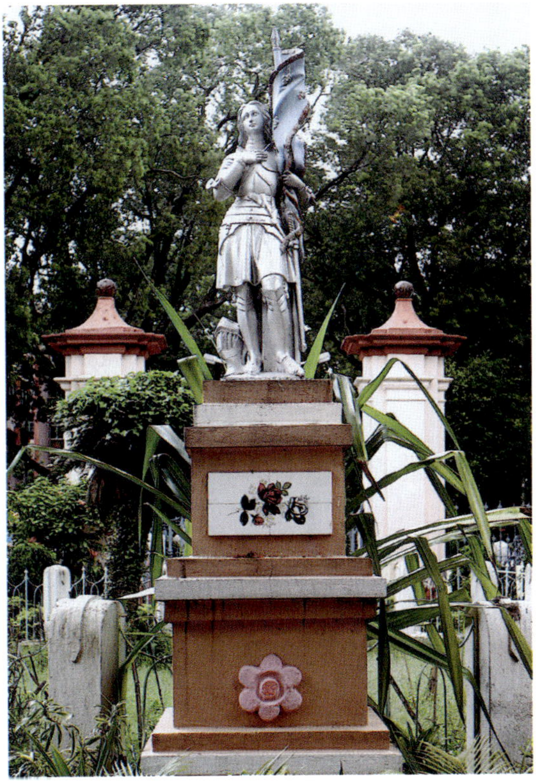
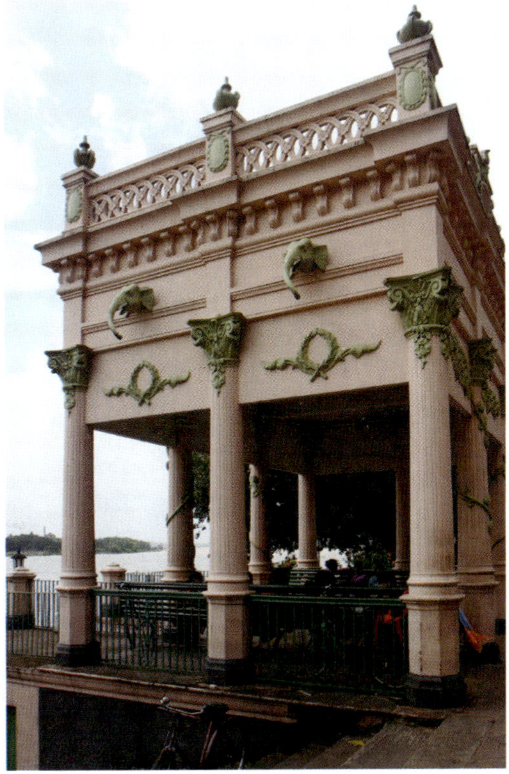
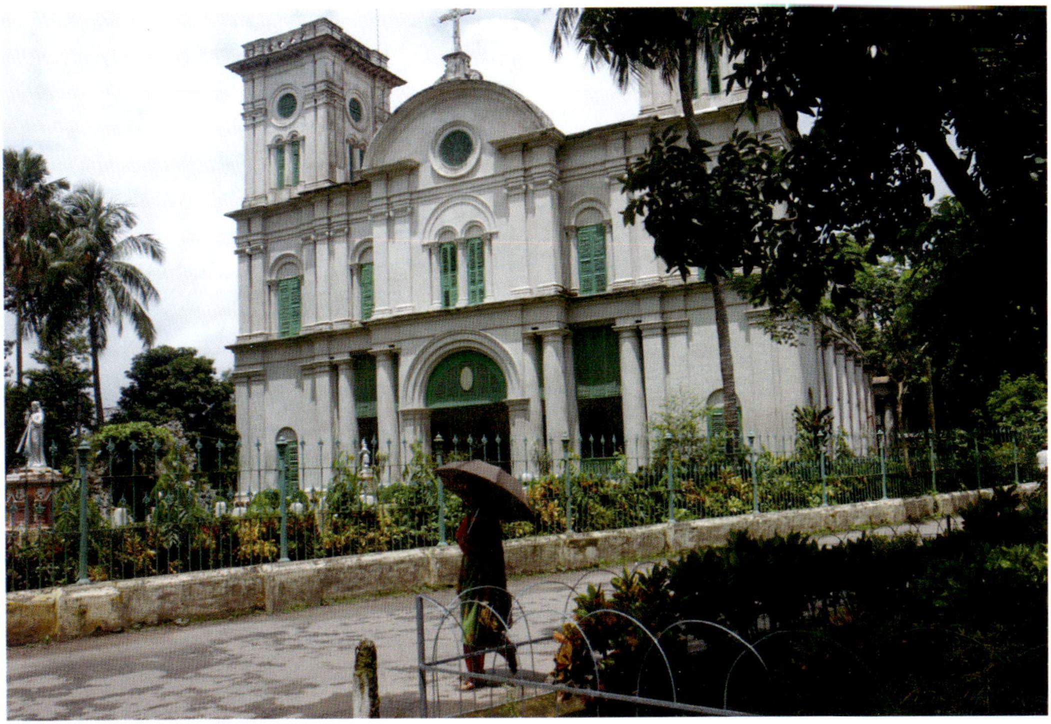

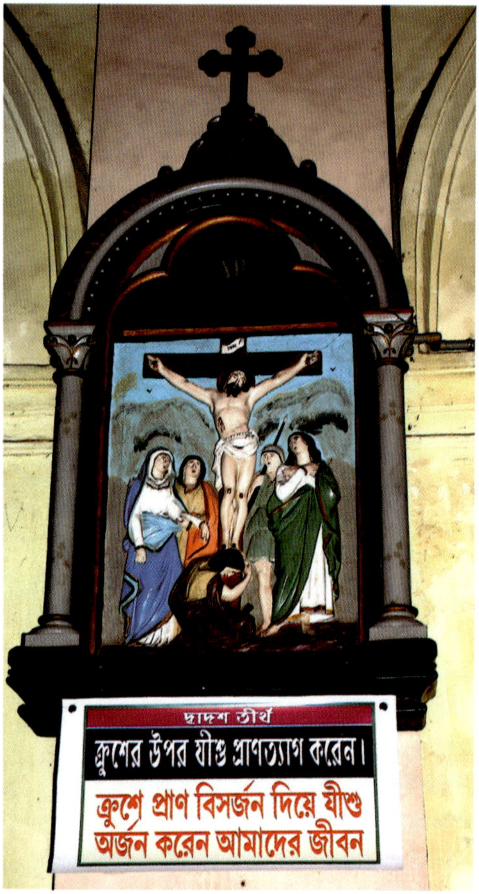

The 12th Station of the Cross

missed. Inside a fence of wrought iron panels supported by stuccoed pillars is a statue of Jesus and another of Joan of Arc. The church is two storied with twin towers either side of a rounded pediment. Green shutters and doors, typical of many Bengali buildings, are a feature of the church.

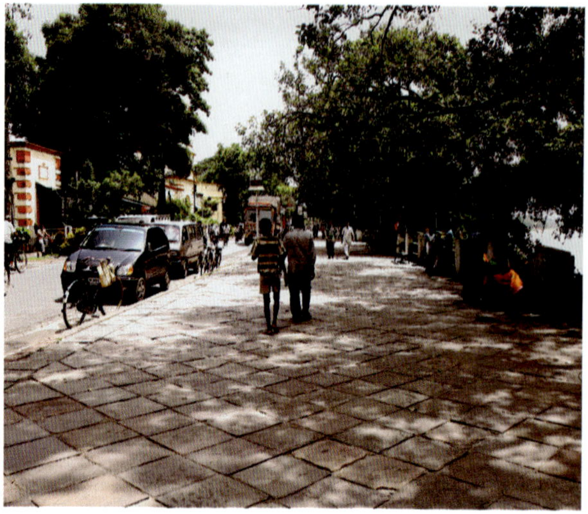

The Strand by the Hooghly in Chandannagar

Along the Strand, not far from the church is an ornate pink French styled pavilion built in the 1920s, the Durgacharan Ghat. It is square and partly juts out over the river. Decorative Corinthian columns and stucco medallions meld with elephant's heads. It is a folly and which makes one think that if the French queen Marie Antoinette had lived in India this is where she would have sat, watching the boats go by.

LAYERS OF MEANING

'Architecture is that great living creative spirit which from generation to generation, from age to age, proceeds, persists, creates, according to the nature of man, and his circumstances as they change. That is really architecture.'

Frank Lloyd Wright, from 'The Realm of Ideas' 1987

The architecture of India's churches has been interpreted in many different ways. Kerala's early Syrian Christians built their churches with local materials in the style of the Hindu temples they saw around them. By incorporating Hindu concepts and rituals to their churches they were and still are the most successful of India's Christians to integrate into Hindu society.

The impact of European culture with the arrival of the Portuguese in the late 16th century brought about great changes. As Portugal staked its claim for a colonial empire in the east and as zealous followers of the Roman Catholic faith Kerala was introduced to Baroque façades being built between the portico and the nave of indigenous churches. It was a simple way to make indigenous churches appear more 'Christian.' At first foreign to the Indian eye, over centuries the style became accepted as Kerala's own.

As the Portuguese continued to introduce their European styles stained glass, pulpits and wooden statues of Catholic saints were introduced. When Kerala's indigenous craftsmen were used to decorate the interiors of these churches angels with Indian faces began to emerge, murals featured the tropical foliage of Kerala, Indian Madonnas appeared and Christian religious figures were dressed in Indian garments, all infused with a bright Indian colour palette.

Moving north along the west coast the Portuguese captured the sleepy tropical paradise of Goa, after which it was raised to be the capital of Portugal's empire in the east. Its position was reflected in the grand buildings and magnificent churches built during the 16th and 17th centuries. Many of these churches and cathedrals survive today in 'Old Goa', a testament to Portugal's need to impose their Catholic faith on India and

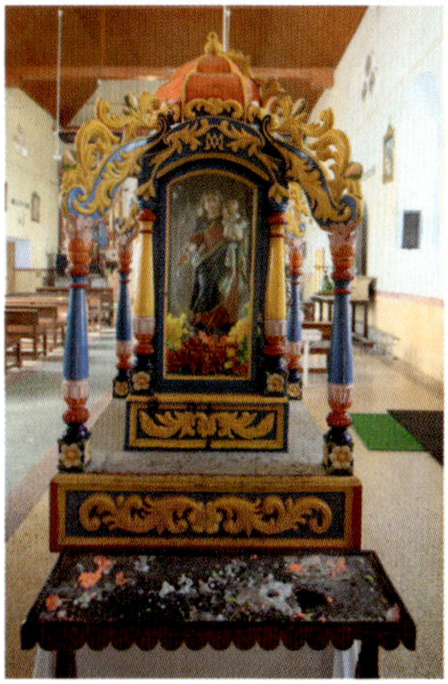

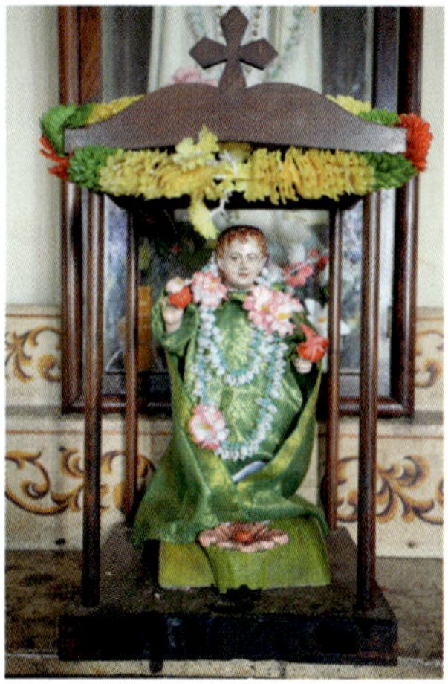

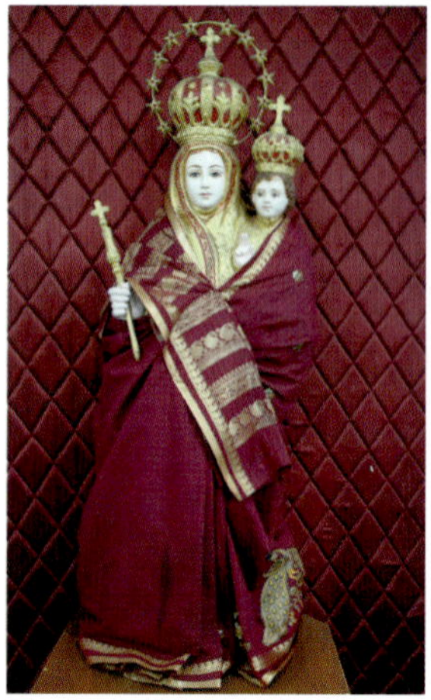

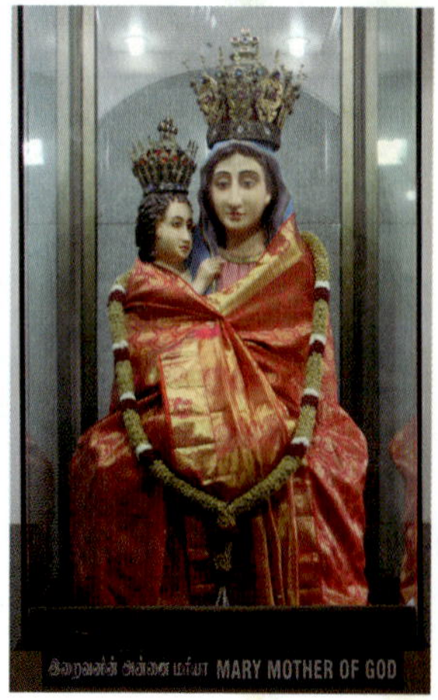

ABOVE (L TO R): *Christian religious figures in Indian dress inside Hindu style pandals*

FACING PAGE TOP LEFT: *Angels with Indian faces*

FACING PAGE TOP RIGHT: *Wall panels with floral motifs*

FACING PAGE CENTRE LEFT: *Cashew nut and foliage*

FACING PAGE BELOW: *Malankara, mythical elephant fish*

to impress and maintain their colonial power which would be the longest in India's history.

Under the later colonial administrations of the Dutch, the Danes, the French and the British different architectural styles for Christian churches appeared across India. It was the British however who had the most enduring impact on India, from the beginning of the 17th century with the British East India Company who developed settlements in the port cities of Madras, Calcutta and Bombay where they built forts, civic buildings and garrison churches, until 1857 when India became a colony of the British Empire. Britain's architecture was meant to express the power of the state in fact the term colonial or imperial refers to this period of architecture in India. British churches however were different, as Britain's objective was trade their churches were built for the British population to worship in, not for the propagation of Christianity as had the Portuguese.

As Christianity continued to expand across India, master stonemasons and members of various religious orders travelled to different regions. Military engineers who served as architects also moved from one region to another. This exchange resulted in established architectural styles becoming superimposed with regional characteristics. More local materials and techniques were used in other words architectural styles became popular in different areas and at different times. An example is the Neo-Gothic

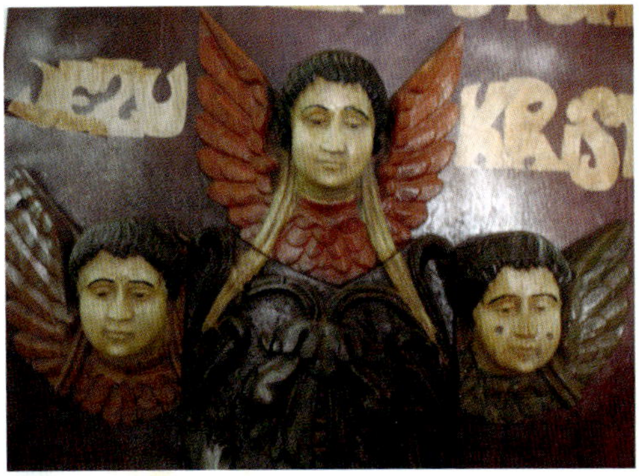

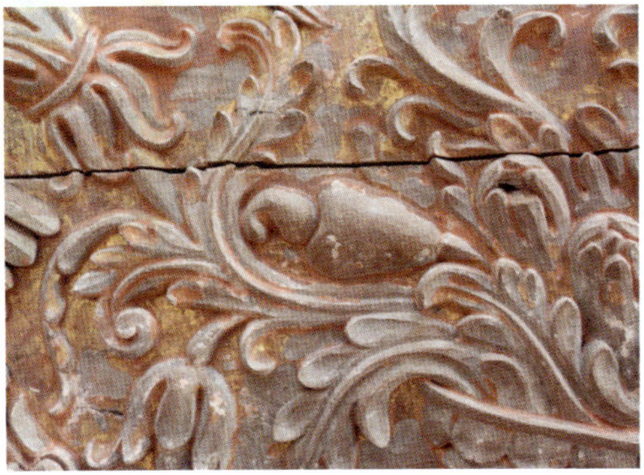

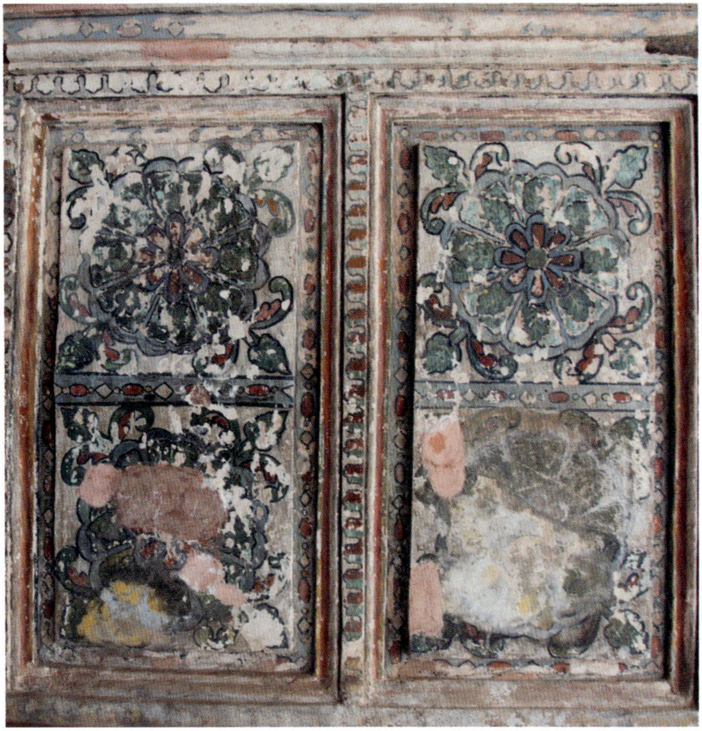

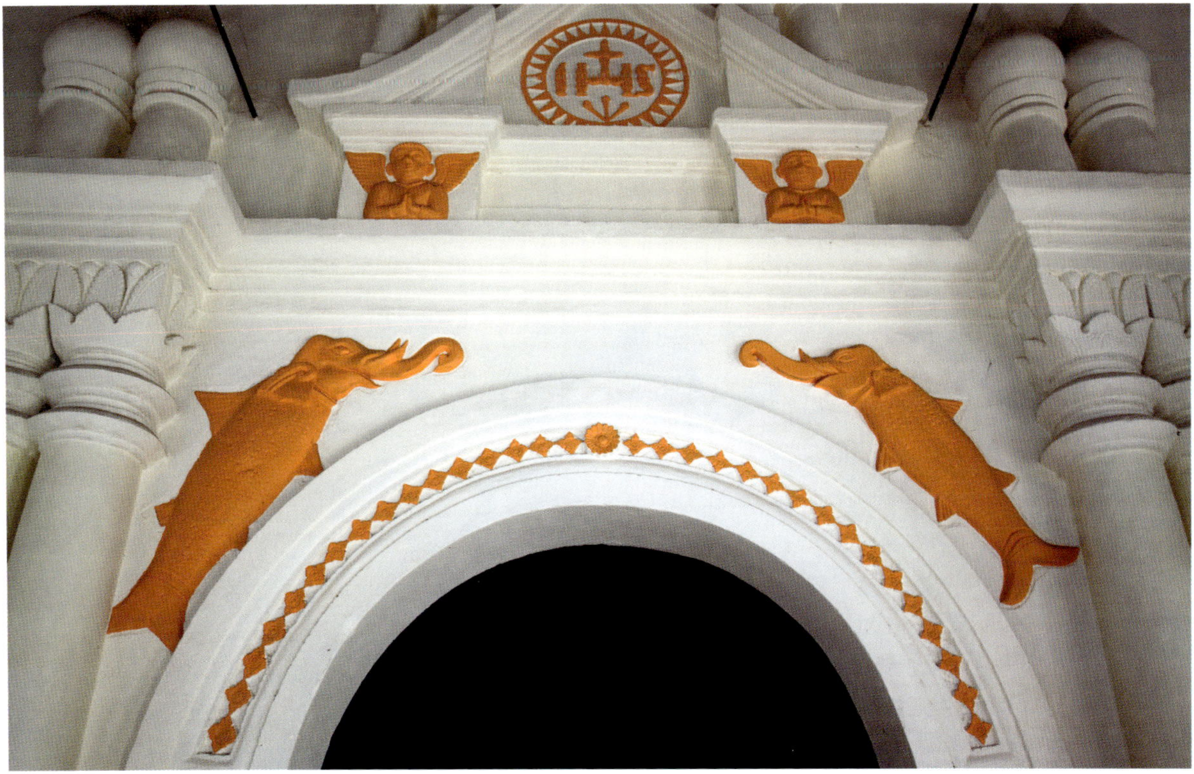
IHS

style chosen in Mumbai also popped up all over India. In Chennai, the Basilica Cathedral of St. Thomas, in Velankanni in India's south, the Basilica of Our Lady of Good Health, and in Kolkata, St. Paul's Cathedral. All are examples of Neo-Gothic architecture on a large scale.

In the hill stations of the vast Himalayan mountain range developed by the British to escape the scorching summers of Delhi and Kolkata Anglican churches can be found in an English landscape of rose gardens, gingerbread houses and a central Mall. From Kolkata it was a difficult five day journey to reach the cool climate of Shimla. However the area was important both socially and politically. By 1864 Shimla had become the summer capital of India. These days it is the Indian middle classes who depart for the hill stations.

Christianity grows in some areas more than others. Our Lady of Dolours in Thrissur, mentioned earlier, has a monumental addition in the form of the Bible Tower while huge churches dominate in the larger cities of Nagaland, a remote tribal state in India's north east known as 'the most Baptist state in the world.' Christianity arrived in the mid-19th century which ended the tradition of headhunting. These days the official religion is Christianity and the majority of the population is church goers. The country now has the largest church in Asia, the egg-shaped Sumi Baptist Church which can seat 8500 people.

Varanasi, the ancient spiritual capital of India and the most sacred city for Hindus seems an unlikely place to find St. Mary's Cathedral. This modern church was built in 1993 by Indian architect A.G.K. Menon. In this building the architect and the cathedral's bishop were 'looking for an architecture for Christianity specifically in the Indian context'. The church incorporates several Hindu elements such as a *mandala* plan from which a multi-layered vertical form rises, like a Hindi *shikhara*, and *jali* screens are incorporated on each side of the entrance which has a sloping tiled roof.

Christianity had been perceived as 'European' but Jon Lang writes that after independence in 1947 India rushed into modernism in their search for identity. In the same year Indian Protestants established their first independent Church of South India, and in 1952 Indian Catholics received their first Cardinal. Independence raised the status of India's Christians. Indian architects began taking over the entire design of the building and were encouraged to design a more Indian Christian architecture. Today Indian architects are building churches that appeal

FACING PAGE: *St. Mary's Cathedral, Varanasi (courtesy Amanda Louth)*

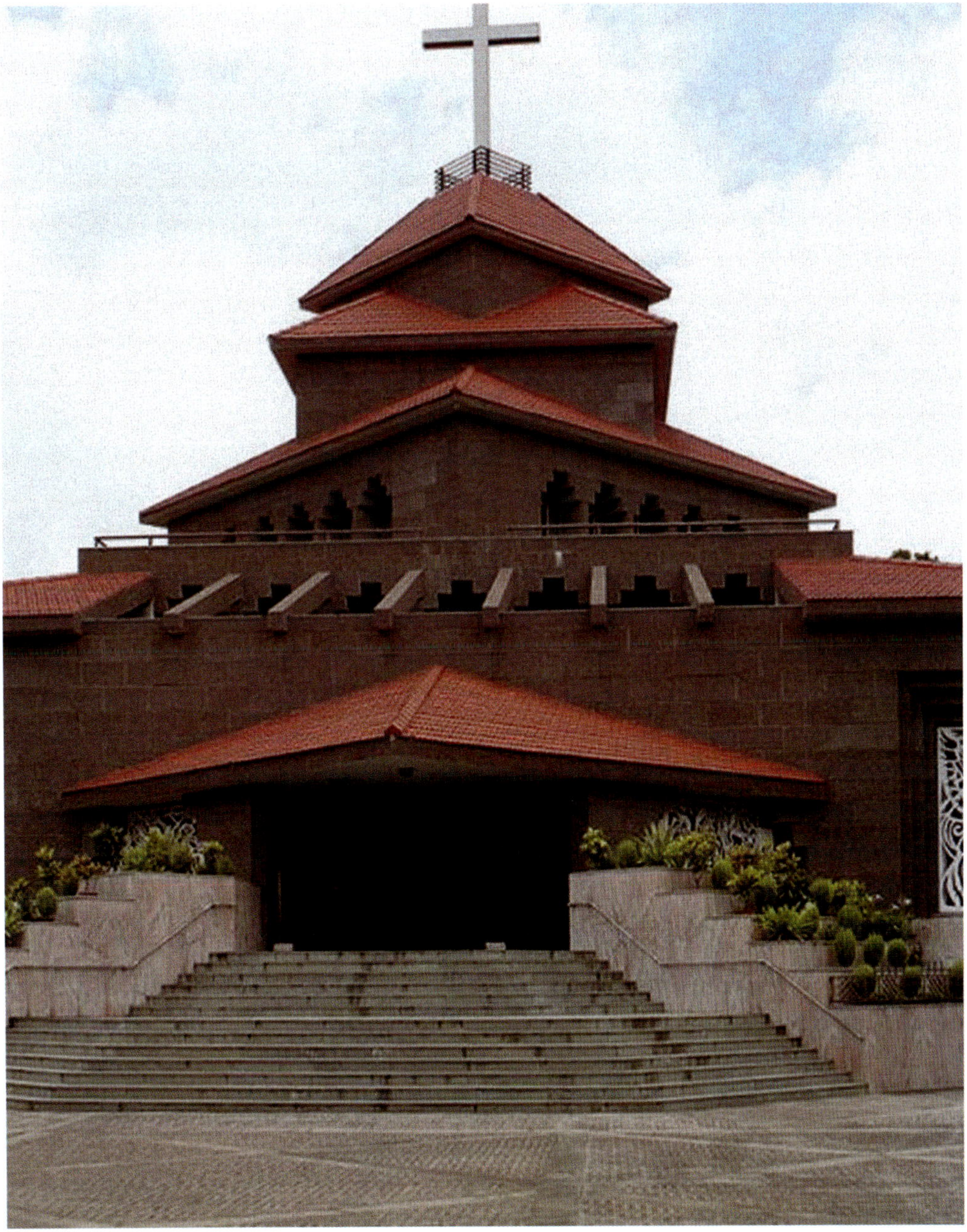

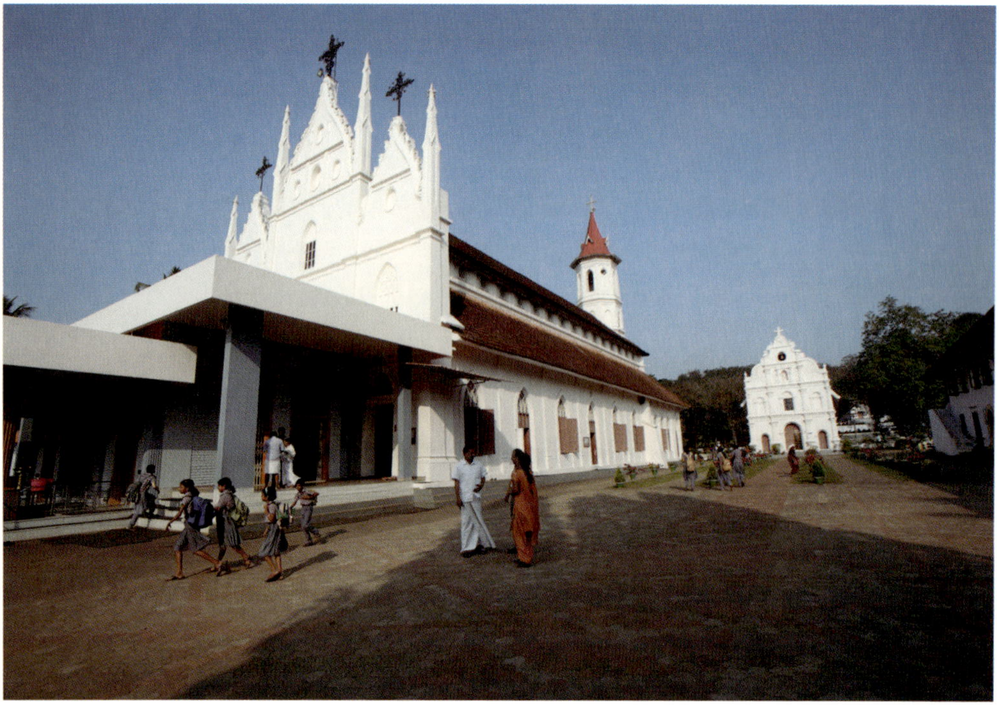

ABOVE: *St. Mary's Catholic Church, Charpunkal*
FACING PAGE: *St. Joseph's Church, Thrissur*

to Indians, with their own style and their own indigenous symbols. Local languages and rituals are being incorporated which may differ from one region to another depending on the existing rites and traditions and the expanse of time Christianity has existed in those regions. In some cases hybrid styles have emerged. Contemporary churches in India are often designed with Modernist leanings of some kind using concrete instead of wood and stone which has allowed a very different, experimental kind of façade and decoration. Interestingly modern temples and mosques remain more or less traditional.

Unexpected church designs pop up all over India today. In Charpunkal the facade of the 15th century St. Mary's Church is Portuguese Baroque in style while the new church alongside built in 1915 has an 'inserted' façade, which harks back to the 16th century and the early days of Portuguese rule, between a modern portico

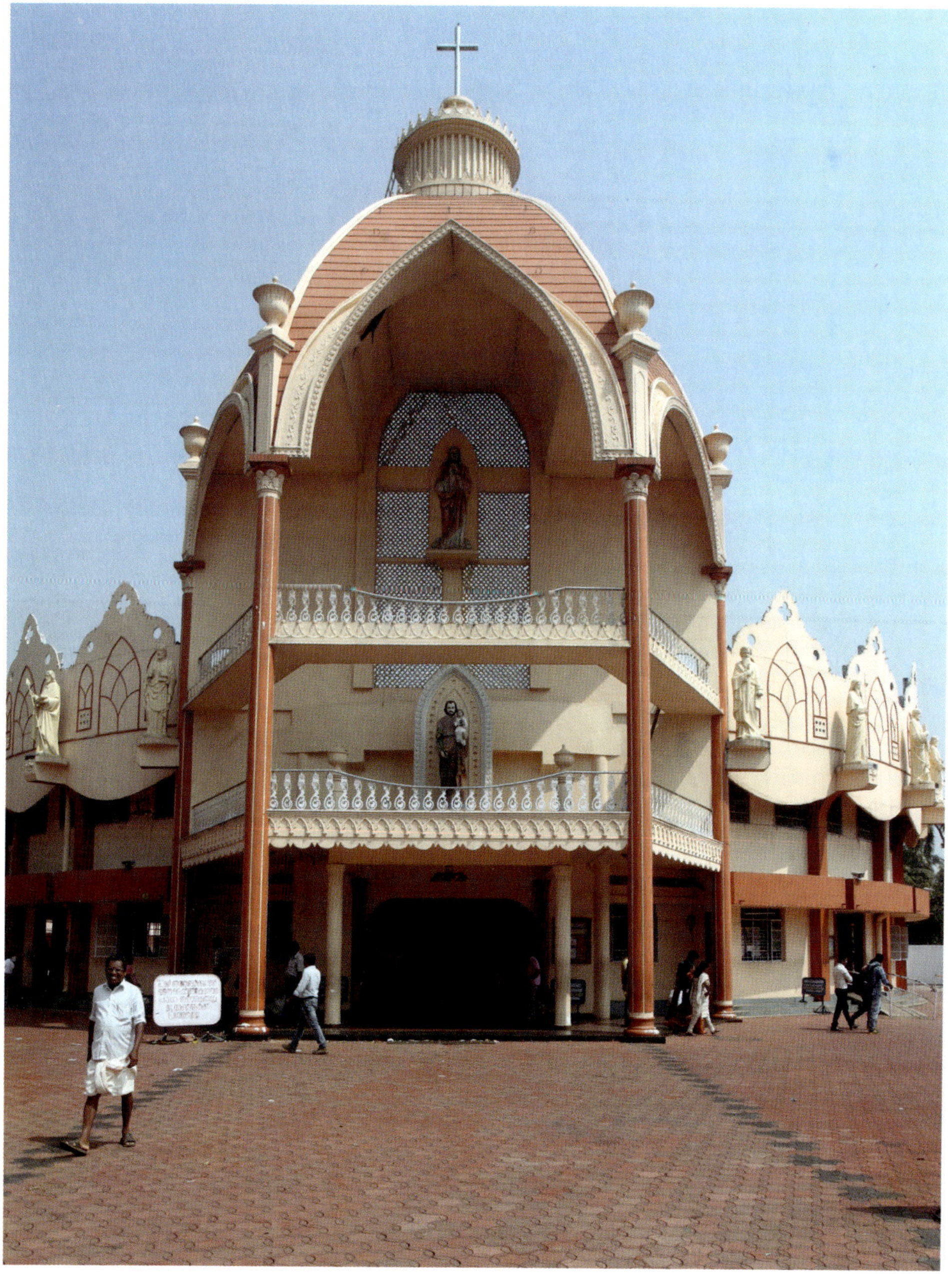

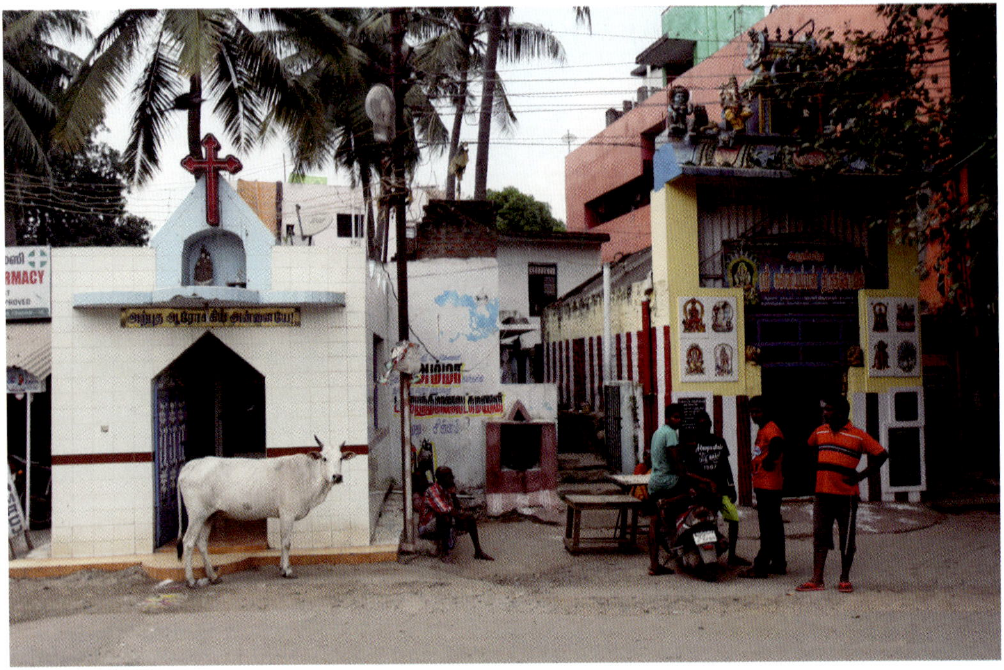

Christian shrine and Hindu temple side by side, Chennai

and the traditionally styled church. Another example is the design of St. Joseph's Church in Thrissur which has components of both a Hindu temple and a Muslim mosque. It is only the cross atop the dome and the Christian religious figures that identify the building as a Christian church.

As shown throughout this book the architecture of India's churches has been interpreted in different ways in different regions and at different times. It is clear that the various colonial powers influenced the evolution of various components of church architecture. Much of India's newer church designs however are imaginative, original and joyful, a move away from the often solemnity of traditional church architecture from Europe. The history of India's fascinating churches is complex and there are other perspectives and more to tell. However that telling will now be up to others.

ACKNOWLEDGEMENTS

In India, my friends and colleagues who have supported my work and made me feel at home.

To my publisher Bikash Niyogi who has championed my books from the beginning.

Also to my editor Mohua Mitra and designer Shashi Bhushan Prasad of Niyogi Books

In Australia my thanks to Emeritus professor Jon Lang for believing in me.

To Amanda Louth, Lynn Sutherland, Judit Korner, Penelope Kourths and the late Belinda Murray for their friendship and continued encouragement.

Finally to my husband Bryan who has unconditionally supported my work in India.

GLOSSARY

Aisle, an extension to the side of the nave or chancel separated by an arcade. Sometimes used for the passageways between the seating.

Altar, the ceremonial table at which the Eucharist (Mass, Holy Communion) is celebrated.

Altar-piece, a piece of art placed on the wall behind the altar (see *reredos*). In the 18th century; these took the form of large classical-style screens.

***Ambum villum*,** diverse offerings of gold or silver tokens, wax forms made in the shape of bows and arrows or human limbs.

Anglicans, belonging to or relating to the Church of England.

Apex, the highest point of an arch.

Aramaic language, the ancient language of the Semitic group which includes the Assyrians, Babylonians, Chaldeans, Arameans, Hebrews and Arabs. Thought to be the language spoken by Jesus.

Arcade; a covered passage with arches along one or both sides.

Ashlar, stonework for monumental architecture, squared building stone cut thin and more or less true on all faces so as to permit very thin mortar joints.

Ashoka tree, a rainforest tree, one of the most sacred and ancient trees in India.

Baroque, a highly ornate style of architecture that flourished in Europe from the 17th century.

Barrel vault, a ceiling or roof consisting of a series of semi-cylindrical arches.

Basilica, an important church building, a beautiful hall designated by the Pope with special spiritual and architectural significance.

Beam, long thick piece of wood or metal or concrete used in construction.

Belfry, a room or structure in which bells are hung, usually part of a church tower.

Broken pediment, a pediment where the apex is missing.

Buttress, masonry built against a wall to give extra strength.

Capital, the head of a column, pillar, or *pilaster*. The form of the capital is often a good guide to its date.

Chancel, the part of the church at the east end, where the altar stands and where the clergy sit.

Chapel, (side-chapel) an area of a church with its own altar, originally for the cult of a saint other than the patron saint.

Chattri, a 'canopy' often found in the architecture of Rajasthan.

Choir stalls, seating running east-west in the chancel or crossing, where the choir sits.

Chunam, a type of plaster used in India, made from ground shells, lime and sand.

Colonialism, the policy and practice of a power in increasing control over weaker people or areas.

Communion rails, in front of the altar at which the congregation kneels to receive communion. First introduced in the 16th century.

Corbel, block of stone bonded into a wall either inside or out, supporting the end of a beam, or a statue.

Corbel table, a series of *corbels,* just below the roof eaves. Used to carry a parapet, a wall plate or wall post.

Correlated parapet, or battlemented or castellated, alternate raised or lowered sections.

Crockets, a hook-shaped ornamentation.

Crossing The area in the centre of a *cruciform* church, where the east-west and north-south arms cross.

Cruciform, cross shaped, often of a church floor plan.

Cusps pointed projections in window *tracery* or in arches.

Decalogue, the Ten Commandments.

Decorated, to add something to an object or place to make it more attractive.

Diaqonikon, the sacristy.

Dormer (window) form of window 'pushed up' through the roof line to bring extra light into the top of a building.

Dravidian, the most basic division of Indian society is of Dravidians and Aryans. Native speakers of any of the Dravidian languages spoken mostly in southern India and Sri Lanka.

Durbar, a ceremonial gathering held by a ruler in India.

Dhwajastambha, a flagpole.

Enna Nercha, annointing an ancient granite cross with oil as an offering to God.

Façade, the front of a building, especially an imposing or decorative one.

Fan vault, form of vault made up of halved concave masonry cones decorated with blind tracery.

Fidalgo, mounted Portuguese noblemen.

Font, container used to hold the consecrated water used in baptism.

Flushwork Decorative patterns in flint flat against limestone, brick or carrstone, used to decorate the outside of some churches

Flying buttress A buttress which stands away from its building, and is attached to it by a bridge.

Freestone, a stone which may be 'freely worked' with metal tools. It has a fine grain. Thin slabs of freestone used as facing are called ***Ashlar***.

Gabled, a portion of the front or side of a building enclosed by or masking the end of a pitched roof.

Galletting Small pieces of flint inserted into the mortar between the large flints.

Gallery, balcony overlooking the main interior space of a building. Usually at the west end of a church, but some occur in the side-aisles. Generally in the 16th to 18th centuries, and removed in the late 19th.

Gallnut, a swelling on a branch that looks like a nut.

Gargoyle A projecting stone, usually carved in a grotesque manner, which throws rainwater away from the walls and footings of a church.

Ghee, clarified butter that originated in India.

Gothic, art, architecture or decoration styles dating from after the Norman period but before the renaissance.

Gothic revival , a 19th century version of the medieval Gothic style. Sometimes called Neo-Gothis. Dates from approximately 1840.

Gradine, a shelf behind the altar, usually part of the *reredos*, on which the cross and candlesticks stand.

Grotesque, decoration which either interweaves human and animal form with vegetation, or a distorted face.

Haykla. the nave of a church.

High altar, the main altar in a church at which the Eucharist (Mass, Holy Communion) is celebrated.

Hood mould, projecting moulding above an arch or lintel used to throw off water.

Incumbent, The cleric in charge of a church. May be called Rector, Vicar, or Priest-in-Charge.

Indo-Gothic, fusion of Indo- Islamic and Indian architecture with the Gothic revival and Neo-Classical styles favored in Victorian Britain.

Indo Saracenic, a fusion of exotic elements from native Indo-Islamic and Indian architecture.

Indigenous, ethnic groups who are the original inhabitants of a given region.

Jagir, a grant of the public revenues of a district in northern India or Pakistan to a person with power to collect and enjoy them.

Kannada, the ancient Dravidian language.

Kurla stone, a beige-coloured basalt

Laterite, a porous stone found between the western *ghats* and the coastline of the Arabian sea. A common material used in Old Goa's religious buildings. It is easy to cut and carve however it is also susceptible to corrosion.

Madbaha, the sanctuary, the consecrated area of a church or temple around its altar.

Makara, mythical elephant fish

Malabar Coast, the southern part of India's western coast, approximately from the state of Goa southward, which is bordered on the east by the Western Ghats range. The includes most of the state of Kerala.

Malayalam a Dravidian language spoken across the Indian state of Kerala

Mandala a spiritual and ritual symbol in Hinduism and Buddhism, representing the universe.

Naga; a fabulous serpent.

Navaratna, from Vedic texts and Indian Astrology, the sacred nine gemstones as per that have a profound impact on human life. In architecture eg. nine verticle stupas on a temple.

Nave, the main body of the church, where the congregation sits.

Nazrani an ethno-religious community of Syrian Christians from Kerala who trace their origins to Thomas the Apostle in the 1st century.

neem tree an attractive heat loving plant with a lovely perfume. A native of India it has been used as a natural medicine for thousands of years.

Nettipattam, a famous and traditional handicraft of Kerala used to adorn the forehead of an elephant during ceremonial occasions.

Nile Tulip, small sub-tropical tree with yellow trumpet shaped. Origins in East Africa.

Nilavilakku , a wick oil lamp.

Pahalavi, an ancient Persian language

Palanquin, a large box for the conveyance of one or two people carried on two horizontal poles by four or six people. Also a mobile altar.

Pandal, a temporary structure set up to venerate a god.

Parapet A raised rim around the edge of a roof. A wall, rampart, or elevation of earth or stone to protect soldiers.

Pediment A triangular or sometime curved head to panelling – used in 18th century altar-pieces.

Pews, seating for the congregation, benches.

Piers, another name for pillar.

Pilaster, a very shallow buttress, which has no structural use; it articulates the building on the outside.

Pinnacles, projecting points at the corners of a tower, or along a parapet, or topping off a buttress.

Plinth, a solid base on which something stands.

Pooram, annual Hindu religious festival.

Porch, covered approach to entrance of building.

Puthan Pally, 'New Church.'

Pulpit, a structure for the Priest to speak from, raised above the congregation.

Protestant, a religious movement started in the early 16th century, a reaction to medieval Roman Catholicism doctrines and practices.

Punka. A fan used especially in India, made of a palm frond or strip of cloth hung from the ceiling and moved by a servant, or *punka walla.*

Qurbana the Eucharist, commemorates the Last Supper, in which bread and wine are consecrated and consumed.

Rafters, the main structural timbers in a roof. Sometimes called principal rafters.

Reredos, a screen or decoration behind the altar in a church, usually containing religious images. Often painted wood, but may be carved and gilded.

Reserved sacrament, the bread consecrated at the Eucharist, and kept for the sick.

Rib vault a vault in which the sections are marked out by raised stone ribs.

Romanesque. a style of architecture in Europe from the mid-11th century to the advent of Gothic architecture. A product of the great expansion of monasticism in the 10th-11th century.

Sanctuary, the area around the main altar of the church, within the communion rails.

Screen, a pierced barrier, often carved wood, dividing a space but allowing vision through to another area.

Shala. carved teakwood portico.

Sari a garment for women in India consisting of a drape of fabric 4.5 metres to 8 metres in length and 60 cm to 1.20 m wide.

Side altar an altar in a side chapel.

Shikara, a type of wooden boat.

***Swadeshi* movement,** a protest movement boycotting British-made goods and using only goods produced in India.

Statapathis, Indian master masons.

Tabernacle, a box to hold the sacrament, (the wine and wafers) which stands on the altar.

Toile, fabric that typically has a light coloured background with overall bucolic scenes in one colour. A favourite of Marie Antoinette.

Tokris, wax offerings in different shapes used for wishes.

Tracery, an open-work pattern in masonry or wood in the upper part of an opening; a window or screen.

Transept, part of a church, built at right-angles to the main structure. May be added to an existing church, or be part of a cruciform building.

Trefoil, a three lobed shape, seen in stained glass windows.

Truss, supporting a structure or framework.

Turret, a small tower, sometimes containing staircases.

Vault, an arched stone roof.

Vernacular, native or indigenous language.

Vestry a room in which vestments are kept, but also used for parish meetings.

Viceroy a regal official who runs a country, colony

Victorian Gothic a 19th century revival version of the medieval Gothic style. Dates from approximately 1840 to WW1. Sometimes called Gothic Revival.

Zigzag course course with abrupt alternate right and left turns.

Vilakukumadam stone crosses.

Numinous the mysterious light that falls from a great height, a device seen in Gothic churches in particular.

***Hooghly* river**, an offshoot of the Ganges in Kolkata.

Koli, fisher-folk tribes

Uralal nercha, the ritual of crawling or rolling to a church to show respect and gratitude.

BIBLIOGRAPHY

Al Sayyad, N, ed. (2001), *Hybrid Urbanism: On the Identity Discourse and the Built Environment.* U.S.A: Praegar Publishing.

Andrews, P. (2010), *Resonance of Church Bells, the Churches of Calcutta Diocese,* C.N.I. Calcutta Diocese Publisher.

Arackal, M, Kurisinkal. F (2008), *Exploring Cochin, Commemoration Volume 450th Anniversary,* Diocese of Cochin, Vasco Da Gama Research Institute of Cochin.

Arnett, R. (1996), *India Unveiled.* Georgia: U.S.A. Atman Press.

Assis Correia, L. (2006), *Goa: Through the Mists of History from 10000BC - AD 1958, a Select Compilation of Goa's Genesis.* Dourada, Goa: Grafica.

Bach, B.P (2006), *Calcutta's Edifice the Buildings of a Great City.* New Delhi: Rupa and Co.

Baillie, F. J. (1851), *Literary Memoirs of Lieut-Col. James Skinner, C.B. for many years a distinguished officer commanding a corps of irregular cavalry in the service of the H.E.I.C.* London: Smith, Elder and Co.

Barlow, G. (1921), *The Story of Madras.* U.K: Oxford University Press.

Basham, A.L. ed. (1975), *A Cultural History of India.* Oxford U.K: Clarendon Press.

Bharadwaj, A (2016), *Seen and Unseen Bangalore.* Chennai: Notion Press.

Bhatia, G. (2003), *Laurie Baker, Life, Works and Writings.* New Delhi: Penguin Books.

Blake, S.P. (1991), *Shajahanabad: The Sovereign City in Mughal India 1639-1739.* U.K: Cambridge University Press.

Blechynden, K. (1905), *Calcutta, past and present.* London: Thacker.

Bateman, J. (1860), *The life of the Right rev. Daniel Wilson, D. D., late lord bishop of Calcutta and Metropolitan of India.* London: J.Murray.

Borden, I. Kerr, J. Rendell, J. (eds). Pivaro, A. (Contributor), (2000) *The Unknown city, Contesting Architecture and Social Space,* Massachusetts: Institute of Technology.

Borges, C. J. Feldmann, H. (eds). (1997), *Goa and Portugal their cultural links.* New Delhi: Concept Publishing.

Busteed, H.E. (2002), *Echoes from Old Calcutta, Reminiscences of the days of Warren Hastings, Francis, and Impey.* New Delhi: Rupa and Company.

Chakraborty, L.S. (2010), *Wicked man on the wall*. Calcutta: The Telegraph.

Chaudhuri. S, ed. (1990), *Calcutta The Living City, Vol 1: The Past*, New Delhi: Oxford University Press.

Clarke, Sundar. (1980), *Let the Indian Church be Indian*, Madras: Christian Literary Society.

Collins, P.M. (2007), *Christian Inculturation in India, Liturgy, Worship and Society*. U.S.A: Ashgate.

Conti, F. (1977), *The Grand Tour, Splendour of the Gods*, U.K: Cassell.

Cooper, I. Dawson, B. (1998), *Traditional Buildings of India*. London: Thames and Hudson.

Correia, L. (2006), *Goa Through the Mists of History from 10000 BC - AD 1958, A Select Compilation on Goa's Genesis*. Goa: The Golden Goa Press.

Dalal, R. (2006), *The Religions of India*, New Delhi: Penguin Books.

De, A. ed. (2008), *Multiple City, writings on Bangalore*. New Delhi: Penguin Books.

Disney, A. Booth, E. (eds). (2001), *Vasco da Gama and the Linking of Europe and Asia*, New Delhi: Oxford University Press.

Dutta, K. (2003), *Calcutta, A Cultural and Literary history*. New Delhi: Roli Books.

Evenson, N. (1989), *The Indian Metropolis: A View Toward the West*
New Haven. Yale University Press.

Farookqui, S.A. (2011), *A Comprehensive History of Medieval India, Twelfth to the Mid-Eighteenth Century*, New Delhi: Dorling Kindersley.

Fernando, L. Gispert-Sauch, G. (2004), *Christianity in India*, New Delhi: Penguin Books India.

Ferguson, J. (1899), *History of Indian and Eastern Architecture*.
New York: Dodd, Mead and Company.

Firminger, Rev. W.K. (1906), *Thacker's Guide to Calcutta*. Calcutta: Thacker, Spink and Co.

Frank, P. (1900), *Fort St. George, Madras: A short history of our first possession in India*. London: Swan Sonnenschien and Co.

Frykenberg, E. (2010), *Christianity in India. From Beginnings to the Present*, New York: Oxford University Press.

Gomes, P.V. (2011), *Whitewash, Red Stone: A History of Church Architecture in Goa*. New Delhi: Yoda Press.

Green, V, A. (1996), *New History of Christianity*. New York: The Continuum Publishing Company.

Gupta, P.D. (2000), *Ten Walks in Calcutta*. India: HarperCollins.

Groseclose, B.S. (1995), *British Sculpture and the Company Raj; Church Monuments and Public Statuary in Madras, Calcutta, and Bombay to 1858,* Newark: University of Delaware Press.

Hall, M. (1992), *Window on Goa, a History and Guide.* London: Quiller Press.

Hargreaves, C. Mathew. K.G. (1975), *25 Indian Churches.* Calcutta, Bishop College and Delhi: Indian Society for Promoting Christian Knowledge (ISPCK).

Headlund, R.E. (2000), *Quest for Identity, India's Churches of Indigenous Origin, the 'Little Tradition' in Indian Christianity*, Delhi: ISPCK.

Holman, D. (1961), *Sikander Sahib: The Life of Colonel James Skinner, 1778-1841*, London: Heinemann.

Irving, R.G. (1981), *Other editions.*

Indian Summer: Lutyens, Baker, and Imperial Delhi, USA: Yale University Press.

Jayapal. M. (2014), *Bangalore Roots and Beyond*, New Delhi: Niyogi Books.

Jenkins, J.P. (2008), *The Lost History of Christianity*, New York: Harper Collins.

Kaye, M. ed. (1980), *The Golden Calm, An English Lady's Life in Moghul Delhi,* New York: Viking Press.

Kumar, R. ed. (2003), *Essays on Indian Art and Architecture*, New Delhi: Discovery Publishing House.

Kurikilamkatt, Dr. J. (2005), *First Voyage of the Apostle Thomas to India: Ancient Christianity in Bharuch and Taxila*, Bangalore: Asian Trading Company.

Lakshmi, C. ed. (2004), *The Unhurried City: Writings on Chennai*, New Delhi: Penguin Books.

Lang, J. (2002), *A Concise History of Modern Architecture in India*, Delhi: Permanent Black.

Losty, J. (1990), *City of Palaces*, London: The British Library Publishing Division.

Love, H.D. (1995), *Vestiges of Old Madras, Indian Records Series*, New Delhi: Mittal Publications.

Mandeville, J. (2005), *The Travels of Sir John Mandeville*, London: Penguin Books.

McCulloch, V. Stott. D. (2013), *Goa with Mumbai*, U.K: Footprint Handbooks.

Medlycott. A.E. (2005). *India and the Apostle Thomas, an enquiry with a critical analysis of Acta Thomae,* USA: Gorgias Press.

Menon, A.G. Krishna, (2003), *The Contemporary Architecture of Delhi: a Critical History,* New Delhi: TVB School of Habitat Studies.

Metcalf, T.R. (2002), *An Imperial Vision, Indian Architecture and Britain's Raj,* New Delhi: Oxford University Press.

Michell, G. (2013), *Southern India, a Guide to Monuments, Sites and Museums*, Mumbai: Roli Books.

Michell, G. (1998), *The Hindu Temple, An Introduction to Its Meaning and Forms,* U.S.A: The University of Chicago Press.

Morris, J, Winchester, S. (2005), *Stones of Empire: The Buildings of the Raj,* U.K: Oxford University Press.

Muthiah, S. (1990), *Madras, the Gracious City*, New Delhi: Affiliated East-West Press.

Muthiah, S. (2005), *Madras that is Chennai, Gateway to the South,* Chennai: Ranpar Publishers.

Newman Fernandes, I.P. (1994), *St. Francis Xavier and Old Goa, A Historical Guide,* Goa: Koinia Publications.

Norman, E. (2005), *The House of God, Church Architecture, Style and History,* London: Thames and Hudson.

Rosengarten, F. Jr. (1969) *The Book of Spices*, Wynnewood Pennsylvania: Livingston Publishing Company.

Pinho,V. (2007), *Snapshots of Indo-Portuguese History – 1,* Goa: Vasco Pinho Publishers.

Pirbhai, R. (2009), *Reconsidering Islam in a South Asian Context*, The Netherlands: E.J. Brill Publishers.

Raman, A. (1984), *Bangalore-Mysore*, Hyderabad: Disha Books.

Sengupta, N. (2011), *History of the Bengali-speaking People*, New Delhi: UBS Publisher's Distributors.

Singh, U. (2008), *A History of Ancient and Early Medieval India, From the Stone Age to the 12th Century*, India: Dorling Kindersley.

Sood, S. (2010), *Landmark Churches of India*, Noida, India: SDS Publishers.

Stephens, H.M. (1897), *Rulers of India*, Oxford: Clarendon Press.

Stephenson, D. (2005), *Visions of Heaven: The Dome in European Architecture,* New York: Princeton Architectural Press.

Sundararajan, R. Mukerji, B. eds. (2003), *Indian Spirituality, Postclassical and Modern,* New Delhi: Shri Jainendra Press.

Tadgell, C. (1990), *The History of Architecture in India*, London: Phaidon Press.

Thapar, B. (2004,) *Introduction to Indian Architecture*, Singapore: Periplus Editions.

Thomas, P. (1964), *Churches in India,* Publications Division, Ministry of Information and Broadcasting, Government of India.

Tillotson, G.H.R. (1989), *The Tradition of Indian Architecture, continuity, controversy and change since 1850*, USA: Yale University Press.

Tully, M. (2012), *India's Unending Journey*, UK: Random House.

Volwahsen, A. (2004), *Splendours of Imperial India, British Architecture in the 18th and 19th Century*, New York: Prestel Publishing.

Watson, F. A. (1974), *A Concise History of India*, U.K: Thames and Hudson.

Yeates, T. (1881), *Indian Church History*, London: A. Maxwell.

Articles

Arakal, M. Kurisinkal, F. (eds), (2008), "Exploring Cochin," Commemorative Volume 450th Anniversary Diocese of Cochin

"Church Portals open for Ayyappa devotees," (2012), *Deccan Herald.*

Das, S. (2008), "Gaur to St. John's", Calcutta: *The Telegraph.*

Das, S. (2010), "Look, Last Supper Restored," Calcutta: *The Telegraph.*

Department of Ancient Near Eastern Art. (2000), "Trade Routes between Europe and Asia during Antiquity." *In Heilbrunn Timeline of Art History,* New York: The Metropolitan Museum of Art.

Keshishian, A. (1994), "The Oriental Orthodox Churches," The Ecumenical Review, Vol. 46, Issue 1.

Marshall, P.J. (2000), The White Town of Calcutta under the Rule of the East India Company, *Modern Asian Studies, Vol.34*, U.K: Cambridge University Press.

Narsimhan, S. (2009), "Plants and Human Civilization: Indian Spices," *Comparative Civilizations Review*: Vol. 60: No. 60, Article 8. Delhi: Department of East Asian Studies, University of Delhi.

Nelson, D. (2009), "India's Scottish heritage remembered in renovation of Calcutta's Raj Architecture," New Delhi: *The Telegraph.*

Stamp, G. (2016), "The tragedy and triumph of a British architect in New Delhi," London: *Apollo, The International Art Magazine.*

INDEX